The Mystery and the World

The Mystery and the World
Passion for God in Times of Unbelief

Maria Clara Bingemer

Foreword by
Peter J. Casarella

Translations by
Jovelino and Joan Ramos

CASCADE Books · Eugene, Oregon

THE MYSTERY OF THE WORLD
Passion for God in Times of Unbelief

Copyright © 2016 Maria Clara Bingemer. All rights reserved. Except for brief quotations in critical publications or reviews, no part of this book may be reproduced in any manner without prior written permission from the publisher. Write: Permissions. Wipf and Stock Publishers, 199 W. 8th Ave., Suite 3, Eugene, OR 97401.

Cascade Books
An Imprint of Wipf and Stock Publishers
199 W. 8th Ave., Suite 3
Eugene, OR 97401

www.wipfandstock.com

PAPERBACK ISBN: 978-1-62564-106-9
HARDCOVER ISBN: 978-1-4982-8496-7

Cataloguing-in-Publication Data

Bingemer, Maria Clara Lucchetti

The mystery and the world : passion for God in times of unbelief / Maria Clara Bingemer ; translated by Jovelino and Joan Ramos ; foreword by Peter J. Casarella.

xxvi + 376 p. ; 23 cm. Includes bibliographical references and index.

ISBN 978-1-62564-106-9 (paperback) | ISBN 978-1-4982-8496-7 (hardcover)

1. God—Worship and love. I. Ramos, Jovelio. II. Ramos, Joan. III. Casarella, Peter J. IV. Title.

BV4817 .B554 2016

Manufactured in the U.S.A. 05/06/2016

Contents

Foreword by Peter J. Casarella | vii
Introduction | xi

1 Premature or Late Modernity: A Question of Culture | 1
2 Secular Culture and the Crisis of Religion | 56
3 Religious or Mystical Experience: A New Moment, a New Configuration, New Challenges | 125
4 Mystical Biographies and Theological Narrative | 224
5 Stories and Experiences of Love | 279
   Conclusion | 325

Appendix: Translator's Note Regarding Sources and Footnotes for Chapter 5 | 329

Bibliography | 333
Index | 369

Foreword

It is a great honor to write a preface for this groundbreaking reflection on the passion for God in times of unbelief (*paixão por Deus em tempos de descrença*). The theme is not new, but the approach through a novel analysis of culture has yielded unexpected and valuable results. Passion for God is what we encounter in the Psalms, a book that contains the prayers said by Jesus himself. The English nun Mary Ward (1585–1645) displays that very same passion when she utters these well-wrought words:

> I think, dear child, the trouble and the long loneliness you hear me speak of is not far from me, which whensoever it is, happy success will follow. . . . The pain is great, but very endurable, because He who lays on the burden also carries it.

Dorothy Day, the American Catholic journalist and founder of a newspaper and social movement called the Catholic Worker, cites the exact same words of Mary Ward as the epigram that introduces her autobiography, also titled *The Long Loneliness*. Dorothy measured her life with passionate words about the spiritual condition of humanity like these. Passionate words for a passionate God describe the life and social engagement of many in an age striving to transcend our disturbingly fluid addiction to consuming without reflection commodified ideas and marketable things.

Dorothy Day is just one of the religious writers invoked in this beautiful text to offer hope in the midst of the crisis. Etty Hillesum, the passionate Jewish diarist of Camp Westerbork (the last stop for the victims of the Shoah before Auschwitz), and Egide von Broeckhoeven SJ, a profound but little-known friend of God who died far too young in a Belgian factory, play equally significant roles. But, in from as director of a research center in Chicago, Dorothy is the witness who captures much that needs to be said about this particular book.

I had the pleasure of hosting the author in the Center for World Catholicism and Intercultural Theology (CWCIT) and enjoying her immense capacity for vibrant intellectual exchange during the months when this manuscript was gestating. This sojourn for her away from Rio de Janeiro offered, I hope, a Sabbath from administrative burdens and also a chance for a living immersion into the very topography of Dorothy Day's youth. I am referring to the fact that Dr. Bingemer stayed in a residence next to Lincoln Park. So to reach her office and write this book she walked on Belden Avenue, the street where, as Dorothy recounts in *The Long Loneliness*, she as a teenager took her baby brother for a stroll. The Psalms and the sermons of John Wesley were a part of Dorothy's Anglo-Saxon, Episcopalian childhood. Before joining the Socialist Party in college and later leaving that affiliation for the communion of being a Benedictine oblate and a disciple of Peter Maurin at the Catholic Worker, Dorothy experienced a rather ordinary, middle-class childhood in Lincoln Park. It was for her the domestic calm before the storm of her long loneliness. For Dr. Bingemer, too, the calm of being in Lincoln Park made way for the storm of passion for God that flows through this book.

Dorothy's childhood took place in the tumultuous early decades of the last century. We too live in turbulent times. Dr. Bingemer precociously asks whether theology in these times should focus on texts or on testimonies. St. Paul made this very point in 2 Cor 3:3 when he configured the testimony of his life as a living letter: "and you show that you are a letter of Christ, prepared by us, written not with ink but with the Spirit of the living God, not on tablets of stone but on tablets of human hearts" (NRSV). Abstract formulae do not move, but St. Paul's and Dr. Bingemer's point goes beyond the desire for an emotive bond with figures like Day, Hillesum, and Broeckhoeven who bear witness to the truth. We are called to read lives, including our own, precisely in order to transcend dichotomies between public and private, between sacred and secular. A certain form of postmodernism proclaimed nothing to be outside of the text, but here a life lived in passionate response to a passionate God is rediscovered at the juncture where text, testimony, and ethical responsibility for the human condition are woven delicately into an intimate and theologically powerful bond.

Forging bonds of solidarity and finding concrete ways to live out the vision of *Ecclesia in America* is one way to offer hope in the midst of epochal change. This project brought the spirit of Rio de Janeiro and that of Chicago closer together, while forging new ties between individuals and institutions. My prayer is that this book will find readers within and beyond the north-south route that joins these two cities. Dr. Bingemer is now an internationally recognized theologian whose early passion for journalism lends to this scientific treatise a uniquely catholic mode of expression. Its passionate and brilliantly intercultural message of hope should not be confined to just academic theologians in Brazil and the United States. This work deserves to find new and unsuspecting readers whose passion for God mirrors that of Dorothy, Etty, and Egide. May the Lord provide safe passage to this message in a bottle as it finds its way to them.

—Peter J. Casarella
Director, CWCIT
DePaul University
Chicago, January 25, 2012
(Feast of the Conversion of St. Paul)

Introduction

THE RELEVANCE OF THE topic, corroborated by much research received by the academic community at several levels and by a significant number of texts approved for publication, not only in Brazil but overseas, demonstrates that the subject of mysticism is, undoubtedly, a major concern for the scientific study of theology and religion.

Our own current time, identified by different designations such as modernity, late modernity, hypermodernity, and postmodernity, among others, reflects significant transformations. It is not so much an era of changes as it is a change of era that is taking place in the Western world, with profound implications for human life, its configuration and its context.[1]

One of the most profound impacts of this change of era was most certainly on religion. If during the Enlightenment human reason began to gain stature and became the fundamental principle ruling human life, and established itself as the indisputable canon of truth, today the change is taking another form. The crisis of modernity was followed by a new state of things, which human knowledge is still far from having definitively assimilated. And it is in the twentieth century that this new process is most clearly seen.

Religion suffered the consequences of this new vision of the world introduced by modernity. In this vision, in order for something to be considered legitimate, it had to submit to the process of rational understanding that characterizes the thinking being. The critique and questioning of tradition and authority grew and strengthened. A new human organization emerged that implied abandoning the old one, which was proclaimed to be based on fanaticism, superstition, and intolerance.[2]

---

1. Cf. *Documento de Aparecida*, the concluding text of the Fifth General Conference of the Latin American and Caribbean Episcopate, 2007.

2. Cf. Castiñera, *A experiência de Deus na pós-modernidade*.

Thus we will consider the period of history that encompasses the fourteenth and fifteenth centuries and extends into the twentieth. Its characteristics were an increase in the autonomy of the human being, great scientific advances, and the use of reason to explain what previously belonged in the domain of beliefs. The human being—and no longer God, as in medieval times—became the being at the center of the universe, at the center of phenomena and events. Human beings were now characterized by a mature consciousness and were subjects of their own history. With emancipation, such subjects became responsible for their own happiness (which was fully and exclusively dependent upon their action and reflection).[3]

Historical Christianity—indisputably the hegemonic and majority religion in the West—saw emerging around it, and even within its ranks, such phenomena as theism, secularism, atheism, and agnosticism. This atmosphere of rejection had a scope that was more than external. It affected the very structure of individualistic thinking, the mental categories of the believers themselves. To them it seemed that the only options were either to reject the modern world and shelter themselves in their faith or to enter into dialogue with the Enlightenment thinking and, apologetically, accept the modern mindset (or at least develop a greater degree of tolerance for the deviations that were invading their sphere of life and knowledge).[4]

Yet religion was not banished from the human horizon as intended by the masters of suspicion. The same Enlightenment thinkers who so criticized the superstitious and magical aspects of the Christian religion now capitulated before the force of transcendence as an essential element of humanity, while looking for a model of God and religion more in line with their mechanistic vision of the physically and technically perfect world emerging from the new sciences. Thus the concept of God began to receive designations such as "the great watchmaker" and "the supreme architect or geometrician" in response to the theoretical necessity arising from a rationalistic vision of the world.[5]

Religion became something belonging exclusively to the inner life of human consciousness, without mediation or intermediary. It came to inhabit a private sphere in which each person believes and welcomes the truths presented, appreciating and discerning them through the prism of reason.

---

3. See Carrara, "A experiência cristã de Deus," 11–12.

4. See Moingt, *Dieu qui vient à l'homme*, for a brilliant analysis of the process of secularization in the Western world. See also Castiñera, *A experiência de Deus na pós-modernidade*, 25.

5. Castiñera, *A experiência de Deus na pós-modernidade*, 26.

Introduction

According to some of the great philosophers who considered this epochal change, such as Nietzsche, Heidegger, and Wittgenstein, the meaning of universal history was undergoing deconstruction and being replaced by a new structure—that of individual history, where its subject reacts to concrete historical circumstances by working out syntheses that are continually being renewed, while refusing to be ruled by established and permanent norms. Knowledge becomes fragmented into several specialties, and occurrences become dependent and relative, according to the particular event, the dialogue and interpretations it provokes, and the understanding of each individual.

The concepts of secularization and progress gain greater centrality once we move from being uniquely "thought" by a God who creates us and gives us existence and movement to being "thinkers," or self-conscious spirits, since "for one who thinks, a thinker is infinitely closer, more present and more certain than one who is thought of."[6]

Yet, finding itself in crisis, Enlightenment reason—powerful and sovereign—questioned the whole previously ruling system of comprehension and understanding. Our era, no longer understanding itself as a domain of reason, witnesses the fragmentation of the great narratives and utopias and is forced to rethink and recast all—or almost all—the concepts that had provided their theoretical justification. The difficulty in finding an appropriate name for the current period is itself an example of its complexity. Modernity in crisis, late modernity, hypermodernity, or postmodernity? In fact, our era is definitively challenged and confronted by a crisis of its model. All that was solid vanishes in the air, and all that was certain—including questions and answers—is subject to doubt, thus shaking the image that human beings had constructed of themselves as absolute subjects and builders of their history. The prevailing feelings are those of distrust and despair. There is a nullification of history as a result of the shattering of political and religious ideals, especially throughout the twentieth century.

Realizing that they have no solid basis as previously thought, and that reason alone cannot answer their great questions about the meaning of life, human beings individually seek a new basis, detached from collective and communal systems and proposals, that would sustain their beliefs and allow them to build their identity with some consistency. But this search ends up transforming the individual into a manifold and fragmented being, possessing not one but several core identities that can be exchanged and replaced according to the needs of each person. The individualistic culture becomes a culture that each person constructs and wants to pursue alone rather than a society to which the individual or group belongs or wants to be part of.[7]

6. Ibid., 41.

7. Cf. numerous books by the Polish thinker Zygmunt Bauman about this unraveling of the postmodern process.

The culture faces a crisis, and the media exacerbate it through an excess of information, making it almost impossible to evaluate and judge events. The result is their banalization, as reality is transformed into virtuality. Nowadays the real consists of images. With so much information we see a pluralism of cultures, which ends up producing subcultures and making impossible a unitary vision of history, as modernity intended.[8] The media, as builder of opinion and identity, has a strong influence on the individual. Following the logic of consumerism, it manipulates and sells whatever image it wants. It moves societies in accordance with the pursuit of its interest, which is usually that of a small group vying for the control of the masses. After all, those who control opinions hold the power.

The motto undergirding our times could well be expressed in these words: "Human beings are those who consume, and the more they consume the happier they are." There is a frightening increase in the availability of goods and services, an abundance of means and a scarcity of ends. Ours is an accelerated culture in which many things can be instantaneously obtained. Business deals, information, communication, and even amorous relationships can be immediately accessed with a click on a computer screen. The result is a maelstrom of questions and answers that casts aside anything that cannot be integrated into the speed cycles to which we are habituated, and that brings about a mood of impatience in human beings.[9]

"The permanent does not endure, and must always be exchanged for something newer and more modern."[10] Technology is what determines the acquisitive power of each individual. The *cogito* of Descartes, which defined the human being as a reasonable being, is replaced by a fast and inconsistent movement that aims to make of the human being a consuming being.[11]

The twentieth century is a godless century in which even the deities are ephemeral and transitory. In identifying itself with objects of consumption, it represents the height of the postmodernization process. It rescues the transcendent but fragments it before the human being and introduces it without a face, without an identity, and without Absolutes. Religious experiences, once apparently banished by modern rationality, begin to multiply again. However, their configuration no longer consists in a relationship with a personal and Absolute God, but rather in another kind of consumption: the consumption of experiences of the senses, which, emptied of their

---

8. See Carrara, "A experiência cristã de Deus," 13–14.

9. See González Buelta, *Orar em um mundo fragmentado*, and all his excellent reflections on this topic.

10. Carrara, "A experiência cristã de Deus," 15.

11. SeebLipovetsky, *L'ere du vide*; Lipovetsky, *Le bonheur paradoxal*; and Lipovetsky and Charles, *Hypermodern Times*, among others.

potential to give pleasure and delight to those who seek them, are exchanged for others equally superficial.

A new conception of the human being necessarily corresponds to a new conception of God. In the construction of a new subject, the idea of an Absolute God comes into question. In modernity this is because "reason demands a rupture with the idea of an Absolute God who gives meaning to earthly things. Reason takes the place of God. We see, then, that in modernity the world is reduced to mere scientific propositions in which reason accommodates to facts without attempting to transcend them."[12]

However, in excluding God as a social reference, the modern human being begins to search for something to take this now empty place. This is being done by the same human being who, as a rational being, is the reference point for everything. The human being is, therefore, the origin, center, and final end of religion. God is a human product because the human condition is the source of religion. The denial of God restores to human beings the attributes of which they had divested themselves while unconsciously projecting them onto an imaginary being—thus restoring the boundlessness of human subjectivity that human beings had previously refused to recognize in themselves.

Yet, in this modern human being one can still identify ideals closely linked to concerns related to faith and religion, such as commitment, responsibility, and ethical consciousness. One finds the rejection of moral norms and dogmatic definitions but also the valorization of human possibility and human dignity. The entire struggle for human rights must be credited to modernity. Human beings have, at last, the opportunity to become the protagonists rather than mere observers of their own history.

In postmodernity there is a partial return to a reference to God, but under different perspectives in which other fetishes and idols share the leading role with the human being. These are individual perspectives, allowing each person to choose how, where, when, and why to pursue a religious way, according to individual desires and needs. The vision of God—and of the human being—is privatized. Behind a reassuring and secure attitude, postmodern human beings find shelter in a newly configured fanaticism. They no longer canonize and deify modern ideals but rather the more immediate things that can be owned and consumed. There follows a succession of fetishes without which they cannot live, such as computers, cell phones, tablets, cars, and all kinds of material objects and gadgets that are elevated to the status of true idols.

---

12. Carrara, "A experiência cristã de Deus," 25.

The postmodern refusal of the idea of God is represented in a practical atheism derived from a spiritualistic narcissism in which the subject has no tolerance for any reference or example other than itself. In this picture no possibility exists for a committed intersubjectivity. The idea of God is not theoretically denied, as in the case of modernity, but is simply rejected or ignored. Not an outright refusal, but a disguised one based on distance and banality.[13]

The weakening of the idea of God also weakens the idea of the human being. In breaking the relationship with God, the human being is reduced to the insignificance of a disoriented humanity in the midst of a multifarious and soothing fog, and becomes a being without reference to the past, without initiatives for the present, and without perspectives for the future.

As previously stated, the human being no longer has one single identity, but several. Yet he or she is not fully defined by them, choosing just one or another of their characteristics and recombining them. Once deprived of an integral personality the human being loses such references as God and the world, and becomes just one being among many, manipulable and reified by ever-changing quasi-scientific theories. Seen only in their biological ambit, treated as mere objects, reduced to a moral relativism in which judgments are purely subjective, human beings find themselves completely fragmented and defined only by their particularities. They also lose their irreplaceable capacity to give meaning to things and, above all, to find transcendent meaning in them.

Designated as individuals rather than persons, human beings do not understand themselves from the standpoint of Otherness and relationality. They use both in a volatile, accelerated, and inconsistent way according to their needs and expectations—a complex of biological and psychological reactions without reference to a transcendent God. They are just individuals closed inside themselves, not open to communication with the other, and incapable of self-transcendence.[14]

Relationships established by the new postmodern subjects are, like the subjects themselves, accelerated and ephemeral. There is no longer a perspective of durability and permanence, whether in a familial, amorous, conjugal, or professional context. The same is true of the relationship with God, pursued only to satisfy immediate needs and temptations. Some new religious proposals, including some coming from self-described "churches," bear this characteristic.[15]

---

13. Ibid., 27.

14. Ibid., 32. Cf. also Rahner on the human being as a being in constant self-transcendence in "Hearer of the Message," in *Foundations of Christian Faith*, 24–43.

15. Cf. García Rubio, *Unidade na Pluralidade*.

At issue here is a culture exclusively of sensations and rights rather than one of duties and responsibilities. It is a light culture, in which happiness is achieved when all desires are realized. But it is not achieved by all, only by those—whoever they may be—who have the means to achieve it. Individual accomplishments are all that matter. Nothing is important if the benefit cannot be seen quickly, precisely, and immediately by the individual.[16]

Postmodernity is, therefore, a generalized crisis with several shades. It is characterized by a prevalence of weak thinking and by an epistemological reversal brought about by a disenchantment with reason—which no longer succeeds in defining what is real, nor offers clear and indisputable foundations and principles. What prevails is contingency, discontinuity, and the provisional. A new sensibility emerges with a preference for the particular, for dispersion, specialization, and fragmentation. From a psychological point of view, postmodernity is further characterized by a loss of meaning, lived out as existential emptiness, often resulting in an escape into drugs, consumerism, and hedonism.[17]

In this panorama the religious crisis is undeniable, but the search for the transcendent and for principles to guide human life persists. At the same time, this search coincides with a desire for immediate personal satisfaction and for solutions to problems, and not always for authentic experience, adherence to religious principles, and affiliation with an ecclesiastic institution. The need to be sheltered and accepted leads postmodern human beings to search for a religion that touches their senses.

If in the modern period all seemed to point to a godless world without any religious perspective, in postmodernity one finds a return to the transcendent. There is an ever greater eagerness for religious practices—an incessant search for the sacred, but without the need to listen to authorities or theologians. It is a search for something that touches the human heart and makes human beings feel desired and loved.

It is in this context that new religious experiences are born and disseminated, generating movements, associations, groups, and various organizations. In this religious environment, people irremediably withdrawn from historical institutions feel free and open to the experience of the Sacred, surrounded by a deeply involving fellowship—something not easily found in other social spaces.[18] It is possible to note among them the need to become, in one way or another, participants, whether passively or actively, thus rediscovering the thread of the meaning of life.

16. Cf. Lipovetsky, op. cit. Cf. also the works of Bauman cited above.
17. Cf. Lasch, *The Culture of Narcissism*.
18. Cf. Carrara, "A experiência cristã de Deus," 48–49.

The God who is sought and reencountered through this new key to understanding is revealed by means of experience, and above all by a sense of the presence of God and of God's energy that surrounds, perfects, and pacifies. It is the divine that animates the movement of life through the cycles of nature. Nature most certainly is part of the divine. All that is real can be unified in God. And it is through the senses that one can enter into communion with God. Reason does not play a very important role in this process. Thus, several denominations and spiritualities have emerged to address the desires and needs that move all human beings engaged in such constant searching.

Completely free to choose what to believe in, human beings are pushed toward a diffuse reality. At the least sign of a crisis they look for spiritual support of several kinds and sources. With this comes a profound need to experience God—but not necessarily God as understood by official theologies and historical institutions.

In spite of scientific advances, the new discoveries did not help human beings understand the cause, the motive for their existence. Science did not succeed in effacing the desire for God in the human heart. Now the search is not for a religion but for a spirituality that may offer a path to an experience that gives meaning to life. This posture of the postmodern person provokes perplexity and amazement inside ecclesiastic structures. If on the one hand the eagerness for such an experience is a positive factor in guiding the believer to return to God and to develop a deeper faith for everyday life, on the other hand the experience sought after and desired is, most of the time, unrelated to moral norms, dogmatic truth, or institutional membership.

Our research and reflection in this book proceeds from this inquiry. Due to the changes that took place throughout the historical process summarized above, what configuration is presented by mysticism in Christianity today? While in the past the great mystics were persons linked to the institution, living out their experiences inside it and being controlled by it, in the twentieth century we see mystical men and women who claim their bond to the Christian faith and the gospel of Jesus Christ but remain outside of the church—either because they do not accept many of its instructions, or because they are not considered by the church to be full members due to their often rebellious and insubordinate behavior.

We wanted to concentrate our attention on this phenomenon, studying how, in a century such as the last, there were so many mystical personalities who could be a shining inspiration for today—precisely because of their difference and "strangeness" regarding the traditional model of what has been called mystical, as well as regarding those who live out this experience.

Introduction

We see with great frequency the devaluation, even deterioration, of words rich in meaning. As a result they begin to be understood in erroneous and inadequate ways. That was what happened to the term *mysticism*: "Deprived of its noble original meaning, it came to connote a kind of fanaticism, with strong passional content and a large dose of irrationality."[19]

Thus the word *mysticism* has remained connected to something supernatural and outside of reality, even generating some fear when mentioned or repeated. For many scholars and critics, mysticism is looked at with a certain suspicion and disdain because, according to them, it doesn't take into consideration the human being as inserted into history. No matter how and in what environment it is mentioned or analyzed (whether Christian or atheist), it is always seen from a perspective that is "dualistic, more precisely one of opposition between the natural and the supernatural."[20]

One of the causes of the debasement of the real value of mysticism occurred in the seventeenth century. In that period mysticism oscillated in alarming ways. For the duration of that so-called "golden century," it was seen as something that merited distrust and was branded as unrelated to Christianity and, above all, to Christian thought.

> In fact, set in the ambit of the exceptional, of the supernatural, mysticism could only remain outside of the common and normal ground of human life, restricted to a marginal place precisely because of its extraordinariness. All this is due particularly to the endeavor by the Counter-Reformation church to control the totality of the religious, philosophical and spiritual life of the Catholic world. And it is not by chance that several voluminous treatises on mysticism were also written in that period, which today give the impression that it was a tremendously complex topic, but were intended to be a response to that effort. That the attempt failed is seen in what came afterwards—the Enlightenment and all that followed it. This explains why only now we begin to discover that in reality the first eleven centuries of Christianity conceived of mysticism in a way that was radically different from the one that has reached us.[21]

Mysticism has often been subjected to a suspicious silence and a stereotypical viewpoint. Thanks to Freud, psychoanalysis has cast much suspicion on the sanity of the mystics, considering them completely passive persons, deprived of will, desire, joy, and sadness, if not neurotic, hysterical,

19. Vaz, *Experiência mística e filosofia na tradição ocidental*, 9.
20. Vannini, *Introdução à mística*, 11.
21. Ibid., 11–12.

and abnormal. They were no longer seen as equal to any other human being. They would go to isolated places, away from the world, to be in permanent contact with God, far from the problems that affect everybody else. This is an equivocal and prejudicial vision that corresponds neither to reality nor to the richness with which mysticism has graced humankind.

In studying the history of mysticism in Christianity—especially its contemporary history—through the writings of its protagonists, our intention is to demonstrate that the elements comprising the mystical experience can no longer be anathematized and devalued as has irresponsibly been done. We will try to demonstrate that the twentieth-century mystics were completely active persons, committed and engaged in the questions of their time. And if we find, throughout the history of Christianity, great mystical personalities who were religious and contemplative monks, we may equally find, on the margin of the church's calendar and canonization proceedings, men and women who lived out both a union with God and a commitment to the world in an extraordinarily integrated and luminous way. The more intimate and closer to God, the more the mystical experience demonstrates the need for it to take place in a context in which it enters into the struggle to make that context better, always taking into account the value and dignity of human life.

Karl Rahner, the greatest Catholic theologian of the twentieth century, says that "the Christian of the future will be mystical, or will be nothing." Rahner expresses what is not so much a foresight as an affirmation of values. If on the one hand the Enlightenment—beneficially—swept away the superstitious elements of religion, on the other hand it helped make clear the mystical core of Christianity from the standpoint of the essential message of Jesus: "The kingdom of God is here and is within you."[22]

In Rahner's affirmation we may begin to understand mysticism in its real context. The inner richness and depth of Christianity must always, by nature, lead to action. This action can assume different aspects, depending on the circumstances. It may assume a markedly religious and charitable character, but it may also be realized in the social and political realm—either way it is the complete opposite of a flight from reality. There are many examples of mystics that would corroborate this affirmation, but their biographies are not well known and are often dismissed as irrelevant and unrealistically idealized.[23]

It is precisely in the testimony of these mystics that we find the best way to understand mysticism and to obtain

---

22. Ibid., 23.
23. See Schneider, *Teología como biografía*.

reliable information about the nature and content of this singular type of experience. In truth, they are the first theoreticians of their own experience. And it is by acknowledging as authentic their experiential testimony (the experiential is the domain of strictly personal experience, but in obedience to a definite structure, while the experimental is the realm of scientific experience with its conditions and rules) and by accepting, in principle, their proposed interpretation that the studious mystics can define the object of their own investigation. For its part, this investigation is necessarily multidisciplinary, since the mystical experience is a holistic phenomenon in which all aspects of the complex human reality are integrated.[24]

Such an experience occurs in the life history of the human being and gives rise to the encounter with the Absolute other. This experience "annuls" the distance between them. The affirmation that mystics do not enter into their own (social, political, economic, and religious) context turns out to be inconsistent. This transformation involves the whole being of those who experience it, completely changing their knowledge and desires within the reality in which they live, so that they can act in a way that surpasses the relativity of the facts and objects that surround them and arrive at the deepest core of the conception of the human being and the world.

Some scholars affirm that from this standpoint it is possible "to exclude from the mystical experience a whole series of extraordinary and abnormal phenomena, spontaneous or induced, that can accompany mystical states but are not only distinct but also separate from them, and that in general are the object of strict regulation and criticism by the authentic mystics themselves."[25] They are excluded, or at least relativized, because the most important thing is not the extraordinary phenomenon but the positive fruits that the mystical experience produces and illuminates.

Individual mystical experiences will be, then, the basis for highlighting recurrent characteristics with universal import. They possess a large variety of terms that gravitate around two poles—the subjective and the objective. It can be said that the mystical experience is "represented by the triangle 'mystic-mystical-Mystery.' The mystical experience, in its original meaning, places itself in the interior of this triangle: in the experiential intentionality which unites the mystic as novice with the Absolute as Mystery; and in the language with which, in a second moment of recollection and reflection, the

---

24. Vaz, *Experiência mística e filosofia na tradição ocidental*, 15.
25. Ibid., 16–17.

experience is named as mystical and offers itself as the object of theoretical explanations of a different nature."[26]

Anthropology, which embraces mysticism in its originality, points to the need for an anthropological conception capable of interpreting mystical phenomena correctly. This is seen throughout its historical-literary process, where the real value of mysticism was often reduced to a mere declaration or to supernatural sensations. The indisputable originality of the mystical experience, as reflected in the authentic and irrefutable testimony of the great mystics, shows itself to be irreducible to narrow reductionist presuppositions. The mystical experience is original anthropological data. Thus its interpretation demands a conception of the structure of the human being capable of accounting for its originality.[27]

Thus, we can say that mysticism is grounded in anthropological data that involves human beings. It opens them to receptivity to the transcendent, and consequently guides them in all their relational aspects, making them active participants in the context in which they live. This is because the anthropological place of the mystical experience corresponds exactly to the intentional space of the dialectical transition from categories of structure to categories of relationship, or from the subject as being-in-itself to the subject as being-for-the-other, for Otherness and its service through charity.[28]

Human beings open themselves to the world in a first relational moment expressed through the category of objectivity, and may open themselves to the other, and to history, on a second relational level that expresses itself through the category of intersubjectivity. Finally they can open themselves to the Absolute, on a third and higher relational level that expresses itself through the category of Transcendence.[29] True mystics are those who live in profound contact with all relational levels of the human being. This contact, however, does not make them passive beings removed from others but rather beings who are active within their own history.

Throughout this twofold movement—toward oneself, toward the other—the mystical experience appropriately finds its own anthropological place. It can be identified as a fertile tension between being and manifestation, that is, between human beings in their finitude and in their particular situations, and the profound dynamism in the direction of the Absolute that engenders their self-manifestation.

---

26. Ibid.
27. Ibid., 18. See also Schneider, *Teología como biografía*.
28. Vaz, *Experiência mística e filosofia na tradição ocidental*, 23.
29. Ibid., 24.

This paroxysm occurs in an emergence of the Absolute, who, being the ultimate limit of the intentional movement of the subject, is for this very reason present at the origin and during the course of this movement and formally present in the acts of intelligence and will through which the subject expresses himself or herself. Here, in the *apex mentis*, the intuition and fruition of the Absolute occur, configuring the highest act in the life of the spirit: the mystical experience.[30]

The mystical experience cannot be separated from anthropological data, since both are profoundly unified in arriving at the diverse relations that involve the whole human being, according to the environment where he or she lives. But, drowning as it is in a sea of all-controlling psychologisms, it becomes in reality a substantively mysterious object and at the same time an instigation to theological research. From a historical perspective, the misunderstanding and condemnation of mysticism at the end of the seventeenth century, with its effective disappearance from the living texture of the culture, correspond fully to the misunderstanding and condemnation of its meaning and its allusions.[31]

This experience, which springs from the spirit, nowadays appears to be

a blasphemy for the devout conscience, which does not consider itself to be an instrumental and servile conscience, based on accommodation, without the courage and honesty to look and see what is negative and hold back from it. For this reason sentimentalism constitutes the essential element of ideologies as well as religions, making them mere superstitions, and extending its influence to include mysticism, which is often confused with the nourishment of the heart, upon which, consequently, falls a righteous distrust of intelligence.[32]

It is important to emphasize, more and more each day, that mysticism, understood as an experience of the spirit, is not primarily or principally sentiment, which can be precisely defined as that which does not allow the spirit to be. Vannini says that

the most complete proof of this is found in the fact that the mystic is speculative, that is, a dialectician, who has the ability to unify antitheses and to feel at home among them, while the sentimental, as is the case with all that is ideological and psychological, is fixed within his or her limitations and incapable

30. Ibid., 25.
31. See Vannini, *Introdução à mística*, 7–8.
32. Ibid., 8.

of unity. And for that reason the being and action of the sentimental are always those of eradication, the evil thinking that constitutes sentimentality operating in conformity with its own essence—since it is made of pain and evil, that is exactly what it produces.[33]

In other words, the issue here is not sensations. The spirit is, above all, knowledge and integration. Movement effectively comes from an act of intelligence, which bends over the experience and, in an enlightened way, redirects everything toward its own reality. Mystics are, thus, much more than simply those who only talk about God. They are those who, without needing many words, reveal God in their lives through gestures and actions inside their own reality. This goes far beyond pure feelings. The mystics allow themselves to be fully involved by the will of God, who is no more than the perfect realization of Love, but Love in a much wider sense than what we are acquainted with. If true mystics were moved uniquely and exclusively by their feelings, they wouldn't be prepared to allow the Spirit of God to act in them, since they would be confined only to their interests.

In the realm of mysticism as it pertains to feeling, sensitivity is not denied. On the contrary, it is reinforced in such a way that the mystic ends up seeking "those satisfactions which he denies to himself in sensation."[34] Thus, one is aware that "all this love and the desire to suffer for love is in fact at the service of his ardent desire for joy, that is, at the service of his own selfishness."[35] The truth is that the true mystic loses "the love for his own soul, his own I, and from this emerges the spirit and the continuous and tranquil union with God in the spirit."[36] From this true experience comes the determination and will to bring the same experience to others through what is lived out in the struggles of daily life, and through the will and desire that spring from the spirit, thus building an earth free of evil.

Thus, by taking into account the whole historical process of the formation of Christianity, we see that its essence lies in the affirmation that Christ is continuously being born in the heart of those who believe. That is, God is made present in the incarnation through God's Otherness, "and becomes the ever deeper Me Myself, the real I, instead of the superficial empirical 'I.'"[37]

This experience can be understood only from the standpoint of the indifference and emptiness produced in full in the empirical I, that is, in the

33. Ibid., 8–9.
34. Ibid., 26.
35. Ibid.
36. Ibid., 27.
37. Ibid., 35.

whole complex of volitions, thoughts, and feelings that characterizes us at every moment but in no way constitutes that which is essential in us, since it is ceaselessly changing. The measure of a life that is involved in this experience will be in discipleship of Jesus, in answering the call to "live as He lived."

Such an occurrence is the Spirit, who according to the Christian faith dwells in each human being and develops in them the knowledge of God. This knowledge, which only comes through experiences, is a continuous movement bringing to maturity the encounter with the other.

Understood in Christian terms, mystics are those human beings who, in their time, achieve a profound experience of deep and loving union with God while living it out in their reality, and are henceforth impelled to transform the reality of the injustice in which they find themselves.

The three biographies and life histories that we will introduce at the end of our reflection—Dorothy Day, Etty Hillesum, and Egide van Broeckhoeven—will serve to concretely and palpably illustrate what we are trying to convey throughout this book.

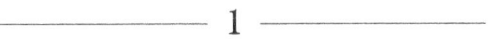

Premature or Late Modernity
A Question of Culture

BEFORE PROPERLY EMBARKING ON an analysis of the issue of mysticism as a pivotal experience to be presented to human beings today, it is important for us to analyze the context in which we live. In this chapter we will try to develop such an analysis, examining the main facts and the economic, social, political, and cultural components that characterized the twentieth century.

During the past century, there was an enormous effervescence of events that changed the sociopolitical configuration of the world. The interpretation of these facts helped to further deepen the crisis in which modern thought already found itself. And it generated the uncertain and unstable environment in which we live today, so-called postmodernity, late modernity, or hypermodernity.

We will try to see how, in this context, what emerges as a foundational and pivotal criterion for human life is no longer Enlightenment reason, but rather an incentive for an unrestrained consumerism that makes human beings believe they will find happiness there. But the degree of frustration brought about by this sterile pursuit unleashes a spiritual anxiety that is reflected in the search for very different forms of contact with the divine and the Sacred.

Thus the change of epoch we are living through has a strong impact on religion and belief, and obliges us to rethink its configuration and the way to live it out and transmit it.

The Death of Utopia and the Predominance of One Model

The word *utopia* was a name given by the English humanist Thomas More (1478–1535) to an imaginary island with an ideal sociopolitical system. It is formed from the negative Greek adverb *ou* ("not") and the word *topos* ("place") and means "that which does not have a place," the *no topos*. This word, which was unknown to the Greek world, was the title given by Thomas More to a work that, according to the author himself, must be considered a "literary trifle that slipped almost unconsciously from his pen" to later gain fame and notoriety. At first, according to More, the work was intended to be only a little lampoon about "the best of republics," situated on the new island, Utopia. The text, published in Louvain, Belgium, in November 1516, would soon find an exceptional audience among European intellectuals and would come to characterize not only a genre but an entire sociological literature. Today, in fact, besides the literature of utopian ideas, there is also a literature of reflection on these ideas. The production on this theme is feverish and dynamic. The utopia has an important place not only in the sociology of retrospective knowledge but also in that of prospective action.[1]

According to the Houaiss dictionary, *utopia* is that which is outside of reality, which never existed in the past and can never exist in the future. It is a plan or a dream that cannot be realized, or that can be realized only in an unforeseeable moment in the future. It also has the connotation of an ideal never achieved and always pursued. That is why, in a more colloquial sense, the word acquired the meaning of an impossible and unrealizable dream. In Portuguese, and in general in the Latin languages, utopia is any imaginary description of an ideal society based on just laws and on politico-economical institutions that are truly committed to the well-being of the collectivity. By extension, a utopia is said to be a project of an unrealizable nature, a project that is the fruit of a noble and generous ideal yet is impracticable. Colloquially, the word *utopia* is thus used as a synonym of *chimera* or *fantasy*.

Returning to Thomas More, *utopia* means, then, "in no place": a place that is not any place, an absent presence, an unreal reality, a nostalgic beyond, an Otherness without identification. To this name the author adds a series of paradoxes with names derived from the prefix *a-*, which in Greek means "absence of": Amaurote, the capital of the island, is a ghostly city; the Anyder is a river without water in its bed; its ruler, Ademus, is a prince without people; its inhabitants, the Alaopolitanes, are citizens without a city; and their neighbors, the Achorians, are inhabitants without a country. "This philological prestidigitation has the admitted objective of announcing the plausibility of a world inside out—and a latent and undeclared objective of denouncing the legitimacy of the theoretically real world, the world of laws."[2]

---

1. Desroche, "Utopie," in *Encyclopaedia Universalis*.
2. Ibid.

After Thomas More, the definition of *utopia* gained in prominence and consistency, and also in complexity. The utopia came to be something like an imaginary plan for another reality, for another society, which would renovate the organizing components and structures of the current reality, such as the economy, politics, and religion. Many utopias have passed through and inspired human history, some with deplorable results, others giving strength to the human project and moving history. The secret of the dynamism of the utopia lies in the Otherness that informs it from inside. For this reason the utopia is not simply a fiction and a fantasy that should not be taken seriously. As Desroche says, "The fantasy in question is that of an imagination which, even if constituted by situations, is not less constitutive of other situations. History makes utopias, but utopias also make history."[3]

Utopias are the engine of history because they make apparent the possibility of an alternative to the way history is configured today. The process would occur in the following sequence:

> the fantasy gave birth to the project, the project to the audience, the audiences to larger circles through publicity, the publicity to plans for realization, the plans to strategies, the strategies to social forces, the forces to an opinion, and this power of opinion to a power of government.[4]

But everything began with a dream, dreamed with others and converted into an alternative and a plan. Following this line, Gramsci says that religion is the most gigantic utopia ever seen in history.[5] In the case of historical Christianity, we tend to agree with the Italian philosopher, since the Christian "alternative" shaped the entire Western part of the world. But it could be argued that in politics, socialism, for example, was also a huge

---

3. Ibid.
4. Ibid.
5. See Gramsci, *Os intelectuais e a arganização da cultura*, 43: "Religion is the most gigantic utopia, that is, the most gigantic 'metaphysics' that ever appeared in history, since it is the most grandiose attempt to reconcile in a mythological way the real contradictions of historical life: it affirms that in fact man has the same 'nature,' that there exists a generic man, created by God as a child of God, and therefore the brother of other men, equal to other men, free among the others and in the same way as the others; and he can in this way conceive of mirroring himself in God, as the 'self-consciousness' of humanity; but it also affirms that none of this belongs to this world or will occur in this world, but rather in another (utopian) world. Therefore the ideas of liberty, equality and fraternity fermented among men; among men who saw themselves neither as equals nor as brothers of other men, nor as free in relation to them. Thus it happened that in every radical uprising of the multitudes, in one way or another, under certain kinds of ideology, these demands were put forward."

utopia. This is confirmed in the large sociopolitical and cultural cataclysm provoked by its fall, which turned a page in contemporary history.

In Marxism, *utopia* means an abstract and imaginary model of an ideal society conceived as a criticism of the existing social organization, with no chance of implementation because of its lack of connection to the political and economic conditions of concrete reality. From this came the concept of "utopian socialism." To other thinkers, such as the sociologist Karl Mannheim (1893–1947) or the philosopher Ernst Bloch (1885–1977), *utopia* means something very different: an alternative plan of social organization capable of indicating achievable and concrete potentialities in a given established political order, contributing in this way to its transformation. According to this last conception, therefore, a utopia would be an engine of history, something that would impel it toward its goal.

The event normally identified as the end point in the crisis of modernity and the beginning of so-called postmodernity was the fall of the Berlin Wall in 1989, consummating a death that had been announced long beforehand: that of real socialism. From that moment, the concept of "the death of utopia" emerged on the proscenium of modern debate, referring to that historical fact, which was of extreme importance in the twentieth century and defined the transition to the twenty-first century.

The twentieth century was born under the aegis of socialism. It was the first century in which capitalism and socialism openly vied for hegemony over the world. The generations of the 1960s and 1970s were protagonists of the revolutionary ideas and movements that emerged in this period, inspired by the writings of Marx, the Russian and Cuban revolutions, and the subsequent guerrilla movement led by Ernesto "Che" Guevara until his death in Bolivia in 1967, and inspired also by the hippie movement, the protests against the Vietnam War, and the rejection of the consumerist society that was the legacy of capitalism in the West. The so-called utopias were now utopias of a new alternative model of society, identified with real socialism and the dream of a society free of the values imposed by capital. The dispute for world hegemony among the great European powers—on one side the former Soviet Union with socialism, and on the other the United States with a capitalist economic plan—would bring the world to a period of cold war, that is, of "armed peace," which lasted for three decades.

In the collision with American capitalism, however, the Soviet model suffered hard blows. And in that process it met its demise after almost thirty years of cold war, with the fall of the Berlin Wall in 1989. The fall of the wall represents the end of the utopias and has also been interpreted as the "end of history."[6] It is the disappearance of subjectivity, in the sense of human

---

6. See Fukuyama, *The End of History and the Last Man*.

will as an agent of the transformation of reality. It equally represents the end of a balance of power that attempted a difficult equilibrium in the Western world. With the fall of real socialism, capitalism triumphantly paraded as the only surviving model and the only model capable of organizing the economy, society, and politics, as well as conquering the countries of the socialist bloc. It is well known how sad and disappointed Pope John Paul II was upon realizing that the society of well-being and the dynamics of consumerism had penetrated his much beloved and very Catholic Poland.[7] The socialist utopia ceased to illuminate the struggle for justice against exploitation, alienation, and oppression. And historical Christianity, which had in some way participated in this utopia—at least through its many followers committed to militancy for social justice—saw itself in crisis, and began retrieving aspects of its faith that were fragmented or actually lost along the way, such as prayer, liturgy, and belonging to a community.[8]

On the other hand, political militancy itself—and within it the militancy of many Christians called "leftist," who were united in being inspired by the gospel and by socialist militancy, or by mysticism and revolution—seemed to have been exhausted as a proposal for a path toward the transformation of the world. Above all, the new generations of militants found themselves very much affected. With this crisis, internationalism and even socialism seem to have been transformed into historical impossibilities. "If capitalism was terrible and unjust, socialism presented itself as impossible," in falling like a house of cards in Eastern Europe.[9]

The end of the twentieth century saw the political elites perpetuated in power, despite the emergence and expansion of new democracies in the world. The new generations failed to find proposals that responded to their anxiety and idealism, and put themselves on "other" trips: drugs and consumerism. The intellectuals, who had been militants of the left, now became "red repainted in green," adhering above all to causes related to environment, gender, race or ethnicity, and betting on criticism as well as the transformation of culture.

The engine of history, which in the socialist model is the class struggle, was replaced in the postmodern era (identified here as after the fall of the wall, although this interpretation is not unanimous among the analysts) by individualized and fragmented relations. The new order, the new ideology,

---

7. See, for example, Bernstein and Politi, *His Holiness: John Paul II and the History of Our Time*, especially ch. 8, "The Angry Pope."

8. Andrade, "Encantos e desencantos: a militância do cristão em tempos de crise"; Andrade, "A crise da modernidade e as possibilidades de uma nova militância cristã."

9. See Emir Sader's article, "Capitalismo: o que é isso?" See also C. Boff, "A Igreja militante de João Paulo II e o capitalismo triunfante."

the supposedly new proposal, was nothing more than a new name for the same old capitalism: neoliberalism and the formation of a consumer society.

Capitalism achieved an expansion never before seen in world history, finding its dynamics in an increasingly global socialization of production and an increasingly privatized appropriation. Centered on the permanent pursuit of profit, it found in financial capital its paradise. Money became more and more virtual, going to sleep on one continent and waking up on another, and not necessarily being channeled into a productive vein. This quick description shows us that the course of the history of an entire era of social struggles and utopias experienced a Copernican turn at the beginning of the twenty-first century, coinciding with the era called—properly or improperly—postmodernity, an era of new political and economic models.[10] It cannot be said, however, that the utopias have died or that they have really arrived at an unshakable "end." If utopia is the engine of history, it will always inhabit the human heart and mind. Now, however, it wears other clothes and shows different faces. It is what is happening today, and with this change comes the challenge to perceive what new utopias are coming to the fore after the fall of the old ones.

The modern utopias appear fragmented and privatized. The new generations are driven to seek alternatives for dealing with current social problems and finding new solutions to these problems. They turn to individual and affective concerns. They struggle with an emptiness of meaning in their lives.

Young people no longer want to change the world. They try to make money in order to have a comfortable life. They no longer take up arms to overthrow dictators and establish a new revolutionary order. Instead they participate in drug trafficking and defend themselves against urban violence, which is growing at a dizzying pace in the big cities of the West, whether in rich or poor countries. Walter Benjamin has already said of modernity that it was born under the sign of suicide. Before him, Freud suggested that modernity was oriented by Thanatos—the death instinct. Based on the reflection of these two thinkers, Zygmunt Bauman comments that the world described by the utopias was a predictably translucent world, where nothing dark or impenetrable was presented to the human eye—a world with nothing to disrupt the harmony, with nothing out of place; a world without impurities; a world without foreigners.[11] A world that would fit in one coherent and holistic narrative.

10.. Aware that authors and thinkers have not come to an agreement on a terminology for the period in which we are living, we have adopted the term *postmodernity* (and sometimes *late modernity* or *hypermodernity*) for a question of convention and clarity.

11. Bauman, *Postmodernity and Its Discontents*, 12.

Others social analysts, however, hold that utopia is not finished. According to L. T. Sargent, for example, a new type of utopia, which he calls "critical utopia," has been created.[12] Since the beginning of the 1970s, writers and theorists on feminism and gender issues have produced a strong and continuous stream of feminist utopias. Furthermore, says Sargent, there are today several communities motivated by solidly established utopias that have already been in existence for a longer period than those of the 1960s. He calls these communities "intentional," that is, motivated to come together by ideas of ecology, justice, spirituality. These communities express the desire of a great many men and women, and even of peoples and nations, to live a better life. They are a sign in the midst of a world that has apparently lost track of the previous utopias.[13] Despite being less well known, these communities show that utopia continues to motivate and strengthen people's search for meaning in this fragmented postmodernity.[14]

Massimo Borghesi, professor of philosophy in Perugia and Rome, Italy, in trying to synthesize what happened from 1968 to 1989 and up until 2008, asserts that we went from a collectivist utopia to an exasperated individualism, and then to the awareness that one is as much an ideology as the other. Marxism is an ideology, and so is the idea that globalization brings heaven to earth.[15] He further argues that, in practical reality, the State is needed as much as the market, the nation as much as supranational reality, secularism as much as openness to religion, and faith as much as reason.[16]

In his criticism, the Italian philosopher vehemently condemns reductionist ideological thought, extending this criticism to theology, which, according to him, was taken in by the thirst for power of the various ideologies that came and went throughout the past thirty years. We think that Borghesi generalizes his critique to theology, and we cannot agree with it. However, we cannot fail to be aware that it represents a whole current of thought that gained considerable strength toward the end of the twentieth century (in the 1980s and 1990s), and that coexists today within society and the church with another that is more in tune with the movement incarnated in liberation theology. The latter has not died, but it suffered a profound crisis with the fall of the utopias. It has been rethought and reconfigured. It seems to

12. See Sargent, "Utopianism."

13. We cite, among other examples, the North American movement known as "voluntary simplicity." Also noteworthy are the "Mariapolises" of the Focolare ecclesiastical movement—"little cities" where, inspired by the communities of the New Testament, the economy of fellowship is practiced. See www.focolare.org.

14. See González Buelta, *La utopia ya está en lo germinal*.

15. See Borghesi, "Da queda do Muro à queda das bolsas."

16. Ibid.

us that Professor Borghesi does not do justice to the progression of some currents in today's Christian theology.[17]

All this demonstrates that the postmodernity in which we live is a multifaceted concept that calls our attention to a set of profound social and cultural changes running from the end of the twentieth century and into the beginning of the twenty-first century, and of the millennium, in many "advanced" societies. Many things are happening at the same time: accelerated technological change, involving telecommunications and the power of the Internet; alterations in political relations; and the appearance of new social movements, especially those related to ethnicity and race, ecology and gender. But the issue is even broader: can it be that modernity itself, as a sociocultural entity, is disintegrating and taking with it the whole sumptuous edifice of the Enlightenment's cosmic vision?

The so-called end of modernity—which cannot be taken literally, since modernity continues to be present in several sectors of modern life—culminates with the end of history as a unity and of the very idea of linear progress, as well as (and primarily) with the advent of mass communications. However, although history is formulated from objective conditions observed by human beings, preventing them from deciding at any moment to work out social relations that come only from their own minds, one cannot forget that these same conditions are created by the social and political actions of these same human beings. Human societies are neither established nor run according to a law that is external to human beings. Hence neither capitalism nor socialism, nor any other ideology or model of society, is the inexorable destiny of humankind. They are rather the result of social struggles between interests and the organized consciousness of social forces.

What cannot be ignored, however, is that the postmodern world has appropriated and assimilated the so-called death of utopia in a way that objectively favors the expansion and predominance of the neoliberal model. This is reflected in the fact that the world's twenty wealthiest countries dictate the economic, political, and social norms to the rest of the nations. This situation is far from just and equitable. It incites reactions from every human being endowed with a consciousness not yet anesthetized by the frenetic and impenitent consumerism that prevails in Western societies.

Therefore we will proceed with our reflection by trying to take a closer look at the impact that all these recent changes have had on culture. The "cultural" effects of the fall of the utopias are as important as—or even more important than—the economic and social ones.

17. Among them we certainly include the Latin American theology of liberation, which was especially strong in the 1970s and 1980s and continues to be alive and active in such Latin American countries as Brazil.

The End of Certainty

The series of books published by Bauman, each title featuring the adjective *liquid* as modifier for a different noun (*modernity, life, fear, love*, etc.), offer a powerful metaphor for the title of this section, in which we try to describe contemporaneity.

We live in a time marked by uncertainty, by insecurity regarding a stable and solid position in society and a clear identity. This is our everyday life. And, according to Bauman, it is more a passive than an active time, a weight that constrains movement. The author characterizes this context as liquid—not the liquid of pure and crystal-clear water, with which we bathe ourselves and quench our thirst, but a sticky, slimy substance that clings to the skin and cannot be removed.[18]

To better explain the idea of the slimy liquidity that we experience today, Bauman quotes Mary Douglas, from her book *Purity and Danger*:

> Only at the very moment when I believe that I possess it, behold by a curious reversal, it possesses me ... The slime is like a liquid seen in a nightmare, where all its properties are animated by a sort of life and turn back against me ... To touch the slimy is to risk being dissolved in sliminess.[19]

The sliminess that Bauman speaks of—following Mary Douglas—and that we adopt in our analysis means a new habitat for what we understand as truth, certainty, belief, and identity. The dispute about the veracity or falsity of certain beliefs is always simultaneously an argument about the right of some to say with authority what others must obey. The dispute, in reality, falls back on the establishment or the reaffirmation of relationships of superiority and inferiority, of domination and submission, among those who hold to affirmations, definitions, and beliefs.[20]

With acute discernment, Bauman refers to Plato's myth of the cave in saying that, if one wishes to build a theory on why a few chosen ones can emerge from the dark cave and see things as they truly are in luminous transparency, one must give equal attention to a theory on why none of the others can do this adequately without someone to guide them—and on why they resist this "guidance," preferring to stay inside the cave instead of

---

18. Bauman, *Postmodernity and Its Discontents*, 26.

19. Douglas, *Purity and Danger*, 53, cited in ibid., 27. Bauman comments that Mary Douglas added a sociological perspective to the brilliant and memorable philosophical analysis by Jean-Paul Sartre of what he calls "le visqueux." Sartre, *L'être et le néant*, 608–10.

20. Bauman, *Postmodernity and Its Discontents*, 113.

exploring what can be seen only in the sunlight shining outside. Bauman adds that if theoreticians of truth were to develop a generalized recipe for leaving the cave, they would promptly argue that the questions involved are not the kind that can emerge from the experience of simple mortals. In this way they would inflate the price of the exit tickets to a considerably higher value, as if to ensure that simple mortals would observe their verdict.[21]

Because of this, what is or is not right, what is or is not true, has today been polarized. And the philosophers dispute this not by building a theory of the truth, but rather a theory of truths, in the plural, striking a mortal blow to the previously reigning certainties. And since the plurality of truths has ceased to be vexing and radically contestable, it will soon be ignored. Because of the possibility that different beliefs not only can be considered simultaneously true, but are in fact simultaneously true, the theory of truth at the center of thinkers' attention today seems to have lost much of its function in disputing the status of any knowledge other than philosophical knowledge.[22]

The impossibility of distancing ourselves from what we believe and take for granted, as well as from the language in which we express it, is assumed here. Using Rorty's image, Bauman says that there is a tapestry of truths and beliefs knit simultaneously by philosophers, intellectuals, and theologians in order to cover the illegible confusion of human discourse with a clean and clear pretense of meaning.[23]

Western culture has been—very understandably—harshly criticized for being racist, sexist, and imperialist. But we cannot deny that it is also a culture very worried about being racist, sexist, and imperialist, as well as ethnocentric, parochial, and intellectually intolerant. In other words, it is a culture that would like not to be what it is, that no longer finds within its reach sure references—such as God, or the truth, or the Nature of things—for presuming what it really wants to and/or should be. It is precisely this legacy, or part of this complex legacy, that increasingly emerges today.[24] We no longer find certainties or absolute truths. We find ourselves in the middle of a plurality in which nothing is categorically affirmed and the ground shifts under our feet.

Ironically, it seems—according to Rorty and other analysts[25]—that today the only shelter for safety and certainty can be found in novels, in works

21. Ibid.
22. Ibid., 116.
23. Ibid., 117.
24. Ibid., 118.
25. See Rorty, "Heidegger, Kundera, and Dickens," cited in Bauman, *Postmodernity and Its Discontents*, 68.

of fiction. Bauman takes an attitude of ironic criticism regarding this theory, saying that one the greatest paradoxes of Western civilization would then be that its truth, the truth of Enlightenment modernity that so much favored certainty and rationality, "would find its home in the same works of fiction against which it fought tooth and nail."[26]

Indeed, while premodern thinkers were taught to see difference with equanimity and to accept the preordained plurality of things as part of God's creation, modernity teaches that it is possible to exclude some realities and build a world according to one's own preferences within a model of certain preconceived ideas. Thus were built the modern edifices of the great narratives, full of certainties, of well-polished and rigorous concepts, and smoothed over by narrations without breaches or insecurities.

One of the great challenges, perhaps without precedent, of the late modernity in which we live is the end of the world we just described. In other words, the diversity we are immersed in is called into question—a diversity situated inside a weak, negligent, and impotent institutionalization of differences, with a resulting fickleness, malleability, and short duration.

If previously the challenge to the question of human identity was how to build it consistently and how to give it a shape that would receive universal acknowledgment, "today the problem of identity emerges above all from the difficulty in sustaining any identity for a longer term, from the virtual impossibility of finding a form of expression of identity which has a chance of being recognized for a lifetime, and the resulting necessity of not embracing any identity very tightly, in order to be able to abandon it in the fastest possible way."[27]

Everything is fleeting, nothing is certain. And the human being, who has no vocation for chaos or anarchy, feels lost in this situation. According to Baudrillard, all beings appear in the postmodern world under the modality of the simulacrum, in other words, as a work of simulation rather than a simple farce or plagiarism. They are like a psychosomatic disease where the patient, despite having all the symptoms, always leaves up in the air some doubt as to whether he or she is in fact sick.[28]

The favored means of expression today is no longer the *logos* (related to speaking, to saying), through which the truth used to be expressed. Rather, it is what is seen, the image, that which has an impact on the senses. Normally it is a directed image, carrying other intentions, and it jeopardizes

---

26. See Bauman, *Postmodernity and Its Discontents*, 118.

27. Ibid., 123.

28. Baudrillard, *Simulacra and Simulation*, 168, cited in Bauman, *Postmodernity and Its Discontents*, 125.

or may even liquidate the symbol, which is open and receptive to interpretation and meaning.[29]

It is no coincidence that in the biblical universe the favored human sense for living fully—the sense that identifies the human being—is hearing, listening. Sight is always under suspicion, due to its high risk of being idolatrous. The desert, the place of conversion par excellence for the people of the Bible, is for the same reason the place of pure listening, the place where truth can be manifested free from the risk of a banal, closed, and idolatrous seeing. What I circumscribe in my field of vision can remain confined within my limits and therefore be manipulated by me. What I am able to see and situate at a particular point in space is smaller than I am. And I modify it as much as I want. Hearing, on the other hand, is made propitious by the Spirit, who, being divine breath, communicates freely and cannot be grasped, nor can its origin be clearly identified. It leaves the human inhabited by the question that touches him or her most deeply, and points to the path of love and life.

Bauman concludes that the truth, banned from vigorous reason and from reality, can expect to find its "second home" only in exile, in the house of art or fiction.[30] We add, however, that truth does allow itself to be found in the deep experiences of the senses that faith calls experiences of God, and that are objects of reflection not only in theology but in all sciences that are called human sciences and are interested in the human being's destiny in this world and at this moment in history.

But religion reduced to a mere human and natural act, without Transcendence, would not take on this challenge. It would explain itself in human terms, and this would result in its depletion. It must return to its source, that is, to the Revealing Word whose mysterious origin teaches human beings about their true origin, their authentic home, manifesting itself as the truth that emerges from deep within history to shine with epiphanic radiance in Otherness, whether human or divine.

The End of Hegemony and the Predominance of Plurality

Among the multiple definitions of culture that today circulate in the world of knowledge, one of them is "the set of distinctive spiritual, material, intellectual and emotional features of a society or a social group, [which]

---

29. See Mardones, *La transformación de la religión*, 51–52.
30. Bauman, *Postmodernity and Its Discontents*, 126.

encompasses, in addition to art and literature, lifestyles, ways of living together, value systems, traditions and beliefs."[31]

What conventionally is called culture, but can have several definitions according to the field of expertise, is something that has suffered great and profound mutations during the transition from modernity to postmodernity. At that point this became an area of the greatest interest for today's human beings. What used to be "social" in the second half of the twentieth century is now "cultural" at the start of the twenty-first century. But the main difficulty with this state of things is that the concept of culture itself is no longer univocal.

Michel de Certeau, in *La culture au pluriel*,[32] warns that the growth of cultural problems occurs in a wide context, defined by the logic of a productivist society that responds to the basic needs of a wealthier population and that—in order to maintain its growth and rate of consumption—must expand and satisfy the "cultural" needs of its consumers.[33] Thus, rather than "values" to be defended or ideas to be promoted, culture becomes a task to be undertaken throughout the whole fabric of social life in order to keep the consumption machine lubricated. "It is a society made up of 'people who want to have something' and less and less of men and women who 'want to be someone.'"[34]

Certeau's analysis, although more than thirty years old, remains—it seems to us—completely current, at least in the Northern Hemisphere, that is, in the developed West, whose cultural standard was homogenized (as Western Christian culture) and exported by means of colonization to the rest of the world, often crushing the indigenous cultures. The current emergence of such cultures—as objects of study and as actors in history—makes it difficult for the concept to remain univocal. In fact, Western Christian society no longer exists. This is corroborated by the author himself, who says that every elucidation concerned with cultural issues progresses on a ground of unstable words, where it is almost impossible to impose a conceptual definition of those words and to articulate a wider sense of their

---

31. This definition is in line with the conclusions of the World Conference on Cultural Policies (Mexico City, 1982), the Intergovernmental Conference on Cultural Policies for Development (Stockholm, 1988), and the World Commission on Culture and Development (Paris, 1993).

32. Certeau, *La culture au pluriel*, 187.

33. Ibid., 188. Among the *cultural* needs to be satisfied, the author cites psychoanalysis, which is current, fashionable, and lucrative for the advertiser and the company. Besides this, he cites the gadgets that industry adds to its production for distribution, etc.

34. Zolkiewski, "Le plan de consommation et le modèle de culture," 346–52, quoted by Certeau, *La culture au pluriel*.

meanings.[35] Thus, "culture" can mean equally: "erudition," the heritage of intellectual or artistic works to be preserved; the image, perception, or understanding of the world appropriate to a particular environment and time—such as rural, urban, or indigenous, and medieval or contemporary; the behaviors, institutions, ideologies, and myths comprising the frames of reference that together characterize a society and distinguish it from others; whatever is acquired and produced rather than inherited or innate; a system of communication according to models elaborated by theories of spoken language. Any one of these levels and/or definitions implies for the researcher an option that will orient his or her reflection and discourse.[36]

As people living in the West—in a time of globalization and new technologies through which the world has become flat and no longer classifiable according to the divisions of a few decades ago[37]—when we speak of a culture that is no longer hegemonic, but plural, we are obviously referring to our own context, the context in which we have lived our whole lives. And that is precisely why the rapid transformations of the last decades alarm us.

It is a culture of passivity precisely because it is a culture of spectacle. Built on leisure as compensation for work, the consumerist culture develops in the spectators—today's men and women—the passivity of which it already is the effect.[38] Michel de Certeau identifies the current cultural strategy as a policy in which two crucial points stand out. The first is the fact that nowadays alienation is linked to cultural isolation. The culture helps individuals escape the hottest issues of society and leads them to consume the emptiness that will nullify them. The second is that the current forms of consciousness—and hence of bonding—have been fragmented and left without defined boundaries. The boundaries among them are found open, forming innumerable interfaces and promoting a new social niche where the actors are difficult to situate.[39]

Finally, culture has become an instrument of power. In his analysis of the relationship between culture and power, Michel de Certeau calls attention to the fact that, as in the case of the folkloric or popular culture of yesterday, mass culture today remains affected by the social coefficient that distinguishes it from an operational culture, which is always set apart. But the cut has been aggravated. Mass culture no longer has a colonizing

---

35. Certeau, *La culture au pluriel*, 189.

36. See Mounier, *Feu la chretienté*. See also Certeau and Domenach, *Le christianisme éclaté*.

37. Friedman, *The World Is Flat*.

38. See Certeau, *La culture au pluriel*, 197.

39. Ibid., 203–4.

function (in both the positive and negative sense of the word: at the same time civilizing and conquering), as was the case, for a long time, of the education that vulgarized and spread the conceptions of an elite. In truth, culture has become more of an object that is profitable and malleable according to the needs of production, and less a weapon of combat.[40]

The powers that be thus make use of culture without being committed to it, no longer dedicated to the discourses they fabricate. Their center of attention is no longer focused substantially on cultural production and cultural dissemination, or only tangentially so. And the products of culture serve the class of those who create them, but are paid for by the mass of those who neither use them nor benefit from them.[41]

The big question that arises—which Michel de Certeau detects—is whether the members of today's society, drowned as they are in the anonymity of discourses that are no longer theirs, and subjected to monopolies whose control escapes them, will find—together with the power to place themselves somewhere in the game of prevailing forces—the capacity to express themselves.[42]

To that end, organs such as UNESCO are constantly concerned with an ever more intense construction of a cultural diversity based on tolerance and respect. After verifying that culture lies at the center of contemporary debates on identity, social cohesion, and the development of an economy based on knowledge, the declaration of the World Conference on Cultural Policies asserts that respect for a diversity of cultures, tolerance, dialogue, and cooperation, in a climate of mutual trust and understanding, are among the best guarantees of international peace and safety. It takes into consideration the process of globalization, facilitated by the rapid evolution of new information and communication technologies. Although globalization represents a challenge to cultural diversity, it creates the conditions for a renewed dialogue among cultures and civilizations defending principles that promote respect for, and tolerance of, diversity.

There is no doubt that plurality is in principle a positive thing, since it enriches human reality, allows the immense wealth of cultural expressions to become public, and provides education regarding fundamental attitudes such as respect and tolerance. However, despite this positivity—which is real and should not be ignored—the ambiguity surrounding cultural reality

---

40. Ibid., 211.

41. See the "cool hunters" or trackers of style, persons who sniff out the tendencies that will govern fashion in the coming seasons. For a better understanding of this genuinely postmodern phenomenon, see the websites www.thecoolhunter.net and www.coolhunting.com.

42. Certeau, *La culture au pluriel*, 215.

today is enormous, and, as Michel de Certeau well demonstrates in his lucid analysis, there is a whole strategy behind cultural production that, albeit plural and tolerant in intention, continues to be, at least in a certain way, exclusionist.

The analyses by the experts of the phenomenon of digital exclusion are well known. It incapacitates large portions of the population, especially in the poorest countries, making it impossible for them to have access to these means, without which today one simply cannot acquire so much as information, let alone culture. In the same way there are very few today who have access to cultural goods and who can make effective "choices" and decisions regarding their cultural life or the way to manage cultural goods, without being hounded and molded by propaganda, by the mass media, etc.[43]

Again, it is Bauman—among others—who shines a new light on this debate, in his chapter "Culture as Consumer Co-operative."[44] He recalls that the notion of culture, as we use it today, was born and took shape in the third quarter of the eighteenth century. This notion was universal, encompassing even the wealthy developed countries at the cutting edge of modernity. The notion of culture, according to the Polish thinker, was thus coined following the factory model, which creates foreseeable and controllable situations.[45] With this meaning, the idea of culture began to be referred to in the singular and, up to a certain point, continues to be so even today. However, this usage appears side by side with another, which is described by the author as implying that each culture is to some degree the product of an arbitrary choice among several possibilities. It is therefore necessary to use the idea of "culture" in the plural.[46] And the metaphor used by Bauman to refer to the new cultural paradigm is "consumer cooperative," where it is very difficult, if not impossible, to separate the "author" from the "actor," since each member is urged to create and to act.[47]

In the "consumer cooperative" metaphor, the more the members of the cooperative consume, the higher is their contribution to and share in the common wealth of the cooperative. Distribution and appropriation are the axes of cooperative activity, not creation or production. And in the effort to increase consumption and profit, its aim is to increase the number of consumers. The true product line of the consumer cooperative is in principle the production of "multipliers," that is, of increasingly more numerous,

---

43. See the analysis by González Buelta, *La utopia ya está en lo germinal*.
44. See Bauman, *Postmodernity and Its Discontents*, 127–40.
45. Ibid., 129.
46. Ibid., 130.
47. Ibid., 134–35.

more demanding, and sophisticated consumers, more and more able to demand and discern.[48]

Faced with a multiplicity of choices the consumer is free to choose, with a freedom tested in the fault lines and in the laboratory of the individual life of each person. It is a freedom that depends upon a multiplicity of possibilities. It lives and multiplies as long as this multiplicity of possibilities is maintained.[49] Therefore, paradoxically, it can become an empty and deceptive freedom, since one does not have the right to put one possibility above the others: choosing one means rejecting others, and this does not enter into the dynamics of the game of consumption. In other words, selecting, rejecting, and canceling are not part of the process. Bauman states concisely that "as in the case of signs, which have the chance to communicate as long as they stay free of meanings, the essence of free choice is the effort to abolish choice."[50]

The momentum of the desire for consumption, stimulated by an ever-growing range of offers, makes self-gratification and satisfaction impossible. Making a decision becomes extremely difficult because it means renouncing other possibilities in order to choose one, or choosing one to be placed above the others. We are enslaved by a "tyranny of possibilities"[51] that constantly hounds us by multiplying the offers before us without leaving us room to choose freely, to say yes or no.

Often we want to say yes to one choice without saying no to the others, leaving all options open. This happens in the act of consuming perishable or volatile goods, but also in affective choices and life options. At one moment we say yes to marriage, or to initiation into a position in life, or to a profession, while deep inside we leave the door open to other options that will come later. Every relationship, job, house, and career seems to have an expiration date.[52]

It is no coincidence that the etymology of the words *decide* and *decision* has to do with cutting off, with separation.[53] Every choice that implies a decision has to consider a plurality of possibilities and routes and to cut off those that are left, in order to remain with just one. It is necessary to

---

48. Ibid., 136.
49. Ibid., 140.
50. Ibid.
51. See González Buelta, *La utopia ya está en lo germinal*, 51.
52. Ibid.
53. See *Dicionário Houaiss*, entry *decido, is, cídi, císum, ère* "to cut, to separate by cutting, to fragment by striking," a composite of *de* + the Latin *caedo, is cecídi, caesum, ère*, with the stem modification -ae- > -í-; in Portuguese and Catalan (*decidir*) there was a change in conjunction; see *ces-*; f. hist. 1532 *deçedir*.

separate by cutting off, sometimes with hard blows, in order to make a real choice and decision.

Sometimes we believe that we decide well, but due to a series of currents that move within us and drag us along, our paths can deviate to ports that we did not choose. And what is at play here are not only the major options, but the quality of our daily lives, which can be inadvertently devalued by the dynamics of the culture that has taken up residence in us.

> Our persona, our "I," saturated with information, with proposals for consumption, with different possibilities for organizing life, with real or virtual relationships, with offers of all kinds, is being converted into a colonized "I." When we are presented with a new situation, we already have an infinity of possible responses filed inside of us.[54]

Colonized means dominated by a foreign power, strange, external to ourselves. To the extent that our "I" is more and more colonized, it is converted into a department store or supermarket display where all kinds of responses appear without internal articulation. They are simply stacked side by side.[55] Our capacity for discernment is dulled and there is no longer an internal scale of values for deciding what is best. At this point, then, we are no longer actors and authors—as Baudrillard would have liked—but computer network terminals obeying commands activated by hands other than ours.[56]

There no longer exists in us a free space for making decisions. Sensations go on as if "accumulating" and adhering to our anxieties and hungers, whether to those which are natural to us and emerge from within us, or to the artificial ones created in us by the consumerist society. Our decisions are thus no longer free, but rather inevitable and imposed by an invisible master that we can no longer detain nor contain. And so we lose control of decisions over our own lives, carried away by the subterranean currents forming inside us.

The avid individualist style of consumption—characteristic of Western civilization—finds itself conflicted in cultures with values and worldviews that generally have deep religious roots. For this reason many people see in the dominant culture a threat of cultural imperialism. From disappointment

---

54. See Gergen, *The Saturated Self*, cited by González Buelta, *La utopia ya está en lo germinal*, 51.

55. See the fine elaboration on this point by González Buelta, *La utopia ya está en lo germinal*.

56. See the commentary on Baudrillard, on this point, by Bauman, *Postmodernity and Its Discontents*, 125.

in the promised but undelivered blessings of a global culture, or from the resistance, fueled by various sources, to a uniform, commercially determined global culture, there come various movements—more or less contradictory—in the form of religious, cultural, national, or ethnic pluralism. This can lead—in the case of indigenous peoples, for example—to a historical process of self-discovery that will help them to avoid entering blindly into the globalization process, or falling into fundamentalism and to a certain extent even into the practice of unprovoked violence.

For these reasons, despite all the tendencies toward standardization, there will be no uniform world culture in the foreseeable future. Before that there will come a pluralization of values and norms that no society will be able to avoid. Since plurality constantly questions the conventional identities until now taken as given, it unavoidably carries not a little potential for conflict. The variety of values and beliefs and their specific influences are now not only a sign of modern societies, but also concern the growing global interdependence in the relationships among societies and peoples.

The problem of global migration is symptomatic of exactly this. There is a growing fear, especially in the wealthy industrialized countries, of cultural alienation and of threats to both internal and external safety, due to the importation of political extremism and to the high crime rates. The political response to this is very often confined to defensive measures, such as restrictions on the right of asylum and aggravation of the conditions for residency through the hardening of visa regulations and border controls. The tendency towards limitation is often justified with a warning regarding the protection of cultural identity.

An anarchistic plurality—in other words, a plurality without a hierarchy of priorities, without reference to a scale of values, and without structural references—ceases to be something positive and liberating and is converted into a reinforcement of the ambiguity that presides over the liquid and "slimy" society in which we live. It imprisons instead of liberating and disorients instead of broadening the inner spaces. Boundaries disappear, individuals grow up uneducated and having only themselves as a reference, avid for pleasure with impunity and without criteria, something that the unlimited quantity of hedonistic offers can provide to them at any time.

As Gilles Lipovetsky says, "Hypermodern individualism is often identified with a chaotic, unstructured, and cacophonic individualism. On the one hand, the sovereignty of the individual grows; on the other, there is the loss of ownership of his person by the individual, who becomes incapable of controlling himself."[57] And what is at play here are not only the major

---

57. See Lipovetsky, *O futuro da autonomia*, 64.

choices that set the direction of life but also the quality of everyday life, which is being slowly eroded by the cultural dynamics that now own and command our existence.[58]

A New Geography

Geography is a science whose purpose is to study the surface of the Earth and the spatial distribution of significant phenomena in the landscape. It also studies the reciprocal relationship between human beings and the environment (human geography). It is a discipline that is almost universal in character. The coexistence of human beings with the world, with matter and life, raises, at the heart of geography, the problem of the relationship between humans and the environment. The question persists today, as it did yesterday, of whether modern and postmodern human beings—who are ever more capable, thanks to their technological expertise, of transforming their environment to the point of destroying or threatening the natural balance—are compromising the complex relationships of cause and effect that are fundamental to our scientific knowledge of the terrestrial globe.

As a synthetic discipline, geography is ambitious, since it comprises global analysis and the explanation of the Earth's surface and of all the earthly phenomena that can be localized, measured, and classified in space, but whose identification has no objective other than specifying mutual and ever-changing relationships. It is at once a natural science and a human science. And this is why it is often misinterpreted, both by the general public and by experts from various disciplines who approach it.

Cultural geography has become today the "geographic exploration of cultural differences and change."[59] To speak of cultural geography is to combine the humanist spirit with naturalist philosophy. Developed to justify nationalism and colonization, this fundamentally cultural human geography was initially conservative and intertwined with racism. It was rejected by many for its nourishing of extreme right-wing ideologies. However, it continues and is perpetuated, for example, by the well known American thinker Samuel Huntington, who speaks of a "clash of civilizations" and of American identity.[60]

In its radical version, cultural geography does not separate the social from the cultural. Culture is at the heart of the structuring process of

---

58. See González Buelta, *La utopia ya está en lo germinal*.

59. See Mitchell, *Cultural Geography: A Critical Introduction*.

60. See Huntington, *The Clash of Civilizations and the Remaking of World Order*; Huntington, *Who Are We? The Challenges to America's National Identity*.

societies, and is no longer invoked as a secondary variable. It is discourse, but also a political issue. It concerns the "culture wars" that express and generate the political, economic, and social conflicts at the core of a specific society. It multiplies the ways of looking at the transnational phenomena of societies and at the relationships of power and control, in order to get a better grasp on the means of production and the structuring of places and spaces. The idea of space as a social and cultural product, a theater of world "standardization," and subject to an increase in mobility, brings the two cultural geographies—the humanist and the radical—closer to each other. The 1990s opened the way for a postmodern current that prolonged the developments committed to this vision.

Today, after the first decade of the new millennium, there is already talk of the "end of geography"—as there was previously of the end of history. It refers to a geography being reconfigured and seeing an end to boundaries, thanks above all to their being redrawn by the phenomena of globalization and migration.[61]

We live in a world where a new geography is in progress, whether in economic, political, or even religious terms. The day of September 11, 2001, of sad memory, showed that what had been called the "Christian West" no longer existed as such. The Middle East, and with it Islam, which burst with noise and violence into the heart of New York, destroying the twin towers of the World Trade Center, confirmed that.

Economically, on the other hand, the new world geography is far from being merely south-south, much less east-west—the main characteristic of the Cold War era—or even north-south—in the sense of the old paradigm of a relationship of dependence between the center and the periphery. Globalization has been charged with transforming all types of hemispheric, continental, or even sub-regional compartmentalization of the world. In other words, economic geography tends to ignore physical and human geography. For example, bilateral agreements such as those between Japan and Mexico or between Chile and China contradict the logic of physical borders. The outsourcing of accountants and engineers and the call centers in India redraw the map of labor.[62]

The hybridity of geographical space translates into the emergence of a highly altered and degraded environment. The deterioration of the urban environment overflows into the countryside and into all spaces, driven by the increasing consumption of raw material by an increasingly globalized industry. Before the disfiguration is complete, there are effects such as

---

61. See O'Brien, *Global Financial Integration: The End of Geography.*
62. See Jank, "A nova geografia do mundo, Presidente do ICONE."

loss of contact with the goods, sounds, and images of local environments, brought about by the strongly hybridized urban environment, and leading to a cultural uprooting of human beings on a planetary scale. Thus the old human-environmental relationship, cast aside by the hybridity and degradation of the environment in a globalized space, must be recreated.

The perception of the problem initially took place in the arena of ethical and theoretical reflection, in relation to a radical condemnation of an economy ruled by the consumption interests of industry, until it was finally translated into a set of measures for landscape reconstruction in the most environmentally degraded spaces. From one moment to the next, we are living in a period of rescue by different practices undertaken in countries where the problem of degradation has been physically felt, by means of advocacy for the conservation and preservation of altered landscapes.[63]

There is a clash, therefore, between the disoriented development of the productive forces of industry and the capitalist relations of production created to regulate them. Consequently, we can see some pressure for the replacement of these relations with others that would reorient and give new direction to the development of productive forces in relation to the capitalist society and the environment, taking into account the possibilities created by science and technology for the new industrial revolution already in progress (the third one) and the globalized financial interests.[64]

Among the factors modifying geography today, the most important is the phenomenon of migration, of population mobility, the so-called "people on the move." It is changing the previously established configuration of the occupation and habitation of the world. For example, Paris, Rome, and other European capitals have today a considerable number—tending to become the majority—of Africans and Arabs. This has an impact on the city's configuration and disposition of living space. In the future it will have a clear impact on religion and the configuration of the population. With its low birth rate, secularized Europe is seeing the multiplication of the offspring of these "other" peoples from different latitudes and longitudes. They are mostly Muslims and consider numerous progeny to be a blessing from God. In this and in other ways they counterpose historical Christianity, previously the majority religion in that region of the world.

On the other hand, there is North America, especially the United States and Canada, which daily receive waves and waves of immigrants, above all Latinos because of their proximity to the borders. The Latino population in

---

63. See the recent books by the well-known Brazilian thinker Leonardo Boff on ecology and the dangers threatening the planet at this moment.

64. See Moreira, "A reinvenção do mundo moderno e a nova forma da geografia."

the United States grows exponentially year by year. And despite the severe American immigration policy, for every hundred who are deported, four hundred new immigrants enter the country. This implies that, in a not so distant future, the Latino population will numerically surpass the current white and WASP majority. Latinos already hold important political posts and leadership positions in companies, although an immense majority still live in conditions far from ideal, besides being under constant threat of deportation as undocumented immigrants, condemned to live in the shadows.[65]

International migration currently constitutes a mirror of the prevailing socioeconomic asymmetries on a global scale. It is a thermometer that points out the contradictions in international relations and in neoliberal globalization. Based on demographic data, we see that dislocation by migration is part of human nature, but today it is stimulated, if not forced, by the advent of technology and the impact of economic problems, in a logic contrary to its preponderance in relation to human beings.

The intensity and complexity of contemporary human mobility raises serious questions regarding its causes. Is it a "spontaneous" or an "induced" phenomenon? Are we facing "voluntary" or "forced" migrations? One has the impression that, rather than the consequence of individual free will, the massive migration to the northern countries is in fact the direct result of the crisis of the current neoliberal model of globalization, which concentrates wealth and subordinates productive and job-creating capital to speculative financial capital. People migrate primarily in search of the jobs and sustenance they cannot find in their region of origin.

On this point, the following affirmation by Robert Kurz is worth quoting:

> It is necessary to stop giving explanations such as "the human being has always made war and has always migrated." This does not help us understand this phenomenon, which is unheard of and has never occurred on such a large scale as now. Migration is nothing new in the history of modernization, but there is indeed an error in evaluation in saying that people migrate freely in search of better conditions. It is a coercive process. The poor

---

65. In the United States alone several hundred are deported every week, the majority of them Mexicans or others from Latin American countries. The population of undocumented immigrants in the United States in 2008 was estimated at more than eleven million. According to the Pew Hispanic Center, in 2005, 56 percent of them were Mexicans, 22 percent were from other Latin American countries (mostly from Central America), 13 percent from Asia, 6 percent from Europe and Canada, and 3 percent from Africa and the rest of the world. See Pew Research Center, "5 Facts about Illegal Immigration in the U.S.," http://www.pewresearch.org/fact-tank/2015/07/24/5-facts-about-illegal-immigration-in-the-u-s/.

are free to sell their labor, but they do this because they do not have the conditions to control their existence. The transformation of capitalist society into a global situation has produced a society of exclusion. The human being participates in a system in which he abstractly sells his labor and integrates a set of gears [put together] to produce an infinite accumulation of capital.[66]

Such a state of things, besides favoring transnationalism and a new model of geographic borders, also favors multiculturalism, since cultures are constantly mixing. On the other hand, however, it reflects the negativity of what might be seen as a new colonization in progress, with indigenous cultures running the risk of being destroyed by the imposition of the dominant and oppressive culture of the country that receives the migration.

This mobility of the world population fosters the emergence of new types of citizens, with new profiles, as the fruit of the current world scenario. Zygmunt Bauman calls attention to the fact that in today's late modernity there no longer exist stable residents. All the human inhabitants of planet Earth are nomads, but nomads who wander in order to settle down and become sedentary. However, in this attempt they find that they are not citizens but *parvenus*, or upstarts.[67]

Bauman also shows that the *parvenu* needs another *parvenu* in order not to feel like one. Thus the nomads dispute among themselves over the right to issue residence permits to one another.[68] "The more they do to turn into something else than they are, the more they are what they have been called not to be. Or have they indeed been called? . . . For the *parvenus* the game is unwinnable."[69]

In the world as it is today, there is no certainty, not even a probability, that there is no place for the outcast, the stateless, the landless, for those without culture or identity. Indeed there are many thousands of migrants who survive in foreign cultures. What seems more plausible, however, is that the path by which the *parvenus* escape from the status of outcast will be closed, requiring them to remain the way they are, making subjective, identity-related mobility impossible for them, even if geographic mobility has been granted them.[70]

---

66. Cited by Marinucci and Milesi, "Migrações internacionais contemporâneas."

67. See the definition of both words in Bauman, *Postmodernity and Its Discontents*, 72.

68. Ibid.

69. Ibid., 75.

70. Ibid., 81.

In this new human geographic panorama, the most appropriate metaphor seems to be that of the hope of arriving at the promised land, which teleologically turned Abraham's adventure into something very different from Ulysses' eternal return to Ithaca. The thousands of Latinos who daily cross the American border, or the hundreds of Africans who disembark on the Mediterranean shores, bring with them a dream: the American dream, or that of working in a developed European country. In sum, something which to them is the promised land, with several components and elements: work, a better life for their children and descendants, etc.

What the dream relies on is the modern hope: to arrive at the promised land, bringing along a feeling of guilt and a sense of failure for not having walked fast enough.[71] This guilt torments and afflicts inwardly, but it also protects the hope from the frustration of seeing that in the end it relied on an unreal dream. For this reason the guilt never disappears and keeps the human beings moving.[72] What awaits them, however, is not deferred gratification, but rather the impossibility of being gratified.[73]

Bauman pronounces in a sour and pessimistic manner on the contempory situation:

> We live in the age of tribes and tribalism. It is tribalism, miraculously reborn, which injects energy and vigor into the panegyric of the community, into the acclamation of belonging, into the passionate search for tradition. In this sense, at least, the grand carousel of modernity brought us to where our ancestors began in days of old. At least this is how it seems.[74]

An Abundance of Means and a Scarcity of Ends

The purpose of an action, of an attitude toward life, of a decision, is the "why," the meaning, in opposition to the "how," which refers to the means, the mechanisms or functions that it sets in motion. The end or purpose is, then, experienced as evidence when some action or dynamism is carried out in order to obtain a result. This has to do with what is undertaken by each one individually, observed by the other in his or her action, and is also

---

71. Ibid., 71.

72. See Camus: "Man is guilty, but only of not having demanded more of himself." Quoted by Bauman, *Postmodernity and Its Discontents*, 71.

73. Ibid.

74. Ibid., 79.

affirmed with respect to the whole established system, living or not, when its parts seem articulated toward a group function.

The means is what makes possible and real the fulfillment of an end. And as there are ordinarily several proposed and used means to achieve an end, there is a traditional and always current debate in moral philosophy on the priority of the means or the ends, and their eventual reciprocal degradation or depreciation. The teleological structure of human action allows for a distinction between means and ends, because it is within the nature of human will to negotiate the means with a view to the end. The means is, on one hand, the instrument for realizing the end, and on the other it is mediation, a transitory action oriented toward a temporal becoming. The ends can be close at hand and can themselves be concrete stages toward the final goal. Or they can be distant and abstract, yet not less real. When this occurs, they are confused with a global project, a value, an ideal.[75] And reflection on the means to reach these ends, not directly configured according to the basic needs of existence, such as eating, drinking, sleeping, clothing and shelter, has other implications in its relation to the means.

The science of economics is intended to administer this complex relationship between means and ends in accordance with its particular instruments. The word *economy* comes from the Greek *oikos*, meaning "things of the house"—"of the house" because many activities that generated wealth in ancient times came from private ownership of the land, or more precisely, from agriculture. In the remote past, ownership of the land was not clearly differentiated from the domicile, since the agricultural space was the house, the livelihood, and the place where the owners put down their roots.

Today, economists know that in economics scarcity is the rule, and abundance is the exception. And the reason for this is very simple; nature's resources are limited and people's needs are infinite. What generates the idea of wealth is scarcity, since one of the premises of value is the difficulty that things or goods require in order to be acquired. Very rarely is something given value that is produced or offered in abundance, because things in large quantities are easy to search for and find, and therefore we attribute less importance to them.

On the other hand there is, besides scarcity, another attribute of economics: the choice of priorities—which, being human, is always infinite—among the finite possibilities for using wealth. Such a choice is associated with the subjective values of the individual and with his or her priorities for the means employed to use wealth. This point is of enormous importance,

---

75. See Antor, "Finalité et Moyen," *Encyclopaedia Universalis*.

considering that we seldom think about how indispensable such choices are for the economic life of society.

The only fundamental equalities which can be attributed to all human beings are those which preserve their basic rights, such as life, dignity, liberty, security, and property—generic principles common to all—in order to make possible the realization and satisfaction of their needs. In the preservation of these rights, all are potentially equal, in proportion to their action. But they are simultaneously unequal. They are equal in the capacity to exercise their rights, yet different in the way they do it. They are equal in the capacity to love and hate, but different in their style and form of expressing such feelings. While equally mortal, they are unequal in the way they die, even if they die from the same cause. They are all individuals, because each human being is similarly endowed with consciousness and individuality; however, each person has his or her own unique way of seeing the world. The common characteristics of humanity do not negate the differences and inequalities inherent in the nature of persons.

This is true not only regarding the material goods which meet basic human needs, but also regarding ways of communicating, learning, relaxing, working, etc. And also regarding ethics, that is, the scale of values which inspires life. In this sense, especially regarding the end represented by education, with learning and instruction closely followed by communication, we live in a historical moment in which there is at our disposal an abundance of means never seen before. In this context, globalization brought with it a range of possibilities never dreamed of by human beings.

In the process of globalization we find the greatest opportunity in recent years for the expansion of communication among human beings, bringing progress to the most distant points on the planet and making it available to all. On the other hand, this generates a series of fears. To many people in the industrialized countries, progress represents failure at work, social disintegration, and the destruction of the environment. Furthermore, in many parts of the world there is a fear of Western cultural imperialism, which spreads without taking other cultures and values into consideration.

However, not all economic development that is judged to be negative by those who are affected by it is attributable to globalization. In many cases the main cause is internal factors. Unfavorable structures of production, a weak politico-administrative system, a badly managed government, or inadequate economic, social, and political measures that generate clearly negative effects—all these weaknesses are frequently amplified considerably by the advent of globalization.

Intimately linked to globalization—which is above all effectively an economic process—another process of dissemination of Western concepts of values and models has, in a certain way, diminished the cultural differences among the regions of the world. Modern means and tools of communication, as well as the export of concrete ideas for specific services, and also expanded tourism, bring Western lifestyles to the whole world every day, and everywhere raise expectations for development following models such as human rights, democracy, and a market economy. This also holds for modes of production and patterns of consumption and leisure. It is due in part to the fact that Western civilization exerts a great power of attraction, even over people from other cultures. On the other hand, this tendency is also consciously encouraged by the industrialized countries, and especially—for commercial reasons—by multinational corporations.

However, the process of globalization is in no way as complete as some would believe. For example, the growing liberalization of trade collides with an extremely restrictive policy of migration which only conditionally allows the poor to look for work where it is more favorable to them. Neither should all the hopes and promises of globalization obstruct the view of the other face of this development, which has very high social and environmental costs. Likewise, the globalized world has winners and losers. And this certainly has much to do with the relationship between means and ends, which is unbalanced in the globalized world.

Technical evolution in the field of communication has brought about an exchange of information at an unprecedented intensity, with consequences for contact among cultures. The fields of telecommunications and online electronic networks have in recent years taken on great importance, and promise to expand a great deal in the near future. In view of such advantages, the other side of global intercommunication is often forgotten. For example, the flow of global information sent through the Internet is very unequally distributed. The United States alone holds 80 percent of it. A similar scenario occurs with cell phones. Most people in the developing countries, whether because of a precarious infrastructure or extremely high usage fees, are excluded from the new communication technologies. Even more notable is the fact that there are almost one billion illiterate people. As long as the majority of humankind remains without access to them, these new means of development will not reach their goal of serving and accelerating human communication as a whole. If this goal is perverted, all they will achieve in the future will be to widen the gap between those with access to information and those excluded from it.

Furthermore, there is the issue of the content transmitted through these new technologies, which is highly ambivalent. On one hand the Internet brings new opportunities, such as the transfer of economic knowledge, the possibility of learning through the World Wide Web, and rapid global communication via email. And the fact that the content transmitted through the Internet is difficult to control, even for authoritarian regimes, has certainly demonstrated advantages and has often been a factor in the success of cooperation in cases of human rights violations. On the other hand, criminal content such as child pornography, racism, pedophilia, incitement to suicide, and glorification of violence can also be channeled through the Internet, at unprecedented levels.

Finally, there are admittedly harmful effects that the Internet can bring to the quality of the mental and intellectual development of its users. If, on one hand, it has infinitely expanded the availability of information, which has become more abundant than ever, on the other hand it has meant a diminishing attention span. One person can watch television, read a blog, and tweet, all at the same time, but his or her level of attention for each activity is extremely limited. In this sense and at this level, the Internet does not bring an end to the problem of scarcity, that is, of having scarce resources for an infinity of purposes. It only transfers the problem to another sphere. What is called, in economics, the "economics of abundance" can be called by others, the "economics of attention," which results in an "economics of assimilation."

The means of communication are constantly gaining in global importance. However, they are largely privatized and therefore subject to the laws of a market yet little regulated. Every domain of information, such as politics, culture, and sports, is being commercialized, and coverage thus becomes highly dependent upon classification, which in turn determines the volume of advertising revenues. Furthermore, the formation of monopolies and their concentration of power in the area of social communication have been greatly increasing through intense competition. The global media market is dominated by several big foreign corporations from which worldwide media distribution passes through distribution centers in the United States, Europe, Australia, and Japan. Developing countries are increasingly gaining in importance, especially regarding the advertising of Western consumer goods. Because of this external dominance, the access to these means by most people in the developing countries is usually limited. Likewise, the modern market offers scarce opportunities or attention in this field to the urgency of the basic needs of the poor.

Kant, as early as 1785, distinguished the means—that which is good and useful in relation to something—from the end—that which is absolutely good, good in itself.[76] The philosopher also spoke of the hypothetical imperative (technical advice, the product of prudence and ability, which expresses the practical need for action as a means to obtain anything one might wish),

---

76. See Kant, *Groundwork of the Metaphysics of Morals*.

and the categorical imperative, which makes absolute demands without a view to a particular end, and thus expresses moral law. One expression of the fundamental principle of the Kantian moral is: "Act in such a way as to never treat the other person simply as a means, but always at the same time as an end." The dignity of the other requires that he or she not be taken as a means or instrument.

However, in the same way, the means must lead to an end which is good and valid in itself. For this not to happen amounts to disrespect for the other person. The true moral problem is presented by the colloquial saying: "The ends justify the means." In other words, one must take necessary and dignified means to the desired end, as long as they are not in contradiction with that same end.

Hence, one neither can nor should use torture in defense of liberty, or diplomatic hypocrisy in the service of peace, or corrupt means to build a social justice program. In the same way, if the ends are not correctly postulated, if they fail to open a horizon that allows human beings to breath freely and to aspire to the highest and most worthwhile things, an abundance of means will serve no purpose and will lead nowhere, but will rather become ends in themselves. This is one of the pathologies of our time: a superabundance of means, but will there be corresponding ends? Inflated means for atrophied ends can be an explosive recipe.

An abundance of means such as is offered by the contemporary world neither fulfills its purpose nor helps in the development of humankind in any way, if it is tantamount to a scarcity of ends. The law of economics for managing scarce resources toward the achievement of unlimited ends cannot be inverted in the fields of justice and human development, as is the case today in a considerable part of the world. Abundance of means and scarcity of ends—when the ends are scarce, or atrophied, or anemic, abundance does not provide quality. And humankind's horizon of meaning becomes stunted. The means lose their purpose and become ends in themselves, benefitting no one except those who conceived of them in this way.[77]

In the Judeo-Christian tradition—in essence theological—the amplitude of the ends is the mover of the use of means. One must take or leave the means in such a way that the end may be achieved, and in discerning this it is necessary to take great care not to use as means what is in reality part of the end: the other in his or her unmistakable dignity, in his or her epiphanic Otherness, made for happiness and Transcendence.

---

77. See Mardones, *La transformación de la religión?*, 51–52.

The Crisis of Memory and of Tradition

Memory is the ability to preserve and retrieve information. This ability, in a broad sense, is not exclusive to human beings. They share it with living organisms and certain machines. However, there is a conception of memory which is indeed exclusively and originally human. Heredity, as the conservation and transmission of information necessary to life, can be considered memory. Adult memory is the result of a genetic evolution that, since childhood, has gone through phases of maturation, of acquisition and appropriation of language, and of the development of logical structures.

With its origin in the Greek words *ána* (emergence) and *mnémè* (memory), the word *anamnèse* means the recollection of a memory. To Plato, it is the restoration of the idea contemplated, before incarnation, by the human soul in the heaven of ideas, whose recollection remains unconscious without the operation of "reminiscence." Aristotle rejects this conception of the *theoria* and makes of anamnesis a faculty, particular to the human being, of voluntarily remembering a recollection of empirical origin and of locating it in time. Thus *mnémè* passes from a potentiality into a state of entelechy.

The word *tradition* comes from the Latin *tradere*, which means to pass on, to deliver, to remit. It is not limited to the conservation and transmission of contents previously acquired. Rather, it integrates new contents throughout history, adapting them to other older ones. Its nature is not purely pedagogic or ideological, but equally dialectic and ontological. Tradition brings again into being that which has already been. It is not limited to knowing/making a culture but is identified with the very life of the community.[78]

Tradition is not strictly limited to preserving the elements of a culture. In a certain way, it "reinvents" and transmits them. Otherwise, traditions from the paleolithic era would still be ours and our cultures would not have appeared or been developed. Societies react to the stimuli that the environment delivers to them, and build for themselves a spiritual instrumentality, not limiting themselves to weapons and tools. The tradition charged with this spiritual equipment cannot be simply interpreted as its mediator, but also as the agent of the heritage that it transmits—through the selection that it practices and through the operations that it performs on the values it considers worthy of being transmitted.[79]

To transmit means to bring into being that which has already existed, and to preserve that which has been transmitted. These are two aspects, one active and one passive, which should not be confounded in the analysis of

---

78. See Pepin, "La tradition," *Encyclopaedia Universalis*, numerical version, 2009.
79. Ibid.

the universal function of tradition, especially regarding its relationship to the life of a community.

The means of the tradition cannot be limited to oral or written communication. Attitudes, behaviors, and examples set by members of a traditional community—in their material daily life as well as in their moral and spiritual life—give witness to their capacity to recreate, in any moment and circumstance, the mythic and symbolic meaning of a behavior or particular gesture. These are not mechanical repetitions of stereotyped acts, but rather the expression of a profound correspondence between what is believed and what is thus recreated. The liturgy or the ritual action may be its culmination, since it carries out in a most perfect and excellent way the celebration and transmission of the "making exist" which any true tradition of the experience of the Sacred requires.

In the fourth century, Saint Augustine had already explored, in a singular and intense way, the psychological dimension of memory, giving dynamism, depth, and fluidity to the places and images that emerged in his consciousness. To Augustine, the writing of his famous book *Confessions* was certainly an important and profound exercise of memory. Some excerpts from this book speak of the importance of the process of memory in the conversion and in the spiritual life of Christianity's great thinker.[80]

Thus, Augustine's emphasis was on memory as psychic activity. He inquired into the vestiges that images leave in the soul. He specified the basis of introspection, the test of consciousness. He put forward a version of Cicero's trilogy, proposing a triad of memory, will, and intelligence. The play of all these ideas, worked out through the heritage and possibilities of many interpretations, strengthened a Christian mnemonic tradition centered in the art of memory as a way to enact "spiritual intentions."

Later, systems of memorization were used to remember heaven and hell. There emerged the idea of purgatory, the liturgy, the memento of the dead. These ways of remembering, these ideas, these places and images are echoed, for example, in the iconography of Giotto's paintings (such as the images of Charity and of Envy) and in the structure and details of Dante's Inferno, and became commonplace in many books published in the

---

80. "I will pass then beyond this power of my nature also, rising by degrees unto Him who made me. And I come to the fields and spacious palaces of my memory, where are the treasures of innumerable images, brought into it from things of all sorts perceived by the senses" (X, 8.12); "[This knowledge is] removed as it were to some inner place, which is yet no place" (X, 9.16); "And what I now discern and understand, I lay up in my memory, that hereafter I may remember that I understood it now. So then I remember also to have remembered" (X, 13.20). See these and other texts cited in Smolka, "A memória em questão," 180–81. [Translator's note: the English is taken from *The Confessions of St. Augustine*, trans. E. B. Pusey.]

sixteenth century. From that century dates the work of Matteo Ricci, a Jesuit who lived in India and China and developed an admirable art of memory in his practice of catechesis. Ricci constructed a palace of memory, linking the knowledge of Christian doctrine with culture, and particularly with Chinese ideograms.[81]

These systems, based on images and the exercise of the imagination in an oral or mental form, were developed at that time along with the prevailing practices of writing. Readings of sacred texts, laws, and memorials strengthened certain ways of remembering, established modes of thought, and produced a memory of a religious and instructional character: it was necessary to learn, repeat, and recite by heart. Now, supported by writing, it is a complete process of the Christianization of memory, configured by Greco-Roman paganism and carried out where religion, worship, ritual, celebration, commemoration, and teaching are salient.

The philosopher Martin Heidegger asserted that "memory is the gathering of recollection, thinking back."[82] By that he meant that it protects and keeps everything which is important, which makes sense, which is preferred to and precedes even the facts as its meaning. Everything, finally, which is presented to thought as content worthy of reflection and of being remembered. For this reason, memory is the condition for the possibility of culture, of civilization, of everything that human beings build on Earth.

In theological terms, memory is what makes it possible not to lose the Word which is revealed and received in faith: the identity of the personal self-revealing God, whose name is spoken, whose face is shown, and who wants to be recognized. Through memory the history of this experience, of this dialogue, of this identity, is narrated and recounted again and again. And all this in order to create memory, to be able to witness to the new generations,

---

81. See Spence, *The Memory Palace of Matteo Ricci*, cited by Smolka, "A memória em questão," 181.

82. See Heidegger, *Qu'appelle-t-on penser?*, 29–30: "Memory is the gathering and convergence of thought upon what everywhere demands to be thought about first of all. Memory is the gathering of recollection, thinking back. It safely keeps and keeps concealed within it that to which at each given time thought must be given before all else, in everything that essentially is, everything that appeals to us as what has being and has been in being [*als Wesendes, Gewesendes*]. Memory, Mother of the Muses—the thinking back to what is to be thought is the source and ground of poesy. This is why poesy is the water that at times flows backward toward the source, toward thinking as a thinking back, a recollection. Surely, as long as we take the view that logic gives us any information about what thinking is, we shall never be able to think how much all poesy rests upon thinking back, recollection. Poetry wells up only from devoted thought thinking back, recollecting." [Translator's note: the English is from Heidegger, *What Is Called Thinking?*, 11.]

and to avoid forgetting what humankind has done and must continue doing: living, suffering, laughing, thinking, speaking, and knowing.

There is the memory of joy, of lived and realized love, of moments lived together. A memory of smiling faces, of words exchanged, of affectionate caresses on the skin, which vibrates with life and pleasure when touched. This is the recollection that helps us live and confers sweetness upon the most difficult daily life.

But there is also the memory of pain, which drags into visibility and into the foreground the suffering of victims confronting powers sustained by the principle of domination. The memory of pain does not speak in abstract terms, of the "human being" or of "humankind." It speaks of the concrete other: of the desperation of widows who helplessly throw themselves on their partner's coffin; of the crying of orphaned children who scream without understanding why their father lies on the floor pierced by bullets and grenades; of the emaciated and starving faces of those who live on continents erased from the map by the major powers. It speaks of the Stalinist purges and of the Nazi Holocaust with its millions of victims, each with a number tattooed on his or her arm, and each marked with a yellow star.

When this pain and suffering are forgotten, a slow process of dehumanization of a people or a culture begins. This is why philosophers such as Adorno and theologians such as Johann Baptist Metz emphasize the importance of the subversive dimension of memory. It is subversive because it does not let the victims be forgotten and places them at the center of attention. It is subversive because it does not allow the evil committed and the justice scorned to disappear into the night of the times. It makes evident the process of the extinction of tradition which begins to grow, threatening to suffocate human dignity and to foster its dehumanization.[83]

Memory invokes anamnestic reason, a way of thinking that does not reduce the subject to a conceptual abstraction without reference to history and social processes. Thus it claims the right to be a critical mediator of human practice. Its instrument is par excellence the narrative. Therefore we can say that the narrative is the residence of memory. This is how Christianity was born—when the disciples of the Nazarene narrated again and again the story of the one who went through life doing good, who was violently and unjustly killed, but was resurrected by God and was now living among them.

The same happens with the victims of history who, named and narrated by memory, remain alive and, keeping ablaze the flame of their existence,

---

83. See Adorno, "The Meaning of Working Through the Past," in *Critical Models*; Adorno, "Education After Auschwitz," in *Critical Models*; Adorno, *Minima Moralia*; Horkheimer and Adorno, *Dialectic of Enlightenment*; Metz, *Faith in History and Society*; Metz, *Memoria Passionis*.

call for justice. It is not simply a matter of a love for tradition, but rather a desire to create a community of solidarity with the victims of history in order to curtail the attempts, at the core of all totalitarian systems, to silence and muzzle the truth. Memory redeems the ardent narrative of the past and makes it current, in order to transform the present. It recollects occurrences with the urgency of the future, bringing about a farsighted solidarity which sees beyond appearances.

A country without memory little by little sees its true identity fade and disappear. This opens the door to undesirable recurrences, and sweeps into the shadows of a misguided oblivion the luminous presences whose lives should be narrated again and again to illuminate the path of new generations.

A world without memory is cruel and inhumane. Unable to identify its roots and origins, it cannot construct its plan and its future. And—instead of a memory which identifies things and puts them in their place—in the face of the great historical dramas that strike and divide countries and political communities, what is left is a traumatic oblivion.

The theme of oblivion and the construction of political memory is central to the work of the historian and to the constitution of citizenship. Chateaubriand (1768–1848), the French novelist and historian, had a heroic vision of the historian's role. In 1807, in a frontal attack on Napoleon, he wrote,

> When, in the silence of abjection, one hears only the sound of the chains of the slave and the voice of the informer; when everything trembles before the tyrant and it is as dangerous to curry his favor as to merit his disgrace, the historian appears, charged with the vengeance of the people.[84]

Paul Ricoeur (1913–2005)—one of the most important contemporary philosophers and the author of a major work on the subject, reflecting on the interaction among memory, oblivion, history, and citizenship—wrote, "The writer-historian creates history. The reader creates history and, creating history, he transforms the creation of the historian into the creation of the citizen."[85] Ricoeur distinguishes several forms of oblivion and of the work of memory, which involve individuals, societies, and the historical field.[86]

Nowadays, the crisis of memory is one of the fundamental elements for understanding the collapse of civilization in which we live. There is a

---

84. See Chateaubriand, *Mémoires d'outre-tombe*.
85. See Ricoeur, *History and Truth*.
86. See Alencastro, "Esquecimento e memória."

patent memory crisis in the globalized society, which has lost its connections and its traditional basis for transmission and reproduction of memory. The cultural domain that set its roots in the globalized society changed the framework that supported the references of memory. The organized group, whose collective memory had been formed within limits imposed by space and time, lost its balance when its borders evaporated. The new means of communication, with its bombardment of information—some true, some less so—makes the present time hesitant and insecure. Thus grows the dissolution of the traditional memory of human groups. We are living in a discontinuous and diffuse new time: a time of consumption which individualizes identities and disarticulates memory.[87]

Collective identities and memories, which had been solidly expressed in monuments, symbols, and values, now find themselves drifting, crumbling, fluctuating in images spread in the millions throughout the four corners of the planet. The stories and myths of a society or group are lost in the midst of the acceleration and massification of culture, while the traditional ways of transmitting group customs are changed through the uniformization of behavior on a global scale. The film or soap opera star, the famous athlete, and the singer become icons of society and bastions of modernity. Their clothes, shoes, words, behavior, and consumption tend to be imitated by the younger generations. In the medium and long term this generates profound changes in traditional memories.

This being the case, the regional or local traditions that had formed the shared culture of a certain group—and consequently structured its memory around permanent references—is progressively disappearing due to the massification imposed on society as a whole. This dilution of cultures into the current consumerist culture is anchored in seduction by products, determined in turn by advertising practices. Such products are globally homogenized, carrying a brand that attributes a symbolic value to them, that is, they are agents of social differentiation for those who acquire them.[88]

It is in this way that collective memory loses sustenance as a factor in social cohesion through effective attachment to a group.[89] Such a union is dissolved as the connection among individuals is lost, as we have shown so far. Regarding memory, what prevails seems to be individual memory, in that it refers to events lived out by the person. Or at most a very reduced group memory, one that is specifically built on the interdependence of a

87. See Rioux, "A memória coletiva," in Rioux and Sirinelli, *Para uma história cultural*, 315–16 and 326.
88. See Fiorucci, "A questão da memória na esfera publica global," 4.
89. See Halbwachs, *Le mémoire collective*, cited in ibid.

limited number of individuals. Thus, what we mean to make clear is that collective memory, which shapes a fuller identity linked to more general aspects, tends to disappear, especially among the younger generations born and raised in this accelerated context.

In the globalized world, therefore, one can observe a growing loss of collective memories and referential traditions, which are dissolved into the mass culture and find no basis of support except in the global culture, which inculcates a forced generalization into a heterogeneous environment. Memory weakens and loses strength, tradition is blunted and impoverished in its creativity for reinventing the past in the present. And it is the people, humankind, that is injured, because of the loss of its references.

Tradition and memory are historical concepts. They are the call that the present sends to the past, or the heritage by which the past survives in the present. For this reason the liquid world in which we live is going through one of the deepest crises of meaning and loss of self-esteem ever seen, in the feeling that the references pertaining to its identity—memory and tradition—are dissolving and slipping through its fingers.

If memory and tradition are not restored, if the process of their annulment and erasure is not stopped and reversed, humankind will be at serious risk of seeing at its core a growth of psychiatric illnesses of all sorts, of which depression will be the main one. The rate of suicide increases just when memory and tradition fade, as if there were an invisible gas, erasing history from people's minds and hearts.

The Crisis of Ethics and the Volatility of Morality

The time we live in is going through several crises. One of them is a profound ethical crisis. Although *ethics* is one of the words most used nowadays—and we find ethics committees in every institution—we now have a kind of ethics that is not in line with the paradigm that has accompanied humankind since ancient times, and that proposes a value system not always strong enough to configure human life.

In premodern times morality was theological—that is, morality was God, and faith conferred virtue. Thus the human being was at the service of God rather than of humankind, which took second place. The advent of modernity unleashed a disconnection of morality from religion, as a distinguishing aspect of the process of secularization. The individual became the sovereign value of secularized lay ethics. In this context, right rather than duty assumed absolute preponderance.

In late modernity, with the crisis of modern reason and its consequences, there was a change in the role of duty, with the imposition of its gradual weakening. Lipovetsky seeks to show a transition to a postmoralist society in contemporary times.[90] In the context of a "twilight of duty" and an "ethics without pain"—concepts developed by Lipovetsky—we are presented with ethical factors in counterposition to the post-duty embedded in the postmoralist tendency in which pleasure is preponderant. This issue was raised in the middle of the twentieth century by the consumerist idea and its inducement to the identification of possession with the feeling of happiness. We are facing a hedonistic society in which "the age of narcissistic happiness is not comparable to the maxim 'it is forbidden to forbid,' but rather to a 'morality' without obligations or sanctions."[91]

The author tackles moralizing tendencies mainly in the field of sexual behavior, where the double standard that has penalized women over men is beginning to be diluted today. Many behaviors previously accepted as normal only for men are now being adopted by women as well.

Morality understood as something extremely individual constitutes a duty to oneself. In other words, it is aimed at personal improvement with an emphasis on individual autonomy. It does not allow for attitudes without restriction, thus it implies ethical restrictions reestablished under the aegis of the normalization of individualist ethics. The author founds his assertions in a discussion of the leading issues of today, such as the right to euthanasia, transsexuality, commerce in organs and the body, hygiene and bodily aesthetics, participation in sports, the use of products harmful to the community, and disciplined work, as well as other issues derived from these concerns.[92]

The morality thus established includes neither sanctions nor obligations. On the contrary, it has the objective of structuring a hedonist-democratic individualism. "It is painless, because it is incarnate in the present time and conforms to the desires of its followers. It also takes part in a communication show, when broadcast through the mass media. This implies a non-binding and remote benevolence, without anything that engages and weighs upon the ego. This morality also presents an economical

---

90. See Lipovetsky, *A sociedade pós-moralista*, 27: "In the postmoralist era, what is in play is a social demand for just limits, a measured sense of duty, some specific laws to protect the rights of everyone—but never the spirit of moral fundamentalism. We certainly advocate respect for ethics, provided that it doesn't require our own self-immolation or an arduous mission to carry out. A spirit of responsibility, yes; an unconditional duty, no! After the magic ritual of demiurgic duty, we see the phase of the ethical minimalism."

91. Ibid., 36.

92. Ibid.

configuration, since it has created a new form of racism. It is no longer skin color or religion that initiates discriminatory racist attitudes. Today, the origin of the incentive for racism is linked to migratory waves related to the economy."[93] It is how much one has that determines which is the superior and which is the inferior "race."

Labor has ceased to be a moral duty to society and is now linked to personal satisfaction, to professional recognition of a career plan for the future. The effects of neoindividualism are present at the heart of labor, with a feeling of more rights and fewer duties. Consequently, a considerable minimum of workers miss work without justification or with a forged note from the doctor. They work thinking about the time of retirement. The mysticism of work as ennobling and transforming the world does not exist. What exists is a confrontation between responsible individualism, which inculcates moral rules, and irresponsible individualism, which seeks to escape from the rules that generate responsibility. The latter, according to Lipovetsky, is what leads to the demoralization of work.[94]

In face of this new ethical configuration, the Lithuanian Jewish philosopher Emmanuel Levinas argues that any ethics that does not begin with the personal cannot be adequately transposed to the public level. Levinas emphasizes the moral obligation to the other, and this other is understood as a face. The *other* and the *face* are generic names, but in each moral encounter these names represent just one being—one other, one Face. Nor can the name appear in the plural without losing its ethical stature, its moral meaning.[95] Collective concepts such as "the people" and "the community," in Levinas' understanding, do not go to the root of true ethics, which must always take place between "you and me."[96] And entering into this moral space means taking time away from daily work and from one's social position, leaving aside mundane rules and conventions. To this ethical encounter of two, the other and I, one must come divested of one's own social apparatus, stripped of status, social distinctions, deficiencies, ranks or functions, being neither rich nor poor, elevated nor humble, powerful nor powerless—reduced to the naked essentiality of our common humanity.

In his essay "La souffrance inutile,"[97] Levinas states that "intersubjectivity in its proper meaning is non-indifference to others." It is a "responsibility

---

93. Ibid. See also Bauman, *Postmodernity and Its Discontents*, 5–16: "The dream of purity," especially 16: "The pursuit of modern purity."

94. Ibid.

95. Ibid., 46.

96. See Buber, *I and Thou*, and all of Levinas' work, which has many points of contact with that of Buber.

97. See Levinas, "La souffrance inutile," in *Entre nous*, 100–112.

to others, but, before the reciprocity of such responsibility, it is inscribed in impersonal law. For this reason, the intersubjective perspective can survive, but it can also be lost in the political order of the city or in the Law that establishes the reciprocal obligations of the citizens."[98] Levinas holds that charity is impossible without justice, but that justice without charity becomes deformed.[99] Recently Pope Benedict XVI, in his encyclical *Caritas in veritate*, agreed with this affirmation, but added that Christian charity goes further than symmetry with justice. It incorporates the unlimited love of the gospel in the Sermon on the Mount. However, he agreed that any charity that is not anchored in justice is not worthy of the name.

The justice of institutions and of the State, founded on reason, must be present to bring about a truly just and responsible world. The uniqueness of the other is not by itself enough for a task of such breadth. In this sense, the other must be seen in the condition of a citizen, not just as an individual, but as a participant in a *polis* for which he or she is responsible—although the establishment of real ethics and justice would be impossible without ethically experienced uniqueness.

Justice, however, will only be such if it is permanently monitored and questioned by ethics, only if it is perpetually dissatisfied with itself. Justice in the liberal State will never be definitive. It is awakened by charity, which comes before justice but also after it.

Levinas says that in the presence of the Third Party,

> we leave what I call the order of ethics, or the order of sanctity, or the order of mercy, or the order of love, or the order of charity—where I am concerned about other human beings, regardless of the place they occupy in the multitude of human beings, regardless of quality and even of our common condition as individuals of the human species. He concerns me as someone who is close to me, as the first to come. He is unique.[100]

The idea of justice is conceived at the moment of encounter between the experience of uniqueness (such as moral responsibility for the other) and the experience of the multiplicity of others (as in social life). And it cannot dispense with either of these two elements. Because if there were no memory of the uniqueness of the Face, there would be no idea of a generalized, "impersonal" justice. Morality is the school of justice. The infiniteness of

---

98. Levinas, "La souffrance inutile," cited in Bauman, *Postmodernity and Its Discontents*, 47.

99. Ibid., 49.

100. See Levinas, *Qui etes-vous?*, cited in Bauman, *Postmodernity and Its Discontents*, 50.

moral responsibility, the unlimitedness (even the silence!) of moral requirements, simply cannot be sustained when "the other" appears in the plural. The epiphany of the face in its density and its "accusation" is indispensable for the existence of ethics and a commitment to justice.[101]

To the question regarding the impotence of ethics for doing good and the risk of frightening the other with an ethical voluntarism, Levinas responds,

> I don't know if this is an insupportable situation. Certainly, such a situation is not what one would call pleasant, pleasant for living, but it is good. What is extremely important—and I can affirm this without being a saint myself, and without the pretension of being a saint—is to be able to say that a human being who really deserves the name, in its European sense, derived from the Greeks and from the Bible, is a human being who considers sanctity as the supreme value, an incontestable value.[102]

Levinas' writings—with the great importance he gives to Otherness—certainly offer a rich inspiration to the analysis of the endemic hesitancy of moral responsibility, as well as of the painless and light ethics of our time.

Thus, to Levinas, the macroethical extension of moral responsibility in relation to the other goes beyond the defense against shared dangers. Let's keep in mind that, to Levinas, the macro equivalent of moral responsibility is nothing less than justice—a quality of human existence that obviously requires the anticipation of global catastrophes as a preliminary condition, but can in no way be reduced to this. Neither could it be considered successful, even if prevention might have been effective in some way.[103]

Therefore, in view of what Levinas says about ethics, one must be aware that ethics is not enough. Especially when it is a light and painless ethics such as that which prevails today, and which certainly is not Levinasian ethics. From a theological point of view, we add to Levinas' ethical primordiality the need for mysticism—the experience of Mystery, of Transcendence—as a source of ethics. Only then does ethics cease to be an ethics of disaster prevention or of institutional safeguards, and become an ethics of caring, of concern for the other, of being affected by what affects the other.[104]

---

101. See Bauman, *Postmodernity and Its Discontents*, 51.

102. See Levinas, *Qui etes-vous?*, cited in Bauman, *Postmodernity and Its Discontents*, 52.

103. See Bauman, *Postmodernity and Its Discontents*, 56.

104. See the thought, and especially the ethical behavior, of persons such as Simone Weil, Etty Hillesum, and others.

If justice is understood as Levinas wished it to be, expanding and generalizing such a strictly selective responsibility, applied to the singular and unique other—then, as is true of this responsibility, justice must emerge not so much from the demands of the other as from an ethical impulse, and from a concern with the ethical self that assumes the responsibility to see that justice is done. In other words, within the conception that permeates all Levinasian work, moral responsibility is asymmetric and nonreciprocal. Therefore it can be derived only from mysticism, which opens the subject toward the Whole.[105]

To do justice is always to demand more of oneself. Only when we know this will the desire for justice be susceptible to immunity from the most striking of dangers: that of self-satisfaction and of a conscience once and for all light, calm, and clean.[106]

Thus it seems plausible that the key to such big problems as social justice and exclusion—which appeal to the ethical element in the humanity of human beings—is found in an (apparently) small-scale problem, such as the moral primordial act of assuming responsibility for the other who is nearby, within reach—for the other as a Face. It is here that moral sensibility is born and gains strength, until it grows and becomes strong enough to carry the burden of responsibility in any instance of human misery and suffering, whatever the legal norms or empirical investigations may say about its casual relations and "objective" attribution of guilt.[107]

An ethics thus understood would be substantiated in a politics that would not only be political, but would be a matrix from which could emerge something like what Paul called "the new creature in Christ" or what Mao Tse Tung called "the new socialist man"—a mature stage of humanity that would replace all kinds of infantilism. This type of politics assumes that things must drastically change, so that a new form of beauty can emerge. And this beauty certainly cannot emerge from a light and painless ethics, where duty and responsibility are doomed to an obscure twilight, as seems to be the case in our era.

The Crisis of the Institution and the New Subjectivity

When the issue of subjectivity is raised here, we immediately touch upon the important, even central, issue of identity. By identity we mean a person's exclusive and unique set of characteristics. And personal identity is the

---

105. See Bauman, *Postmodernity and Its Discontents*, 62.
106. Ibid., 69.
107. Ibid., 70.

consciousness that someone has of himself or herself. Consequently, identity is the set of characteristics that are unique to a person (such as name, occupation, gender, fingerprints, physical defects, etc.), that are considered to be exclusive to him or her and are therefore taken into consideration when this person needs to be recognized. As for external visibility, identity is the circumstance in which an individual must be who he or she claims to be or who someone else presumes that he or she is.

Depending on the field of knowledge, the concept of identity receives new traits. For sociology, identity is the sharing of several ideas and ideals by a specific social group. Thus, the individual not only shapes his or her own personality but also receives it from the environment in which his or her social interaction is realized.[108] For anthropology, identity consists in the sum—never completed—of an aggregate of the signs, references, and influences defining the relational understanding of a particular entity, whether human or nonhuman. It is perceived, by itself or by others, through its difference in comparison to others. Hence, identity is always related to the idea of Otherness. The existence of others and their different characteristics is necessary in order to make it possible for me to identify, by comparison and differentiation, the characteristics by which I identify myself.

Subjectivity is understood as the individual's intimate space from which he or she relates to the world, to others, and to himself or herself. This relational pole that is human subjectivity determines both the singular characteristics that shape the subject and the formation of beliefs and values shared at the cultural level, which in turn constitute the historical and collective experience of groups and populations. Subjectivity is the internal world of each and every human being. This internal world is composed of emotions, sentiments, and thoughts. Through our subjectivity we build a relational space, that is, we relate to the other.

It is important to note that the idea of identity here is not linked to the propositions of Aristotle—unity of substance and/or identical forms—or to the notion of equality or anything close to it. We admit that identity itself can be established or recognized as based in any conventional criteria. But the criteria need to be mutually "established" and "recognized." It is a symbolic construction—viscerally linked to interpretations given to reality—which configures the vision of one's own position in the world. It is a way to differentiate oneself and to differentiate others from particular criteria. And one cannot speak of identity, but rather of identities, since there are several levels in its construction. One can speak of a "national identity," connected to patriotism and to the nation, of a "regional identity" (such as, for example,

---

108. See also Mannheim, *Ideology and Utopia*.

the idea of a Mineiro, a Nordestino, or a Gaúcho in Brazil), or even of a "social identity," which applies to the different positions that each individual occupies in society. In this sense, what is relevant to the discussion here is the fact that, even if this traditional identity does not disappear completely, it suffers visible transformation. The memory shared by a particular group is not preserved in its purity. It suffers unavoidable external influences and cultural impositions.[109]

One can already see, simply through interdisciplinary interfaces and definitions, that identity and subjectivity are concepts that constantly and intensely touch each other. In ancient philosophy, the question of identity belonged to metaphysics, and idealism was constituted as a way to maintain a balance in the realm of external structures. Modern and contemporary philosophy finds several variants in the conceptualization of identity, depending on which school of thought or which author one is working with.

Here we are following Paul Ricoeur, who speaks of "personal identity" as "ipseity," which is different from "selfhood."[110] It is an identity that answers the question "Who?" and refers to the person as a responsible being, capable of answering for the other and being responsible for this other. Thus, in asking "Who am I?" the gaze is directed to me, but in the light of what the other demands from me. In other words, the question "Who am I?" refers to the person as such, as responsible for his or her free action. In the dimension of "selfhood," the question for identity is formulated as a "What?," that is,

> that which is the same thing which remains despite the continuous changes. What is its permanent essence in the midst of its transformations? And the answer does not point to the person as such, to himself—even more profound, but to what is or has ceased to be, to that which does not change in the midst of the mutations that affect it.[111]

Although we are aware of his divergences with Ricoeur, Levinas—another contemporary philosopher whose thought we have been following in this reflection—says something that, as we see it, is fundamental to the question of identity as subjectivity:

> Identity is not a harmless relationship with oneself, but is being chained to oneself. . . . Liberty is immediately limited by its

---

109. See Fiorucci, "A questão da memória na esfera pública global."

110. See Ricoeur, *Soi-même comme un autre*.

111. See Scannone, "Identidad personal, alteridad interpersonnal y relación religiosa."

responsibility. In this resides its enormous paradox: a free being who yet is not free because he is responsible for himself.[112]

In short, selfhood attaches itself, above all, to permanence or to the stability of the same character or the same proprieties of the person during his or her constant mutations. As for ipseity, it refers to the same person, or subject, as ultimately responsible for his or her actions and omissions. Both types of identity are related, although there is, according to Ricoeur, a considerable hiatus between them. The mediation of this hiatus then happens in narrative identity, in the life stories narrated to another (dialogue, interlocution, etc.) or to oneself (journal, autobiography, etc).

According to the Argentine philosopher Juan Carlos Scannone, "Neither the classic metaphysics of substance nor the modern philosophy of the self-conscious subject adequately accounts for human personal identity insofar as it is personal (*ipse*). In other words, they don't give a conclusive answer to the question: who?"[113]

For this reason some philosophical systems today are opting for a new paradigm: that of Otherness. This reflects an attempt to surmount the Cartesian axiom "I think," founded and centered in oneself. The intention, consequently, is to discover that human beings are not definable only by their cognitive and thinking capacity, but by their Otherness and intersubjectivity. Otherness, therefore, would constitute human personal identity.[114] Such Otherness can be interpreted in different ways, which, however, are not mutually exclusive. They could be "the Otherness of being—or of reality—with respect to the subject, of the body itself, of the face of the other, of the community of communication, of the ethico-religious we, of the voice of conscience, of phenomena saturated with benefaction, including religious manifestations of the sacred, etc."[115]

Levinas clearly opts for responsibility for the other as the basis for human society. And this society would be constructed from a transcendental perspective, which for him consists in the epiphany of the Face of the other. It is only here that the relationship I-other is established, leading to rational law and political structure as a guarantee of liberty—which "presupposes" that each individual enters freely into relationship with others

112. See Levinas, *Le temps et l'autre*, 93.

113. See Scannone, "Identidad personal, alteridad interpersonnal y relación religiosa."

114. See the philosophies of Ricoeur, who proposes the recognition of oneself as another, and of Levinas, who constructed his whole philosophical system upon an ethics derived from the epiphany of the Face of the Other.

115. See Scannone, "Identidad personal, alteridad interpersonnal y relación religiosa."

in such a way that the law and the structure are possible. But this relationship, this dialogue with the other, is characterized essentially by the absolute quality of the ethical relationship, which for Levinas is the relationship "par excellence."[116]

It is in its fragility and vulnerability that the Face—the Face of the other—is a constant temptation to murder.[117] Through its appearance as a naked, powerless, and needy Otherness—like the biblical characters who personify the poor, the foreigner, the widow, the orphan—the face invites or even challenges the ego as it strives to achieve more happiness and power, seizing the other in his or her weakness. The naked and mortal face seduces me, reducing me to myself, and leading me to acts of violence and even to murder.[118]

And what is most intoxicating about this seduction is the fact that the violent ego realizes that it is in no way forbidden, and is actually possible, to manipulate others in their weakness.[119] According to Levinas, this is the heart of responsible, dialogical, and nonviolent ethics. In the vulnerability exposed in the Face of the other, I discover myself as a potential murderer. And I discover, at the same time, that the poverty of the other is a substantial strength, a radical resistance to my totalizing and reductionist cupidity. The Face of the other thus appears as "opposition," insofar as it places itself in front of and "against" me, confronting me as a radical interdiction, as a resistance to all my obsessions.[120] And this resistance, this force, this accusation raised against me in my violent potentiality, does not come from the free choice of the other but from his or her essential Otherness, in the destitution that proclaims itself as a protest against the violence of the ego.[121]

Levinas' reflection reaches its peak of radicality and seriousness at this point. The encounter with the face of the other accuses the ego, which discovers itself to be egocentric and a potential murderer. The shame that this provokes is ethical. The eye-to-eye encounter with the other causes the ego to acquire a guilty conscience and makes the other appear as a "judge," radically and permanently—not temporarily—questioning the ego.[122] This judgement brings about a crisis in my belief in my presumed rights and my license to practice and defend them. It even questions whether my being, as

---

116. See Levinas, *Liberté et commandment*, 267–70.
117. See Levinas, *Ethique et Infini*, 90.
118. See Levinas, *De Dieu qui vient à l'idée*, 244–45.
119. See Levinas, "Ethique et philosophie première," 124.
120. See Levinas, *En découvrant l'existence avec Husserl et Heidegger*, 173.
121. See Levinas, *À l'heure des nations*, 141.
122. Ibid., 141–42.

ego, is something I have a right to, or if I would not "be killing by the very fact of my being . . . or if through my being in the world, I am not taking someone else's place . . . if I do not suppress the other in my being and in my thoughtless attempt to establish my effort to be?"[123] Thus, I remain under the accusation of the Face, in a way that inverts my subjectivity from the nominative "I" to the accusative "me." I can no longer, in my formerly self-sufficient and violent ego, conceive of myself as the first principle (*archè*), as the measure of all things. Rather I am myself questioned and persecuted, measured by the other, by the face of the other that judges me.[124]

For Levinas, no peaceful relationships and societies are possible without that basic conception. Before the appearance of the other, my liberty is still innocent and without a sense of guilt for its own violence. But through the encounter with and the appeal of the other, my liberty receives a shock and sees in the face of the other, as in a mirror, its own egoism and violence. Thus—according to Levinas—an "inside-out conversion" takes place, that is, a catharsis of the savage and dogmatic effort to be, through which the spiral of violence and war can finally and actually be interrupted and broken.[125] The only basis for a truly ethical justice is the unconditional responsibility made known to the ego at the appearance of the face of the other.

However—Levinas points out—none of this can be realized unless the ego accepts this responsibility and takes it into its own hands, disrupting the unjust chain of the usurpation of life and allowing the other to experience "justice."[126] Thus, a truly human society is possible only when based on a law that takes the Otherness of the other as its first and deepest principle, in a fundamental ethical relation of justice through which Otherness can be recognized and its recognition realized.[127]

Here are the beautiful and exacting words that Levinas uses to define his utopia for society:

> For people to meet one another without conflict and in a reciprocal recognition of the human dignity of each, by which each one is equal to any other, it is necessary that we feel responsible for this equality, a responsibility that goes so far as to renounce

---

123. See Levinas, *Ethique et infini*, 129, 131.

124. See Levinas, *Autrement qu'être ou au-delà de l'essence*, 140.

125. See Levinas, *Autrement que savoir*, 64; Levinas, *Humanisme de l'autre homme*, 49.

126. See Levinas, *Difficile liberté*, 187.

127. See Levinas, *Du sacré au saint*, 21.

equality for oneself and to demand "ever more," "infinitely more" of oneself.[128]

I am thus responsible for the others, above all in their suffering and mortality. The death of others, therefore, cannot result in my indifference, but must be more important and more painful to me than my own.[129] I am thus questioned in my endeavor and my hunger to be, whose Cain-like form makes me refuse to be the guardian of my brother and afterwards tempts me to kill him. The others are there and call for me to be with them at their death, and I cannot do anything against this inexorable enemy except to respond "Here I am," so that my proximity may bring some light and a more bearable death.[130] It is an entirely gracious, asymmetrical, and non-reciprocal movement, since, given the inexorability of death, the others cannot reciprocate.[131]

Levinas also claims that no institution, macro or micro, can be considered exempt from this responsibility for the other. Only in this way can real, strict justice be brought about, in a society with no distinction between these who are near and those who are far away, but where it remains impossible to overlook the nearest. The equality of all is limited by my inequality, by the preponderance of my duty over my rights. Only self-forgetfulness can mobilize justice.[132] This makes clear that, for Levinas, interpersonal relations serve as a basic norm for a society of many. We are created totally and above all for the other and not for ourselves. Being many, we must set limits on our creaturely positivity and assume a wisdom of love that implies a justice that reflects love. Justice consists in the delimitation of love for the neighbor, rather than the delimitation of mutual animosity. Thus, love and justice are inseparable and simultaneous, love being impossible without justice, and justice without love for the other capable of degenerating into violence.[133]

Our society, in postmodern or late modern times, presents us with some serious questions concerning this understanding of identity and subjectivity. The crisis of the institution is intensely felt, impeding, or at least making difficult for the individual, the possibility of attention to and interest in the proposals that would offer them an identity and a sense of their deeper subjectivity.

---

128. See Levinas, "La laïcité et la pensée d'Israel," 50.
129. See Levinas, *Autrement que savoir*, 91.
130. See Levinas, "Intentionalité et sensation," 34–54.
131. See Levinas, *Autrement que savoir*, 76; *Ethique et infini*, 128.
132. See Levinas, *Autrement qu'être ou au-delà de l'essence*, 203.
133. See Bloechl, *Liturgy of the Neighbor*.

Premature or Late Modernity

In the first place, there is a change in contemporary historical consciousness. While in the past the belief in progress as growth encouraged and enhanced an optimistic view of the future, today this conception finds itself in decline and breaking down. This began after the crisis of the 1970s, reaching its peak with the fall of established socialism. It now points to the collapse of a philosophy of history laden with optimism, as it was previously.

The unpredictability of a future for the progress of society, which previously seemed foreseeable, disorients people, making them turn within themselves, to intimacy, rather than to the public role that they could play in society and in culture.[134] We also see a return to the past, called—appropriately or not—the "return of the Sacred" or of religion, as one of the symptoms of this return. Undeniably, there is an ascent of the religious in the current individual consciousness of identity.[135]

Despite the rise and the process of relative stabilization of democracy, the democratic state is neutral from the perspective of the ultimate sense of reality, life, and the cosmic vision. And this situation is consolidated in democratic and pluralistic societies. Religion is a strictly individual matter, as the preservation of the "secularity" of the state is fundamental.[136] The problem of the meaning of life is also strictly individual. No worldview or concept of the good can be privileged above others. "The State would be simply the impartial arbiter of freedom of expression and the peaceful co-existence of various religious convictions."[137]

In this democratic-pluralistic society, where institutions daily face profound crises and a loss of credibility,[138] a radical individualism reigns regarding the meaning and purpose of human beings, their identity, and their actions. Therefore the meaning of life for each person must be found not in the institutions, but through his or her personal search. And it must be identified from a plurality of answers, among which this individual must discern and choose his or her own course and what he or she desires for his or her life.

In this context, while ideology and science find themselves at a very negative level of appreciation due to the hard blow they suffered at the end of the twentieth century—which transformed history from progressive

---

134. See Mardones, *La transformación de la religión*, 204.

135. See, for example, Gauchet, *Un monde desenchante?*, 13f.

136. Consider, for example, French society as characterized by this. See, however, the nuance introduced by Mardones, *La transformación de la religión*, 205–6, as commented upon by Gauchet.

137. Ibid., 205.

138. In recent research carried out in Brazil on which institutions deserved greater credibility, politics took the last place.

optimism into a distressing enigma for the human being—religion enjoys a more favorable status. This clearly has to do with a religion of a quite different cut from the way it was previously conceived. It is a religion without strong beliefs or structures, without stable institutions, yet with credibility.

But undoubtedly the end of the "terrestrial eschatologies"—another name for the "fall of the utopias"[139]—and the consequent disenchantment it provoked, had repercussions in philosophical thought and unleashed upon humankind a great inquietude and even a spiritual thirst. We are in a moment of late modern subjectivity when "the multiplicity of lines of individualization converge in the Mystery of the profundity of the self in relation to the invisible."[140]

The relationship between personal identity and religion is therefore not an impossible equation, but is, on the contrary, extremely present in the moment in which we are living. Even the apparently more "material" concerns, such as the care of the body, or the practice of meditation with Eastern techniques, allow us to foresee a return to the hidden face of things and a new appreciation for knowledge that is not purely cognitive.[141]

The emergence of a new subjectivity is under way, and it does not waver from the course of spiritual thirst or even from the spiritual search. This search aims for liberty in the face of the plurality of responses coming from inside and outside the religious traditions and institutions. And, despite the risk of superficiality and alienation carried at its core, this search brings with it a gauge of the sensibility through which is felt a subjective anchoring with anthropological roots and references, many of which even plunge deeply into old spiritual traditions. This is undoubtedly a new opportunity to search for an authentic identity in the midst of a complex and reenchanted world.

The Nebulousness of Transcendence and the Deconstruction of Faith

The thirst for Transcendence and spirituality found in the postmodern contemporaneity in which we live has, however, contours that are very different from those of the postmodern religious sphere.

While the followers of traditional religion adhere to a single religion and stay with it, and atheists and agnostics reject belief in or adherence to any religion, it is different with human beings who have lived through the

---

139. See Gauchet, *Le désenchantement du monde*, 17.
140. See Mardones, *La transformación de la religión*, 207.
141. Ibid.

crisis of modernity or were born at its climax, and are swimming in the waters of postmodernity. They are like "pilgrims" who wander among the meanderings of the different proposals that make up the religious sphere. They see no problem in moving from one religion to another, or even in building their own religious composition with elements from various proposals.[142] Or even in declaring themselves to be without religion, but not without faith, as shown by a recent survey on the new ways of believing.[143]

In Brazil, recent research projects have tried to identify the self-representation of several groups of people regarding their religious affiliation. The objective was to understand the reasons why they identify themselves in the way they do. The findings showed that 41.4 percent of the total considered themselves without religion because they had their own religiosity, without a link to any church. For 29.4 percent, having no religious beliefs and not frequenting any religious institution was the main justification for seeing themselves as without religion. Another 23.2 percent claimed that they had no time to attend church, and for that reason considered themselves without religion.

It is evident that for many people, the fact of not having a religion does not mean disbelief or the absence of a specific religiosity or of contact with transcendence. On the other hand, simply not attending church makes people declare themselves to be without religion. In many cases, these people maintain or preserve some practices of their previous religion, even though they distance themselves from the institution as a whole. This process of self-naming through a declaration of belonging could be motivated by religious pluralism. Thus, in a country where people identify with increasingly numerous affiliations, there seems to be a social pressure that forces individuals to position themselves in this camp. Along with this there is a simultaneous rejection of and search for religious institutions, as well as a general conception that belief can do without the institution and can

---

142. Cf., confirming this point, Hervieu-Leger, *Le pèlerin et le converti*; See the reflection on the thought of this author by Teixeira, "O Sagrado em novos itnerários," 17–22. See also, in a more Brazilian vein, the concrete question of syncretism and double belonging. The bibliography is vast, making impossible its full listing here. On the issue of double belonging, we recommend the thesis of Rocha, *Teologia e negritude*.

143. See the recent research of CERIS (Centro de Estatísticas Religiosas e Investigação Social) on the new ways of believing: *Mobilidade religiosa no Brasil*, 2005, which follows a previous one, *Desafios do catolicismo na cidade* (São Paulo: Paulus, 2002). The research on the New Ways of Believing, or Religious Mobility in Brazil is a qualitative study consisting of 435 interviews held in the six main Brazilian metropolitan areas with followers of Catholicism (RCC and CEBs) and Pentecostalism (Assembleia de Deus), and individuals without religion. The citations below are taken from this research.

be reformulated, often according to the life context of each person and his or her subjective needs. It is evident that there is no need for a process of disbelief in a transcendental dimension, but rather an explosive search for religious experience, which can occur through institutions, although not exclusively through them.[144]

These recent studies have demonstrated that being without religion does not necessarily translate into disbelief or nihilism, but often into a search for other sources for promoting peace, well-being, and balance, giving priority to the universal values shared by religions, but reaching beyond them rather than being confined to their frontiers and limits. Among the reasons for being religious without religion is the augmentation of the I—in other words, the existential need to seek one's own formula for the meaning of life, without linking it to a group or association, or to an institution. It appears that there are more and more people who believe in God, but who don't feel comfortable in an institution and are looking for their own path.

However, just as there is a way to leave the Catholic religion, one also discovers a reverse path: those processes of conversion and strengthening of faith that pursue traditional pathways and knock on the door of the old traditions, among them the Catholic Church. Traditional Catholicism is often not translated into practicing Catholicism. But those who arrive at, or return to, the Catholic Church can bring a stronger motivation than those who simply remain there, often because of family tradition or just inertia. They return precisely because they wish to find a space where they can fully live out what they have rediscovered.

For a better understanding of the direction and challenges taking place today in the Christian faith, one must first consider a conceptual distinction: the distinction between faith and religion. The two concepts are connected but not interchangeable. Demarcating their boundaries and frontiers can help us understand the situation of historical Christianity today and clarify how we are questioned as followers of its proposal.[145]

In this complex and plural contemporaneity of ours, the challenge to belief has been the subject of many works by renowned current theologians.[146] And it continues to be an ongoing challenge to theology. The

---

144. See for instance, Burity, "Religião e política na fronteira"; See also Rodrigues, "Os sem religião no Censo nacional"; Siqueira, "Pluralidade e trânsito religioso entre as novas religiosidades."

145. See the comments on this distinction by Moingt, *Dieu qui vient à l'homme*, vol. 1, ch. 2, especially "Foi et croyance, Évangile et religion," 82–93.

146. Cf., among other works, Moltmann, *God for a Secular Society*; Vaz, "Religião e modernidade filosófica"; Panier, "Pour une anthroplologie du croire"; Gauchet, *Le désenchantement du monde*, 231, 234, 236.

process of secularization impelled by the modern crisis presents several characteristics apparently seen as incompatible with consciousness of the presence of the Sacred, with living the faith, and even more with the practice of religion, especially institutionalized religion.

The secularization and disenchantment of the world continue on their path despite the crisis of modernity and the power of reason. Meanwhile religion, transubstantiated into many different forms not compatible with the premodern ones, continues to be ferociously questioned. Even if the "masters of suspicion" find themselves at least partially denied—given that the prophesied irremediable decline of religion has not come to pass, and a "return of the Holy" can be verified—the question remains whether this crisis of religiosity implies a crisis of faith in equal proportion.[147]

Postmodernity rescued the Holy, but it is a Holy without Absolutes and without a face, not on equal terms with the content of the faith experience as understood in Christianity. The question that remains after these introductory reflections is not only whether we can identify faith with religion. The central point of our inquiry is: If we verify that faith can no longer be identified with religion, what then is the configuration which, among so many denominations in the most diverse combinations, would most faithfully correspond to the proposal of Christian revelation?

Even if religion is defined and understood as a "set of beliefs related to what humankind considers supernatural, divine and Holy, as well as the set of moral codes and rituals derived from these beliefs,"[148] one cannot say the same about faith. Faith is fundamentally a response to a proposal made for the liberty of the human being, who is called to respond to it with all the dimensions of his or her being. Hence, it is a second moment, a later consent to something previously proposed by the other. Believing is therefore not a human initiative searching for a space where one can discharge anxieties and frustrations, but on the contrary, it is fundamentally a receptive and welcoming attitude that generates a radical surrender, commitment, and engagement with life.[149]

---

147. See Moingt, *Dieu qui vient à l'homme*, vol. 1. ch. 2, "Le retrait de la religion," 81–130.

148. See the definition found at https://en.wikipedia.org/wiki/Religion.

149. See Rahner, "O homem como ser de responsabilidade e liberdade," in *Curso fundamental da fé*, 50–53, and "Características da vida cristã," in ibid., 466–75; Libânio, *Eu creio, nós cremos*, esp. ch. 9, "A liberdade do ato de fé e sua motivação última," 191–212, and ch. 21, "Nós cremos na perspectiva da libertação," 437–66. See also Theobald, *Le christianisme comme style*, esp. vol. 1, 16–205, "Ouverture," and vol. 2, part 4, "Le christianisme comme style," 701–837.

All the meaning, all the importance and relevance of faith, therefore, comes from the fact that it is an experience that seconds a proposal coming from Someone. Someone who is not equal to me or to anyone. The most important thing in the dynamics of faith is, then, to ask from whom comes the proposal I respond to, and what consequences this believing unleashes in my life. In answering these questions, we arrive at what fundamental theology calls Revelation.[150]

As Christianity understands it, Revelation is the Word of God that breaks its eternal silence and erupts into human time and space. The nucleus of the Revelation is thus God, the very God who communicates to the human being God's Mystery, God's project, and God's invitation to a full life—a life that represents a covenant and fellowship with God and the surrender of life, energy, and desire for the construction and implementation of a world ruled by justice and peace.[151]

The Revelation comes to the human being as a Grace that surprises and summons freedom. It is a gracious and freely offered proposal, which asks for an equally free response as the fruit of the Grace that precedes it. Thus, God's Grace is not only the fact that God makes such a proposal to the human being, but also the fact that the latter, limited and finite, can hear it, receive it, and respond to it by faith, in the absence of evidence and empirical proof. The desire to believe is itself given by God, whose Grace and mercy precedes everything. However, the act of accepting or rejecting this freely given offer is unique to human freedom, which is summoned and questioned in a definitive way. The decision to say "yes" or "no" belongs to the human being and nobody else, although always supported and helped by the Grace of God.[152]

Being first a gift, faith is also a task. If it is true that we receive this gift of faith from God with no merit on our part, it is also true that it implies responsibility as well as concrete and radical effort. This is the criterion for verification which demonstrates that this faith is something real. It is not a

---

150. See the reflection by Estrada, *Razones y sinrazones de la creencia religiosa*, 221. The author ends his book with the words, "Much more important than telling others what they should believe or think is to affirm that it is important to believe in something and someone, that it is necessary to question the values that guide life, and that only through personal interiorization is it possible to place oneself in an existence with one's autonomy and protagonism, instead of allowing oneself to be led by advertising fashions, the manipulation of consumers, and egocentric pragmatism. From here God can emerge as a question, a space would open for God's revelation, and the religious experience of humankind would be made possible." See also Rahner, "Em busca de síntese do conceito de revelação," in *Curso fundamental da fé*, 207–12.

151. See Rahner, "O ouvinte da Palavra," in *Curso fundamental da fé*, 37–59.

152. Ibid., 47.

product of our imagination or an alienating experience but an experience of commitment. Nor is it a frenetic and illusory self-seeking, but rather a surrender and response to something that came to us from the other. Faith is therefore the subjective correlate of Revelation, that is, Revelation that has reached its recipient, that has arrived at its goal.[153]

Religion is the basis for the doctrinal, ritual, and moral support by which this faith is expressed within a society that is human and needs to organize its most important experiences. Religion is necessarily organized and structured as an institution. This is extremely important if the faith of the coming generations is to find a space and a community to provide the foundation and condition for its growth. Yet, and for this same reason, any religion is a human product, inserted into time and into space and therefore subject to changes and adaptations. This has happened and does happen with all religions. It has also happened and is happening with the Christian faith and revelation, which today confront a historical moment of great and profound change in their shape and form.

As we proceed, we will try to examine at length the global situation of religion in the contemporary world and how the mystical experience can find a way through such a complex panorama.

---

153. See Libânio, *Eu creio, nós cremos*, ch. 7, "Estrutura subjetiva da fé: dimensão antropológica," 151–70; see also Rahner, *Curso fundamental da fé*, 57–58, and all his profound elaboration on the fact that the human being is a subject under alien control and carried by the Mystery.

2

Secular Culture and the Crisis of Religion

IN THE WORLD WE live in, reconfigured by the contours we examined in chapter 1, religion appears as a powerful force that touches and affects human desire. But in the midst of secularity and pluralism, it seems to have lost the power to configure the behavior of society. The situation of religion today will be the subject of this chapter.

Contemporaneity preserves religious symbols, often transforming them into touristic and historical monuments. And people go their way with independence and freedom regarding what the religious institution seems to be saying to them. On the other hand, the search for God and the desire for spirituality grow in equal proportions, emerging on many shores that are no longer solely or primarily the historical churches.

Given this state of things, historical Christianity, more than two thousand years old, will have to rethink itself, and perceive what central point it must communicate to the men and women of today if it is to motivate them to be guided in their lives by the way called Good News, which was capable of turning a decisive page in history and of molding the life and culture of a large part of the world.

Secularity and the Apogee of the Real

Religion is the most omnipresent and the most universal of the elemental characteristics of humankind. All human actions, from the most sublime to the most commonplace, have been identified with religious phenomena.[1] Even today, in a time of full secularization, religion continues to be the object of observation and study, often becoming what redefines modern and postmodern preoccupations, at least in the last resort.[2]

---

1. See Bauman, *Postmodernity and Its Discontents*, 166.
2. Ibid., 170.

Even when its importance is denied, religion more than ever constitutes part of the current of everyday life. And this is because death, despite having been relegated to the business of professionals (doctors, intensive care personnel, and funeral homes), continues to assault the imaginations of people who, day after day, continue to feel frequently and fragmentarily threatened in their desire to live. Although the death of a loved one has become a private and secret affair, human death as such has become a daily occurrence—in the news media, in the congestion of large metropolitan areas, and in the violence and injustice on display in our societies—much too common to cause fear. It is just one show among many.[3]

Meanwhile human beings, ever more eager to own and benefit from a life they feel is threatened, and not knowing how long life may last, need a "mountaintop" experience. Such experiences are no longer offered by institutional religion—through the practice of meditation, spiritual seclusion, and their attractions—but have migrated to the arena of worldly seductions, to the desire for earthly goods. They have developed into the driving force of intense consumerist activity.[4] This was a long process, which first began with a denial of religion, along with the revelation and faith that inspired it, just to restore it later in another place.

As we reflect on the historical sources of the phenomenon of secularization, we can place them at the roots of modern culture. Secularization is the product of an understanding of the world as no longer based on myth (*mythos*), but on rational discourse (*logos*). This vision and the process that disenchants myth and establishes the primacy of *logos* come from ancient philosophy and lead to a certain demystification of knowledge, and to a liberation of ordinary life from theological norms.

Bruno Forte, in his book *Trindade para ateus*,[5] reflects on the multiple difficulties faced by the believer in the midst of modernity's process of secularization. Among them he lists immediacy, secularist restlessness, the triumph of powerful reason, and the fecundity of the Enlightenment. These factors give rise to the atheist ideologies of the masters of suspicion (Marx, Freud, and Nietzsche), which, in turn, lead to the dissipation and almost disappearance of inquiry through the Senses—the only ground from which the quest for Transcendence and for the belief in and the naming of God can take off. Bruno Forte states that "this is the true mortal disease that permeates the societies of Europe and the whole secularized world"[6]

---

3. Ibid., 175.
4. Ibid., 180.
5. See Forte, *Trindade para ateus*.
6. Ibid., 137.

in our moment in history. And although this question may present itself in different forms, according to the circumstances, we tend to agree with such an affirmation.

The same phenomenon continues even in the midst of the so-called crisis of modernity. It would be too complex to analyze here all the aspects of this "crisis." That would require the analysis of all the faces by which the crisis makes itself visible and palpable in our historical time. We cannot do this, nor is it our objective within the limits of this analysis.[7] What matters here is for us to understand how the axial dislocation—of the question of the sacred, the Divine, and God, and of the conception of a theocratic world into one of an anthropocentric world that proposes the human being as the measure of everything—makes itself visible. After that, we will see how this same transition, in turn, admits a questioning and a crisis that will destabilize modernity, which appears so solidly established.

Father Henrique de Lima Vaz, in his monumental text "Religião e modernidade filosófica,"[8] places the dawn of modernity not at the beginning of the sixteenth century but much earlier, in the time of Plato. The modern, according to Father Vaz, was already for ancient philosophy the new thing that arrives and questions the present in its established situation. To what we call modernity and place at the beginning of the sixteenth century, he gives the name "modern modernity."[9]

The characteristics of this long period of history would thus be:

1. The transition from theocentrism (God as the measure of all things) to anthropocentrism (the human being as the measure of all things).

2. The transition from tutored science to emancipated and autonomous science, searching for its own method and path without asking for permission from institutional religion (see the case of Galileo).

3. The transition from heteronomy (the primacy of the other as ruling life, the other understood as God, the church, institutional religion) to autonomy (the subject as the sovereign of his or her own life, following a chosen way in full freedom, and not having to be accountable to anyone).

4. The transition from a conception of religion as the explanation of the world, to a conception of the world and reality as self-explanatory for

---

7. For a deeper understanding of the so-called modernity crisis, see Azevedo, *Entroncamentos e entrechoques*. See also Mardones, *Las nuevas formas de la religión*; and Taylor, *A Secular Age*, among others.

8. Vaz, "Religião e modernidade filosófica."

9. Ibid.

the human being. This is sometimes called the "disenchantment of the world."¹⁰ The world is no longer explained by supernatural premises and parameters. It is no longer inhabited by supernatural beings that magically explain, transform, and illuminate it, as had been believed since the time of Thales of Miletus, five thousand years before Christ. All explanation must be found at the very heart of reality, in the constitution of the world itself.

5. The transition from a conception of learning and knowledge as centered in theological reflection (the University where theology is queen of the sciences and the center around which irradiates the very idea of the University, exactly as it existed in the Middle Ages) to a conception centered in human beings and their surroundings (anthropology, the human sciences, the social sciences, and the exact sciences) as the perspective from which the world and reality is conceived and understood. Religion and theology are just another field of learning, all of which is compartmentalized and organized into separate specialties.

6. The transition from a conception of the world where faith in God and in the church as an institution is at the center of everything, of all fields of knowledge and all of life, to a conception where human reason is central. The Cartesian "I think, therefore I am" is the motto of modernity. The human being as a thinking being is at the center of modern, secularized modernity.

This new way of conceiving the relationship between the "secular" and the "divine and supernatural," a relationship of the "profane" with the "Sacred," unavoidably raises the question of the space remaining for the sacred in a world and a reality thus conceived. What faces can still introduce the Sacred to our contemporaries in understandable and assimilable ways? What faces of the Sacred can still interface with a secular mentality structured in such a way?

Since it is a long historical process, secularization grows in complexity as time goes by, and after more than four centuries it no longer admits a univocal interpretation. On the contrary, it reveals itself to have acquired, over time, a plurality of aspects. And, because of this complexity, it has been crossed by numerous interfaces by which it can be discovered and understood, on a new basis and with different cues for reading.

If we consider the process of secular culture from the point of view of theology, we will discover the inadequacy of a model of understanding shaped by the idea of conquest, that is, a vision of secularity as a harmful

10. See Gauchet, *Le désenchantement du monde*.

system, implying that it needs to be evangelized at all costs to bring about a recovery of the hegemony of faith and religion in the world. This is no less true for a hierarchical model, which would put secularity at a lower level as a benefactor of humankind, while a society ruled by a religious model would be superior and should be preserved no matter what. Equally inadequate would be a model in which levels are superimposed upon one another, which would give rise to a confusion of concepts rather than making them clear and consistent. What is important is to look at the phenomenon of secularization relative to faith and religion as a relation between two faces that touch each other, thus opening up the possibility of new syntheses.[11]

Even in a first approach, one is already conscious of the existence of a positivity that is very much present in the process of secularization. It has to do with a phenomenon that is not at all negative—as it was considered for a time, especially according to Christian thought—but which, on the contrary, introduces some faces of visibility that challenge faith, religion, and theology in a fecund and vital way.[12]

Most especially, regarding historical Christianity, we could enumerate some of those interfacing points where we find, visible and flourishing, the presence of secularization as a positive challenge to theology:[13]

1. The conception of creation: the process of secularization helps humanity to remember a truth that the biblical revelation has always affirmed: the created world is not sacred. Neither is it divine or supernatural. Nothing except God is divine, and any attempt to see tangible, immanent, and provisional realities as sacred deflects the focus of transcendence away from the right understanding that there is only one God, that this God is not identifiable with anything that exists, and that all things are the work of God's hands. Creation can, therefore, be a way to arrive at God and to see God's presence in the world. In fact, many forms of spirituality see nature as the source of the Sacred and of the experience of the Sacred.[14] But it is definitely earthly, not divine, and therefore is secular even in its sacredness. A theological interpretation of secularization, underlining the desacralization of the world, refers to the condemnation of idolatry, which was ceaselessly denounced by

---

11. See on this matter Queiruga, *Fin del cristianismo premoderno*, esp. the chapter titled "La Modernidad como cambio radical de paradigma," 17–21.

12. Ibid.

13. We basically follow here the elaborations on this matter in the works of Queiruga, especially *Creio em Deus Pai* and *Fim do cristianismo premoderno*.

14. See the entire ecological current and the holistic spirituality that flourishes nowadays as a result of this vision.

Israel's prophets. On the other hand, by affirming the existence of only one God, distinct from the created world, biblical religion initiates a process of understanding the world from the perspective of both the human person and the Creator. The world is not God, but neither is it a power hostile to God. The world speaks of the one who created it and proclaims the glory of God.

2. The conception of history: neither is history, in its processes and injunctions, divine. It constitutes the ground for human operations and interference. It can and must be transformed and changed by the human being. Secularization was clearly important enough in the twentieth century for a theologian such as Karl Rahner, among others, to affirm as a basis for his understanding of history that there are not two histories: one transcendent and the other profane. Chronological history—where humanity struggles, building the present and desiring the future—is by now already the history of salvation, permanently running the risk of becoming a history of perdition.[15] In history we find manifestations of the sacred, although history itself is not divine. And in the biblical Revelation, God reveals God's self to Israel inside its own history, remaining present in it and guiding its people by the internal workings of that same history.

3. The understanding of the worship of God and the dignity of the human being: in the process of the biblical Revelation the human being comes to perceive that Sacred spaces are indeed relative and provisional, and do not contain and arrest the divine. In truth, the divine is more certainly found in the humanity of the human being. Relocated from the temple to the human being, the axis of the sacred will be a *leitmotif* of the biblical revelation, and, above all of the New Testament,[16] revealing injustice and idolatry to really be two sides of the same coin—or better, of the same sin. In losing the right way to relate themselves with God, human beings lose as well the right way to relate with the other, that is, with their neighbor. The struggles for justice and human rights against all forms of oppression are in truth sacred struggles, even when they take place in complete secularity. The process of secularization brings the issue of the primacy of the human being—that is, of Otherness—into the center of Christian theological reflection and into the life of faith.

---

15. See Rahner, *Curso fundamental da fé*.

16. See the parable of the Good Samaritan (Luke 10:30–37). See also the text of the last judgement in Matt 25:31–46, among others.

4. The Mystery of the Incarnation understood as a secular Mystery: the Mystery that is at the center of the Christian faith is, in truth, understandable and even credible from the standpoint of secularity. The mystery of the incarnation says that since everything has been deeply touched by God, everything has positive value. Nothing is less dignified, less noble, less valuable for being in the midst of the secular. All was assumed by the Word made flesh in the fullness of time. Therefore everything, without exception, is seen through the screen of secularity, including even God, whose person and presence give it positive value via the kenotic process of descent into the human core. In Christianity, the incarnation confirms the dignity of the world and of humanity and its differentiation from God. Secularization thus emerges as the continuation, in time, of a "de-divinization" of the world and of the human being on the part of none other than God. This desacralization is positive since it allows God, in the fullness of God's divinity, to gloriously shine in the midst of the creation, at once as wholly other and as radically near to humankind.[17]

In view of these considerations, we believe that a possible opening can be found in Christianity and throughout the biblical revelation for an interface with a mundane and secular conception of the world, in which religion and religiosity do not impose themselves as constituting a univocal and essential understanding. In fact it can be said that there is already, even in the biblical text, an emancipation of the human being in relation to God and religion. The process of secularization does nothing other than reinforce this on a new and more universal basis. Presenting a positive rather than only a negative face, secularization reminds us that the emancipation of the human does not necessarily mean the sunset of God. And also that if secularization can be seen (in many of its faces) as the enemy of a certain conception of religion, particularly institutionalized religion, that doesn't necessarily mean that this same secularization, in some of its other faces, cannot live together—that is, interface—at an acceptable level of cordiality with the human experience of faith.

The assimilation of this state of things is not yet complete in the faith community and in theology. One still sees hesitations, fears, and denials, as well as attempts at an impossible return to premodern Christianity, with the hope of rescuing, from there, the hegemony that institutional religion enjoyed in other periods of history. On the other hand, modernity itself is in deep crisis due to the demise of the utopias on which it had built its model,

---

17. On this and other references to secularization, see Bingemer and Andrade, *Secularização: novos desafios*.

and to the emergence of a new subjectivity that questions the conception of the human being as basically configured by rationality, while claiming the right to values that would seem to belong to the past, such as affectivity, graciousness, and contemplation.

As a result, our current context has received several names—such as modernity, late modernity, hypermodernity, postmodernity, and liquid modernity—and it is a "movable"[18] context. And this brings significant transformations to human life, its configuration, meaning, and self-understanding, together with a feeling of great uncertainty, insecurity, and even anxiety.[19]

One of the deepest impacts of the transformations of the current time is undoubtedly their effect on religion. If during the Enlightenment—as we have seen—human rationality became more and more visible and gained the status of the central governing principal in human life, what we see today is different. The crisis of modernity made way for a new state of things that human knowledge is far from having assimilated deeply. And it is during the twentieth century that we see this new process with greater clarity.[20]

Religion suffers the consequences of this new world vision. In a modern perspective, for something to be considered legitimate or true it must go through the process of rational understanding—as an antidote to the fanaticism, superstition, and intolerance that religion was always accused of bringing with it.[21]

This valorization of the rational caused human beings to consider themselves autonomous and emancipated. Science and technology, instead of beliefs, would solve their problems. The individual, possessing ever more power through science and technology, would be the center of the universe, of phenomena and events, taking the place of God. Human beings alone would be responsible for seeking and finding happiness and the meaning of life, with their capacity for thinking and reasoning.

Yet, just as at the beginning of modern times the theocentric conception fell into a deep crisis and lost the power to explain the world, so now something similar is happening with Cartesian reason. It is seen as insufficient and as having failed, in a certain way, in its project.[22] This comes about

---

18. Here we use the word *movable* with the meaning of "changing," "insecure," "volatile."

19. Ibid.

20. See Muller-Armack, *El siglo sin Dios*, on the idea of the twentieth century as the century without God.

21. See Castiñera, *A experiência de Deus na pós-modernidade*.

22. See Damasio's remarks on this point in *Descartes' Error*. He states that the absence of emotion and feeling can destroy rationality. See also the affirmation of Simone Weil in *Sur la science*: "A aventura de Descartes acabou mal," "Descartes' adventure finished in a bad way."

as a symptom of the birth of a New Era, the one in which we live today. We have seen that, with the utopias in progressive collapse, with certainty disappearing, and with an incredible abundance of means being put to meager, scarce, and poor ends, contemporary human beings look anxiously for experiences that may give meaning to their lives with the message that it is still worthwhile living on this planet.[23]

Institutions, organized belief, and "religious organizations," with their message of the perpetual insufficiency of the human being, are no better positioned to facilitate and communicate these experiences, especially to those excluded from the "gains" of civilization. Neither are the achievements of human rationality.

Human living has come to be considered synonymous with enjoyment of the delights of consumerism at the reach of one's hands. Living fully would mean satisfying the endless avidity of human desire in a very material way. A certain deification of the capacity and power of consumerism is elevated to something similar to real religion, a major cult in mass societies. Thus, it is no longer a matter of "I think, therefore I am" but of "I consume, therefore I am." Implicitly or explicitly, this is the commanding motivational word in human life today. We find ourselves standing before a kind of sacralization of commercial and consumerist relations.[24]

Yet, religion as a relationship with Transcendence has not been abolished from the human horizon, as the "masters of suspicion" had always prophesied.[25] The same modern thinkers who so much criticized the superstitious and magic elements of Christianity are now called to recognize the strength of Transcendence as a constitutive element of humankind. Even avowed atheists, such as André Comte-Sponville, speak of an "atheistic spirituality" that offers human beings some experiences which cannot be classified as rational or natural.[26]

---

23. See Baumann's expression, *Postmodernity and Its Discontents*, 180.

24. See the excellent reflection on this issue by Mardones, *La tranformación de la religión*, 48–49. On 50, Mardones says, citing Vattimo, that "at the root of consumerism there is a Christian stamp, reoriented toward immanence, a fruit of European and Western curiosity in exploring alternative worlds." See also the excellent study of consumerism by Cavanaugh, *Being Consumed*.

25. On the expression "masters of suspicion," see Ricoeur, *Freud and Philosophy* and *The Conflict of Interpretations*.

26. See Comte-Sponville, *L'Esprit de l'athéisme*: "Quite frankly, do you really need to believe in God to realize that sincerity is better than lying, that courage is better than cowardice, that generosity is better than selfishness, that sweetness and compassion are better than violence or cruelty, that justice is better than injustice, and that love is better than hate? Obviously not! If you believe in God, you recognize these values in God; or maybe you recognize God in them. It is the traditional picture: your faith and your

Religion becomes something private, belonging exclusively to the inner forum of human consciousness, without mediation or institution. More and more it is to be lived out in the sphere of private life, where each person believes and welcomes the truths presented, appreciating them and discerning them according to the affective affinities or gratifying sentiments that come from life experience.

A godless century, in which even the deities are ephemeral and transitory—consumer goods—the twentieth century takes the postmodernization process to intense levels as a challenge to human thinking. It rescues Transcendence, but rejects its traditional form, introducing this same Transcendence without a face, without an identity, without Absolutes. Religious experiences proliferate once again where they seemed to have vanished. Yet they assume a different configuration: consumption of sentient experiences, which speak to the senses and are interchangeable with others that are equally superficial. And the result is an exhaustion of the potential for fulfillment and delight, thus creating a more and more "frigid" society.[27]

Observing all that is happening in religion today is tantamount to taking into account what is happening in society, or at least in so-called Western and Christian society.

> Therefore, when we say "religion" in this Western late modernity, we are utilizing a generalization of the predominantly Christian phenomenon that configured it in terms of civilization. And if not exclusively, then at least primarily, we have before our eyes the dominant religious fact among us, which is historical Christianity, whether Catholic or Protestant.[28]

In traditional societies religion holds a monopoly on the worldview. The consequence is that religion there is more than religion. It plays such an important social and cultural role that practically all social realities (political, economic, juridic, or artistic) as well as behavioral realities (family, psychological, or symbolic) depend on it for legitimacy. Religion is what sets the rhythm of time with the tolling of bells—for the morning mass, the angelus, and the vespers, for the deceased or for religious feasts—and signals the different moments of the day, the week, or the year.[29]

---

faithfulness go together, and I am not the one to criticize you for that. But those with no faith, why couldn't they perceive the human greatness of these values, their importance, their necessity, their fragility, their urgency, and respect them for that?"

27. See on this point the acute and pertinent analysis of Heisig, "The Recovery of the Senses."

28. See Mardones, *La tranformación de la religión*, 8.

29. Ibid., 18–20.

With modernity there came a transition to a social situation in which religion no longer occupies the center of the scene, having been replaced by politics and economics. It no longer dictates behavior, which is now ruled much more by the new psychoanalytic maxims, the mass media, or by new technologies such as the Internet. Religion, so to speak, is pushed to the periphery, ceasing to play the principal role and moving to a secondary place.

For the West—the part of the world where historical Christianity had clear and strong roots—this process implied a complete social and religious restructuring and reconfiguration. Religion lost the cultural plausibility and the leadership to intervene in society and its processes. "The religion of modernity is a decentralized religion which loses strength in the hearts of the faithful."[30] And in spite of the postmodern turnaround that rescued the search for Transcendence—and in some measure even due to that turn—it arrived at the twenty-first century with a very low level of institutional communication with the more advanced modern culture.

The reaction of institutional religion to this situation has been the rejection of modern sensibility. Today we observe the recrudescence of ultraconservative groups, together with the neoconservative groups that are regaining visibility in the Western religious scene. We also see the exponential growth of the Pentecostals of both denominations, Catholic (Charismatic Renewal) and Protestant.[31] With the Second Vatican Council, historical Catholicism undertook a serious task of dialogue with modernity, including new theological elaborations. But this task remained inconclusive in view of the "return to great discipline" during the pontificate of John Paul II[32] and the consequent intensification of the contraposition between modernity and Christianity.

According to some authors, what really happened after the Council was an attempt to "adapt" the historical Christian religion, whether Catholic or Protestant, to the new state of things brought about by modern secularization. Yet one of them comments, "when adaptation is such that for the sake of it one surrenders the identity of the faith, we are facing a cognitive capitulation."[33] What we see today is that the symbolic religious capital is no longer in the hands of the churches, and has been coopted by other actors and subjects—such as the sects or the media—which manage it in different ways.[34]

30. Ibid., 28.

31. See on this matter Comblin, "As religiões hoje"; see also Comblin, "O Cristianismo no limiar do terceiro milênio," 147.

32. See Libânio, *A volta à grande disciplina*.

33. See Mardones, *La tranformación de la religión*, 30–31.

34. See the book by Campos, *Teatro, templo e mercado*, on the Universal Church of the Kingdom of God.

Secular Culture and the Crisis of Religion

According to the French sociologist Danièle Hervieu-Léger, secularization today can be defined not as the loss of religion in a society definitively emancipated from any code of belief imposed from above, but rather as a general process of institutional deregulation of belief.[35] There is an increasing deinstitutionalization, that is, a growing withdrawal of individuals from religious institutions, to which they no longer turn as the regulating and legitimizing agency of their religious practice or formulation of faith.

On the other hand, individualism and the call for a more authentic conduct prevail in a climate that favors affectivity. Expression of feelings is no longer taboo. On the contrary, it is sought by those tired of the modern rational rigidity, and thirsty for an affective interchange and experience searching for ways of expression. Although criticized by some authors as "hedonistic individualism" centered in the "I" and avidly pursuing self-realization, self-expression, self-experience, and such, this tendency points to what may be called the "expressive revolution," which involves issues of gender, a primary matter of debate today.[36]

Furthermore, the generational breach perhaps appears nowhere as intensely as in the field of religion. There is a profound crisis in religious socialization, that is, in the transmission of the Christian message to succeeding generations who no longer adhere to dogmatic formulations or moral norms. They seek an experience that will touch them emotionally. The official Christian institution has failed to find a way to do that.[37]

The situation of religion in the Western world today is, then, characterized by the loss on the part of ecclesiastic institutions of a good portion of their hegemonic religious monopoly. The religious initiative finds a new elaborating and irradiating center in the individual. An individual who seeks Transcendence or greater meaning in life will often choose a religion, reordering and structuring it, and giving it form, at the margin of the institution. A religion lived out in this way will not necessarily be configured faithfully according to the historical Christian model. It could be a plural religion that includes other elements, synthesized where religiosity appears nebulous and fluctuating, reconfigured as open and without well-defined frontiers or boundaries.

The secularization that generated this state of things not only questioned the existence of Transcendence, but also deregulated Transcendence wherever it was accepted and believed. It brought into crisis the traditional

---

35. See Hervieu-Léger; Mardones, *La tranformación de la religión*, 36.

36. Ibid., 39, on the crisis of masculinity and the claims of men regarding the expression of sensitivity. See Nolasco, *De Tarzan a Homer Simpson*.

37. See Mardones, *La tranformación de la religión*, 40.

ways of believing, and introduced new ways that are quite different from the previous ones.[38]

Religiosity, once disconnected from the institution that gave it structure and stability, begins to acquire from society an unstable and "wandering" form, a mixture of syncretism, eclecticism, and even a double or multiple religious affiliation.[39] This diffuse and fluid religiosity, which develops at the margin of institutional religion, presents a certain symbolic nebulosity and a consumerism of sensations generating indifference and incredulity in the more critical and skeptical individuals and groups. On the other hand, it is often the breeding ground for new religious and mystical experiences provoked by artificial elements and substances, some of which can be classified as hallucinogenic.[40]

This leads to a dangerous distinction between religion—with tradition, code, and institution—and a new emerging "spirituality," belonging more to the emotional arena, without tradition, and spontaneously born of a purely subjective and emotional experience.

Anthropocentrism and Human Autonomy

While in the Middle Ages God was the measure of all things, in modernity the human being came to be this measure. The famous drawing by da Vinci of the Vitruvian Man[41] describes well this conception. It is a nude male figure separated into two superimposed positions, with the arms inscribed in a circle and in a square. This drawing has been interpreted to represent Leonardo's conception of the map of the human body as a cosmography of the *minor mondo*, to the extent that he believed the human body could be considered an analogy of the universe.[42]

The anthropocentric paradigm allowed all areas of knowledge, especially the reflection on faith or theology, to achieve a veritable Copernican revolution, starting from a human perspective (human reality, context, and condition) in order to be able to speak intelligibly to the modern world—and to persons molded and configured in the kiln of modernity and secularization—about

---

38. Ibid., 42–43.

39. Ibid., 70. See also Fernandes, *Novas formas de crer*.

40. See for instance the Brazilian ecological religion called Santo Daime, or the União do Vegetal, also Brazilian. On Santo Daime, see Araujo, *Navegando sobre as ondas do Santo Daime*; Lodi, *Estrela da minha vida: histórias do sertão caboclo*.

41. A famous drawing based on calculations by the Roman architect Vitruvius, made around 1490 in one of the artist's diaries.

42. See http://leonardodavinci.stanford.edu/submissions/clabaugh/history/leonardo.html.

transcendence, religion, and the divine Mysteries.[43] But it also brought—in large part because of the dialogue with an anthropology not informed by faith—the risk of a conception of human beings as needing, in order to affirm themselves as free beings responsible for their destiny, to distance themselves from any and all tutelage, above all from religious tutelage.

Modern humans came to be generally considered as beings who have dismissed God, who have emancipated themselves from religiosity, and who no longer consider their lives dependent on this aspect—whether they are called atheists, agnostics, theists, polytheists, or are simply indifferent to religious questions. But we can see that this definition is not so easy to make. These human beings, in reality, find themselves in a situation that besides presenting them with the option of desacralized secularization, confronts them equally with a crowded pantheon of new gods, which postmodernity tries to "sell" to them every day. And they—whether atheist, agnostic, or believer—feel vulnerable before these new idols and divinities that are offered daily to their potential for belief. Ultimately they may find themselves perplexed before the emergence of a new plurality and a new religious consciousness, which increasingly complicates their visual and affective field as well as their thirst for Transcendence.

Traditional sacredness presented a heteronomous face, that is, one that presumed adherence to a set of norms and truths which, coming from outside, imposed themselves on the human being as indispensable for the experience of faith and the practice of religion. Today, after the advent of the crisis of modernity, heteronomy is in the shadows, and in its place, clearly and unquestionably, rises autonomy—the liberty of human subjects to define their options, to choose their own way and their own destiny, without being subject to any authority outside of themselves and their conscience. Modern philosophy reinforced this affirmation and thus had an impact on, and consequences for, theology.[44]

With the fall of the old paradigms and the advent of new ones, and with the increasing complexity in the sphere of religious life, the place and role of autonomy and heteronomy present themselves in a different way. It is important, once again, to look at the definition of the relevant terms to verify what is understood by each, and to clarify the concepts by which we comprehend the processes of the world and the historical moment in which we live.

---

43. See on this point the verifications in the manuals of introduction to theology, and their analysis of the theological method before and after the Council. Cf., for instance, Boff, *Teoria do método teológico*; Libânio and Murad, *Introdução à teologia*.

44. See above all the works of Feuerbach, Nietzsche, etc.

The idea of the human influences the concepts of *authos* (same), *heterós* (other), and *nomos* (law). Premodernity and, within it, the classical and traditional theologies, understood religion as a set of external norms that must be followed for the worship of the true God to occur. Modernity brought about a dislocation regarding this conception, in placing the axis of the sacred in the profoundest depths of the human subject, understood as conscious and productive freedom—productive, in a way, of its own *nomos*, its own law.

The fragmentation of the modern in the hard-to-define postmodern poses both the problem and its questioning in a different way. Currently, amidst secularization and religious pluralism—that is, amidst the fragmentation inherent in postmodernity—human beings rediscover the primacy of Otherness, and revalue the experience of this same Otherness. And from this standpoint they discover themselves as relational beings, intelligible to themselves only through relationship. As they do, the *authos* interfaces with the *heterós*, opening a space for a new *nomos*, a new law. A new moment emerges: that of subjectivity, which must live together with the intense individualization that brought to human beings the enormous loneliness of their egos.

Some modern philosophers have centered their reflection on autonomy, seeing it as the sovereign and solitary capacity of individuals to decide their destiny without recourse to any other source of influence. For some of them this logic went as far as anathematizing Otherness as a threat to human happiness. One cannot forget, for instance, the clamor of Jean-Paul Sartre, through the mouth of the character Garcin in the play *No Exit (Huis Clos)*: "Hell is other people!"[45]

Yet other contemporary philosophers follow a totally opposite line. One of them is Emmanuel Levinas, who clearly opts for the element of responsibility for the other as the basis of a human society. For him, this society would be built on the transcendental basis which consists of an epiphany of the Face of the other. It is only there that the I-other relationship can be initiated, resulting in a rational law and a political structure as guarantors of freedom—a freedom which "presupposes" that each individual enters freely into relationship with others in a way that makes possible both the law and the structure. This relationship, this dialogue with the other, is essentially characterized by the absolute configuration of the ethical relationship, which, according to Levinas, is the relationship "par excellence."[46]

---

45. See Sartre, *Huis Clos*.
46. See Levinas, *Liberté et commandement*, 267/18; 270/21–22.

The naked and mortal face of the other seduces me and reduces me to myself, revealing to me my potential for violence as well as my loneliness.[47] But it seduces me with the illusion of freedom in manipulating the other for my own benefit. The most intoxicating thing about this seduction is that the ego discovers and understands that this is not in any way forbidden, but on the contrary, it is effectively possible to manipulate the other in his or her weakness.[48] Here one finds, according to Levinas, the heart of a responsible, dialogical and nonviolent ethic. In the exposed vulnerability of the Face of the other, I discover myself as a potential murderer. At the same time I discover the poverty of the other as a substantial force, a radical resistance to my totalizing and reductionist cupidity. The Face of the other thus appears as opposition, insofar as it places itself in front of me and against me, confronting me as a radical prohibition and a resistance to all my intentions.[49] And this resistance, this force, this accusation, which rises up against me in my reductionist and violent potentiality, does not come from the free choice of the other, but from the essential Otherness of the other, from the dismissal that proclaims itself a protest against the violence of the ego.[50]

Levinas thus arrives, with his reflection, at a radical inversion of the Cartesian cogito, in affirming that to be human is to remain under accusation by the Face of the other. Human subjectivity inverts from the nominative *I* to the accusative *me*. No longer can I, in my previously self-sufficient and violent ego, conceive of myself as the origin (*archè*), the measure of all things, but rather I am myself being questioned and measured by the other, by the Face of the other who judges me.[51]

Before the appearance of the other, human freedom can still present itself as innocent and without a sense of culpability in its own selfishness and violence. But through the encounter and appeal of the other, such freedom receives a shock, seeing in the face of the other, as in a mirror, its selfishness and violence. Thus, according to Levinas, there occurs a "conversion from the inside to the outside," a cathartic inversion of the barbaric and dogmatic effort to be. Only in this way can the spiral of violence and war be finally interrupted and broken.[52] The only basis for a truly ethical justice is the unconditional responsibility conveyed to the ego with the appearance of the Face of the other.

47. See Levinas, *De Dieu qui vient à l'idée*, 271, 244–45/161–63.
48. See Levinas, *Éthique comme philosophie première*, 124.
49. See Levinas, *En découvrant l'existence avec Husserl et Heidegger*, 173/105.
50. See Levinas, *Hors-sujet*, 141.
51. See Levinas, *Autrement qu'être ou au-delà de l'essence*, 140/109.
52. See Petitdemange and Rolland, *Autrement que savoir*, 64; Levinas, *Humanisme de l'autre homme*, 49/97.

If the ideal or purpose of the human being is the I in and of itself, then heteronomy and Otherness—which appear as the norm—can indeed be experienced as slavery, as alienation before the other who obliges, oppresses, and alienates me. If the ideal and purpose of the human ego is the good, the building of community, and the establishment of relationships of solidarity and freedom to be lived out in reality, then the Otherness of the other becomes—with all its risks, dangers, and conflicts—the condition for the possibility of the I, something that establishes and anchors it, and allows it to be and to exist.

In times when human autonomy is exalted, accompanied by a profound identity crisis of the human condition, perhaps the stumbling block lies in overcoming the understanding of autonomy and heteronomy as two irreconcilable poles, with no possible exit from the impasse. Ethics, in truth, calls attention to this point when it places at the center of thinking and living the primordial nature of the other and the other's rights, which questions and summons the ego. The biblical vision tries to take a step in this direction by saying that freedom, rather than coming purely from the outside, is inside the human being. It is like an inscription engraved there of the epiphanous questioning that makes manifest the Face of the other—of the poor, the widow, the orphan, the stranger—establishing for the believer the only law, which is the law of love, as in Exod 22:22, Deut 16:11, and Ps 146:9, among many others.

Love is understood there not as a search for pleasure or the satisfaction of instincts and needs. It brings with it a stamp of sacredness when seen from the standpoint of an exit from oneself, of the free delivery of oneself, and of oblation—all at the service of building human solidarity in new relationships.

Modern anthropocentrism, for all its importance in contributing to the idea of human beings as free and no longer subject to external laws alien to their subjectivity and dignity, runs the risk of reducing itself to an atrophying and individualistic loneliness.

The objectivity of the world—a product of modernity—is an extreme result of the separation of human beings from the institutionalized belief in God, a separation that liberates them and establishes them as the subjects of their knowledge, making them autonomous before the divine intelligence and normativeness. God—or Transcendence—has withdrawn from the world, leaving human beings on their own in their search for meaning.

The end of anthropocentric humanism (with its perverse androcentric and ethnocentric deviations) opens the way for a new vision, a new perception—which would consequently become a new experience—of a humankind that has survived the decline of the utopias and the change of

Secular Culture and the Crisis of Religion

paradigms, and feels an emergent desire for an encounter with Transcendent Otherness, which reason can neither explain nor circumscribe.[53]

The Hegemony of Reason, the Power of Science, and the Misconduct of Practice

Scientific knowledge depends on a society in which discoveries are made while their content remains neutral, belonging neither to nation nor class. Yet as a body of knowledge science never ceases to be strictly associated with power. The resistance of the scientific world to Einstein's discovery of relativity is an eloquent example of this point.[54] And World War II, one of the gravest chapters in human history, represented, among other things, a sealed alliance between knowledge and power, with science and technology used to perpetrate one of the greatest cases of genocide ever seen by humankind. Likewise, the long Vietnam War demonstrated that the contributions of mathematicians, physicists, chemists, and biologists can result in the production of the cruelest and most destructive weapons, such as napalm and missiles, among others.

There is a fundamental confusion of content between science and technology. Technical progress is accused of causing damage to humankind, when the true responsibility for such harm belongs to the political and economic structures that influence policies regarding scientific work and research.

The use of computers in the economic field has magnified the importance of numbers and calculations in facilitating their performance. But precise machines are of no use in achieving exact calculations in optimal time if the data used are false or misguided and thus not conducive to an accurate result. Economic models are not immune to ideology. By the use of certain simplifications and approximations—think inexactitude—results can be obtained which do not correspond to the proposed hypotheses and are more in the service of a political choice than of objective truth.[55] For this reason, and given the privileged condition of exact scientific research—which tends to make researchers into unintelligible communicators using a language that nobody understands, and whose claims are therefore difficult to contest—the

---

53. See on this point Bingemer, *Um rosto para Deus?*, ch. 1.

54. See for example Einstein's relativity, the objection of Cesar Lattes, and the proposal of Andre Assis; see http://stoa.usp.br/cienciacultura/weblog/82774.html.

55. Examples could be multiplied. Economic data are often expropriated by the executive power, and the information that reaches the population about inflation, the GDP, etc., is often false, or at least distorted.

natural sciences today are often at the service of a political power interested in a rupture between the keepers of knowledge and the people.

The human sciences have as their objective a knowledge of the behavior, human activity, and all that human beings produce, such as language, art, and history. They also manage privileged resources for their work, although in general more modest ones than those of the natural sciences. But in distinguishing between the two areas a question of principle arises: the proof of truth in the human sciences is not obtained by *strictu sensu* experimentation, as in the case of the natural sciences. Experimentation, when employed, cannot be carried out without the consent of the individual or group. And the human subject will be changed in the course of the experiment. That is why the results in the human sciences are always dynamic, and continually changing. Any *a priori* attempt to establish a structure to fix them in some political, economic, and social model can lead to alienation and a repressive culture.[56]

Science is one of the movers of the development of humankind and of life. Its progress has been responsible for great improvements in human life, especially during the last century, although the fruits of this progress have not been equitably shared in the world. On the other hand, the misuse that is often made of scientific knowledge was, also in the twentieth century, a cause of the worst afflictions ever suffered by humankind. For this reason, even if the progress of science—made possible by modern rationality—is highly positive, even if we agree that science is the mover of socioeconomic development, the efforts by several countries and regions of the world in the field of science still remain far below minimum desirable levels.

The recent phenomenon of globalization, unleashed by the demise of the utopias and the progress of information and communication technology, led to the opening of national economies the world over, and never ceases to engender international commercial and financial relations, as well as a transnational genesis of knowledge and a new worldwide division of labor. The "end of geography" is provoking the beginning of a new conception of the world, where scientific activities must be reorganized.[57]

Strong interdisciplinary and transdisciplinary capabilities, which require innovative mechanisms, will be needed to facilitate the investigation of complex problems that go beyond the immediate spatial and temporal horizon. On the other hand, science should always be carried out more ethically and with more conscience. Research must be transparent and socialized. It

---

56. Many military regimes that ruled Latin American countries in the decades of the 1980s and 1990s were examples of this point.

57. On the question of the end of geography, see our reflections in the first chapter of this book.

should be concerned not only with quality, but also with communicability.[58] Scientific discoveries must serve humankind, now living through a delicate and important moment in history.

The moment in which we are now living is, from an economic and technological perspective, one of neoliberal globalization. The dynamism of the capitalist free-market economic system, with tools for the systematic application of a functional science and practice, has acquired planetary dimensions. This hegemony corresponds with a univocal way of thinking—reinforced by the fall of the socialist block—which destabilized the world balance of power. There remains only a neoliberal thought, expanded and generalized. The law of the market is seen as no less evident than the law of gravity. And if socialism fell because it lost—engulfed by the thirst for power and totalitarianism—the mystique that sustained it during its first years, it must be admitted that neoliberalism, which is nothing more than capitalism with a few ornaments, is deprived of ethics.

This entire state of things could not have escaped being a powerful influence on culture and values. We are facing a technological leap and a shaping of scientific thought that do not control themselves, and nobody yet knows the consequences of this lack of control. And there are reasons to be afraid. As Hans Jonas says, the mere possibility of a threat of danger must become an element of ethical reflection.[59]

To this globalized and technoeconomic situation corresponds a type of rationality, and consequently a way of understanding reality, called the functional conception of reality.[60] It is focused on dimensions that are measurable, strategic, and functional. It specializes in the instrumental point of view of adequate means to reach an end. But it misunderstands those same ends and their ethical objectives. It remains at the level of the means, analyzing and evaluating reality according to the criteria of efficacy, profitability, pragmatism, and functionality.[61]

This functionalist homogenizing of the world produces several perverse effects. The first consists in valuing only that which is measurable and can be expressed through numbers, statistics, and instrumentality. All that results from abstraction, from Mystery, from inspiration, and from poetry is set aside as useless, as something that cannot be controlled by instrumental reason, which—with its diabolical and reductionist pride—imagines itself

---

58. See Mayor, "Science," in *Encyclopaedia Universalis*.

59. See Jonas, *The Imperative of Responsibility*, according to Mardones, *La tranformación de la religión*, 50.

60. See Mardones, *En el umbral del mañana*, 124.

61. Ibid., 125.

to be rendering a service to the world, driving out the superstitions and magic conceptions of life that keep people infantile.[62]

Furthermore, with it comes a withering of traditions and memories, a dessication of the search for the meaning of life—a constitutive aspect of the human being that gives nobility and dignity to human life itself. All that comes from memory, from the cultivation of the riches of aboriginal cultures, and from enriching traditions—the breeding ground of human creativity—is diminished, devalued, and confined to an insignificant place in reality.[63]

This is a society of sensations, immersed in the consumerism of mercantile fetishes, generating injustice, nihilism, and a sterile *ag-nosía*.[64] Universalization, catapulted to the highest power by the social media, uniformizes behaviors, anti-values, and sensations, based on triviality and vulgarity.[65] There is a sameness in fashion, tastes, flavors, music (especially music for young people), and movies—which are primarily formatted after the North American model. The United States is the matrix that exports this culture, which is avidly consumed especially in the developing countries and is even conquering old Europe.

The linguistic phenomenon itself says something about this. The *koiné* of modernity is English.[66] Nowadays even those who do not know English, but need to work with the Internet or computers, have adopted English words with pronunciations in local vernaculars—creating a new Esperanto based in banality. Not infrequently one can hear words such as *delete*, *copy-paste*, *link*, and others from the mouths of ignorant men and women who surely do not know even half the wealth of their own native language. It is a case of babelization through uniformization rather than through diaspora, and this dialectic communitarianism is far from leading humankind to greater understanding and solidarity.

The modern dream has preserved some of its very positive foundations, such as the primacy of reason, the advent of technology, and the autonomy of science. But it has lost the purity of its objectives and its ethics. In place of the wholeness made possible by human reason, by technology, and by the digital and communication sciences, what we see is the dissolution

---

62. Ibid.
63. Ibid., 126.
64. Ibid.
65. Ibid., 127.
66. *Koiné* is the technical term most commonly used to refer to the Greek of the Hellenistic period. This Greek word simply means "common." Hellenistic Greek, or *koiné*, is the popular form of Greek that emerged in classical post-antiquity (c. 300 BC–300 AD).

of the whole in the plurality of multiple fragments and a variety of partial perspectives. Modern historical continuity, which unfolds in a continuous linear progress, is replaced by discontinuity, a plurality of fragmented visions of the world—a post-history or the end of history.[67]

From the point of view of religion, especially in the Judeo-Christian tradition, the relationship between faith and reason has luminous and shadowy points, pros and cons. The undue tutelage of reason by faith that continued for a long period of history, generating an equally undue subordination of scientific reason to faith, played an important role in the acquisition by reason of a consciousness of its autonomy. The result was a conflict that entailed a total rupture of the relationship between faith and reason, and the replacement of the supremacy of faith by the supremacy of autonomous reason at first, and later of scientific reason, only to degenerate eventually into that of instrumental reason. The prestige and success of scientific thought led to the identification of reason with scientific reason, leading science to be considered the only valid form of knowledge. To summarize, we are confronted with an epistemological monism.[68]

This sterilizing conflict is overcome when instrumental reason finds itself in crisis and performs self-criticism. Then the affirmations of the human sciences—relegated to second place by the hegemony of the "precision" of numbers—as well as the affirmations of faith and of religion, begin anew to find some possibility in the realm of reason. The need for an articulation of meaning is felt,[69] and religion becomes a theme even in the writings of the great agnostic thinkers of today, who speak of it in a nostalgic, but not a polemic, tone.[70]

A positive and effective articulation between faith and science is needed for the development of an ethical vigilance over the practice of science without taking anything from its autonomy. In this way, it is possible to articulate the presence of faith with that of philosophical reason and that of scientific reason.

---

67. See Mardones, *Hacia donde va la religión?*, 28–29.

68. See Velasco, *El malestar religioso de nuestra cultura*, 156, who further says that the reality to which this reason gave access was proclaimed the only valid form of reality, producing an ontological monism.

69. See Ladrière, *Articulation du sens*.

70. See Habermas et al., *An Awareness of What Is Missing*; Eagleton, *Reason, Faith and Revolution*.

Plurality and the End of Unicity

Pluralism has been present in the history of Christianity since its beginnings. Already in its first centuries, Christianity, born in the heart of Judaism, needed to find ways of self-expression in the pagan and polytheistic world of ancient Greece and Rome. To that end it had to make use of the categories of the ancient pagan Greek philosophy, and was compelled to dialogue with the different gods of that world, to be able to make visible and audible the experience of its God. A delightful and powerful example of this pluralism and of the entry of Christianity into it is the episode of Paul in the Areopagus in Athens with his announcement of the unknown God, described in Acts 17.[71]

This pluralism seems to have become obscure in the Middle Ages, when the Western world was massively and almost totally Christian. Those who professed different creeds were considered heretics and infidels, to be combated and eliminated.[72] The Protestant Reformation reintroduced the question of pluralism, rupturing the univocality of Christendom. The process of secularization, with the autonomy of reason, rationalism, and the crisis of the institutions, brought new elements into an area where homogeneity was already, if not ruptured, at least questioned.

Today this pluralism appears to be reconfigured. We are seeing a privatization of religious life, which accompanies the autonomy of the modern human being *versus* the heteronomy that ruled the theocentric medieval world. Each composes its own recipe for transcendence, and the field of religion resembles a huge supermarket, as well as a place where traffic comes and goes.[73] Modernity did not liquidate religion. On the contrary, religion rose anew, with new strength and a new form. It is no longer institutionalized as before, but rather plural and multiform, wild and even anarchical, and lacking the conditions to return to its premodern ways.[74]

The question of sacredness introduces, then, another face, which goes together with that of modern secularity. It generates suspicion and atheism wherever Transcendence is subjected to unrelenting criticism by the Enlightenment's reason and logic. It is the face of plurality. It implies the

---

71. Acts 17:1ff.: Paul in the Areopagus of Athens, speaking of the unknown God from the standpoint of the Greek polytheism.

72. See Bingemer et al., "Violência e não-violência na história da Igreja"; Bingemer et al., "Violência e não-violência na história da Igreja (II)."

73. On religion as supermarket and as place of traffic, see Libânio, *Crer num mundo de muitas crenças e pouca libertação*, and Certeau, *La faiblesse de croire*.

74. See Bingemer, *Alteridade e vulnerabilidade*; see also Libânio, "Fascínio do Sagrado"; Couto Teixeira, "O Sagrado em novos itinerários."

existence of an interface of different attempts at interreligious dialogue, of multireligious practice and of double belonging, and of the religion of the other as a condition for the possibility of living out one's own faith in a more radical and deeper way.[75]

In phenomenological terms, the category of religious pluralism simply refers to the fact that the history of religion portrays a plurality of traditions and a wide range of variations inside each tradition. Philosophically, however, the term refers to a particular theory of the relationship among these traditions, with their different and competitive characteristics. According to this theory the great religions represent a variety of conceptions and perceptions of, and responses to, the ultimate and mysterious divine reality.[76]

The issue of religious pluralism is increasingly prominent in today's world, itself a pluralist one, assaulted by an explosive resurgence, unrestrained and almost barbaric, of religiosity. Not only do the ancient and traditional religions appear to be growing in importance and becoming a strong voice for historical Christianity, but new religious movements are springing up from all sides—inside and outside the ecclesiastic communities—causing perplexity and questioning among the followers of the traditional and historical churches.[77]

It is clear that, on the one hand, historical Christianity is aware that it has lost its earlier secular hegemony, especially in the traditionally Catholic Latin Mediterranean countries—where Christian affiliation was more an inheritance by birth than a free choice by adults. To be a Christian today is not that obvious, and Christianity is called to find its place among of a plurality of other religious traditions and confessions of diverse hues.

On the other hand, this religious plurality raises some very serious questions for Christianity regarding the very contents of its faith. For a real dialogue in a multireligious world, historical Christians must be willing to find new words to express ancient and traditional ideas and to make them understood.

The question of God and the experience of God is one of those delicate issues to which theology must devote special attention as it approaches interreligious dialogue. If an interface is really theological contact and not an imposition, it presupposes an openness to dialogue, which in turn implies a renouncing of the preoccupation with an explicit adherence to the past.

---

75. See on this issue Bingemer, "Religions and the Dialogue among Cultures."

76. See J. Hick, "Religious Pluralism," in Eliade, *Encyclopedia of Religion*, vol. 12, 331.

77. See on the new religious movements, Campos, *Teatro, templo e mercado*; Luz, *Carnaval da alma*; Hortal, *O que fazer diante da expansão dos grupos religiosos não católicos?*.

There must be, here, a spiritual and mystical aspect that humbly and confidently seeks an experience of God common to more than one tradition.

Undoubtedly, historical Christianity is called to find its place in the multireligious fabric that permeates society today. In so doing, it is invited to participate in a common project in which religions would play an important role in promoting the good of humankind as a whole. According to important contemporary thinkers, the traditions of the entire world are being called to contribute to the elaboration of a new world ethic. And they cannot refuse or ignore this call.[78] Nor can they comply by letting go of that which constitutes the profoundest depth of their identity.

It seems, therefore, that Christian faith, Christian theology and Christian mysticism today must deal with the question of their identity, which is sometimes lost and fragmented amidst a sea of experiences presenting themselves as religious but not necessarily embracing Otherness—which in its total freedom reveals itself as Holiness, or an absolutely other Otherness. If we easily legitimize any experience of seduction by the sacred, we run the risk of baptizing many deities with this name, but not touching that which for us and for contemporary followers of other religions can be understood as the experience of God.

The ascent of multireligious sacredness does not necessarily imply the sunset of adherence to traditional religion, with all the consequences this would bring. But it does imply a constant and acute discernment, to the effect that the living of the faith and reflection on it must be, more than ever, submitted to a reflection on the very heart of its identity. The fecundity attained by the interface among religions runs the risk of becoming diluted as long as the face of sacredness remains diffuse and lacking any contour, resulting in the failure of any effective attempt to fulfill the dream of the creation of a robust and consistent synthesis.

In the dialogue about and the desire for an interaction and encounter among religions, one experiences a tearing asunder of love and truth. At the profoundest depth of the extraordinary desire to meet the other, one can also find the desire to learn through the other things that only the Spirit of God can teach. But for a dialogue to take place, one must engage in it without losing the identity of one's own experience, even if—fortunately—this requires always being open to learning through the other how to wait for the future that we are all called to build in rich reciprocity, but which, on the other hand, is and will be graciously given to us.

---

78. See Küng, *Christianity and the World Religions*.

The Profanity of the World and the Silence of God

In the current picture of religion as a whole, the situation of Judeo-Christianity could be summarized as follows: after the predominance of the conviction, which lasted for centuries, that other religions and religious traditions gravitate around Christianity—considered the center of all the world's religious phenomena—it must be recognized that the center around which all the religious traditions gravitate, including Christianity, is God. Called by different names by different traditions, whether One or plural, God or the Supreme Being, Allah, Yahweh or Abba, God is the nucleus of the gravitation of religions.

Theology is called to say a word about the fundamental question of the idea of God. Secularity was intended to banish faith in God from human consciousness. But is it possible that the secular world could be a world without God, or a place from which God has been made absent?

The concept of God, or the Transcendent, or the Ultimate Reality, is considered fundamental by all religious systems, because it gives meaning to the world in general and to human life in particular. The authentic religious question thus continues to be—despite the process of modernity, the crisis of secularization, and other phenomena to some extent analyzed by the great commentators—precisely the question regarding to what or to Whom human beings can authentically give the name of God.

One of the intentions of modernity was to remove the question of God from the horizon of humankind. The expectation was for a civilization of rationality and emancipation at all levels, in which humankind, having grown out of its childhood, would no longer feel the need of a Supreme Being or an Absolute Subject to dictate norms of behavior and organization.[79]

The crisis of modernity and its later reconfiguration into a new stage called—appropriately or inappropriately—postmodernity, far from bringing this process to an end, instead took on its main characteristics and proposed to radicalize the cultural and conceptual death of God. With the reappearance of religiosity, atheism did not disappear from the Western horizon. It is no longer a matter merely of the modern atheism of the masters

---

79. See the innumerable authors who work on this aspect of secularization as a change of perspective for the understanding and assimilation of religiosity. See also Moltmann, *God for a Secular Society*; Westhelle, "Modernidade, mito e religião"; Lacoste, *Dictionnaire critique de théologie*; Eliade, *Encyclopedia of Religion*; Poupard, *Diccionario de las religiones*; Queiruga, *Fin del cristianismo premoderno*; Queiruga, *Creio em Deus Pai*; Derrida and Vattimo, *Religion*; Martelli, *A religião na sociedade pós-moderna*; Gómez de Souza, "Secularização em declínio e potencialidade transformadora do Sagrado"; Gómez de Souza, "Secularização e Sagrado"; Ricoeur, "L'herméneutique de la sécularisation," 60; and Bingemer and Andrade, *Secularização: novos desafios*.

of suspicion, or their predecessors and followers. New forms of atheism have appeared on the horizon that question, in depth, the more traditional religious institutions, above all the three monotheisms. Nor is it a case of pure and simple religiosity. On the contrary, we are facing a religious indifference that is not at all concerned with arguing about the existence or nonexistence of God.[80]

Modernity proclaims the disappearance of God and any trace of God's existence. Furthermore, while modern atheism denied God and affirmed a human project (the death of God would be the price paid to allow human autonomy and freedom to emerge and fully develop), postmodern contemporary atheism and religious indifference threaten, once and for all, to do away with humanism, by questioning the stability and the very existence of the foundations of society as well as the global nature of reality.

Contemporary atheism does not expect to inherit anything from the death of God. In this respect it is not the atheism of dispossession and repossession from believer to nonbeliever, from the religious to the secular, from faith in God to faith in the human being. On the contrary, it remains tied to a nostalgia and to other—theoretically "truer"—values, as well as other "more authentic" cultures.[81]

Postmodern thought, characterized by the deconstruction and relativization of the apparently solid conceptual edifice of modernity, questions any attempt to speak of the ineffable Absolute—called God, among other names, by the Christian and other religious traditions. It considers any discourse that tends toward universalization and totalization to be reductive and inadequate. The result is indifference and disenchantment. That being the case, an apparently new—but actually very old—track is opened for Christian thought and discourse, leading to the Mystery and plurality as a confession of the impossibility of thinking and speaking consistently about the Being, no matter in what way one seeks to comprehend the Being.[82]

From this it follows that not only reason and reflection, but also the desire and thirst for the infinite and Transcendence, find themselves trapped in a perplexity that can have a reverse effect on faith, trust, and

---

80. See recent works on contemporary atheism, such as Forte, *Trindade para ateus*; Bingemer, *O impacto da modernidade sobre a religão*. See also the recent works of the so-called New Atheists: Harris, *Letter to a Christian Nation*; Hitchens, *God Is Not Great*; Dawkins, *The God Delusion*; Onfray, *Atheist Manifesto*.

81. See the atheism of Dawkins in *The God Delusion*, in which he professes a belief in the truth of scientific naturalism as the only valid one.

82. See the numerous works that analyze this phenomenon: Dupuis, *Rumo a uma teologia cristã do pluralismo religioso*; Teixeira, *Teologia das religiões*; Texeira, "A experiência de Deus nas religiões"; Hébrard, *Entre Nouvel âge et christianisme*; Amaral et al., *Nova era*; Schlegel, "Retour du religieux et christianisme," 92.

amazement before the mystery. And this could have the result—albeit inverted and paradoxical—that the experience of and discourse about God may encounter, in these times which at first sight appeared to be so hostile, an unimagined possibility of fecundity.

Theoretical and Practical Atheism

In a secular and plural society such as ours, atheism—seen by some streams of faith and theology as the great enemy to be combated—is just one among other temptations that daily stalk believers and their faith.[83] This is a consequence of the crisis of Western culture, which goes hand in hand with the religious crisis. The prophecies of the masters of suspicion are partly fulfilled and partly denied. The conviction that religion is important can accompany a rejection of institutionalized religion. Religious faith, religious affiliation, and belonging to a religion do not necessarily harmonize with honesty and ethics—contrary to the simplistic idea that all that is good, just, and kind comes as a consequence of religious experience, while the atheist is unjust, unscrupulous, embodying the practice of evil. Thus, explicit atheism can live together with implicit belief, just as an explicit believer may be an implicit atheist.[84]

The atheist challenge has, therefore, a positive face at the core of the process of secularization. And the atheist, far from being just an enemy to be attacked, becomes an interlocutor who questions. This face, in turn, unfolds in several ways that help create an interface of the faith lived out in a secular context, with the more profound identity of that same faith. In so doing it rescues the origins of the faith in order to creatively live them out today.

Atheism can bring about a purifying criticism of the images one has of God. It can help believers not to be satisfied with whatever conception of God is presented to them, and never to cease their quest to discern whether their apparently religious experiences are indeed experiences of God.[85] Therefore it can prevent us from taking possession of God. It can help us criticize the blemishes of institutionalized religion, and to inaugurate a New

---

83. See Forte, *Trindade para ateus*.

84. See the category coined by Rahner, "anonymous Christians," which consists of all human beings who effectively realize their existential-supernatural dynamism—all human beings who, although not confessing Christ by mouth, actually live out the grace of Christ in their lives. This theory has met some rejection by the most radical sectors of religious pluralism and interreligious dialogue. See also the book by Queiruga, *Creio em Deus Pai*, on this topic.

85. For a differentiation between the religious experience and the experience of God, See Vaz, *Experimentar Deus hoje*. See also Anjos, *Experiência religiosa*.

Era of knowledge, free from religious tutelage.[86] It was this endeavor that led to the emergence of reason and to the Enlightenment, which—in spite of all the criticism it has received, and in spite of the failure of its model to explain the world—introduced important changes in the history of humankind. It is this same questioning that functions today as an important critical factor in the prevention of abuses in the name of religion and faith.

The New Atheists of the twenty-first century seek arguments that disqualify all forms of religious discourse. We find in the writings of the New Atheists an open denunciation of the kind of religion that could foment violence and hatred.[87] It is a critique that gives less emphasis to the problem of ontology and concentrates on a more militant and pragmatic atheistic discourse. The problem for the New Atheists is less the existence of God than the existence of religions.

Not wanting to be the direct heir of the atheistic movement that led to the proclamation of the death of God, contemporary atheism does not appear to configure itself as waving the flags of unbelief, secularity, and faith in humankind. It invokes other—true and authentic—models and systems in support of its affirmations.[88]

Its intention is apparently to structure a world without religion. Thus a discussion of God becomes irrelevant, since in attacking the teachings and dogmas upon which religions are founded, one could avoid the dissemination of the idea of God. The construction of a society without religions would be the condition for a world of peace and tolerance, since many conflicts in today's world have religion as their backdrop. In this way, neo-atheism would be a militant rewriting of laicism.[89]

Recently, the popular press and discussions on the Internet have been paying considerable attention to the professions of faith and atheist declarations of Richard Dawkins, Sam Harris, and Christopher Hitchens, whose books were bestsellers. Yet the media seldom examines in depth the presuppositions of these authors. The fundamental failures and fallacies of the new atheism are found especially in its unshakable belief in scientific naturalism. This is the belief that nature is all there is, that God doesn't exist, and that

---

86. In some authors who work more closely with the Eastern religions, polytheism is also seen as a purifying and critical agency. See Heisig, "Six Sutras on the Dialogue among Religions."

87. See Dawkins, *God Delusion*, 387–95.

88. See the atheism of Dawkins, *God Delusion*.

89. The attempt to build a world without religions reintroduces, according to the analysis of the Jesuit theologian João Batista Libânio, an antireligious consensus of a militant character, already encountered in history, which identified secularization with atheism. See Libânio, "Fascínio do Sagrado."

science is the only way to truth. Although the New Atheists reject the God of the creationists, fundamentalists, and terrorists, it is worth noting that they debate only with extremists, and not with eminent theologians and serious thinkers.[90]

In effect, the New Atheists are saying that if it is true that God exists, we should allow the identity of this God to be determined, once and for all, by the fundamentalists of the Abrahamic religious traditions. It would appear that they opted for this strategy because at heart they have a poorly disguised admiration for the simplicity of their opponents' conception of reality. The best proof of their attraction to an uncomplicated cosmic vision can be found in their adhesion to a system that is also basically fundamentalist and even more simplistic, known as scientific naturalism.[91]

In classical times, fields of knowledge such as art, religion, and philosophy (or science) remained united and not fragmented as today. Each one of them, in its own language, addressed the same themes regarding the noblest interests of the human being: where did we come from, where are we going, what is the meaning of life, what values are worth defending, how can we avoid wasting our life during the time that has been given to us, how should we behave in front of others? Also: is there in history any decisive model that should be imitated? Or: how can we live out the great passions, and how can we deal with anxiety, and what can we do with freedom, if indeed freedom is possible?

The nineteenth century came to an end with a verdict as simple as it was consequential: God is dead. Nietzsche did not desire God's death; he only declared it. God no longer mattered, and no longer changed the destiny of the planet, whether in scientific or moral affairs. It was the century of atheism and scientific enlightenment. Why then, a hundred years later, did the New Atheists come to the fore, desperately trying (and succeeding) to market their bestsellers in an attempt to pull atheists out of the closet, and lead them to publicly acknowledge their atheist pride, in imitation of other minorities who considered themselves marginalized?

In his *Atheist Manifesto*, Michel Onfray affirms,

> The three monotheisms, animated by the same genealogical death drive, share a series of identical forms of aversion: hatred of reason and intelligence; hatred of freedom; hatred of all books in the name of one book only; hatred of sexuality, women, and

---

90. See the recent works, already cited here, of the so-called New Atheists: Harris, *Letter to a Christian Nation*; Hitchens, *God Is Not Great*; Dawkins, *The God Delusion*; Onfray, *Atheist Manifesto*.

91. See the entire issue of the journal *Concilium*: "Atheists of What God?" (2010/4).

pleasure; hatred of the feminine; hatred of the body, of desires, of drives. In place of all this, Judaism, Christianity, and Islam defend faith and belief, obedience and submission, taste for death and longing for the beyond, the asexual angel and chastity, virginity and monogamous fidelity, the wife and the mother, the soul and the spirit. In other words, life crucified and nothingness celebrated.[92]

It is true that recent events have brought more reasons for a renewed interest in this concern. They include fundamentalist Islamist terrorism; the speeches of former President George W. Bush, who appealed to God as he considered occupying the oil-rich countries that he declared to be dangerous; the American fundamentalism that advocates the teaching of creationism in the schools; the French democracy that forbade Muslim students to wear a veil; Jews and Arabs—descendants of Abraham—hating and attacking each other while teaching innocent children to write messages in missiles; and bishops of recent denominations who seem primarily interested in tithing and profits while vying for power in partisan politics. Religions today undeniably have a great deal of exposure, and in one way or another attract a profusion of criticism.

What is surprising about contemporary atheism is its optimism and its almost naive faith in scientific explanation, thus running the risk of producing a new idolatry.

The point of contact between atheism and Christian faith would be the defense of all human possibility. In this respect, the great interlocutor for theology would be anthropology.[93]

For Queiruga, atheism at its core does not seek the denial of God, but of a religious discourse that has become idolatrous. At the heart of this attitude is a struggle for spaces that do not suppress the autonomy of the human being. For this reason the great challenge for Christian theology is to see to it that modernity—and its byproduct, postmodernity with its obvious consumerist culture—returns to the Gospel of Jesus and discovers there that the divine discourse in his narrative takes shape in a full affirmation of humanity. The "Abba" God of Jesus Christ did nothing other than to defend human beings before religious persons and mechanisms seeking to deny them. Only thus can we appraise the affirmations of contemporary atheistic criticism and the need to sustain an authentic dialogue. No serious science—whether in the field of the natural sciences, genetics, or the

---

92. See Onfray, *Atheist Manifesto*.

93. See the works cited above of A. Torres Queiruga, especially *Fim do cristianismo pré-moderno* and *Creio em Deus Pai*.

humanities—can persist today anchored in prejudice or the ancient rivalry of science *versus* religion, as stated by Queiruga in this long quotation:

> Nothing helped more than the modern critique of religion toward the rediscovery of something deeply fundamental in the Christian experience of God: that his revelation and his presence in our history has no meaning other than our Salvation. Salvation with a double value: denial of all denials of man and affirmation of all that is positive in the human . . . Saint Irenaeus of Lyons expressed it in insuperable terms as early as the second century: "Gloria Deis, vivens homo"—the glory of God is man in the fullness of his life. If we Christians succeed in demonstrating, with our theory and practice, that God is the ultimate denial of all the denials of man, then a strictly common ground will open upon which we are able to meet one another in the most profound search for the nonbelievers. For we are together in the fundamental: the defense of man and his potentialities . . . Modernity is relatively new, and the great historical misunderstanding by which, for many, God appeared as the enemy of man, will not be eternal. Personally, I do not renounce the hope that . . . the modern sensibility will end by creating the experience—or more nearly approximating it—that God does not deny man, but affirms him.[94]

We might add to the statement of this Galician theologian that—although many of them lack scientific consistency—the accusations of the New Atheists at least serve to question us and provoke us to a more radical conversion and to a more coherent living of Christianity as a faith, while learning how to keep at a distance and to relativize what in many of its religious expressions is indeed relative and must be set aside.

Thus, both atheism and Christianity need to subject themselves to mutual criticism. They stand together in facing the failure of the Enlightenment, and can equally stand solidly together—and make a valuable contribution—in confronting the proliferation of new religious proposals that often insert themselves into the secularized world as an escape from the frustrations of everyday life.

Therefore, it would not be pertinent to admit as unequivocal the premise that we live in a time of the debilitation or disappearance of faith in God and reflection about God. Even if it is true that the modern era proclaimed the inevitability of a decline of religions—to the point of supporting the thesis of the death of God—the identification of modernity with atheist

---

94. See Queiruga, *A revelação de Deus na realização humana*, 38–39.

humanism carries with it an unsupportable reduction. In effect, the project of modernity engendered religious indifference more than a denial of God. At the same time, the crisis of this project demonstrated that a society that does not find its foundation in Transcendence—whether or not it gives it the name of God—is destined to slowly and inexorably disintegrate.[95] True or not, and no matter how well grounded—the proclamation of the advent of so-called postmodernity and the supposed "return" of the religious allows for the perception that it is quite inadequate to decree the banishment of God from the human horizon. On the contrary, the search for God continues to agitate the heart of humankind, regardless of the risk of finding themselves irreparably outdated, a risk that is run by all the official or unofficial discourses on God by certain institutions.

To summarize, if atheism—as understood in modern terms—continues to be an issue whenever the problem of God is mentioned, one needs to acknowledge that it is no longer the only issue. Furthermore, one may also recognize that such atheism is not a completely negative presence in our modern culture. Indeed, faced with the silence of the traditional premodern God, modern culture is challenged to discover a new image of God in a secular and plural world. It may be possible to find a conception of God evolving from a personal God—as proposed by premodernity—toward a God who is more impersonal and therefore more distant from the Christian tradition.[96] But for the postmodern man and woman, would it not be a fascinating opportunity to discover the one whom, in the first hour of our era, Paul of Tarsus tried to make known to the Athenians, as he sought a way to give a name to the unknown God whose temple he found while walking through their city?[97]

The great theologian Karl Rahner rightly affirms that even if the word *God* and the memory of it were definitively banished from human thought and discourse, that would not prove the nonexistence of God. On the contrary, it would be human beings who would have disappeared and sunk into nothingness, failing in their project and vocation. The truth is that it is God who constitutes human beings in their identity and continuous self-transcendence.[98] The pinnacle of Rahner's text is as follows:

95. Ibid.
96. See Mardones. *La transformación de la religión*, 34.
97. Acts 17:22–24, the famous episode of Paul in the Areopagus of Athens.
98. See Rahner, *Curso fundamental da fé*, 178: ". . . we have no experience of God of the kind we have of a tree, of other human persons or of other external realities which, although they simply may never exist for us without words, nevertheless by themselves impel the birth of a word for them, because they simply emerge in the realm of our experience at a determined point in space and time, and thus, by themselves, immediately

It [the word *God*] is always exposed to the protest of Wittgenstein, who demands that silence be kept on what cannot be spoken of with clarity and yet violates this maxim in the very fact of expressing it. The word itself, if well understood, agrees with this maxim, since it is *the last word preceding the silence* that is speechless and wordless in adoration before the ineffable Mystery.[99]

If on the one hand it is true that "only desire is capable of qualifying the relationship of God with the human being," on the other hand the relationship established by this desire places the human being before the same "difference" of God, the difference of the other's desire, an encounter that is made possible only through self-renunciation, conversion, and abandonment of one's own desires. This is the only way, in most religious traditions and especially in the Judeo-Christian tradition, to open a space for what God may desire in the human being, and, following that, to permit human beings to desire nothing except God, more and more identifying their desire with divine desire. In this experience it is the human beings who are taken by God, and not the contrary. And their experience, if genuine, entirely escapes domination and control by human rationality.[100]

Therefore, if the experience of God takes place at the level of desire, unable to take place in any other way, it also needs to be said that it comes about as Mystery—revealed Mystery, the Mystery of love that approximates salvific movement. But always Mystery. There is no natural and logical transition between the experience of everyday life and the experience of God, even though the one is the place of advent of the other. One could speak of it as analogical knowledge, based on the fundamental perception that nothing, no reality, is capable of expressing Transcendence. Thus, with respect to the whole human experience of Transcendence, the word *Mystery* is best suited to define the discovery of God as the Absolute who attracts and invites to the experience.[101]

---

compel a name to be given to them. We can, therefore, say that what exists in the most simple and inescapable way for man with respect to the question of God, is that the word 'God' exists in his spiritual and intellectual life." And he continues: if someone wishes to avoid it, "not only must one *expect* that in the existence of man and in the language of society it would completely disappear, but also one must contribute to this disappearance by keeping complete silence, thus abstaining from declaring oneself an *atheist*. But how would that be done, if others, who could not definitively emigrate from their linguistic field, continue to speak of God and are concerned with this word?"

99. Ibid., italics mine.

100. See the most recent work by Domínguez Morano, *Los registros del deseo: del afécto, el amor y otras pasiones*. See also Bingemer, *Alteridade e vulnerabilidade*.

101. See the text by Rahner, "The Need for a 'Short Formula' of Christian Faith,"

In view of its mysterious communication, silence, rather than words, is best suited to the experience of God. Silence is a companion of the experience, and of the intimate understanding one has, or can have, of the Mystery, in experiencing it. In it lies the possibility for the human being to appreciate and finally perceive the insufficiency of words and concepts to express it, keeping silent in order to really posses it. There is a Mystery of death immanent in human consciousness and language when it comes to speaking of God, or better said, to speaking of the experience as the possibility of knowing the Absolute. This is a recognition that everything has its beginning prior to humankind, which in one way or another arrives only later, and too late to be fully pertinent to the Mystery and to enter into a full relationship with it.[102] One must, therefore, always seek it and wait for it in the humility of a poverty conscious of its finitude.

The God of Judeo-Christian revelation is different from the gods of all the other peoples of Antiquity. This God does not reveal God's self only in the laws and cycles of nature, but through men and women and in contingent events in the history of humankind. This is the God of the People, who speaks God's name and shows God's face in events through which God's self is revealed to all kinds of creatures. This God is from the beginning the God of Abraham, Isaac, and Jacob and the Father of Jesus of Nazareth, who transcends all natural phenomena and liberates the people from malevolent powers, oppression, and death. Unlike the gods of nature, this is the God of history.

This identification of God with the powers of nature and the liberation of God from this idea by the people of Israel, prepare the way—remotely but fundamentally—for the dialogue of this God with the emancipated world and the human beings of modernity. Humanity lies, from the beginning, at the center of the experience of the people of Israel. The experience of the biblical human being is that of a past definitively left behind, and that of a

---

which says, "Man—whether he expressly affirms it or does not affirm it, whether he represses this truth or allows it to emerge to the surface—always finds himself exposed, in his spiritual existence, to a Sacred Mystery which constitutes the foundation of his existence. This Mystery is the most primal, the most evident, but because of this also the most occult and ignored; a Mystery which speaks while keeping silent, which 'is there' while, being absent, it reduces our own frontiers. And all this because, as an inexplicable and unexpressed horizon, it ceaselessly embraces and sustains the small circle of our everyday cognitive and active experience, the knowledge of reality and the act of freedom. We call it God."

102. See the recent film *Die große Stille (Into Great Silence)*, filmed in a Carthusian monastery by Philip Gröning, who, in order to make it, interned himself for six months at the Carthusian monastery in Grenoble, France.

future that must be searched with hope of finding it. The future is something new. It is not a cyclical, perpetual, and constant return to an eternal past.

Modernity and secularization carry something of this teleological conception of time. But they distort it with the notion of progress and efficacy. Progress is the *leitmotif* of modernity as much as *equilibrium* was the *leitmotif* of premodern civilizations. However this same modernity is in tune with the biblical revelation regarding the valorization of history. At a time of changing paradigms, when the emergence of a postmodern paradigm is portrayed as announcing the end of history, it is important to rescue the positiveness of this category as a help in the understanding of the moment in which we live.

Our premise is that Christianity dislocates sacredness from the Sacred place, the temple, to the world and humankind. Classical and traditional theologies understood such dislocation as a set of external norms that should be followed to ensure the worship of the true God. Modernity brought about a new dislocation that places the axis of sacredness in the most intimate depth of the human subject, understood as conscious freedom and, to some extent, the producer of its own *nomos*, of its own law.

Thus, in Christianity the human being is seen as someone who is free. But free to love. Freedom is conceived neither as an oppressive heteronomy—an external law that destroys subjectivity—nor as a superego that crushes subjectivity, but rather as a free gift from God, who again and again places the human being freely on the path of love, moving toward the other in an essentially plural human context.

The Emptiness of Meaning

A first approach to the theme of the meaning of life "cannot be anything other than a reference to the question regarding meaning in its condition as primordial for the human being, in an entirely unique way."[103] It is a universal question that no human being can avoid at any moment of existence. Furthermore, it is more radical than any other question, because it refers to the open space of "questionability" that continues to confront human beings even after they have answered the concrete issues raised for them by the very fact of being alive. Therefore the question of the meaning of life embraces all previous questions and at the same time transcends them. Likewise it highlights a radical problematic—the mysterious condition of life itself. I didn't ask to be born and I don't want to die: this is the arc of the human question of Meaning. The question of the meaning of life qualifies

---

103. See Velasco, *Mistica y humanismo*, 203.

the human being as such, because among the created beings, only the human being raises it. Moreover, it underlines the definition of human life and the human creature as created Mystery, which necessarily leads to the question of the Uncreated Mystery, which is God.[104]

The question of meaning is raised in notably different ways, according to the historical era, the context of life, the situation of the person or group which formulates it, and the dimension of existence where it emerges. It is born of the discovery that we all make at some moment, which leads us to question life. In this questioning we ask ourselves if life means anything, or if it is no more than an absurd and meaningless succession of brute facts. In view of the attitudes and demands brought about by our existence on earth, and the difficulties and suffering that accompany it, all human beings must certainly have asked themselves at one time or another if life is really worth living at all.[105]

However, although it is a question for all times, it seems clear that the question of meaning became more insistent and serious in the modern era. The discourse about the death of God had as a consequence for human beings the sensation of loneliness and orphanhood. They lost a God who was the key to all previous attempts at answers. Based on this, many would speak of the crisis of meaning as characterizing the spiritual situation of our time, leading to a diagnosis of our developed societies as suffering from a "sickness of meaning."[106] And the human being would be seriously tempted to define as "absurd" a life that seems so meaningless and cruel as to provoke a sensation of nausea.[107] More than a concept, meaning is a word-symbol applicable to all kinds of metaphoric descriptions, but resistant to a clear and exhaustive analysis of its content.[108]

We can speak of meaning as relating to the orientation of a reality in movement. In this sense, the meaning of life refers to the direction of the course of life. The valley through which human life runs had an origin that we don't fathom, and we don't possess it because we were not active participants in its beginnings. We are belated beings who arrived after the beginning of the world and after our parents had met each other. The past is given to us without our interference. Our existence has a certain end: death. It is as certain as its moment and circumstances are unforeseeable—certain death,

---

104. See Rahner, *Foundations of Christian Faith*.

105. Velasco, *Mistica y humanismo*, 204. All the great thinkers did so: Plato, Heidegger, Blondel, Camus, Descartes, Spinoza.

106. Ibid., 205.

107. See the work of such famous thinkers of the twentieth century as Albert Camus and Jean-Paul Sartre.

108. See Velasco, *Mistica y humanismo*, 206, citing Olegario de Cardedal.

uncertain hour. It is a final limit that we don't control, since even in the case of our own death we are not active subjects, but must passively receive it—incapable as we are of avoiding or postponing it indefinitely no matter how much we try.[109] Biologically speaking, death is, in this directional sense, and contrary to our liking, the meaning of our life.[110] Willingly or not, we walk toward it. And death will be the criterion of discernment of our life.[111]

Even without denying that death is the only destination of human life as a biological reality, one has to emphasize that this is so in a very unique way as compared to other living beings. Human beings don't just die. Of all the animals, only they know they are mortal. For them a consciousness of mortality is incorporated into their lives like a shadow over their entire existential journey. And since death is the only inevitable thing in human life, this known and certain end questions human beings as to whether life does or does not have a meaning. Is life worthwhile or not, if the only certainty one can have is that one day all this will end, and that we are going to die like all the other beings of creation? The way human beings react to this fact—the attitude they take in confronting it—brings about, for human thought and being, the placement of the problem of the meaning of life in a new semantic field: that of signification. I didn't ask to be born and I don't want to die. The fact of questioning death, of not wishing for it or desiring it, of doing anything to avoid it, of ritually celebrating it, or of trying to communicate with those who are already departed—all this raises the question whether human beings understand themselves as made for life and not for death.

In the second place, the definition of meaning can refer to the signification of a word, a phrase, or a text, as when we encounter a new word, or a word in a language we do not know, and ask: what does it mean? What is the meaning of such a text, of such a parable? Life, which is in effect the events of a biography, but more than just the facts that compose it, means something to those who live these events. In this conception, the life of each person is full of significant realities, of signs and symbols that give it a unique singularity. Also, still in this constellation of significations, meaning is that which—with the capacity of the human being to signify and symbolize—brings about the emergence of each person's own symbolic condition. This is, if not the most important, then certainly one of the most important indications of the *plus* that is present in human identity, signified by that

---

109. Ibid., 207.

110. Ibid.

111. See Sartre, in the play *No Exit*: "On meurt toujours trop tôt—ou trop tard. Et cependant la vie est là, terminée: le trait est tiré, il faut faire la somme. Tu n'es rien d'autre que ta vie." (One always dies too early—or too late. And yet life is there, ended: the line is drawn and one must do the sum. You are nothing more than your life.)

which illuminates one's own world and by whose light one understands and lives out one's own being in the world.

This *plus*, this *more* with which the human being is endowed, makes possible the phenomenon of truth in its primary sense of the unveiling of reality, of the revelation of the Mystery—which is fundamentally nothing more than, on the one hand, the problem of knowledge, and on the other, in the light of faith, the problem of Transcendence. Faith summons transcendence—which is understood as personal and relational—from God. It is here that human beings, in their relationship with the world, open themselves to the possibility of meaning. It is from here that emerges in and for them, and above all before them, the anguished question of meaning, because of all that is threatened by the possibility that the answer to this question may be nonexistent or negative. The question of meaning therefore comes to all human beings shadowed by the real possibility of the absurd, of a lack of meaning, and of chaos.

Human beings can adapt themselves to anything that their imagination is capable of representing, but not to chaos.[112] They have no vocation for either chaos or anarchy. From this derives the imperious need to find a justification for life, a guiding thread that allows them not to feel lost and disoriented when threatened by events and circumstances that put them in question, shaking their utmost foundations. In this second semantic field of the word *meaning* we see the radicalism that human existence implies for the question of meaning.

According to Juan Martin Velasco, the events and circumstances that threaten the integration and reconciliation of human beings with the meaning of life can be summarized into the three most important ones: (*a*) when human beings face insurmountable limits to the understanding of certain facts in their life;[113] (*b*) when, for no apparent reason, unjust suffering shakes or destroys the cognitive and affective factors that until that moment had allowed the integration and conciliation of what apparently could not be integrated or conciliated, making it tolerable; and (*c*) moral evil, particularly injustice. What is threatened here is not only reason or human feelings, but also the need to perceive a radical and intimate meaning in facts apparently deprived of such meaning, a need which is an integral part of human beings and resides in their moral conscience, to which whatever is good and just belongs.[114]

---

112. See Geertz, "Religion as Cultural System."

113. See the famous saying of Pascal: "Le silence éternel de ces espaces infinis m'effraie" (The eternal silence of these infinite spaces frightens me).

114. See Velasco, *Mistica y humanismo*, 209.

There is a third field for understanding what meaning is: the sphere of values. To ask, in this context, if life has meaning, is to ask if life is estimable or good, and to ask, given the difficulties—the considerable exertion, fatigue and suffering—that all human life bears with it, whether life is worth living at all. Meaning as value, the positive condition that human things and experiences may have, appears amidst a wide range of possibilities. Several contemporary thinkers have reflected on this.[115] It is important to pay attention to the hierarchy of needs and the consequent scale of values that derives from it. An exclusive consideration of need would lead to a culture reduced to immediate satisfaction, and would recognize the value of usefulness and efficiency as the only value. The meaning of life understood as value in relation to human needs would have as its final product a perfectly satisfied subject. In truth, that would be a satisfied robot, an automaton but not a person.[116]

The result of such a model of life would be boredom and disgust, as well as disappointment and therefore a descent into the emptiness of meaning. But the word *value* could likewise designate goodness of a different order. Human beings do not just aspire to satisfy material needs and interests. They not only have needs, but are also inhabited by desires. Indeed the human being is, in a certain way, a desiring being, a being of desire, and as such is capable of a relationship with the ends toward which the desires are oriented, according to an absolutely original configuration. Human beings are individuals in search of goals for their lives. In recognizing values in this way, they direct themselves toward ends perceived as capable of making their lives worthwhile, valid, and meaningful. Such ends demand that the human being actualize the value that these ends incarnate (beauty for the artist, charitability for the philanthropist and the saint, etc.). Values of this order do not fulfill the desire, but deepen and sharpen it.

As Levinas says, "The difference between need and desire lies in the fact that desire can never be satisfied; that desire, in some way, is nourished by its own hunger and augmented by its own satisfaction."[117] In this conception, meaning is present not as something oriented to me and dependent on me in its condition as value, but as something that orients me to myself, serves as my compass, and thus gives value to my life.[118]

Likewise, in this conception meaning is given uniquely by Otherness, and does not come from itself. The other is the interlocutor *par excellence*, the

---

115. Ibid., 211. Among other contemporary thinkers who reflected on this, the author cites Levinas, Maslow, Rof Carballo, and Habermas.

116. See Marcel, *Homo Viator*.

117. See Levinas, *Ethique et infini*, 97.

118. See Velasco, *Mistica y humanismo*, 211.

one before whom and for whom all human works and deeds are carried out. The presence of the other is indispensable if my gestures and my actions are to occur. The other is neither a cultural signification nor a simple objective datum of reality, but is fundamentally meaning, to the extent that the other gives meaning to my actions. I am what I am for and with others (father, mother, son, daughter, friend, brother, sister). The absolute newness of the other—continually self-giving in the world—consists in the fact that what is phenomenal in the other, the concrete existence of the other, is the face. The face is not just manifestation and epiphenomenon, nor is it just being there. Its worldly and palpable significance finds itself subverted and dominated by its *ab-soluta* presence (loose and free) in the world, not being integrated into it (and without any possibility of being included in its totality). Its newness consists in presenting and manifesting itself as new, and always so. The epiphany of the Face of the Other is visitation, and therefore, as a phenomenon, it is image. The epiphany of the Face of the Other is life.[119]

Here consciousness as an ontological concept loses its primacy. It is no longer intentional consciousness, but a consciousness that is called for, required, and demanded. The I cannot evade responsibility before the other. In this sense the I identifies itself with an ethic and a morality that are not casuistic, in the full sense of the term. As in the foundational and paradigmatic bible story of Cain and Abel,[120] the response to the Creator's question about the existential location of the other (Where is your brother?), cannot be evasive, and not an answer but rather another question, "Am I my brother's keeper?" The answer has its source in the ethic that defines the human being as responsible for the other, as one who responds for the other, and who is, yes, the brother's guardian.

In this privileged place of experience, human beings perceive and experience themselves as valuable subjects. And their lives have value to the extent that they accept and receive this supreme value from the Otherness which challenges and questions them. Meaning, in this understanding of value, consists in the self-discovery oriented toward a reality in which they must always and continually transcend themselves. Thus they instill meaning into the experienced Transcendence, and are attracted to it. With the word *meaning* something precisely human is named, something that bestows specificity on the person before all other living and created beings.[121] The word *meaning* expresses the idea that the human being is and exists as more than a fatality, and as more than a mundane and biological being.

---

119. Ibid., 213. See Levinas, *Humanismo do outro homem*, 58.
120. See Gen 4.
121. See Velasco, *Mistica y humanismo*, 214.

And further, the human being cannot be happy with just being and existing. For men and women, being human requires truly being—as much as being good—being worthy of being. Meaning is the word for this *plus*, this excess of being that reveals itself in the form of truth, beauty, and goodness, like streaks and flashes of a plenitude to which one cannot cease to aspire.[122]

What human beings can do in relation to this is to pay attention to the exuberance inhabiting them and telling them that living as a human being is more than simply existing and simply being in the world, and more than satisfying their urges and basic biological needs. The question of meaning carries a disproportion between the fact of being, and the more-than-being to which life aspires whenever someone desires, and strives for, a good, right, and just existence, which is therefore worth living and replete with value. The cultivation of the question of meaning is, therefore, a way of cultivating attention to that upon which rests meaning and the question of meaning.

Human beings are not content to live in a manner that is really nothing more than survival. They need quality of life—a quality that is not exhausted at a certain level of well being, of satisfaction of basic needs, or of comfort. Human beings are not limited to the framework of direct motivation, of seeking all that can quickly satisfy their most immediate needs. The measure of this quality of human life is the aspiration for what philosophy calls the Good and revelation calls Love—a measure without measure.[123] Life is not just a striving toward the end result of short-term aspirations, but a fecund striving, which is its source and its mover, its inspiration and its aspiration.[124] A life so driven, that aspires to so much, is a life full of meaning, a happy life.

Throughout, meaning is immanent to life, always directing and urging it further, toward a constant Transcendence. This direction and meaning take place even in the absence of certainties and securities, as is the case with our society today.[125] Because it takes place as conscious human experience, meaning infuses the frustrating and somber certainty of death with the doubt and the suspicion that it is not, and cannot be, the end of everything. And this gives one the strength to fight and combat it, to refuse to tolerate it, indeed to wholeheartedly reject it, with all one's strength and understanding.

---

122. Ibid., 214–15.

123. Ibid., 216. See Saint Augustine: "Loving without measure is the measure of love."

124. Ibid., 217.

125. Ibid., 279.

In an existence thus understood, death is incapable of exhausting its possibilities, since life is based on values full of meaning and dignity that go beyond the natural and biological fact of death. A life of this kind offers reasons for living, and says that these same reasons deserve the sacrifice on their behalf of comfort, well-being, and even life itself—insofar as it is chronological and spaciotemporal.[126]

Therefore human beings, in their irreproducible originality, upon gaining consciousness of themselves before all the other realities of the world, become aware of the marvel of their reason and the reach of their desires, and discover themselves to be constituted of a total inner disproportion between what they are, what they are called to be, and what they could be.[127] This explains the nostalgia for eternity, the paradise that inhabits even those who do not believe.[128]

This paradoxical condition, divided, strained—and above all beautiful—is the human condition. It is what makes the question of the meaning of life appear inevitable and constitutive. Obviously, this question could be evaded, distorted, and suppressed, but at the price of blunting and atrophying the most precious and marvelous potentialities of the human being. On the other hand, although this question is constitutive of the human being, there are no scientific reasons or rationale on which to ground that which transcends the mundane and the relative. Only in graciousness can one find the answer to this question, which notwithstanding sustains the whole of human life.

Humankind has always tried to answer this question. And the way most frequently followed for this purpose has been religion. All religions touch on the question of the meaning of life. And sociologists identify the close relationship between religion and the meaning of life as the most important function that religion has performed in human history.[129]

Many philosophers, even atheists and nonbelievers, express the same conviction. For instance, Wittgenstein affirms that we can give the name God to the meaning of life, that is, to the meaning of the world. Therefore, according to him, to believe in God is to say that life has meaning.

---

126. Ibid., 218.

127. See Gesche, *O ser humano*, 10: "Reality is not only that which is, but above all that which could be."

128. See Velasco, *Mistica y humanismo*, 219–20, citing Cioran, *Del inconveniente de haber nacido*, 225: "I couldn't stand a stay in paradise, not even for a day. How can I then explain my nostalgia for it? I don't explain it; it has always lived in me, it was in me even before I was myself." See as well the recent books by Habermas et al., *An Awareness of What Is Missing*, and Eagleton, *Reason, Faith, and Revolution*.

129. See Velasco, *Mistica y humanismo*, 221.

Confronted with this meaning one must keep silent, as we are thrust into the order of mysticism.[130]

In theology, this question has been dealt with as part of the theme of Salvation, which is present in all religious traditions. It identifies life as biological and worldly, insufficient, illusory, and unsatisfactory. The existence of evil makes it so, and religion comes to rescue it from this evil and redeem it, revealing to human beings that they are finite and unable to understand themselves without reference to God, the nostalgia for whom remains the only refuge for human desire.

Some eminent Protestant and Catholic theologians have expressed their convictions on this question. Paul Tillich affirmed that religion is a fundamental orientation that encompasses and carries all other functions of the spirit to the absolute. Thus, for him, to be religious is to be passionately committed to the question of the meaning of life. And for Karl Rahner the question of an Absolute meaning must be always understood as a question about God. For him these two questions are identical.

Theology has struggled—especially after the Second Vatican Council—to demonstrate that it is necessary to reject all attempts to manipulate the word *God* in order to cram with immediate and manipulable meaning a frustrated and disoriented human life.[131] There are many nonbelievers who live meaningful lives. For example, there are nonreligious and even atheistic spiritualities that allow many to orient their lives according to values such as justice, peace, and solidarity. The same can be said of the search for truth by honest science—science worthy of being called honest—and of the aesthetic experience, a place inhabited by so many "real presences."[132] This is also true of the experiences of Transcendence that open horizons to human beings and enrich them internally, even if they do not give them the content and the name of God.[133] These have been designated lay spiritualities, spiritualities without God, or simply spiritualities, as alternatives to the religious way to meaningful existence.

Apart from the adherence to a confessional structure there is a spirituality, a mysticism that unites all human beings who arrive at the fundamental choice to withdraw from selfishness and to open themselves to love. In this choice there is no this or that member of this or whatever religion. There are only human beings who opt to exit from themselves, in an attitude of

---

130. See Wittgenstein, *Tractatus Logico-Philosophicus*, 186.

131. See Gesche, who affirms that God is not a functionary of meaning: *O Cosmo*, 289. See also the commentary of Velasco in *Mistica y humanismo*, 226.

132. See Steiner, *Real Presences: Is There Anything in What We Say?*

133. See Comte-Sponville, *L'Esprit de l'athéisme*. See also Fiores, "Espiritualidade contemporanea," 462–63.

oblation, as the only way to find meaning in their lives.[134] These are persons who raise today, as they did yesterday, the same question that was articulated in the first half of the twentieth century by the French writer Albert Camus: "Can one be a saint without God?"[135]

This is often a matter of a mystical life lived outside any church and on the margin of any religion. At the same time, it implies the demise of ideology of any kind, and the rupture of all impoverishing and reductionist models. It is not a question of a way of thinking, a philosophical system, or a new school. It consists in the exercise of freedom, in the living out of the fundamental ethic, and in carrying out a good and just life that finds its meaning in this exercise. The accomplishment of freedom is, therefore, the condition for the profound discovery of the meaning of life.

The Atrophy of Freedom

Freedom is the set of recognized individual rights, separately or collectively considered in the context of the political authority as well as the state. It is the power that enables citizens to exert their will inside the boundaries established by law.

Freedom, in philosophy, is negatively designated as the absence of submission, servitude, and determinism, that is, it qualifies the independence of the human being. In positive terms, freedom is the autonomy and spontaneity of a rational subject. In other words, it qualifies and constitutes the condition for voluntary human behavior.

It is not a matter of an abstract concept. It is important to observe that philosophers like Sartre and Schopenhauer try, in their writings, to attribute this quality to the free human being. Neither is it a matter of a separation between freedom and the human being, but rather of a synergy between both for the self-affirmation and existence of the ego. And in the equation between freedom and the will one can observe that the will to be free becomes the driving force and, paradoxically, the instrument for the liberation of the human being.

According to Thomas Aquinas, human will is "always inclined to want the good in general."[136] To want pure evil for himself or herself is something that the human being, whether a man or a woman, "cannot" choose. Even when committing an obviously bad act, such as suicide, the human being is reaching for happiness, for the good, seeking to feel alright with himself

---

134. See Velasco, *Mistica y humanismo*, 228.
135. Camus, *La Peste*.
136. *S Th* III, q. 18, a. 1, 16.

or herself. It is clear that it is sometimes a case of a pathology, such as masochism, which finds pleasure in pain. Yet deviant behaviors occasioned by psychological pathologies have no effect on human freedom, since these behaviors are not caused by them.

However, Saint Thomas goes on to say that, although inclined to always want the good in general, the human being is not inclined to choose just one single good. The thrilling and stimulating truth about freedom is that the possibilities for the choice of whatever good is most suitable for the human being are almost infinite. It is like having one destination and innumerable itineraries to get there. One has only to choose. Certainly, there are times when it is not possible for us to choose between one and another good. We can only accept and want—without passive resignation—what we have been given and cannot change. But when the choice takes place by a process that leads us to free action or thinking, it is important that this choice be made well. From the fundamental option, freely taken, will come others derived from it which we must choose in life. Thus the meaning of life will continue to emerge and rise to the surface of consciousness.

Human autonomy has become a tyranny of possibilities.[137] The possibilities multiply, and freedom, pursued and cornered, tyrannized by an infinity of choices, unable (or unwilling) to choose, atrophies instead of expanding. Sociologically this is explained by the configuration of the world we live in. Seductive and tempting sensations overwhelm us and shape our interior universe. They try to control our feelings and freedom by creating addictions that are extremely difficult to liberate ourselves from.[138]

Instead of deciding the rhythm and direction of life, we are led by a torrent of external sensations and stimuli that stun and disorient us, leaving us no space for personal reflection or for appropriate and mature decisions. This uninterrupted torrent impacts our affectivity and freedom, and paralyzes even our thinking. Pascal's critique of *divertissement* is testimony to this.

The etymology of the word *diversion—divertissement* in French—already says well what is at issue, and why this central question enticed and intrigued the great Christian thinker Pascal. "To divert" means "to deviate from." On the etymology of this word Pascal built an ethical and moral category.[139] Diversion in the sense of amusement is the practice of escape, which is typical of human existence. It diverts us from that which afflicts us and from whatever reality is not pleasurable. It prevents us from thinking truthfully about our existence and from liberating our freedom so that it

---

137. See González Buelta, *Caminar sobre las aguas*, 56.
138. Ibid. See also, by the same author, *Orar en un mundo roto* and *Ver o parecer*.
139. See Pascal, *Pensées*.

will be fully exercised. Pascal affirms that "men, not having been able to cure death, misery and ignorance, try to build happiness by not thinking about them."[140] Human beings today, as apparently also in Pascal's time, cope badly with silence, lack of recreation, loneliness, and the encounter with themselves. They always need to be "in a state of diversion, of amusement, of *divertissement*" in order not to think about serious things and not to have to make weighty decisions.

With the contemporary technologies of a consumption society, and in a culture of leisure, opportunities for amusement are made available to human beings as an escape from the unpleasant situations that are part of everyday life. Loud music deafens them so that they are oblivious to reality. They isolate themselves to avoid receiving questions from the real world.[141] In this feel-good culture of entertainment, of continual frenetic stimulation, it is very difficult for one to live freely and to reach the depths of the self, the place where great decisions, expressive of a liberated freedom, are made.[142]

Feeling good implies disengagement. It calls for discarding relationships that no longer seem interesting, replacing still useful consumer goods with new ones, and seeking ever new leisure pastimes to substitute for old ones, whether outdoor activities, good reading matter, or a good movie. It is very difficult for human beings today to renounce what is incompatible with decisions that would give direction to their lives.[143] Choices are made with all doors left open. Renunciation becomes a word without meaning. Freedom is conceived as doing whatever one wants, and not as the capacity to choose what is most humanizing and fosters personal growth. And decisions, once taken, are not sustained for long.

In theological terms, the church, through its teachings, has constantly spoken of the drama that the loss of the meaning of sin represents for the human person today. With the explosive refutation of a repressed mentality for which everything was, or could be, sin, now, in contrast, nothing is. In an irresponsible transgression, the unpunished enjoyment of all that exists, especially of what was forbidden, makes up a part of the postmodern *modus vivendi*. In the joy brought about by the pleasures of an irresponsibly exercised sexuality, by eating and drinking more than is necessary, without restraint, and by the wasteful enjoyment of the pleasures of a good table, what "transpires is less the legitimate use of the privileges of existence than

---

140. Ibid., B 168.
141. See Buelta, *Caminar sobre las aguas*.
142. Ibid.
143. Ibid.

a way of exorcizing death, and of rushing into an uncontrolled race without return no matter what."[144]

For his part, Pope Pius XII had already said that "the sin of this century is the loss of the sense of sin." And Benedict XVI, in 2009, declared,

> In our time, to form with rectitude the conscience of the faithful constitutes without doubt one of the pastoral priorities because, as I have already had occasion to say time and again, to the extent that one loses the sense of sin, the sense of guilt, unfortunately, increases.[145]

The religious crisis we are going through therefore walks hand in hand with the discovery of a nature that little by little has replaced God and rehabilitates the body without restriction, occasioning a reversal in the modes of life and thought. The metaphysical history of freedom is, so to speak, the history of its covenant with subjectivity. It implies, therefore, a series of frontiers that do not necessarily coincide with progress in the phenomenological description of the concept, nor even with significant articulations at the ethical and political levels.[146]

The fluidity of the social and ethical fabric in which we live in today, instead of freeing human beings from all the social and moral shackles that have kept them imprisoned, actually atrophies their freedom. Without feeling the density of the real, the epiphany of Otherness and the voice of conscience that would lead them to make decisions and to regulate their actions, what occurs is an atrophy of freedom, which finds itself the captive of a way of life closer to animal instinct than to human autonomy. Human freedom atrophies and regresses to the shrinking point of someone who does not think, does not hope, and does not love, and who is thus not able to live or be free in the human sense. Here, Transcendence, even if named and professed, is in need of the Absolute to give it consistency and veracity.

The Thirst for the Absolute

In a moment of decline and change of paradigms and models, one observes in contemporary society, which had considered itself free from oppression and the "opium" of religion, an understanding of the human being as a relational being open to a heteronomous autonomy, that is, an autonomy ruled

---

144. See Certeau, "Péché," in *Encyclopaedia Universalis*.
145. See the pronouncement of Benedict XVI, March 14, 2009.
146. See Ricoeur, "Liberté," in *Encyclopaedia Universalis*.

by Otherness. Unrepressed and uncontrollable, the seduction of the Sacred and the Divine bursts forth again.

The resacralization of the same world in which modern reason hastened to proclaim its disenchantment and its secularity complicates the possibility of diagnosing it clearly. After their attempted banishment by secularization, the reappearance or re-emergence—more than the return—of the religious, of the Sacred, of the thirst for the Mystery and for mysticism in different ways, indicates a return (or a permanence) of contemplative need, an apparently new emergence of values such as graciousness, desire, sentiment; and the rediscovery, in a new dimension, of nature and the relationship of the human being with the planet.

The source of every religious experience finds a common denominator in seduced desire, in the fascination with and irresistible attraction to the Mystery of the other, whose beauty and difference involves, seduces, and incites passion, and who provokes an uncontrollable urge for closeness, embrace, and union.[147]

This Mystery that attracts and seduces, however, does not cease to cause fear and to provoke—from poor and impotent humility—a reverent and trembling distancing (See Exod 3:6–7): "And Moses hid his face, for he was afraid to look at God." It is the very violence of the attraction that overwhelms and appears like a voluminous and fearful torrent, or like a devouring fire that consumes but at the same time inebriates and delights. It is thus felt to be as radically threatening and inexorable as death itself, even if its secret is the source of life. "And so it is that the wife in the Song of Solomon, lovesick at the vision of the Beloved, moans, 'I am faint with love' (Song 2:5), and exclaims, 'love is strong as death, passion fierce as the grave'" (Song 8:6). Saint John of the Cross, at the highest point of his mystical union and of his ineffable and unitive experience with God, plays with the words death-life in trying to describe the at once pleasurable and painful experience brought to life by the love of God.[148]

---

147. The *Dicionário Petit Robert* defines *seduction* as action to seduce (to lead astray), to corrupt, to drag, but also to attract, to enchant, and to fascinate; and *desire* as awareness of a tendency toward any known or imaginary object.

148. See the famous poem of the Spanish mystic John of the Cross, "Llama de amor viva": "Oh llama de amor viva / que tiernamente hieres / de mi alma en el más profundo centro / pues ya no eres esquiva / acaba ya, si quieres / rompe la tela de este dulce encuentro / Oh cauterio suave! / Oh regalada llaga! / Oh mano blanda! Oh toque delicado / Que a vida eterna sabe / y toda deuda paga; / *matando muerte en vida la has trocado* . . ." (*Obras completas*, 891). See also Bataille, *O erotismo*: "On erotism one can say that it is the approbation of the same life in death" (11), and "when it is an issue of the mystical experience as both negative and positive, such as suffering from absence and continuity of being" (19–21).

It is a fact, then, that the divine Eros is always self-presented as stronger than the human being, overcoming human resistance and self-imposing God with majesty. Under the touch of God's love, at once gentle and violent, the prophet bows his head and surrenders himself, exclaiming: "O Lord, you have enticed me, and I was enticed; you have overpowered me, and you have prevailed" (Jer 20:7). And under God's leadership the unfaithful wife does an about-face, abandons her lovers and submissively allows herself to be led in nudity into the wilderness, and to renounce the first love of her youth (see Hos 2:16ff.).

At the same time, possessing an irresistible power of attraction, the other Beloved, after conquering the human heart, hides away from the possibility of being reached by the one in whom an inextinguishable flame of desire was ignited, although being self-revealed as the Non-manipulable one, over whom the human being has no power. On the contrary, it is made very clear that the human being must live as dependent on this god. A god thus desired and experienced does not succumb either to the frenetic impatience of the human subject or to the impassioned anxiety of humankind. Being absolutely free, God will respond plentifully, according to God's own desire, to the expectant and humble poverty that never ceases to seek and hope for God wherever God allows God's self to be found, in order to receive Salvation (health) and holiness.[149]

For the human being attracted to God, therefore, God is an object of desire and not of need, of the realm of graciousness rather than of the necessary, the intelligible, or the controllable. God is incomparable, and is not counted among what are conventionally known as basic human needs: eating, drinking, and everything without which biological life weakens and dies. From the perspective of—so to speak—animal life, God does not appear as a useful or necessary factor.

However, in spite of God's lack of usefulness, divine Eros has, over all that is human—that is, corporeality animated by the spirit—a power of attraction and seduction that arouses desire to paroxysmal heights, and can lead to the most radical and the most heroic renunciations in the name of a faintly perceived possibility of participating in God's divine life and of experiencing the unity offered by God, even if only for one minute.[150]

---

149. See on this theme *Dictionnaire de spiritualité* (DS), vol. 91, col. 38, entry "sacré."

150. See the lives of saints and mystics as well as the testimony of martyrs. For complete citations from a huge bibliography on this phenomenon in the Christian tradition, see DS, vol. 10, col. 727–28, *Martyre*, a variant of the word that refers to the experience of martyrdom as an experience of profound union and identification with Christ. Not only does the martyr experience the presence of Christ, but there is even a transubstantiation of the martyr's "personal martyrdom into the person of Christ, which is what

The Sacred is not useful. It adds nothing to biological life. It doesn't promise success, longevity, or tangible pleasure. On the contrary, it demands the surrendering and renunciation of the most tangible and palpable goods, and even of the most legitimate liaisons of the human heart (family, friends, etc.). Neither is any other reality allowed to surpass the sacred, on pain of refusing to be reached as the only Absolute capable of responding to and satisfying the human heart's thirst for love.

In spite of such terrible demands, today as always—even after the whole secularization process of modernity and the categorical affirmations on religion by the masters of suspicion—we still find persons capable of passing hours and hours in worship, celebration, and ceremonies of praise. These are persons who, in the name of their faith in this useless God, are capable of delivering their lives in a sacrifice that makes our modernized, consumerist, and comfort-seeking minds and bodies tremble. They are capable of meeting death in a state of happy exaltation, and of considering as an immense Grace the renouncing, for the love of this invisible and useless object of desire, all that brings sweetness, comfort, and well-being to human life.[151] They are persons willing to channel all of their affective potential and almost all of their time, energy, creativity, and religious ritual resources into singing hymns of adoration and participating in long hours of collective prayer as physical and spiritual therapy and healing; or willing to prostrate themselves during unending hours in contemplation before the tabernacle or before nature; or capable of ruminating at length on some verse of the Bible, on a small prayer, or on the five Mysteries of the rosary. The truth is that the men and women of today, like those of all times, continue to experience the drama of feeling themselves limited and fragile, and yet made for union with the Limitless. At their profoundest depth, they perceive themselves as inhabited by an ardent and uncontrollable desire to commune with this incomprehensible reality called the Sacred—who, although incomprehensible, is not felt as less real—to touch, and be touched, by the Infinite Beauty; to tremble with love upon being touched by the divine holiness,

---

sustains some under torture and which in truth is for him the continuation, in this way, of his saving passion." See Festrugière, *La sainteté*, in which the author develops a comparative inquiry between the Greek hero and the Christian saint.

151. See Bataille, *O erotismo*, 20–21. On divine erotism: "Certainly, what the mystical experience reveals is an absence of an object. The object identifies itself with discontinuity, and the mystical experience, once we have the strength to perform a rupture from our discontinuity, introduces in us the feeling of continuity. Sacred erotism, present in the mystical experience, requires only that nothing should disturb the subject of the experience." We allow ourselves to disagree with the author in his reference to the Christian mystical experience, since we consider that there exists in it a "real and fully present" and "visible" presence of the object of desire: Jesus in his humanity.

by the Invisible Mystery who attracts and seduces, and whose life calls for participation and integration. It is this Mystery of Otherness who, in graciousness, offers them profound fellowship. Then love proceeds to govern their lives and transform them according to the inexorability and radicality of the Mystery's will.

From this thirst for the Absolute that dominates the plural and secularized contemporaneity in which we live, we infer that the paradigm of Otherness and intersubjectivity returns to the center of the debate and of the reconfigured way of thinking.

To our contemporaries' thirst for the Absolute, historical Christianity must offer this Absolute in the form of love. The monotheistic Abrahamic religions (Judaism, Christianity, Islam) have, in the human encounter with the one prophetically revealed Unconditional God, the foundation of the universal normativeness of their *ethos*.[152] Among them, the Christian faith affirms that the encounter with the God of Jesus Christ is the radical experience of existence, a foundational theonomy of personal freedom and responsibility, an experiential grounding of the person in the Unconditional, which at once grants him or her both freedom and limitations.[153]

A Greek term—already present in the Greek translation of the Jewish Torah and central to the New Testament—designates the foundation of the *ethos* of early Christianity. The word is *agape*, usually translated as "love." The intention was to signify a concept of love for which the more common Greek words such as *eros, filia,* or *storgé* seemed neither adequate nor appropriate. In agape/love the emphasis is on disinterested and oblatory generosity—without any extraneous interest or the possibility of joy and satisfaction other than love itself—and on the willingness to move away from oneself and toward the other. The non-profaning Otherness is the starting point for this self-offering, which has its roots in a self-giving God. This self-revealing God is perceived and adored as actually being love. This is expressed with obfuscating clarity in the first epistle of John: "Whoever does not love does not know God, for God is love" (1 John 4:8).

One of the constants of this conception of love is its universality. It vetoes any exceptional treatment of persons in the exercise of the most characteristic property of Christianity: the effectiveness of love. From this effectiveness no one can be excluded—none of the ontologically deprived human beings, not even enemies or criminals. All are called to find the citizenship of repentance and reconciliation in unconditional love, which is the always-open Door of pardon: the Resurrected Crucified. The Gospel of Jesus

---

152. See Küng, *Proyecto de una ética mundial*, 75.
153. See Mathon, "Sainteté," 704. See also Festugière, *La Sainteté*.

Christ has an extravagant eagerness to saturate with love even the darkest corners of reality, which are included in the embrace of the Grace always larger than sin and the destruction of solidarity: to pray for the enemies, to offer the other cheek to the aggressor—here is the disconcerting circle that closes around those who are "freely shackled" by the God of Jesus Christ.

A second constant is its preferential commitment, its partiality. The agape/God came into the world not to save the "righteous," but the "sinners," committing God's self above all to the destiny of the weak, the sick, the poor, the marginalized, and the excluded. The Logos of God, which carries life within it (John 1:4), is committed to those for whom God's gifts are the most assaulted, and is engaged on the side of the victims of human lovelessness—while always keeping open, even to the aggressors, the Door of repentance and pardon. This means loving solidarity, which brings comfort in the midst of suffering and sharing in the midst of deprivation. Through God's experience in the flesh, the Otherness of sufferers becomes a mysterious process of substitution,[154] which faith and the paradigm of Christ reveal to be rooted in the liberating power of agape/love.

Another constant is the rupture of all merely human boundaries. Incarnate in the created, agape/love explodes, in pain and joy, the boundaries of their living space. Paul of Tarsus knew how to magisterially express this intense and liberating rupture as an internal struggle, where so often "I do not do the good I want, but the evil I do not want is what I do" (Rom 7:19). The Christian discovers the enabling of this "good I want" by participating in the mystical body of the Resurrected Lord, who vanquishes death and the "evil I do not want." To overcome evil with good (Rom 12:21) is not to avoid assuming all the vulnerability and mortality of the human condition up to its ultimate consequences. It is to plunge the cross into the foundation of the *ethos*.

The enormous challenge and gift that Christianity sets before its followers finds an obligatory reference in the cross. These challenges and gifts frighten us when we are about to live them out, aware of the fragility of our options, of the lack of coherence in our lives, of the meager courage that animates our intervention in the world and in history, of the considerable vanity that inhabits our hearts. To live out the Christian *ethos* is to live in the epicenter of a conflictive situation: the crisis of the human, leading to an opening up to the divine as a total surrender. In this crisis the agape/God had the first word: that crazy love adventure of the Incarnation—a craziness

---

154. For a deeper understanding of the question of substitution, see Levinas, *Autrement qu'être ou au-delà de l'essence*, ch. 4, "La substitution."

that found in the ancient saying of the first church fathers a disconcerting expression: "God became man so that man could become God."

The Old Testament presented a picture that is not very different, in delineating rationality and practice as mysteriously rooted in messianic spirituality. Christianity deepened it even further, taking it to the level of a paroxysm. In the Incarnation, God's Love ironically subverts the entire order of worldly expectations: one must redo the normal human perception of Divine Majesty and Omnipotence. The God of Jesus Christ is a God who humbles God's self to the level of abjection, plunging—together with humankind—into an abyss of humiliation, passion, and death in order to lift up humanity in the Glory of the Resurrection.

Is it necessary to turn one's back on culture in order to follow the ways of God? The answer is no. A painful no, one which imposes on believers today the subversive task of preserving the dialogical relation between culture and holiness, finding in the "holy craziness" of Revelation a vibrant way of life for the world: ". . . the 'crazies for Christ' come to intervene, at least indirectly, in the order of culture, of science or of civilization, to warn against any type of absolutizing or sacralizing of human creations."[155] Their objective is to cross the desert of secularization with a proposal and an identity.

Even if the world had been as good in the past as is sometimes affirmed, it is in the current world that Christians are called to live and bear witness. In other words, to recognize the value of the profane does not mean to succumb to the logic of secularism or to renounce being a "figure of the logic of graciousness,"[156] which demands acceptance, without reservation, of all the risks involved in demonstrating the "crazy love" of the Incarnation. It is precisely this that the saints, prophets, and mystics who are present in this world do as a manifestation "of the One who refuses to be manipulated, or appropriated, or exchanged for whatever it may be."[157]

It has always been thus in the history of Christianity, which can be interpreted not only as the history of sin, as was often done by the prophets of chaos and the detractors of faith and religion. It can also be understood as the history of holiness—whether or not officially recognized by the institution. The universal character of the call to holiness—so acutely expressed in the first epistle of Paul of Tarsus to the Thessalonians: "For this is the will of God, your sanctification" (1 Thess 4:3)—affirms the possibility for the whole of humanity to reach holiness through a life in the Spirit of God. In the midst of the conflictive and often disconcerting secularization and plurality of the

---

155. Ibid., 65.
156. See Valadier, *Igreja e modernidade*, 87.
157. Ibid., 120.

twentieth century, there are—in the heart of a postmodernity fashioned by redeeming faceless and formless Absolutes—some examples of persons who realized this possibility.[158]

The authentic religious relationship, although tending toward sacrifice and self-denial, is one of personification, and consequently of personal identity and personalization, leading asymptotically to the most intimate and profound depths of the human heart. In order to better understand this, we should start from an ethical, interpersonal and inter-subjective phenomenology of Otherness, such as, for instance, that set forth by Emmanuel Levinas. Then it will become clear that Otherness is constitutive and a constituent of personal identity: both that of other people and that implied in the religious relationship.[159]

Religion can, indeed, depersonalize and de-identify human beings if they become fusional, nostalgic for the womb, or affected by other pathologies discovered by the psychology of religion.[160] Yet philosophy and theology try as well to answer the question of religion as a possibility of personalizing and subjectivizing the individual. This can be noticed in the so-called prophetic religions—Judaism, Christianity, and Islam.[161]

Modern philosophy was born from a Copernican turn that generated a new moment: the moment of the subject, who takes leave of the condition of object with a qualitative leap forward.[162] This second moment generates a second paradigm, that of personal conscience.[163] About this, Levinas says that the authentic person takes on, above all, an accusative declension, "Here I am!" as the responsible answer to others, but also to the historical event and to the voice of conscience. And, we could add, even to the implicit or explicit call of the living God.[164] This becomes clear in the book

158. See Thils, *Existencia y Santidad en Jesus Cristo*, 363–74.

159. See the reflection by Scannone in the articles "Filosofía primera y intersubjetividad" and "Racionalidad Ética, comunidad de comunicación y alteridad."

160. See Domínguez Morano, *Crer depois de Freud*; *Orar depois de Freud*.

161. See on this point Velasco, *Introducción a la fenomenología de la religión*; *El fenómeno místico*.

162. See Libânio, *Formação da consciência crítica*, where he distinguishes three moments: of the object, of the subject, and of the social.

163. Although Descartes clearly distinguishes between the self-transparent "I think" and things that are not self-conscious, he nevertheless highlights self-consciousness as a criterion of truth and certainty to the point of falling into idealism. He does not *distrust* the *illusions* of consciousness, as the masters of suspicion—Marx, Nietzsche, and Freud—were soon to do. Therefore, he remains in the immediacy of the *cogito* without passing through, by means of a critical discernment of suspicion and of reflexive mediation, the shared Otherness of others, of language, of culture, and of history.

164. See Scannone, "Identidad personal, alteridad interpersonal y relación religiosa."

Autrement qu'être ou au-delà de l'essence,[165] where Levinas affirms that the Messiah is not someone who bursts into history but is indeed all those who take upon themselves the pain of others. As Levinas understands it, such a human-divine figure would correspond to the human vocation, under the primacy of Otherness, yet an Otherness that is not purely human, because it implies at its core both messianic mediation and the divine.

Modern philosophy, in large part, still does not incorporate the interpersonal and inter-subjective movement of Otherness. As a paradigm, it sometimes recognizes the mediating role of Otherness in the formation of the self-consciousness of the subject. Yet, up to that point, it does not sufficiently take into account interpersonal Otherness. It equalizes all differences, not only between the one and the other, but also between the other and others, reducing them to pure negations (I–not I). It conceives of interpersonal Otherness merely as the abstract negation of the abstract identity of the I, in order to synthesize both in a dialectical identity.[166]

This moment is supplanted by a new turn: the turn from the moment of the subject to the moment of inter-subjectivity.[167] This turn is taken above all by Levinas, when he speaks of the humanism not of the I but of the other person. It is also taken by Ricoeur, who speaks of himself as the other. Habermas presents a new rationality—a communicative one. In the current Latin American philosophies and theologies, priority is given to the we over the I, with emphasis on the commitment of the community to the practice of justice. There is therefore a way, in the search for the Absolute with a face, that does not lead to a neutral Otherness but rather to the ethical and interpersonal Otherness of the Face of the Other (and of others)—as expounded especially by Levinas, for whom God left God's mark on that same face.[168] Nowadays there is an effort to discover in all these phenomena, and in the so-called saturated phenomenon of theophany,[169] the (explicit or implicit) religious relationship as an Otherness that establishes personal identity at a more radical level. Through these contemporary thinkers one can see the religious relationship as in some way interpersonal, not only in the prophetic religions, but even in those that do not explicitly recognize a personal God.

Ricoeur takes the opposite route, going from ontology to ethic and finding in consciousness not only self-identification but also an ethical

165. Levinas, *Autrement qu'être ou au-delà de l'essence*.

166. See Scannone, "Identidad personal, alteridad interpersonal y relación religiosa."

167. We believe that, although this is not exactly what Libânio identifies as the social model in *Formação da consciência crítica*, n. 6 [footnote 165], it is an approximation and gives a better account of what we want to say here.

168. See our affirmation above.

169. See Marion, *De surcroît*.

mandate[170] that can be interpreted both in the sense of an order (commandment) and in that of a sending or mission (the accomplishment of a call, and thus the achievement of self-fulfillment). In this way the passive moment of being-affected interprets itself as a situation of listening by one who finds himself or herself ethically questioned in the second person.[171]

For this French philosopher, such a commandment precedes the law—that is, prescription and prohibition—since it orders and solicits the living of a good life, in the Aristotelian sense of good living. According to him, this ethical option of a "a good life with and for others, in just institutions" structures the possibilities most appropriate to each individual, but adds to this first ontological moment the ethical relation of Otherness. Furthermore, for Ricoeur this ethical mandate becomes prohibition and interdiction only due to human violence, thus taking the form of a negative imperative: "thou shall not kill!"[172]

This mandate implies a relationship not only personal (since it is constitutive of the person), but above all interpersonal, as suggested by the metaphors of voice, call, and debt. Moreover it expresses itself and plays out in an absolute and unconditional way. Ricoeur recognizes and affirms the irreducible Otherness of the call of conscience. But he finally leaves open the issue of whether the other, the source of the mandate, is just the Face of the Other person—who can look at me and take care of me (as affirmed by Levinas); or whether it includes parental and ancestral figures with whom I identify myself—buried, forgotten, and possibly repressed in the superego (as Freud says); or the living and personal God of religion (as Saint Augustine or Newman would say); or whether it is simply the case of an empty place, prior to any other thing, a *tabula rasa*, where the subject will build his or her relational capability from its beginnings. In this hypothesis, being-affected under the modality of being ordered or sent is—philosophically—a condition for the possibility of identification, no matter what. I am who I am from the standpoint of the mandate I receive from the other. In sum, I am who I am from the standpoint of the other and not from my own.[173]

No longer in the realm of philosophy but rather in that of biblical faith, Ricoeur takes a new step toward a deeper understanding of ipseity.[174] He

---

170. He calls it "injonction." [Translator's note: in Portuguese and in French there is no distinction between the English words *consciousness* and *conscience*, both being translated as *consciência* in Portuguese and *conscience* in French.]

171. See Ricoeur, "De la morale à l'éthique et aux éthiques."

172. Ibid.

173. On this, see Scannone, "Identidad personal, alteridad interpersonal y relación religiosa."

174. See Ricoeur, "Le sujet convoqué."

discovers and interprets the *ipse* as a "called subject," or better said, as an "I-myself-sent" ("soi mandaté"), thanks to the election, vocation, and mission received from the God of Israel, and discerned—in the light of the biblical narratives of prophetic vocations—in the call of conscience.

For his part, Levinas does not hesitate to refer the ethical mandate above all to the interpersonal relationship with the other. According to him, the true I-myself of personal identity does not primarily decline itself in the nominative ("I think" [*Ego cogito*], "I act," "I work"), but rather in the accusative ("Here I am!")—"I" as the responsible answer before an ethical questioning by the Face of the Other.[175] Thus it is that authentic human subjectivity is not thought of from the standpoint of the sameness of the essence, nor from the standpoint of the modern subject as self-conscious center and source of his or her actions (thinking, acting, or doing). It is, rather, thought of intersubjectively and ethically from the standpoint of the other, and in radical passivity, which is to say, as an answer to the ethical call of the other, who takes all the initiative.[176]

For Levinas, Otherness is essentially constitutive of personal identity. He interprets it as interpersonal according to the ethical relationship that, although interrelational, does not mutually relativize persons but rather respects their unconditional character. For this reason he speaks of a "relationship without relationship" or "absolved from all relationship"—that is to say, from all relativization of myself and/or the other to mere moments of a totality (dialectical or not). Unconditional personal identity relates to the Unconditional, that is, to the Absolute.

Thus, the subject is thought of neither as a substratum nor as the center of his or her actions, but as ethically subject to others through his or her responsibility for them, up to expiation and substitution.[177] This constitutes the personal identity of I-myself when, paradoxically, it departs from itself and gives up its selfish spontaneity and egocentrism, in answer to the ethical mandate that attributes it to the other. Here resides that which makes a person unique and irreplaceable in his or her ipseity, and—in this sense—personally identifies him or her. For no one other than this person, and only this person, can answer this call, this commandment, and this mission pertaining to each of the others, in a concrete face-to-face relation that here and now critically questions him or her.[178]

---

175. See Levinas, *Totalité et infini*; See also *Autrement qu'être ou au-delà de l'essence*.

176. All the works of Levinas repeatedly affirms this.

177. See Levinas, *Autrement qu'être ou au-delà de l'essence*.

178. Levinas uses the strong term "hostage" to define the situation of the I in relation to the other.

For Levinas this radical exit from oneself should come about without any recovery or return. For this reason it does not de-identify, but, on the contrary, constitutes the authentic subjective ipseity and identity. This is because the mandate from the other "does not limit my freedom, but rather engenders my goodness." In other words, it liberates me, in that most intimate and personal I-myself, from all self-complacency and narcissism, by arousing a gracious goodness toward others.

Ricoeur disagrees with the position of Levinas, which, he claims, reduces the Otherness of conscience to the Otherness of others. On the other hand, Ricoeur himself—while recognizing that others are the obligatory route to the experience of being-sent ethically—nevertheless affirms that this experience presumes, ontologically, an attestation of itself as self-love. This could be another way of saying, without Levinasian radicality, that exiting from one's self constitutes and presumes the I-myself. Going beyond Levinas, Ricoeur would add that it also presumes a non-egocentric self-regard. Fundamentally, it would be the commandment to "love thy neighbor as thyself."

But Levinas does not dwell only on the human other. In the ethically summoned face one discovers the mark of the infinite, also found in the disinterested response, "Here I am!" that is responsibly attentive to the other. For Levinas, what takes place there is not only the mark but also the witness and glory of the Infinite. For the attribution to the other, and the personalized election of the I-myself as called and mandated to be responsible for the other and others, are immemorial, original, and previous to any freely assumed commitment. They refer to the Infinite as metaphysically anterior to finite beings and to their conscience and freedom.[179]

However, just as Ricoeur leaves open the final interpretation of the Otherness of the conscience, Levinas also affirms the ambiguity of these marks, which may or may not be religiously interpreted. For him God cannot be shown or demonstrated as if God were an object or the conclusion of a syllogism. As a man of faith he preserves God's intangible Sanctity, calling it *illeité*.[180] According to him, there is neither demonstration nor proof of God, but only ethical witnessing in responsibility for others.

It would be pertinent to add that although the witnessing and marks mentioned above do not rationally demonstrate the existence of God, they nonetheless provide that it would not be absurd and may even be reasonable to believe. In other words, they admit interpretation in a religious key. That being the case, the personal identification of each I-myself (*ipse*) that comes about through the responsible answer to the original call of the others (and,

---

179. See Scannone, "Identidad personal, alteridad interpersonal y relación religiosa."
180. See Levinas, *De Dieu qui vient a l'idée*.

with them, from the voice of conscience itself) would not only be necessarily constituted by interpersonal Otherness in the face-to-face with other people. It would also be constituted, in the ultimate instance, by interpersonal Otherness with the living God, in whom it is reasonable to believe.[181]

Scannone—whose thinking we have been following here—taking a coherently Levinasian line but going further than Levinas himself, adds that only a personal Absolute justifies the ethical mandate while unconditionally questioning the free person. If that is the case, the religious relationship solicits, touches, and engenders that which is most personal and personifying in each I-myself (*ipse*) of each person.

The same line is followed by Jean-Luc Marion, who radicalizes this proposal.[182] Based on the understanding of the phenomenon as given to human experience and of a phenomenology of the gift, Marion conceives the I above all as receiver and witness of such a gift. In other words, the I is affected by it, because the initiative and the possession of priority belong to the gift of the phenomenon. The I does not decline itself in the nominative—*Ego cogito*, as in Descartes—nor even in the accusative—as in Levinas—but in the dative of one who receives and receives oneself.[183] Theology, faced with philosophical reflection, allows itself to say that we would find here the philosophical ground of the New Testament's affirmation that "we love because God first loved us."[184]

Thus the personal identity of each person is conceived neither as that of a substratum or a center of actions, nor as the subjective self-conscious act of thinking, but as pertaining to that which Marion calls *adonné*, which is at once the receiver and the giver of the gift.[185] It receives itself with that which gives, due to the very fact of the gift. Marion compares this gesture with a screen (*écran*) that is needed if the light that illuminates it is to manifest itself. Thus the gift of the phenomenon becomes manifestation and intuition without giving priority to the subject, which in truth is the receiver-giver (or, as Scannone says, the co-given).[186]

Although this can happen in any experience, for Marion it happens above all in the phenomena he calls saturated, that is to say, saturated with intuition because they are as much so as a gift. Marion lists among them, besides the body itself, the flesh of the subject, the historical event, the work

181. Ibid.
182. See Marion, *Étant donné*. See also Marion, "Métaphysique et Phénoménologie."
183. See ibid. and *De surcroît*.
184. 1 John 4:19.
185. See Marion, *De surcroît*.
186. See Scannone, "Identidad personal, alteridad interpersonal y relación religiosa."

of art, the Face of the Other, and above all the phenomenon of revelation or theophanies. He shows phenomenologically that in all these cases intuition (and therefore the gift) exceeds and surpasses subjective intention. Such phenomena not only remove the focus from the subject, but also surpass their previous horizon of understanding, as well as all *a priori* and all concepts that try to enclose and circumscribe them. From here—as Ricoeur says about the symbol—they always "make one think" without exhausting oneself in concepts. For in these "saturated" phenomena, coming from an irreducible Otherness, an unexpected novelty happens, thanks to an incalculable or nondeductible graciousness. For Marion, the religious phenomenon of revelation or theophany—and we would add, of the mystical experience—condenses and exceeds, in itself, the property of all the other saturated phenomena.

For this reason Marion applies the metaphor of the call that, preceding any response, is never totally the same. Yet the human being can begin to fulfill it, and thus go on to fulfill himself or herself as a person, even if not yet completely. However, for Marion the call is anonymous, since it calls *to*, giving a proper and personal name *to* the one who is called, without however identifying the one who calls. The response is the same one that, recognizing the call with its "Here I am," gives it a name, and in so doing interprets it, acknowledging it: "There you are!"

In the case of theophany, faith dares to name it "God" or possibly "holy Mystery."[187] No matter what, the receiver-giver or co-given continues to be fully himself or herself, and to personify himself or herself in a free response to the call that precedes it and echoes in it. The response is not only to the clamor of his or her conscience and to the questioning of the other about redemptive responsibility, but—in the religious phenomenon that surpasses all the other saturated phenomena—it is above all to the election, vocation, and mission that he or she receives (and believes himself or herself to receive) personally, in the name of the superabundant gift that occurs in the religious and mystical fact.

All this, formulated by philosophical thought, is recognized and named in the prophetic religions as the revelation and self-communication of a personal God, conceived inclusively as Mystery. However, one must admit that this is so not only in the prophetic religions but also in polytheism and in other traditions, which—out of respect for the Mystery itself—do not conceive of it as personal, although behaving as if it were. In this case it is a question of naming and language, that is, of discerning the extent to which we can name the holy Mystery with human language without falling into

187. See Rahner, *Foundations of Christian Faith*.

idolatrous anthropomorphisms.[188] Yet, as far as we can see, interpersonal Otherness is constitutive of human or personal identity. And the religious relationship—once made explicit—does not alienate the human being, but, because of the unconditional Otherness that is its undeniable premise, personifies him or her.[189]

This is even more so in the case of radical dispossession and self-delivery, without return, to the holy Mystery—whom we call God.[190] What takes place here, more than anything else, identifies the human person and makes that person who he or she is, since union and distinction mutually fertilize each other and proliferate in fruits that nourish them in reciprocity and solidarity. We believe that the faceless Absolutes of postmodernity could hardly show the human being a way similar to the one we have described above. Any redemption of Transcendence nowadays will be obliged to take into account this journey as an integral part of the experience.

The Primacy of Experience and the Crisis of Institutions and Dogmas

Until the Second Vatican Council, there was a suspicion in theology regarding experience. Rationality superimposed itself, and experience remained under suspicion of a lack of rigor and method.[191] The philosophy of the time contributed to this state of suspicion.

In the nineteenth century, Schleiermacher interpreted religion as pure intuition and feeling, separating it from dogma. He held that the highest experience of religion was found in the feeling of union with the infinite. Defining religion as the feeling of absolute dependence, he considered Christianity simply as the highest expression this feeling had adopted.[192]

At the end of the nineteenth century and the beginning of the twentieth, other factors strengthened the Catholic fears about the terminology of experience. Some modernists overemphasized the place of individual religious experience and minimized the value of common affirmations of faith in Christian life. Similar anti-dogmatic tension comes up in the work of William James, *The Varieties of Religious Experience*.[193]

188. See Scannone, "Do símbolo à prática da anologia."
189. Scannone, "Identidad personal, alteridad personal y relación religiosa."
190. Rahner, "The Need for a 'Short Formula' of Christian Faith."
191. Much of our elaboration here is indebted to the excellent article by O'Collins, "Experience."
192. See Schleiermacher (1768–1834).
193. See James, *The Varieties of Religious Experience*.

Eventually a more positive vision of experience began to take hold and to affect Catholic theology little by little. Authors such as Newman (in *Apologia pro Vita Sua*), Kierkegaard, Dilthey, Husserl, Blondel, Max Scheler, Jaspers, Marcel, Heidegger, Merleau-Ponty, and Gadamer also helped promote the theme of experience within the area of theology that reflects on Revelation and the faith, that is, on the foundations of knowledge of this faith. The same thing happened with the debate regarding understanding and interpretation fomented by the existential hermeneutics of Bultmann.[194]

There were other influences as well, such as the work of Otto[195] on the place and importance of the numinous (the fascinating and tremendous Mystery) in religious consciousness, the increasing dialogue with other religions, the ever-growing opening to the psychology of religion, the impact of sociology, and in general the omnipresent influence of the experimental sciences. These influences produced great changes in Catholic reflection on the human experience of God.

Sometimes the religious dialogue with other Christian communities and traditions brought about the re-emergence of the same question. The same is true of the biblical and liturgical movements inside Catholicism itself. It was difficult to speak of a divine pedagogy in the Old Testament, of the apostolic witnessing of Christ (1 John 1:1–3), or of liturgy as a theological source, without moving, or having to be moved, to the realm properly called experience.

Researchers and thinkers such as Mouroux, Bouillard, Congar, and above all Rahner[196] developed this theme even before the Second Vatican Council, in sixteen documents. Among them, the constitution *Dei Verbum*—concerning the problem of Revelation and its sources—speaks of Israel and its experience with God's ways (no. 14), and of the several causes of development in the post-apostolic traditions, one of them being the "intimate meaning of the spiritual realities" that believers "experience" (DV 8). The language of experience naturally reappeared in this very important document of the Council, which deals with divine self-communication (DV 6) in the history of salvation (DV 3, 4, 14, 15, 17) and invites human beings to freely entrust their whole persons to God (DV 5).

Nowadays the persistent fear that in some way experience and reason, or ecclesiastic experience and authority, are opposites and may even mutually exclude each other, appears to have practically disappeared. In his teachings,

---

194. See O'Collins, "Experience."

195. See Otto, *Lo Santo*, 19–21.

196. Cf., for example, Mouroux, *L'expérience chrétienne*; Bouillard, *Révélation de Dieu et langage des hommes*; Congar, *Les voies du Dieu vivant*; Rahner, *Ecrits de théologie*.

John Paul II often employed the language of experience. His second encyclical (*Dives in Misericordia* [1980]) uses the word thirteen times in reference to religious experience, in both its communal and its individual aspects.

If the audience of theology is made up of non-abstract human beings in their concrete historicity, then it is certainly fitting to speak of experience and to ask ourselves where and how we experience the Mystery of God. How do we know that we are experiencing God, and correctly interpreting this experience? What in our human experience gives credibility to that experience and to the message we receive and claim is contained in the Bible, the book of God's people?

This message derives, in the first place, from the experience of God as lived out by the people of God, by the prophets and other personages in the revealed history of the Old Testament. For its part theology studies the foundational revelation conveyed through the unique experience of God by Jesus of Nazareth, through the experience of His disciples, and through the experience of the apostolic church as it carried out its mission under the power of the Holy Spirit.[197]

The post-apostolic tradition can be considered the collective memory of those privileged experiences that constituted the foundational relationship that reached its definite and unsurpassable zenith in Jesus Christ and the coming of the Holy Spirit. Tradition, in all its written and non-written forms, means the transmission from one generation to another of the collective, and specifically Christian, experience of God in Jesus Christ.[198]

Since the theme of experience constantly touches the central points of the revelation of God in Jesus Christ and of God's credibility and communication, theology must carefully analyze what is presumed by the human and religious experiences. And in its reflection and analysis, it will necessarily arrive at the conclusion that not every human or even religious experience can be called an experience of faith or an experience of God.

Only some human experiences are explicitly and consciously experiences of the Sacred (or religious experiences) or, still more rarely, experiences of Meaning (or experiences of God). They presume and thus imply situations where we feel the revealing and salvific self-communication of God inviting us to renew a commitment to faith,[199] resulting directly in the assumption of a life-transforming commitment.

---

197. See Libânio, *Teologia da revelação*; and from the same author, *Eu creio, nós cremos*.

198. Ibid. See also Queiruga, *A revelação de Deus na realização humana*.

199. See Vaz, "A experiência de Deus," 34ff.

There is a special language that is frequently used to describe the explicitly religious experience, or, even more, the experience of God, such as mountaintop experiences, limit situations, limit experiences, cutting-edge experiences, and in-depth experiences. These deeply felt experiences can be identified, as well, in the movement from death to life, from the absurd to the meaningful, and from hate or loneliness to love and community. In Christian terms, such an interpretation recognizes a Trinitarian aspect in all religious experiences, since they lead us to the fullness of life (the Father), to the ultimate meaning and truth (the *Logos*), and to the fullness of Love (the Holy Spirit).

In the end, experience did not turn out to be the only way to develop a theology. It is true, however, that a clear and careful analysis of religious experiences can serve as a fertile approach to this endeavor. Today, besides reflecting on the concept, theologians are called to establish criteria for interpreting and evaluating religious experiences.

Father Henrique de Lima Vaz, in his memorable text "A experiência de Deus" (1974),[200] conceives of the experience of God as one of plenitude or of radical meaning, but distinguishes it from religious experience, which would be an experience of the Sacred. The experience of God would thus be a totalizing experience, that is, one that would not confine itself to only one dimension of existence but would inundate the totality of the human life.

According to Vaz, the Christian experience of God has to do with the presence of Radical Meaning in a particular and historical existence, that of Jesus of Nazareth, which is expressed in a conditional and historical word: the word *Revelation*. The word of God accompanies God's people, leading them toward the realization of the promise, developing a logic appropriate to the experience of faith that it engenders in the history of this same people. In this sense the Incarnation of God in Jesus Christ, the culmination of this dynamic, will be the full manifestation of Radical Meaning, not only through a reality and its expression, but entirely identified with it.

It is in the vulnerable and mortal flesh of Jesus of Nazareth, and in His Spirit that blows wherever he wants and pitches his tent in human flesh, that the experience of the unseen God will take place. And it is here that the logic of the Mystery, the logic of the ineffable,[201] will finally be inaugurated. This logic is a way to relationship with the other—who, in the case of religious experience, is God—as the constitutive element of the mystical experience. In the case of Christian mysticism, there is an anthropological component at the center of the identity of this other, this Otherness, since the experi-

---

200. Ibid.
201. See Pastor, *A lógica do inefável*.

enced God became flesh and showed a human face. Therefore nothing that the mystical experience reveals can deviate, abstract, or even distract from that which constitutes the humanity of the human being. Paradoxically, it is in the deepest similarity with the human that the God of the Christian revelation shows God's difference and absolutely transcendent Otherness.

Even more than in other times, Christian mysticism nowadays is challenged to rediscover its place and its ways, and to see the human being as the necessary way to the divine. It must ask itself: what are the ways that will show us the differences that are emerging today with vigorous questioning, when speaking of the human? And more: how can these ways lead to the fulfilling experience of union with God or to the knowledge of God through experience? What human desires are the basis for the experience of God?

Relationships between faith and the world of desires are intimate. Intimate, yet complex and often incomprehensible. Many are the ways faith can take in this world, at times through a genuine labyrinth, with the risk of going the wrong way. It is easy to go astray, and sometimes fatal. We all remember situations in which beliefs led to all kinds of alienation, and even destruction.[202]

Nevertheless, faith is capable of generating attitudes, behaviors, and life choices of a nobility and quality seldom offered by other dimensions of human existence. It is enough to remember Francisco Xavier, who died at forty-six years of age at the gates of China, where he went alone, moved only by the desire to bring the gospel to a continent that still knew nothing about it. Teresa of Avila and other mystics experienced ecstasies of such height and profundity that they wanted to die just to be with the One who brought such joy and delight to their bodies and hearts. The memories of the martyrs of yesterday and today are full of stories of Christians who would rather be thrown into the jaws of the lion or into the fury of bullets than deny their faith. Likewise, faith can bring self-denial to ferocious levels, as in the case of Saint Jerome, who crawled naked on thorns, and of Saint John Berchmans, who chastised himself until his body bled. In human history there are few areas where passion, fervor, and desire appear with such intensity as in the life of faith. It is desire, in its multiple derivations, that constitutes the basic energy through which faith authentically moves mountains.[203]

Desire, in a certain way, is the maternal procreator of faith. It welcomes human beings upon their arrival into existence and forms their first relationship with life and the world. What happens at the anthropological level also happens at the level of the experience of faith. To believe means

---

202. The reflections following the events of September 11, 2001, confirm this point.
203. See Domínguez Morano, *Crer depois de Freud*; *Orar depois de Freud*.

to possess a basic trust in life. It means to count on a conviction that is secure, although not demonstrable, that—although at times difficult to understand—life and the world do have a meaning, a logic, and a purpose.

> In consolation or desolation, in anger or ecstasy, to believe means to feel anchored, desired, and loved. Therefore, whoever believes knows that he or she can ask because he or she will receive, search because he or she will find, and knock because the door will be opened. Whoever believes knows that even when we are persecuted we do not despair; that we are pursued, but not abandoned. By faith we feel safe. We are convinced that no matter what may happen, in the end we will not sink into a bottomless well, but rather will be supported and protected.[204]

There is Someone, an other, with whom we neither merge nor confuse ourselves, and with whom dialogue and conversation can occur in any situation. Through the desire that leads us to this Primordial Otherness, we recognize the mysterious presence of God and hear God's word. However, as the great spiritual masters convincingly show, this does not imply an easy way, and one must pass through dark nights, long silences, etc.[205]

Desire can take shape in our personal history in many forms and hues, such as the desire to consume, to possess, to enjoy sexual pleasure, to know, to create, to fight, or to serve—until death. Religion has often brought misguidance to the intense impulse of human desire. Mystical experience, grounded in a faith in the other who is not I—the absolute Freedom that comes to meet my conditional freedom—teaches how to regulate desire and to discern impulses. In other words, it teaches how to organize and center existence on a fundamental axis of life rather than death.[206]

In any case, it is in our own profoundest depths—where the most authentic passion for the Absolute pulsates—that the voice of God makes itself heard over human life, expressing God's desire, which is both sovereign and loving. The God of Revelation is undoubtedly a desirous and passionate God. This is not a God who shows God's self as the unapproachable Absolute, but rather one who incessantly and passionately searches for the human being—God's most loved creature—desiring to be given to him or her for encounter and union.

204. Ibid.

205. See the dark night, so well conceptualized by Saint John of the Cross. More recently, public opinion was shaken by the book of Mother Teresa of Calcutta's letters, in which she confesses, to her spiritual counselor, to passing through total darkness in her spiritual life, even to the point of doubting the existence of God. See Teresa, *Come Be My Light: The Private Writings of the "Saint of Calcutta"*.

206. St. John of the Cross. See Morano, *Crer depois de Freud*; *Orar depois de Freud*.

When this divine Desire finds the answer of faith, which works through Love, the mystical experience comes about, created from *pathos*—passion and profound pleasure, fulfillment and oblation, which is what makes the Revelation credible and worthy of faith, because it is incarnate in concrete persons. That was what happened with those who lived with Jesus of Nazareth. They were seduced by his person and by the message of his singular relationship with the God whom he called Abba-Father. It is what happens with the witnesses of yesterday and today, who are—according to Pope Paul VI in the apostolic exhortation *Evangelii Nuntiandi*—the only masters to whom our contemporaries listen without skepticism or cynicism.[207]

The Christian faith has been since its beginnings a faith in the witness of others. The disciples believed in Jesus, whom they recognized and proclaimed as a Faithful Witness.[208] The women believed that the tomb was not the place for one who was alive, and bore witness to that. The apostles—after some reluctance—believed the women. Thus began the journey of this proposal of life which proceeded to conquer the known world of those times simply by the strength of the word of several frail human beings who said: "This is true because I saw it, I experienced it. I gave testimony, and for it I am willing to die."[209]

Therefore the Christian faith, since its beginnings, has been a faith of witnesses and not so much of texts. The metalanguage that is theology, added to the language of faith, also makes truer and more verifiable the affirmation that what is needed is a theology not of texts but of witnesses.[210] In light of the witnessing of men and women who were reached by God in the midst of history, the difference between faith and religion, between faith and institution, becomes more evident. It becomes even clearer what constitutes the deepest identity of all of us, the men and women of faith who are called to be, and help others to be, in this confused and diffuse

---

207. "And before anything else, not wanting to repeat all that has already been recorded previously, it is appropriate to emphasize the following: for the Church, the witness of an authentically Christian life, delivered into the hands of God, in a communion which nothing must interrupt, and dedicated to the neighbor with a limitless zeal, is the first means of evangelism. . . . Thus it will be, through her behavior, through her life, that the Church must, more than anything else, evangelize this world; that is, through her witness lived out with fidelity to the Lord Jesus, a witness of poverty, of disinterestedness, and of freedom before the powers of this world; in a word, a witness of holiness" (*EN* 41).

208. Rev 1:5, 3:14.

209. See González Faus, *Calidad cristiana*, 85–103: "Antropología cristiana y martirio."

210. This expression is found in the most recent works of theologians such as Metz and Sobrino.

contemporaneity in which we live. It is they who show us that Christian faith still has a role to play today, provided it doesn't lose its identity in the current nebulous times. Yet there are some new and little known profiles among these witnesses that may be propitious for experiencing the God of the Judeo-Christian revelation, who spoke God's name in the history of the people of Israel and of Jesus of Nazareth.

3

Religious or Mystical Experience

A New Moment, a New Configuration, New Challenges

IN THE PREVIOUS ANALYSIS we established that at this moment experience returns with unusual strength when one wants not only to think about reality, but also to envisage religion inside this same reality. In this chapter we will focus on the category of experience. We will begin by defining the concept at several levels, seeking above all to place it in the areas of philosophy and theology—the areas within which we are working. To that end we will refer to several basic sources such as dictionaries and encyclopedias for different definitions of experience, and apply them to the particularities of our reflection.

Next, we will try to see how experience, in the context we live in, is often superimposed on and confounded with several interpretations. We will examine these different interpretations in an effort to establish human experience as a category that will allow us to enter into a deeper reflection on religion and theology.

In this chapter, which is the heart of this book, we will single out and demarcate the religious experience, the mystical experience, the experience of God, and the Christian experience of God. That done, we will consider the importance of the narrative of the experience of God today in making possible a true access to the Mystery of God, which is sometimes barely perceptible in the current unstable context.

Experiencing Everything: The Tyranny of the Provisional

Our era is marked by a loss of the value and the meaning of various words. Among them, one of the most salient is the word *experience*. It has become vulgarized to the point of losing its original meaning.

It is therefore necessary to revisit some sources that will allow us to identify its precise etymological origin. In doing this, we come across the complexity of the term. There are several definitions of experience, from the colloquial (an act of experience; something that is lived out or lived through), to an acquired professional, athletic, or artistic capability (a specific type of knowledge or expertise that is acquired through systematic learning and improves over time; a practice), to wisdom brought about by maturity and many years of life, or by the exact sciences (empiricism, scientifically controlled experiment), and to philosophy (knowledge obtained through the senses; knowledge that is all-encompassing and not organized; or wisdom spontaneously acquired throughout life; an attempt, effort, or test).[1]

The term in fact has a double etymology. The Latin word *experientia*, from which the word *experience* is derived, comes from the original Greek term *empeirismos*. But it derives, as well, from a more specific use of the word *empirical* as related to sciences such as medicine, whose capability comes from practical experience rather than theoretical instruction.[2]

The *Encyclopaedia Universalis* indicates three areas that intersect with conceptual notions of experience: the philosophy of spirit, the philosophy of knowledge, and the philosophy of science.[3] Thus, mental pursuits are called experience. As in the case of sensations, these seem to indicate an immediate relation of the spirit with a datum, and their content is intrinsically subjective and qualitative. For the theory of knowledge, experience would

---

1. See *Dicionário Houaiss*, digital version, 2007, entry "experiência." [Translator's note: in Portuguese, the word *experimentar* ("to experiment") carries connotations closer to the word *experience* than does the equivalent word in English.]

2. The Online Etymological Dictionary (http://www.etymonline.com/index.php?search=experience&searchmode=nl) gives us, for example, the following information: experience 1377, from O. Fr. experience, from L. experientia "knowledge gained by repeated trials," from experientem (nom. experiens), prp. of experiri "to try, test," from ex- "out of " + peritus "experienced, tested." The v. (1533) first meant "to test, try"; sense of "feel, undergo" first recorded in 1588; empirical 1569, from L. empiricus, from Gk. empeirikos "experienced," from empeiria "experience," from empeiros "skilled," from en- "in" + peira "trial, experiment." Originally a school of ancient physicians who based their practice on experience rather than theory; expert (adj.) c. 1374, from L. expertus, of experiri "to try, test" (see experience). The sense of "person wise through experience" existed 15c., reappeared 1825. Expertise (1868) is from Fr. expertise "expert appraisal, expert's report." And the Centre National de Resources Textuelles et Lexicales (http://www.cnrtl.fr/etymologie/experience) defines expérience, subst, fem. Étymol. et Hist. Ca 1265 "connaissance acquise par la pratique" (Brunet Latin, Trésor, éd. Carmody, II, XXXI, 24: longue experience); 2. 1663 "fait de provoquer une observation dans l'intention d'étudier certains phénomènes" (Pascal, *Traité de la pesanteur de la masse de l'air*, ds Oeuvres complètes, éd. L. Lafuma, 245). Empr. au lat. class. experientia "essai, épreuve, tentative."

3. See Engel, "Expérience," *Encyclopaedia Universalis*, numerical version, 2009.

not only be all immediate—as opposed to inferred—knowledge, but also mediated knowledge, that which is inferred or induced from sensorial data, learned rather than innate or inspired. The writer identifies here four characteristics of experience. In the first place they are immediate, that is, they occur directly in human subjectivity. In the second place, phenomenologically, their contents are intrinsically qualitative. Third, they are private and nontransferable. And fourth, conscious experiences are, in a certain sense, infallible. The subject may forget, or not clearly remember, the content or the circumstances, etc., but will always attest, with complete certainty, that the experience happened to him or her.

In the *Dicionário básico de filosofia*,[4] we find the following definitions of experience:

> Experience. We distinguish in the word "experience" a general meaning (experience) and a technical meaning, approximating experimentation (experiment). [See n. 1, translator's note]
>
> 1. In its general meaning, experience is a spontaneous or lived-out knowledge acquired by the individual throughout life. It appears in relation to ongoing life (we say: "a person of experience"), or in relation to the theory of knowledge. For empiricism, all knowledge derives from experience. For rationalism, on the contrary, experience teaches us nothing. It is itself what has to be explained, as there is no experience that is not impregnated with theory.
>
> 2. In its technical meaning, experience is the act of observing or experimenting, with the object of forming or checking a hypothesis. Thus, experience (in the sense of *experiment*) is the act of provoking, on the basis of well-determined conditions, an observation that may result in knowledge about the nature of the phenomenon under study.
>
> 3. Concepts: "Experience is a principle, which instructs me in the several conjunctions of objects in the past" (Hume). "No a priori knowledge is possible for us, except that of possible objects of experience"; "Experience is empirical knowledge, that is, knowledge that determines objects through perceptions" (Kant).

All these definitions help us understand more deeply the complexity of the topic we are considering. Nevertheless, we must later enter into an area that is not deeply contemplated by any of these definitions. It is the area of

---

4. See Japiassú and Marcondes, *Dicionário básico de filosofia*.

mysticism, of the experience of God and the Absolute, which is studied and reflected upon by philosophy and, above all, by theology.

Now, however, we will concentrate on perceiving our era as a historical moment in which experience has returned with vigor to the forefront and to the heart of knowledge and debate. While reason was sovereign during the past four centuries—when nothing could be considered true without its blessing—apparently now the parameters have been altered. This was especially so in the last four decades, after May 1968, when the sexual revolution became official and it was important to "make love, not war."[5] The hippie movement, and all the other libertarian movements that were in the vanguard of these events, would say, "It is necessary to try everything. And it is not obligatory to decide on anything."[6]

Since then we have perceived a development in this situation, in which the thirst for new and diverse experiences increases as the limits to continuous and unruly experimentation disappear. Try everything and choose nothing seems to be the law that governs this moment. In consequence, the bitter fruits that we taste are: the volatility of commitments in general, whether professional, amorous, religious, or of any other domain; consumerism on a geometrically increasing scale that becomes an end in itself; the ever shorter horizon of areas of experimentation and the atrophy of the goals that guide such experimentation.

Ours is a culture of constant harassment. Not only sexual harassment—which can bring financial reward and prestige if the legal process is "well managed." We are speaking of harassment in all sectors of life. At the same time that privacy is glorified, it has become a rare article at the level of personal existence. Harassment, in this case, enters the most private corners in the home without permission and without ceremony. There is harassment through commercial products, through ideas, through the senses, through proposals and through religion. Such harassment corrupts and imprisons the senses, which are the channels through which experience could really take place and lead us toward a more fulfilling life.

González Buelta affirms that "we constantly receive proposals that arrive at our senses through publicity, or simply through the exposition to us of the consumer society as it moves through our streets."[7] And he continues: "It is a culture of persecution. We are subjected to the 'tyranny of innumer-

---

5. We are referring to a mid-1960s slogan featured in a song by John Lennon and used by the thousands of protesters who rallied against the involvement of the United States in the Vietnam War. With this movement, "sexual permissiveness" reached its height in what was until then a predominantly puritanical country.

6. See on this point the fine analysis by González Buelta, *Caminar sobre las águas*.

7. Ibid., 50.

able possibilities.'" At all hours of the day, and in almost all spaces, "through cellular phones, the telephone, the Internet, the newspapers, the mailbox . . . we are receiving offers: insurance companies, alternative remedies that are only sold 'online,' vacations with tempting discounts."[8]

Besides the seductive intoxication that this harassment sends out to people, there is the problem that everything is offered while all doors are simultaneously open. One cannot choose, but one must rather accumulate one thing after another, this and also that. One must consume as much as possible, for as long as possible. Step by step, more and more. One does not make a choice, and leave aside other options. On the contrary, one hopes to succeed in acquiescing, in trying out and consuming all that exists in the world in the shortest time possible, in order to continue consuming and to enlarge one's own consumerist capacity—and to atrophy one's own capacity to decide.

This is true about experimenting with *things*. It would not be so serious if it did not apply equally to *persons*. In the area of affection, one finds ever more experimentation without commitment—involving oneself and another in an adventure completely lacking in responsibility. It is an experiment to see if it works. If it doesn't, something else will be tried. Commitment becomes tiresome after awhile, provoking the feeling that it is no longer possible to continue. We each go our own way, experimenting with things that are newer and therefore more enjoyable—and when we tire of this one, we try another. And another, and another. We leave behind the wreckage of ruined affections, of lacerated psyches, and of mortally wounded emotions. And traumatized children who seek to find compensation in drugs for the disruptions they had to confront before they were mature enough. And depression, emptiness, and suicide.

The etymology of the word *decision* shows us what is hidden in its radicality and profundity. Decision comes from the Latin *decidere*, which carries at its core the difficult and sometimes painful, but necessary, meaning of cutting, splitting, segmenting. Deciding in favor of one thing, therefore, means cutting off the other. Deciding in favor of one person means to save oneself for that person, since the others cease to be an option no matter how attractive they may be. But the culture of harassment does not allow such a thing. Relationships, work, places, and attributes—everything seems to have an expiration date. The machine of consumption must continue turning rapidly in order not to lose its balance.[9]

---

8. Ibid.

9. Father Fernando Bastos d'Avila compared the consumer society to a bicycle that, in order to balance, must maintain or increase its speed. Decreasing its speed will destabilize it, and stopping will cause it to fall.

All this has a deep impact on the identity of the human being, who is aware of not knowing who he or she is, of existing only in relation to a perpetual thirst for new objects to consume. The human being discovers that his or her most intimate identity is that of someone weary of so much information, of so many proposals and different possibilities for organizing his or her life in real or virtual relationships. When perceiving a new situation, the human being encounters an infinity of possible answers that are already registered inside himself or herself, and cannot decide permanently and consistently on any of them.[10]

Indeed, experimenting with everything, yielding to the harassment of the culture that has settled in our Western societies, entails the risk of finding oneself with a nebulous identity, without effective and firm ties, without solid references, without alternative attributes and choices, and without the capacity to make decisions regarding one's own life. It means being carried along in life by several currents that surge in various directions: currents of fashion, of publicity, of trends, and of aesthetic patterns.[11] But also by currents that are internal and "underground, that have been taking shape inside us, and that, when rising to the surface, can no longer be contained. We end up as slaves and not as the owners of our lives. The autonomy that we desired so much has dissipated, crushed by a culture which no longer allows or permits us to be ourselves."[12] And what is worse, it makes us lose sight of the meaning of life. As Lipovetsky says, if on the one hand the sovereignty of the individual increases, on the other hand this individual more and more loses the ownership of himself or herself, thus becoming incapable of self-control and of the possession of his or her own identity.[13]

In this game what is at play is the totality of human life, not only the important choices. The quality of everyday existence can be devalued without the person being aware of it, due to the emotional, affective, and cultural dynamics that have been taking up his or her internal space and have finally occupied it fully, after expelling the I to an unknown and nameless exile.[14]

In truth, the desire to experiment is natural and innate in the human being. But today it is stimulated in exponential proportions and endlessly provoked by the culture in which we live. The result is that this culture,

10. See on this point, see Gergen, *O eu saturado*, esp. 79–121.

11. Cf., as an example on the issue of fashion, Lipovetsky, *The Empire of Fashion*; on the currents that dictate the standards of beauty, see Novaes, *O intolerável peso da feiura*.

12. See González Buelta, *Caminar sobre las aguas*.

13. See Lipovetsky, *O futuro da autonomia*, 64. See also, from the same author, *L'ere du vide*.

14. See González Buelta, *Caminar sobre las aguas*.

with so much undefined and infinite desire, with neither restraint nor criteria for discernment, has become frigid and sterile. And, of course, sterilizing as well.

Those who reflect on the quality of human life often refer to the consumerist society as a beast that devours everything with its insatiable appetite. But the enormous losses that this society, thus structured, brings to humanity are not always denounced in the same way or with the same intensity.

Consumerist madness has as its counterpart an immense loss that makes obsolescent everything vital and new, including the senses and desire.[15] In this process an asceticism is brought forward that takes a direction opposite to that of the classical asceticism of the religious traditions. It is a case of a discipline that seems highly responsible for something that runs the risk of taking shape as the death of desire and vitality.

According to Heisig, the asceticism of contemporary life is a caricature of the most rigid classical religious asceticism. Its practice is in large part inconsistent, which makes it even more dangerous.[16] The intensity of the isolation, the mortification of the appetites, and the frigidity of the senses required of those who choose to live in the center of the civilized world, are better measured by the amount of torpor induced by these things than by any afflictive austerity destined to maintain the physical body in a state of vigilance and alertness. Far from the ideal of the discipline of the sacraments, the asceticism of everyday life is nothing more than routine, an external sign of an internal aridity.[17]

The symptoms of this situation can be identified as the deterioration of dialogue between persons, since its form and content are apprehended unilaterally by the market media, which metabolizes them into uncontrolled syntheses; the repression and debilitation of the learning of love by objective norms which prevent a true and mature education of the senses; the increasing unwholesomeness of nutrition, sterilizing the sense of taste for the majority; a life that is intramural, sedentary and confined, in environments that are artificially cooled or heated and deprived of contact with nature, thus weakening the olfactory sense and its capacity to pick up simple and natural aromas, and dampening the ability of the body to vibrate with the rhythm of seasonal change.[18] Furthermore, since music and song are identified with the mechanical equipment marketed to reproduce them, the pleasure of live

---

15. See on this point Cavanaugh, *Être consommé*, esp. 148–54.
16. See Heisig, "The Recovery of the Senses: Against the Asceticisms of the Age."
17. Ibid., 224.
18. Ibid.

performances becomes a luxury entrusted to the care of professionals, to be enjoyed only by the minority who can pay the very high price of the shows.[19]

Human touch comes in contact only with artificial things such as fabrics and materials of all kinds, desensitizing its capacity to identify natural surfaces and textures. Even the human body—and especially the feminine body—is no longer authentically natural, due to prostheses, silicone, and other grafts to which women subject themselves in the name of an aesthetic that is imposed upon them.[20] Thus, when a man touches the body of his beloved, he encounters not only flesh, but silicone, metal, or some hidden graft that disguises the real physical person he desires to be close to for mutual pleasure and true joy.

Machines that save time and amplify the capacity of bodily limbs and organs also cut off the basic rudiments of Grace and the rhythm of work, and—besides reducing the number of jobs available for those who depend on them—redefine work as a repetition that impedes thought and automatizes the body.[21] The identification of work with wages results in the loss of the most basic gratifications of productive and creative labor. Oppressed by the need to provide the basic needs of life for themselves and their families, human beings do not manage to think or create. Transformed into machines, their bodies experience other forms of reification as objects of specialization.[22] Indeed, submission to work quantified by time and its physical demands leads to an obligatory renunciation by the individual worker.[23]

Appetites, after so much persistence in satisfying them, are simply becoming anesthetized. The more the human spirit is oppressed by the superhuman rhythm, the more it drags along as if sleepwalking. This affects the whole person, who ends up in the realm of things rather than in the realm of spirit.

According to James Heisig, choosing against poverty and privation need not wait for reform of the prevailing social structures.[24] A revolution can be inaugurated merely by seeking out a life that is simpler and perhaps more satisfactorily human. A simpler life would necessarily stimulate us to use our senses more, and would alleviate a good part of the unhappiness

19. Ibid.

20. See Novaes, *O intolerável peso da feiura*. See also a more recent work by the same author, *Com que corpo eu vou?*

21. See Simone Weil and her experience in the factory. See Weil, "Expérience de la vie d'usine," 295.

22. See ibid. See also Charlie Chaplin's famous film *Modern Times*, in which the worker ends up being so identified with the machine that it becomes his true identity.

23. See Heisig, "Recovery of the Senses," 224.

24. Ibid., 225.

that seems to constitute postmodern life, where depression is the sickness of the century and the suicide rate increases exponentially in the developing countries.[25]

In making this choice we may be surprised by the state of frigidity in which we find ourselves, and by the paralysis and dullness of our senses, which have been incapable of being exercised for the only function appropriate to them: that of feeling. Our society appears to be anaesthetized, as if it has unlearned how to feel. While classical asceticism taught how to discipline a body that seemed desirous of feeling and enjoying too much, perhaps now an asceticism is needed whose objective is to relearn how to feel and enjoy.[26] To relearn how to listen to the sounds of nature and to good music; to see the infinite range of colors of the trees, the birds and the sea; to smell the aroma of the first morning coffee, of the oil being heated in the kitchen in preparation for cooking a meal, of the wet earth after a rain; to taste pure whole wheat bread without butter; to sip with delight a cup of cool water on a hot day; to touch the fur of a pet and feel its softness; and above all to touch the bodies of our loved ones with hugs, kisses, and with hands interlocked, feeling the fellowship of the flesh that symbolizes the spirit.

From all this we see that we are living in a culture in recess from desire. Among the many fears that invade and saturate our culture, perhaps one of the greatest is the threat of the extinction of desire—the fear of an impotence brought about by progressive apathy, of a failure in the strength and capacity to experience the interior expansion—sometimes painful but always uplifting—provoked by desire.[27] Our aggressively eroticized societies—where eroticism has become, through excessive advertizing, a banal and cheap commodity—are truly tormented by an obsession with the lack of desire. This obsession, which would seem to be a case of hyper-sexualization, is in fact just the opposite. So much talk about sex raises the suspicion of a lack of sexual performance. Unrestrained talk and exhibition of eroticism give the impression of an effort to conjure and exorcize the fear of failure in the desired capability.[28]

In his book *La tyrannie du plaisir*, Guillebaud affirms that "this humanitarian rhetoric applied to desire is part and parcel of a new concern:

---

25. According to Deutsche Welle, every thirty-five seconds a person commits suicide. In Germany alone, the rate is one every forty-five minutes. The rate of suicide is higher in the industrialized countries, and proportionally highest in Eastern Europe, while in absolute numbers China has the highest rate. See http://www.dw-world.de/dw/article/0,,605532,00.html.

26. See "Recovery of the Senses," 225.

27. See Guillebaud, *La tyrannie du plaisir*, 114.

28. Ibid.

that of a slow emasculation by default, an inexorable weakening of our impulses."[29] The challenge is "no longer to fight against the repression of desire but rather to keep it from running dry."[30]

Perhaps the suppression of restraints, prohibitions and limitations has brought us to this point. Nowadays transgression is no longer perceived as a combative impulse, but, according to the author, as "a nostalgia for lost sin," that causes the transgressing act to lose its potential interest and urge.[31]

Indeed, this could be a symptom of an extenuated desire. If the horizon of restraint is more and more diffuse and distant, and if sex has become a Russian roulette in which dangerous relationships are sought without protection, or a banal habit that no longer excites the body, then it involves a pulsation more of death than of life. And what is agonized here is precisely desire, bored with having all the doors open, and dying from starvation disguised as overdose.[32]

Quite a few thinkers have recently focused on this question. The conflict between desire and excessive permissiveness seems to confirm the belief that permissiveness and immodest exhibition deprive desire of its positive and elevating strength. Along these lines, Georges Bataille himself, who reflected extensively on erotism,[33] affirmed,

> As I understand it, sexual disorder is cursed. In this regard, in spite of appearances, I am opposed to the tendency that seems dominant today. I am not one of those who see the neglect of sexual restraints as a solution. Indeed I think that human possibility depends on such restraints.[34]

In truth, the dissolution of desire goes hand in hand with the dissolution of restraint. With restraints, the object of sexual desire is valued. When all restraints disappear from the horizon, and everything is permitted and even glorified, the result is the animalization of the human being. What really distinguishes the human being from the animal is, among other things, limitations on the free and merely instinctive satisfaction of immediate biological needs, including sexual activity. Limitations give new value to

---

29. Ibid., 115. [Translator's note: the English translation is from Jean-Claude Guillebaud, *The Tyranny of Pleasure*, trans. Keith Torjoc, New York: Algora, 1999. Page 93. Accessed online May 2014.]
30. Ibid. [Translator's note: see footnote 29. Page 93 in English translation.]
31. Ibid.
32. Ibid., 116.
33. See Bataille, *O erotismo*.
34. Ibid., 16, cited by Guillebaud, *La tyrannie du plaisir*, 116.

what for the animal is nothing but an instinctive, transitory, and irresistible impulse, and without meaning beyond the genital.[35]

Therefore, the intention to experience everything may finally amount to experiencing nothing. Skimming over many things, circling around many persons, carrying on many marginal relationships, may result in nothing consistent and lead to an extremely painful and unbearable frustration. The innumerable sensations that are introduced into our natural hungers—or artificial ones cleverly created by the consumerist society—often come to impose decisions that are not positive ones, as they are not truly our own. They come from outside and are alien to our own identity and to our real desire.[36]

In these days when we find society so sick and deprived of true fulfillment and satisfaction; when eagerness for consumption freezes and paralyzes our best appetites—for love, for gratitude, for fulfillment, for contemplation; when the predatory attitude of humankind threatens to extinguish or reduce to alarming levels the planet's resources; when this situation threatens to lead us to an authentic frigidity of the senses;[37] we are called to carefully examine the distinctive consequences of these multiple impacts. Experimenting is good and necessary. But the emotions and sensations caused by the experience are distinct in themselves and must be consciously and carefully analyzed.

In the contemporary mystics, the true masters of what is essential, we may discover what is truly understood as experience, and discuss it in human terms.

Experiences, Emotions, Sensations: A Necessary Distinction

According to the dictionary definition, emotion is an act of dislocating, of moving. Likewise, it is the agitation of feelings, an affective or moral disturbance, a perturbation, a commotion. In psychology, emotion is an organic reaction of variable intensity and duration, usually accompanied by changes in breathing and circulation, etc, and by great mental excitation.[38]

We define emotion, then, as a subjective experience, associated with temperament, with personality, and with motivation. The English word

---

35. See Guillebaud, *La tyrannie du plaisir*, 116 n. 17.
36. See the remarks of González Buelta on this point, *Caminar sobre las águas*, 13.
37. See on this point Heisig, "Recovery of the Senses," 223. See also Bingemer, "A aplicação de sentidos."
38. *Dicionário Houaiss,* digital version.

emotion derives from the French *émovoir*, which comes from the Latin *emovere*, where the initial *e* (a variant of *ex-*) means "out," and *movere* means "movement." The word *motivation*—related to emotion—is also derived from *movere*.

There is a distinction between emotion and its results or consequences, especially regarding the behavior generated by the emotion, and the emotional expressions. A certain behavior is often the direct result of a person's emotional state. Just think of someone crying, struggling, or smiling. However, one can experience an emotion without the corresponding behavior. Thus we see that emotion is not merely the behavior that derives from it. Nor is the behavior an essential part of the emotion.

Emotion can be more generally defined as a neural impulse that moves an organism into action. It is distinct from feeling, in that it is related to a neurophysiological state. Feeling, on the other hand, is emotion filtered through the cognitive centers of the brain, producing physiological in addition to psycho-physiological change. Daniel Goleman, in his book *Emotional Intelligence*, deals extensively with this distinction.[39]

Experience is not synonymous with emotion, although an emotion can be an important part of an experience. An experience can be accompanied by internal movements that characterize an emotion, without being completely reduced to it. On the other hand, a purely emotional reaction that is not worked through by consciousness and rationality will never become an experience in the deepest sense.

Sensation is a process by which an external or internal stimulus provokes a specific reaction, producing a sense perception (such as a visual, gustatory, or olfactory sensation) or a sensation in the brain (such as a sense of hunger, anxiety, or freedom). The word *sensation* can also refer to immediate and intuitive knowledge; to a significant experience that mobilizes affections and emotions; or even to the surprise and strong impression caused by unusual events.

The etymological origin of the word *sensation* is the Latin verb *sentire*, leading to the conclusion that sensation means to perceive through the senses. It has to do with the impression produced on the senses by objects and other external stimuli, causing pleasure or suffering. The same can be said of a psychological state with a strong affective component.[40]

Sensation is, therefore, the physical reaction of the body to the physical world (governed by the laws of physics, chemistry, biology, etc.), resulting in the activation of the primary areas of the cerebral cortex. It is a

---

39. See Goleman, *Emotional Intelligence*.
40. *Dicionário Houaiss*.

simple experience produced by the action of a stimulus (whether external or internal, such as light, sound, heat, etc.) on a sense organ, transmitted to the brain through the nervous system. Our organism constantly receives an infinite number of stimuli (sensations), although we interpret only the necessary ones. The stimuli (sensations) received are the same for all. What changes is the perception and interpretation given to them.

Although sometimes considered the starting point for the construction of experience and knowledge, sensation is not an immediate datum of consciousness. Sensation is presented to our spirit only in a more complex form, that of perception. We can only speak of sensations in perceptions if we consider them in and of themselves, without taking account of what they mean. The principal sensations of the body are the visual, auditory, tactile, gustatory, and olfactory sensations.

Sensation, therefore, is not synonymous with emotion, and much less with experience, since it is applied to and stimulates only a part of ourselves—our five senses, and only at their biochemical levels. If we were to reduce emotion to sensation, and even more, if we were to reduce experience to sensation, only low and unsatisfactory levels of experience would be possible. The gateway to experience is not sensation. Nor is it emotion. It is desire.

Current society is betting on sensations that can transform a human identity based on desire into a merely consumerist identity. We consume unnecessary objects as a result of the excitation of sensations that are confused with desire. The market functions to create fictitious needs through the mechanism of publicity and social exhibition. At bottom, what is consumed is not so much objects, but sensations. More and more, the mass media market propagates a world culture of stimulated and seduced sensations, maintained by means of an unlimited offering of sports, music, television and movie shows featuring iconic characters that promote identification while generating fictitious and frustrating needs. Schultze says that this is a society of sensations, and one that does not postpone gratification but rather seeks the immediate satisfaction of desire.[41] Caught in the midst of an uninterrupted torrent of objects, sensations and seductive promotions, human beings in this late modernity—especially in the more affluent societies and social classes—are caught up by unrestrained consumption and by

---

41. Schultze calls the society of today a society of sensations, that is, a space in which people are tasting a variety of sensations that constantly attack their vital palate. See Sulkunen et al., *Constructing the New Consumer Society*, cited by Mardones, *La tranformación de la religión*, 208.

seductive and harassing sensations[42] that atrophy the possibility of experiencing the desire that would open the door to deep experiences.

Human life, in this context, proceeds amidst a kaleidoscope of multiform and multicolor sensations and objects, where pieces are moved in a persistent and ephemeral game. Life is tantamount to an endless process of consumption of new items. What matters, says Bauman, is not so much the accumulation of objects but their consumption, the hasty and indefinite tasting of them without metabolism.[43] What is important is to consume for the sake of consuming. The process finalizes itself. Its end is its own means. And the worship of omnipotent sensations grows in an exponential rhythm and culminates in idolatry.[44]

Originally, sensation meant perception. Nowadays sensation is primarily understood as that which, magnetically and extraordinarily, attracts perception—the spectacular, the evocative, that which shines. There has been a linguistic dislocation with the word *sensation*—from perception of the totally common to perception of the uncommon, and finally of this uncommon characteristic—following the pattern that prevails today, from the general to the particular.[45] Dislocations such as this, says Türcke, are normal in all living languages. What merits attention in this case is that the dislocation of meaning is small, with a linguistic abbreviation for social dislocations, rejections, exclusions, and revolutions on a larger scale.

Current technoscientific progress has subverted all that seemed to be natural: work and property relations, habits, rituals, foundations of belief, common rhythms and styles of life, speed, ways of thinking and perceiving. "Nothing is obvious any more. The inconstant has become the only constant: the state of general unrest, of excitation, of effervescence."[46] And the result is an "excited society," as Türcke says in his book of that title.[47]

We live in a culture where every minute our senses are attacked by new sensations. It is indeed an excited culture, where the attack on the senses is intended to create attitudes and behaviors. The publicity headquarters, the editorial offices of illustrated magazines and the laboratories of industry are constantly creating new and seductive sensations that impact affectivity in irresistible ways.[48]

42. See ibid., 208–9.
43. See Bauman, *Society under Siege*.
44. See Mardones, *La tranformación de la religión*, 209.
45. See Türcke, *Sociedade excitada*, 9.
46. Ibid.
47. Ibid.
48. See Gonsález Buelta, *Caminar sobre las águas*, 12.

It is a culture in which form is more important than depth, in which the packaging is more important than the product. "Its seductive mission is as important as that of perfumes and lotions. Bottles and packages increasingly ensure that, with hardly a glance, we know what to expect them to contain."[49] The consumer

> will perceive the packaging before the product, and even before verifying if such a product will truly serve him or her. The external form, which transmits an external stimulus about the interior contents, is the first contact. The elements of design of the carton, the texture and feeling of the paper, the quality of the print . . . all these allow for the prediction of the efficacy and luxury that the product may provide.[50]

All this is to seduce irresistibly, provoking sensations of pleasure and the irresistible urge . . . to shop.

This culture disrupts inner life, since the sensations are at times so intense, refined and continuous that they can enter into us without becoming conscious perceptions, and much less elaborations of real thought. It is risky to live permanently in the continuous flux of sensations that reach our senses without our reflecting on them or discerning them. As González Buelta says, "The seductive sensations begin to circulate inside us, already converted into seduced sensations, forming part of our interior universe. They sow their seeds in the furrows of our natural hungers and in the artificial ones provoked by the same market. And—more serious—they may go on appropriating our feelings and our decisions."[51] They proceed to install in us a way of life no longer governed by a desire that is felt, perceived, and reflected upon, leadimg to vital decisions and attitudes. This new way of life makes it difficult for us to face reality and work out its challenges. It continues generating in us debased and compulsive behaviors.[52]

The essential effect of the manipulative use of these means is the promotion and development of a culture of sensations through external stimulation, and arbitrary control of the alternation between attention and inattention.

These means offer sensations that prompt a search for renewed sensations and ever more sensations, always stronger and more unusual.[53]

---

49. See Lana Parrilla, fashion director at *Harper's Bazaar (Brasil)*, cited by González Buelta, ibid., 12.

50. Ibid., 13.

51. Ibid.

52. Ibid.

53. See Haroche, *L'avenir du sensible*, 225.

In this process, lives become liquefied.⁵⁴ They flow unhindered in the unstoppable stream of invasive and bewildering sensations, without space or time for personal reflection, for mature and appropriate decisions, or for the search for the meaning of existence. Without being aware of it, we adopt new ways to live out our identity, which also becomes liquid and inconsistent.⁵⁵ Our inner life is invaded and reduced to an intimacy that misunderstands the body.

A phenomenon concomitant with the consumption of sensations is its diminution of the capacity to reflect. It "distracts" in a Pascalian sense,⁵⁶ that is, it engages and entertains so much that no space and no time are left for either reflective assimilation or discernment. And herein lies the greatest danger in the hasty tasting of sensations: it leads to *divertissement*—in the sense of alienation—of the spirit, which spends the whole time focused on frivolous exteriority, removed from deeper concerns and from the search for meaning. Pascal goes further. He deepens the idea that this unpleasant reality is not a circumstantial evil such as, for instance, grief or a failure of any kind. That would just be unhappiness,⁵⁷ which is part of our existence. Our condition would be that of a fallible and mortal being, exposed to sickness, to the agony of loneliness, and to multiple worries, besides being deprived of the only being who could bring fulfillment, that is, deprived of God. Our condition would be that of a miserable being, condemned, in order bear such misery, to do whatever it takes to avoid thinking about it. Pascal says, "Unable to cure death, misery, and ignorance, men adjusted by being happy not to think about it."⁵⁸

Although we do not follow the pessimistic Jansenist line of Blaise Pascal, we must admit that there is reason in much of what he says about systemic and alienating "self-distraction" as a way of not having to face reality. The configuration of the current affluent society in which we live leads us away from an attitude of attention to reality, especially to its somber face. What Simone Weil values as one of the greatest human capacities, the

---

54. Cf., in Bauman, the words "liquid modernity," "liquid life," "liquid love," etc.

55. See González Buelta, *Caminar sobre las águas*, 5.

56. See Pascal, *Pensées*. In Pascal's time "to divert" meant "to deviate from." Pascal built a moral category based on this term. *Divertissement* (diversion in the sense of amusement) is, in this sense, an act of avoidance, typical of human existence. It is used to avoid thinking about something that afflicts us or about an unpleasant reality. See Manon, "Le divertissement. Pascal." See our comments on this in chapter 2 of this book.

57. We translate here *malheur* as "unhappiness," although we are aware that it is not a satisfactory translation. Others might prefer "disgrace" or another term we have already used, such as "misfortune."

58. See Pascal, *Pensées*, 168.

capacity for attention, is not practiced.[59] At the core of this culture of sensations is a strategy of flight from reality as well as from the suffering and injustice of this world.[60]

The rupture of this materializing and idolatrous immanentization of life can apparently come about only through the reintroduction of the primacy of desire. In philosophy desire is a propensity toward an end considered as source of satisfaction. It is, therefore, an aspiration, a tendency toward what we do not have. It is sometimes a conscious tendency, and sometimes unconscious or repressed. When conscious, it is a mental attitude that accompanies a representation of the hoped-for end, which is its mental content.

Desire is distinguished from its accompanying physiological or psychological need in that it is planted in the center of human affectivity. Desire makes it known to us that we are incomplete, wanting, limited and finite. A being who is lacking in nothing would not desire anything. Such a being would be perfect, a god. This is the reason that ancient Greek philosophy considered desire a characteristic of finite and imperfect beings, who are not the Good but can desire it, who do not possess Beauty but can desire it and seek it.[61] As Saint Augustine says, "What is desire if not the appetite to possess what is still missing?"[62]

Desire is an integral part of the subject, of the person. And it is what energizes his or her inner life and growth as person, as well as his or her continuous self-transcendence. It is not part of the world, except to the extent that the subject is part of the world. It is an attitude of the subject in relation to the world. It is subjective and not objective. In sum, desire incessantly whispers in the ear of the human person what his or her condition is: that of a created, human, finite and limited being. But capable of desiring the Unlimited, the Infinite.

The subjective desire for Transcendence, and the opening to the inner life through the Mystery, may be the force capable of shattering the enslaving obstacle of materiality and consumerism. Thus it is that the turn to the

---

59. See Weil, "Lettre a Joseph-Marie Perrin," in *Attente de Dieu*, 137–74: "Je parle de l'attention la plus intense, celle que l'amour accompagne et qui se confond avec la prière. S'il n'y avait pas un tel bloc, on ne regarderait que là où on voit déjà de la lumière, et -ainsi on ne progresserait pas." (I speak of the most intense attention, that which love accompanies and which is confused with prayer. If it were not for such a confluence, one would look only where one already sees the light, and there would be no progress.) [Translated into English from the author's Portuguese translation.]

60. See Mardones, *La tranformación de la religión*, 210.

61. See https://en.wikipedia.org/wiki/Desire.

62. See *En. in Ps.* 118, 8, 45, cited in Martin, "Désir," in *Dictionnaire de spiritualité*.

inner life seen today in the human being who values it—to the extent of making it almost a new paradigm—has as a consequence criticism and rejection by a society of consumerism and external sensations.[63] Those who practice it with minimal seriousness either drop it or keep themselves at its margin. True opening to desire, therefore, contradicts the market's logic and alters the mercantilist relations of consumption, aligning itself with those who desire and work to build another type of society and culture.

The restoration of the capacity for desire in the individual and society follows, therefore, a direction contrary to the stream of constant excitation of sensations, against the predominance of a liquid emotionality without discernment and without the capacity to decide, against unrestrained consumption as a search for happiness, and against the reduction of the human person to a mere passive consumer of products that are imposed on him or her by this kind of society. Therefore, the turn toward inner life, toward contemplation, toward meditation, that can be seen today in society as a whole, constitutes a counter-cultural movement.[64]

On the other hand, to recover the capacity to desire is also to recover for the senses themselves what they were really made to do: to see, to hear, to feel, to taste, to touch. To hear the beauty of music composed under the inspiration of the artist, but also to hear the appeals that issue from one's own inner life, as well as the clamors of the neighbor for justice and fairness. To see the beauty of nature, of works of art, of human beings in their diversity, but also to see the sick reality of this world, and not to flee from the vision of the suffering or the unjust and premature death inflicted on so many people. Christian spirituality and the spiritualities of all religious traditions lead to attention and concentration and not to evasion of reality.[65]

Therefore it is difficult to accuse—as has often been tried—mysticism and contemplation of being an alienating and evasive practice. On the contrary, a truly illuminating and spiritual experience opens the contemplative sensibilities and intelligence to the realities of everyday life and to the practice of compassion for the neighbor. It is not a flight to the stratosphere, but rather a return to earthen reality with its wounds and injustices. If the spiritual experience itself does not produce the ability to perform a structural analysis of unjust or painful facts, it undeniably tunes one's sensibility to perceive them. With this sensibility, complemented by a political-structural analysis of reality, one who experiences his or her inner life inhabited by Transcendence will certainly be better equipped for political consciousness

---

63. See the book by Aleixandre et al., *La interioridad: un paradigma emergente.*
64. See Mardones, *La tranformación de la religión*, 210.
65. Ibid., 211

of social phenomena and for intervention in the polis with transformative and solidary action.[66]

To value internal experience, which consists of desire and of emotions discernible by consciousness—and takes a direction opposite to that of the aggressively seductive and seduced sensations—is anything but alienation. The true interior revolution, mysticism, is not the enemy of political commitment. On the contrary, it provides ammunition for the well grounded suspicion that many militant political actions, having lost their referential of grace and contemplation, have sunk into a voracious and ferocious activism that has ended up devouring their physical, psychological and spiritual strengths.[67]

What is finally behind consumerism and the culture of sensations in the excited and effervescent society in which we live, is a veil to hide the painful and tragic dimension of human existence. "Under an emotional and intellectual screen, besides the enormous leaden weight of the culture of image and entertainment, runs the equivocation that today one lives in a uniform, radiant and 'happy' society. And this equivocation unanimously hides the somber side of human life."[68]

The thirst for Transcendence, an undeniable symptom of the late modernity, hypermodernity, or postmodernity in which we live, is evidence that all the possibilities of erotism and consumption are not enough for the human being. As Gauchet says,

> If revolutionary criticism of bourgeois society and its mendacious idealism was carried out under the flag of materialism, today we are facing a critical-revolutionary process that unfolds under the spiritual banner. Today we even discover a great and fundamental affinity between them both.[69]

It appears urgent, in this moment in history, to undertake the reconstruction of human subjectivity in such a way that it can resist and confront the reductionism of a society sickened by consumerist indigestion and by its evasiveness regarding its own injustices and wounds. We are seeing an anthropological atrophy that undermines the human being and

---

66. Ibid.

67. See the two articles by P. F. C. de Andrade on this theme: "Encantos e desencantos: a militância dos cristãos em tempos de crise," and "A crise da modernidade e as possibilidades de uma nova militância cristã."

68. See Mardones, *La tranformación de la religión*, 211.

69. See Gauchet, *Un monde désenchanté?*, 19. Besides Gauchet, see Touraine, *Um novo paradigma*; Habermas, *The Structural Transformation of the Public Sphere*; Durand, *L'imagination symbolique*, referenced by Mardones, *La tranformación de la religión*, 211.

society in preventing them from confronting their own crisis. This human atrophy masks the crisis of relationships, the functionalist colonization of more and more vital and social spaces, and the misery of a superficial and supposedly happy life.[70]

Behind these tendencies one glimpses a historic reaction of the human being against the malaise of such reductionism, which demands a transformation of the religious experience through a change of emphasis from exteriority to interiority. When we look at this question through the prism of historical Christianity, we realize that this turnaround requires a profound institutional change and a qualitative leap in religious consciousness. This new religious consciousness demands today a profound transformation in its relationship with the Mystery that surrounds and supports it. If the days are numbered for the external political dominance of religion, especially the Christian religion, one can see that it is nevertheless challenged to take a broad and fruitful road in the process of its inner deepening.

Experience: A Human Privilege

Therefore, beyond semantic or merely linguistic definitions, it is important to take a look at the definition of experience as employed by philosophy and theology, including in this definition the transcendent dimension of the subject who experiences it.

The false opposition between experience and knowledge is the first obstacle to the attempt to clarify the notion of experience. Experience is, indeed, a face of thought that turns to the presence of the object. With this, one observes a direct relationship between the fullness of the presence and the profundity of the experience, which is mediated by the discernment of this fullness through the act of thinking. The etymological origin of the word *experience* offers a good way to arrive at its essence. Both the Greek *empeiria* and the Latin *experientia* speak of trying, of proving, of verifying, which means to investigate an object in all its meanings. This is what is suggested by the German word *Erfahrung*,[71] which means to take a voyage of discovery in search of the meaning of things.[72] Thus, what characterizes experience is the discernment of the object, which on the one hand liberates knowledge from the precarious and confused character of mere sensation, and on the other, fills in the emptiness of purely logical forms.

---

70. Ibid.
71. See Houtepen, *Dio, una domanda aperta*, 376–79.
72. See Mieth, "Alla ricerca di una definizione del concetto 'esperienza.'"

Religious or Mystical Experience

One can see then that experience is articulated between two well-defined poles: the object, which is the phenomenon, and the subject, which is the science or consciousness that turns to the object to discern it and likewise to be discerned by its presence. Every experience is always threatened either by the ineffablility of the presence or the formalism of the language. Therefore the ambiguous character of experience is inherent in the condition of our own knowledge, which sometimes presents itself as receptive, and sometimes as active. The balance between the two poles is constantly set and reset. In this way, experience moves between these two poles as a permanent requirement for lucidity and realism.[73]

It is understood, then, that experience as a modality is also a source of immediate knowledge. It does not take place through the discursive activity of intelligence—such as the conclusion of a syllogism—through later reflection, or through the acceptance of knowledge by reason of either institutional authority or historical tradition. It is rather a matter of a simple and immediate perception of something, which imparts strong certainty based on specific evidence. Naturally, this perception has an intellectual dimension, but it is, in itself, inclusive of the whole human being, of his or her intelligence, will, and sensibility in the broadest and most complete sense of the term.[74] It is not only the perception that enters into it, but also the thinking that understands it as such. For this reason one can affirm that every human experience is interpreted experience. There is no experience without interpretation of its object by its subject. One does not have an experience and later make a reading of what was experienced, in a neutral way, without interpretation. Experience is, therefore, neither objective only nor subjective only. We conclude that an experience takes place when a person perceives himself or herself in relation to the world, to himself or herself, and to God, and reflects on this and expresses it in appropriate language.[75]

Experience, especially when understood as a search for meaning, is a path to the understanding of the human condition because it reveals what the human being, even without knowing it, is looking for. What the human being really desires and searches for is the fulfillment of his or her heart.[76] And only Transcendence can accomplish that, since the human being "is a

---

73. See Vaz, "A experiência de Deus."

74. See Stirnimann, "Linguaggio, esperienza e incontro com Colui che parla," 185.

75. See Mouroux, *L'experience chrétienne*, 21: "Il y a expérience quand la personne se saisit en relation avec le monde, avec soi-même, avec Dieu."

76. See Gelabert, *Valoración cristiana de la experiencia*, 19. See also the famous statement of Saint Augustine: "You have made us for Yourself, O, Lord, and our heart is restless until it finds its rest in You."

being in continuous self-transcendence."[77] While sharing with the animals the cycle of life and death, human beings are not ruled by instincts as they are.[78] Like the animals, they will one day die. The difference is that they know they will die.

The human desire for that which does not pass away, for that which is Unconditional and Eternal, is concomitant with the mortal and finite human condition. Therefore, in desiring to experience anything, human beings are desiring the Radical Meaning of their existence—that which will tell them that the cycle of life is not absurd: growing up, getting nourishment, reproducing, aging and dying. Thus, whatever fails to speak to the desire for life of the human being—even while sleeping—and whatever fails to illuminate or clarify unexplained experiences, is an empty pronouncement that says little, or perhaps nothing at all.

Experience is also consciousness of reality, of access to the reality that affects the subject. If we note that consciousness is consciousness of something by someone, we realize that in experience the subject is affected by reality. This suggests the indispensable role that the subject plays in the experience. There is no experience without an object-subject interaction. And here arises the first problem: the conditions of the subject may interfere with and/or disturb the process of objectivization of the experience.[79]

The real presents itself in different ways according to our relationship with it. This means that every possible experience assumes, as a necessary correlate, acceptance by the human being. The attention and sensibility, the intensity of desire, and the quality of attention of the human being, condition the quality of the experience of reality, its interpretation and expression.

But what reality is at issue, here and now? The whole of reality and its dynamism, no matter how one reaches for it or what perspective is adopted in regard to it. By *real* we mean not only the objects that are external to the human being, but also the phenomena of his or her inner activity. Saint Thomas Aquinas spoke of experience in reference to knowledge through the senses, as well as of the experience of things that exist by virtue of the presence in the soul of their essence.[80]

The experience of reality is dynamic. The perception of a datum is not sheathed in previously acquired representations. One can also identify in the object potentialities that escape the external senses. This is possible because

---

77. See Rahner, *Curso fundamental da fé*, 42.

78. See L. Boff, "Constantes antropológicas e revelação," where he makes a comparison between the tick with the human being.

79. See Gelabert, *Valoración cristiana de la experiencia*, 20.

80. Ibid.

any object is spontaneously compared with others. It is valued and evaluated in relation to others and may acquire the status of example, which is already the beginning of universalization. The human being has an inquisitive cognitive dynamism that does not allow for satisfaction with a fact or a datum in a pure state. On the contrary, we desire to know total reality, to establish connections and proceed further. This reality that we try to know will always and definitively appear as something complex. For this reason access to it may reach different levels and present itself from several perspectives.[81]

One can distinguish four levels of access to the real, or levels of experience: the empirical, the anthropological, the metaphysical, and the theological.[82] The simple mention of these levels already indicates the complexity of the problem and suggests the conflict that would be created in absolutizing one of them, thus depleting all experience. Or in denying or demeaning the others based on the supposed primacy of one of them (including the religious).

> The experience that the human being makes of reality conditions his or her whole life, because he or she moves in it, with it, for it, and before it. Thus, from this totalizing involvement in the experience, one understands the impact it has on the entire life of the human being. Reality is something that the human person dominates, and yet it influences him or her, and shapes his or her life. It conditions it, limits it, and makes it possible. It is manipulable and at the same time it inevitably escapes, which means that, at least in part, it is mysterious. This mystery of reality can be considered provisional by the fact that it never finds itself completely subject to the domination of human power (the theistic perspective), at least in definitive terms (the atheistic perspective). In experiencing reality, therefore, the human being, besides experiencing his or her own capacity to transform reality, already confronts the Mystery of the world, indecipherable and at times frightening and challenging.[83]

With these characteristics, experience is the origin of knowledge. This would be experience understood and explained (through intellectual activity), first to oneself, and then to others. For this reason, all this knowledge founded in experience, or at least this search for a foundation, requires the experience of an Other. Knowledge without experience is pure verbalism,

---

81. Ibid., 21.

82. Here we follow closely the typology presented by the author we have been citing: Gelabert, *Valoración cristiana de la experiencia*, 21ff.

83. Ibid.

empty concept, and illusion.[84] But when we go from the philosophical-anthropological level to the theological, we see that experience is inseparable from the Otherness and relatedness that constitute human identity. This Otherness refers to the human as a prototype. In biblical terms, experience is loving knowledge, and knowing is inseparable from loving.[85]

The words used to convey the experience of faith are taken from the language of human experience (father, son, love, reconciliation, justice, light, life, etc.). All that exists, including Transcendence and the Mystery, is referred to human beings and their existence, and dedicated to answering the questions that human beings raise about themselves and about reality.[86]

When human beings have an experience of God, the structure of this experience includes no language about God as an object among others. It includes, rather, an experience of radical meaning, which makes possible the existence of the multiple languages that compose the interpretative horizon of the human being, as well as a revelation of God in the form of a particular language.[87] The experience can also be dealt with as a way or as an appropriation. On the one hand it can be understood as the search for a truth, or the apprehension of a reality.[88] On the other hand (and in other words), when one speaks of experience, particularly in its spiritual and religious sense, its implied concrete totality must be respected: "It is the whole human being, in some aspect and for a time, who is engaged here."[89]

The opening of the human spirit to the Ultimate, to the Last, to the Radical Meaning of reality, in its own dynamism, tends toward an intangible horizon—toward the plenitude of the being and the good that mobilizes human intelligence and freedom, and is present in each cognitive and volitional act as a condition of its own possibility. This infinite horizon toward which the human being is structurally turned, is none other than the real God, experienced as near and immediate, and ground for the hope of reaching God as a resting place and final point of the human pilgrimage.

What we said above allows us to glimpse some recurring characteristics of the whole human experience, which offers us the substrates of that which would, then, be religious experience. This is not experienced only at the natural level of reality, but accedes to the supernatural realm. It does not

---

84. Ibid., 27.
85. See Moltmann, *Trinity and the Kingdom*, 10.
86. Ibid., 28.
87. See Labarriere, "L'homme et l'Absolu."
88. Mouroux speaks of *trajet* or *possession*. See *L'expérience chrétienne*, 6.
89. See Mouroux, "Language catéchétique et expérience chrétienne," 255.

approach provisional objects, but opens to and penetrates the Absolute, the Ultimate of all reality.

Religion, throughout all of human history, has always tried to organize this experience of Transcendence and to systematize it as norms, rituals and doctrinal conceptualizations. But no such organization could take place without religious experience, which is fundamental to all the great traditions, and which bears witness to the fact that human beings are distinct from all other creatures because they can experience that which—or the One who—transcends them and is greater than all that can be imagined and conceived.

That is exactly what Christian mysticism shows us: that human experience is really total and complete only when it transcends itself in God, who is always greater than all that human beings are willing to experience.[90]

Religious Experience: Seduction and Fear

It was at the beginning of the twentieth century (more specifically in 1917) that the famous book by Rudolf Otto, *Das Heilige* (*The Idea of the Holy*),[91] attempted a more vigorous definition of religious experience without going directly to the more confessional domain of a particular institution. According to Otto, religious experience carries an incommensurability between all that it reveals of the understanding or reason, and the set of phenomena that refer to the act of experiencing as such. Therefore, such an experience escapes any rational approximation. It does not give prominence either to the order of truth (for instance, the metaphysical experience of the true God, as in Descartes, or the arguments of ontological proof), or to the order of ethics (notably, as when Kant tried to anchor it in the postulates of practical reason), or even to the theological order or that of the organization of the senses.

For Otto, religious experience cannot be reduced to an idea, concept, abstract notion, or moral precept. All these operations of thought are too pacific to be adequate for what flows torrentially and abundantly when the Sacred is manifested in a singular experience. Furthermore, religious experience escapes good sense. Otto shows that it is a terrible and devastating experience for those on whom it pours. The experience referred to by the Pauline expression as that of the "living God," is, for the human being, one of a terrifying and crushing power, beyond any mental mediation (see Heb 10:31). For Otto, this

---

90. Ibid.
91. See Otto, *Idea of the Holy*, especially 14–21.

is the experience of Divine Omnipotence. What is found throughout such an experience belongs to the order of the "totally other."[92]

Singular and finite beings suddenly find themselves in the presence of a reality irreducible to anything they find important in the cosmic or human order. What is then lived out and experienced in this interlocution escapes all thought and all will. This radical ontological estrangement, erupting in the realm of human experience, may cause in the being who suffers it a paradoxical attitude, at the limit of the bearable, that could lead an insufficiently prepared mind to dementia. On the one hand there arises a feeling of fear, of Sacred terror—the crushing feeling that Otto designates as *mysterium tremendum*. On the other hand there emerges an imposing feeling of irresistible attraction, in a being torn from ordinary life, an urgency to see even with the risk of dying—an irrepressible feeling that Otto defines as *mysterim fascinans*.[93]

This extreme ambivalence that the experience of the Sacred carries was named by the author as numinous. Everything happens as if the numinous effect were caused by sudden access to the experience of a reality that no category can delimit. It is a sudden change in the level of consciousness manifested by a conflict of attitudes, indicating the irreducibility of such an experience to the reciprocal positions of the I and the world. It cannot express itself except through a contradictory feeling—expressed as well with contradictory words—that takes over the whole being who experiences it: a terrifying attraction, a terrible impulse, etc. This feeling lies well beyond the vital antagonism of surviving-dying, which forms the psychic basis of consciousness. Nor does it lie in an interior-exterior type of relation, such as plays out in the face-to-face between the human and the divine. It is rather an experience of the relation between two orders, two types, two levels of reality: a superior one and an inferior one. This crushing revelation is that of a power that is radically other, lived out by human beings as if on the edge of an abyss, as if balancing themselves on their own nothingness.[94]

Rudolf Otto, together with William James and Baron von Hügel,[95] insisted on the fact that Christianity, in spite of being the highest religion, was even so a type of religion, and nothing else but that. His main concern was to rescue religion from the claws of the reductionists, to reclaim its role as an *a priori* category of feeling, preceding but not independent of rational

---

92. Ibid.
93. Ibid.
94. Ibid.
95. See James, *The Varieties of Religious Experience*; See Hügel, *The Mystical Element of Religion*.

explanation. The essence of religion for Otto must, therefore, be found in the pre-rational feeling of the numinous, which should be understood as "creature-consciousness" or human "creatureliness," which is experienced in the presence of the *mysterium tremendum,* the transcendent source experienced as "totally other."[96]

Otto says that mysticism occurs when the element of distance, difference, and lack of proximity recedes and the all-powerful force of the numinous induces the human subject to see this as the only reality, and therefore to seek self-annihilation.[97] He synthesizes his vision of mysticism as follows: "As a provisional definition of mysticism I would suggest that, while sharing the nature of religion, it shows a preponderance of its non-rational elements and an overemphasis on them in respect to the 'overabounding' aspect of the 'numen.'"[98]

Otto says further that "it is clear that the deity as an immanent principle is distinct from, and means something other than, the transcendent God. The starting point and the essential distinction is not that the mystic has another and new relationship with God, but that he has a different God."[99] Otto's position has the advantage that he can claim as truly mystical some phenomena such as yoga and even certain aspects of Buddhism.[100] Its disadvantage is that, at least among Christian mystics, the majority have insisted that the God experienced by them was at the same time transcendent and immanent, rather than two different beings.[101]

In Otto's typology there are, therefore, two highly interpenetrated modalities: the extrovertive way, or the mysticism of the unified vision, and the introvertive way, or the mysticism of introspection. These modalities are contrasted with three lower forms: illuminism, emotionalism, and natural mysticism.[102]

McGinn considers Otto's categories ambiguous. If we accept that the vision described by mystical language is not so much the content of mystical experience (which mystics have always held to be incommunicable), as it is the transformative process achieved by mystical knowledge, as recent researchers have argued, then Otto's intercultural typologies will collapse.[103]

---

96. See Otto, *Idea of the Holy,* ch. 5.
97. Ibid., ch. 6.
98. Ibid., ch. 11, 88.
99. Ibid., ch. 13.
100. Ibid., ch. 14.
101. See McGinn, *Foundations of Mysticism,* 328.
102. Ibid., 328 n. 15.
103. Ibid., 20.

The philosopher of religion Louis Dupré, in his note in the Encyclopedia of Religion, attempts a historical retrospective on mysticism in the West. Although not as complete as McGinn's survey (at the end of *The Foundations of Mysticism*),[104] it has the advantage of opening up the range of reflection, including in the category of mysticism a broad series of experiences, including the non-Christian.[105]

Beginning with the mystery cults of ancient Greece, Dupré tries to demonstrate that mysticism—understood as union with the Mystery—is a component of all religions.[106] Dupré observes that in the Greek mystery cults, *muein* (to remain silent) probably referred to secret initiation rites. But later, especially in neoplatonic theory, mystical silence came to mean wordless contemplation. Western Christianity, mainly due to the impact of Augustine, eventually came to understand the mystical phenomenon as related to a subjective mental state. Thus Jean Gerson, a chancellor of the Sorbonne in the fifteenth century, described mystical theology as "experiential knowledge of God through the embracing of unifying love."[107]

For his part, William James, in his work on the varieties of religious experience,[108] identifies four characteristics:

1. Ineffability: the private, or at least incommunicable, quality of the experience.

2. Noetic: not an increase in theoretical knowledge, but inspired knowledge, a unique and comprehensive sense of integration that belongs definitively to the noetic order.

3. Passivity: of a gratuitous nature, undeserved, whether or not the privileged subjects had applied themselves to ascetic exercises or meditation techniques.

4. Transitoriness: the most controversial, since many great mystics remained for long periods in states of consciousness altered by their experiences.

Dupré adds a fifth characteristic to the typology of James, that of Integration. He holds that, once expanded beyond its ordinary limits, mystical consciousness in one way or another succeeds in surmounting previous obstacles to its integration into a higher reality. This does not mean that all

---

104. Ibid.
105. See Dupré, "Mysticism."
106. Ibid.
107. Quoted in ibid., 245–46.
108. See James, *The Varieties of Religious Experience*.

restrictions cease to exist, maintaining the indisputably religious character of an experience that presumes the Otherness of the Absolute. But the experience makes itself felt as all inclusive, and therefore of indisputable plenitude.[109]

However, Dupré cautions, there is a common ground upon which the most diverse spiritual theologies stand. At least in the West, theoretical reflection on religion remains faithful to the general principle that only subsequent interpretations can distinguish one mysticism from another. It is here that the author introduces an acknowledgment of the existence of a mysticism called natural.

> Natural mysticism is the intense experience through which the subject feels himself or herself in fusion with and/or confused with the cosmic totality. . . . But in the religious experience a sense of Transcendence persists throughout the experience of cosmic union, . . . with respect to nature as a whole as its undergirding principle. . . . In this sense the difference between the religious and the nonreligious is particularly difficult to maintain.[110]

And there is always more. Today, besides the experiences that Dupré calls natural, there are also experiences resulting from psychopathological conditions, or even experiences of expanding consciousness caused by the ingestion of herbs, or artificially provoked by active hallucinogenic substances and principles, some of them with great number of followers.[111]

In truth—and what we have seen so far strengthens this affirmation—one has to admit that mysticism belongs at the core of all religions. Religions that had a historical founder, all of them, started with a powerful personal experience of immediate contact with the deity. But all religions, no matter their origin, maintain their vitality only insofar as their members continue to believe in a transcendent reality with whom they can in some way communicate through direct experience. Thus, to the extent that a religion

---

109. See Dupré, "Mysticism," 247.

110. Ibid.

111. We are referring here, in the first case, to ecological religions such as Santo Daime, the União do Vegetal, and many others on the rise in Brazil. We also take into account, especially in the second case, the experiences with mushrooms used in patients with incurable infirmities such as cancer for the purpose, according to researchers, of provoking in them a transcendental experience that might alleviate their suffering and eliminate their fear of death. See the research of David E. Nichols, of Purdue University, among others, on psilocybin and hallucinogenics previously used for religious purposes and now used in the treatment of terminal cancer. For example: Griffiths et al., "Psilocybin Can Ooccasion Mystical-Type Experiences."

becomes secularized in the radical sense of the term—that is, as it loses this dimension—the tendency will be for it to dwindle and then disappear.[112] Dupré cautions that any mystical system is less concerned about logical consistency and rigorously defined concepts than about adequate translation of the actual experience. Since what is central for the mystics is the experience, it is to it that the reflective and explanatory systems constantly and continuously turn in order to guarantee its permanence in religion.[113]

All forms of religious mysticism lay claim to a direct contact with the Absolute, according to the author. However, the way a mystical current or experience defines the Absolute depends on its particular perspective. Judaism and Christianity are religions of the word; Buddhism is a religion of silence that renounces all ways of naming the Absolute. It is evident that this will impact the way these two types of religion define what the mystical experience means to them.[114]

Evidently, here as in other cases, an external observer is incapable of perceiving, and, even less of deciding, the extent to which a religion, its dogma, and its institution emerge and grow inside the current mystical experience. What matters is the possibility that such religious proposals represent a direct and intense contact with the Absolute. And what matters even more is the methodical and articulate way that a particular religion offers to bring it about.[115]

Situated as we now are in the vast world of religious experience, we ask about the criteria employed by the subjects of such experiences to distinguish authentic experiences from those that they themselves consider inauthentic or deceptive.

The first criterion, a negative one, appears with all clarity: the value of an experience does not depend on the extraordinary phenomena that accompany it—especially if they are bodily ones (ecstasies, stigmas, delirium). Likewise, an experience that is not accompanied by extraordinary phenomena must submit to a careful discernment. This is required by the profound and global character of the experience and by the quality of the Presence that is felt in it, as well as by the existence of a series of states of mind, the effects of consciousness and feelings, and the internal movement produced by the invisible presence, through which it is diverted from its fundamental option.

---

112. See Dupré, "Mysticism," 248.
113. Ibid.
114. Ibid., 250.
115. Ibid., 251.

A second criterion has to do with the language that describes the experience. When it is described, it is usually compared to more evident experiences—those that proceed from the evidence of the senses—for the purpose of declaring the certitude that it produces the experience of God, and produces it more strongly than all the others. This Presence imposes itself upon consciousness in such a way as to bring with it the immediate perception that such certainty cannot be the result of conscious effort.[116]

The experience reverberates as well in the human will (and this is the third criterion) in the form of affective movements along with the intense feelings that it provokes: peace, pleasure, fulfillment, joy, etc. In the analysis of these emotions and states of mind the spiritual masters fine tuned their criteria of discernment.[117] When mystics describe these feelings, they usually do so in terms that Velasco calls "affective ambivalence." He refers to the contradictory and paradoxical expressions used by the mystics, such as "delicious wound" (John of the Cross), "savory torment" (Teresa of Avila), etc.[118]

But the decisive criterion—here numbered as the fourth—is without doubt that of love. The experience is nothing but the living out, through all the human faculties, of the radical experience provoked by love as felt and lived out. This love cannot be only the object of ecstasies and spiritual feelings, or even of passionate narratives. It must be translated into works. Thus Saint Teresa says, "The Lord wants works," telling her sisters that they must put aside devotion when a sick person needs their prompt attention, and they must even fast so that such a person can eat.[119] Thus also Saint Ignatius, in the final meditation of the Spiritual Exercises, says in describing

---

116. For instance, the following quote from Teresa by the author in 6 M 3, 4 and in 5 M 1, 10: "Queda por una parte gran certidumbre, que no tiene fuerza la duda . . . no porque es vision, sino una certidumbre que queda en el alma." Or Saint Ignatius, in the *Exercises,* explaining consolation without a preceding cause as a source of the first period of election: [329] ". . . proprio es de Dios y de sus ángeles en sus mociones dar verdadera alegria y gozo spiritual, quitando toda tristeza y turbación, que el enemigo induce; del qual es proprio militar contra la tal alegria y consolación spiritual, trayendo razones aparentes, sotilezas y assiduas falacias"; [330] ". . . sólo es de Dios nuestro Señor dar consolación a la ánima sin causa precedente; porque es proprio del Criador entrar, salir, hacer moción en ella, trayéndola toda en amor de la su divina majestad. Digo sin causa, sin ningún previo sentimiento o conoscimiento de algún objeto, por el qual venga la tal consolación mediante sus actos de entendimiento y voluntad"; [175] "El primer tiempo es quando Dios nuestro Señor así mueve y atrae la voluntad, que *sin dubitar ni poder dubitar,* la tal ánima devota sigue a lo que es mostrado; assí como San Pablo y San Matheo lo hicieron en seguir a Christo nuestro Señor."

117. Velasco, *El fenómeno místico,* 63. See Saint Ignatius of Loyola.

118. See Velasco, *El fenómeno místico.*

119. 5 M 3, 7–9, 11; See Velasco, *La experiencia cristiana de Dios,* 65 n. 17.

love, "[230] Note. First one should pay attention to two things: The first is that love can do more through works than through words."[120]

It is an error to think that religious experience only occurs in the narrowing circle of persons who define themselves as religious, or that it is reduced in the lives of such persons to well developed practices of prayer and contemplation. If that were the case, a considerable number of men and women who do not define themselves as religious, and of those among the religious who simply call themselves believers, would be irreversibly condemned to be deprived of such experiences. They would find themselves reduced to living with no contact with Transcendence, or to believing only with the support of the witness of those who, by virtue of extraordinary grace, would have the privilege of seeing and experiencing.[121]

Prayer is certainly a privileged place for the experience of God. It was described by Saint Thomas as *religiones actus*, or putting religion into action. On the other hand, since it has to do with the recognition of the Absolute, of the absolutely valuable, of the *unum necessarium* for human beings, it becomes indispensable for human beings to recognize that they are leaving behind a life centered on utility, on function, and on possessions, which are part of everyday life, and passing—through a certain breach in level—to the order of the Sacred. Thus, we see the importance of prayer expressly cultivated for the effective practice of the experience of God. Prayer is, then, the privileged place for religious experience.[122]

Nevertheless, the possibility exists for the experience of God to be realized in all places and moments of life, and for the effective articulation of distinct experiences of God in the unity of a life wholly accompanied by this Presence, from which it proceeds and toward which it is oriented. This articulation produces the achievements of a human life endowed, in all its dimensions and actions, with the profundity and meaning that allow attention to the Presence without thereby losing the variety, richness, and realism that bring about attention to and care for the world, and relationship with brothers and sisters.[123]

As it is true that God cannot be the object of any action and that God makes God's self present while invisible, one can affirm that through transformation all human beings, in the entirety of their everyday lives—including their bodily senses—participate in the experience of God.[124] Karl

---

120. Velasco, *El fenómeno místico*, 59–64
121. Ibid., 66.
122. Ibid., 67.
123. Ibid., 68.
124. See Augustine, *Confessions*, X, 6.

Rahner wrote on several occasions about the experience, in the midst of life, of God, of the Spirit, and of grace, which constitute what he calls "the everyday mystic."[125]

It is worth asking to what extent can we talk of a real experience of God "without knowing that it is God whom we experience."[126] Concerning these nonreligious experiences of self-transcendence, the experience of God would never allow the human being to transform God into the direct object of an act of knowledge or desire. The difference between these and the highest mystical experiences is not that through some of them one comes to know God but not through others. It rather lies in the fact that

> being human experiences—as always—they have their origin in the founding Presence that constitutes the human being and are lived out by the consent of this origin and source, or then by self-sufficiency and the exclusive reference to the I itself, and likewise interpreted in the more or less clear and explicit light of this acknowledgment, evoking in a more or less vague way some kind of Transcendence, or then calling upon natural, psychological, or other orders of explanation which reduce them to merely human experiences.[127]

In the interpretation of the experience, then, lies the key to its identity.

In cultural situations such as the current one, where the secularization of society and culture has been followed by the tendency of many people to interpret their lives without reference to religion, it is often in a personal situation that something entirely new is desired in relation to the experience of God. Indeed, many of our contemporaries, disengaged from any religious affiliation, carry out their lives without ever referring to the symbols and categories by which religious topics are interpreted. Are these people condemned to be completely deprived of any experience of God? We submit that human beings do not understand themselves without an opening and reference to the infinite, and that this reference is not lacking simply by virtue of the fact that it is not identified. But if they fail to acknowledge their divine condition, their theandric nature (See Panikkar), then one must admit that the option upon which rests any experience of the deity is lacking. An analysis of the experience of such persons shows that many of them, who ignore or reject the designation of God as the transcendent reality, still acknowledge—in certain spheres of human experience—the presence of a reality that imposes itself on human beings and provides a

---

125. See Velasco, *El fenómeno místico*, 85.
126. See Ruiz de la Pena, *El don de Dios*, 398.
127. Ibid., 70.

definitive orientation for their lives. This happens, for instance, when these humans come upon values whose dignity they cannot fail to recognize, or when they are confronted with actions that, no matter how advantageous they are, impose an Absolute ethical interdict on them, or with others that, no matter how inconvenient, impose on them the desire to live a dignified life. In such situations they achieve an act of Transcendence that leads them to acknowledge, in the Good that has come upon them, an absolute reality. And an acknowledgment of the Absolute can also come about in the very domain of philosophy, in the experience of being, and in its disclosure in truth. The same is true for the aesthetic experience, and for the relationship of respect and love for the other.[128]

It is evident that such experiences present a clear phenomenological distinction among themselves and in relation to the religious experience of God. But in all of them there is a structural similarity in what constitutes the central moment in religious experience: its movement of Transcendence, its radical decentering (one speaks of philosophical faith and of moral atheism in referring to some of them) and the fact that such religions incorporate ethical experience and love for others as criteria for the authenticity of religious experience. All this seems to indicate that through them the secular human being can be led to the same Absolute identified by the religious human being as God. Thus, in a nonreligious way, the secular human being may be having an experience of God.[129]

As a result of the process of secularization and the end of the hegemony of historical Christianity, reflection on mysticism turned not only toward religion as a social phenomenon, as in the work of Rudolf Otto, or toward religion as associated with cultural differences, as in Mircea Eliade. It also turned—to the extent that religion is thought of as plural—toward the perception, in the mystical experience that takes place inside religion, of inter- and trans-religious tendencies that explode the boundaries carefully kept by religious traditions and reaffirm the universal character of the experience of God.

Along with thinkers—such as Rudolf Otto, Mircea Eliade, and others[130]—who developed their reflections with the intention of universality, wishing to encompass religion as a whole, the twentieth century also knew thinkers from other religious traditions who reflected on and wrote

---

128.. Ibid., 72–73, 90.

129. In Christian theology there is an illustrious precedent of this thesis, in the category created by Rahner of "anonymous Christians." See Rahner, "Anonymous Christians," in *Theological Investigations*, vol. 6, 390–98.

130. See Eliade, *The Two and the One*; *Myth and Reality*; *The Sacred and the Profane*; and *Briser le toit de la maison*, among others.

Religious or Mystical Experience

about religious experience, such as Gershom Scholem and Hans Jonas, both Jewish.

Gershom Scholem insists that "there is no mysticism as such, there is only the mysticism of a certain religious system, Christian, Islamic, Jewish mysticism and so on."[131] Besides this particularization, Scholem refuses to restrict mysticism to the experience of union with God. He emphasizes that "mysticism is a definite stage in the historical development of religion and makes its appearance under certain well-defined conditions," that is, at a particular moment in the evolution of religious consciousness.[132]

Scholem ventures, as well, a more multicolored and dialectic vision of the relationship between mysticism and society. He says, "All mysticism has two contradictory or complementary aspects: the one conservative, the other revolutionary."[133] To be understood, mystics must speak the language of tradition, but in so doing, they find themselves confronted with certain choices and problems. Insofar as the mystic identifies the source of mystical communication with the original revelation based in tradition, institutionalized mysticism can serve as a conservative force renewing and strengthening that which tradition, as Scholem argues, has generally done in the history of Judaism.[134]

Hans Jonas—another prominent twentieth-century Jewish thinker, especially regarding post-Holocaust Western society—says that the myth and the objective representation of "a way of being in the world" usually precede in time the mystical objectification "that may appear as an internalized version of the same motif."[135] Jonas presents an important critique of the usual vision, which presents mystical theory as nothing more than a secondary reflection, a projection of mystical "experience."[136]

There are still those who conceive of the question of religious experience in comparative terms, distinguishing natural from religious mysticism. One of the most important scholars of comparative religion is without doubt the British thinker Robert Zaehner. As articulated by McGinn in his

---

131. See Scholem, *Major Trends in Jewish Mysticism*, 6. See the comments by McGinn in *Foundations of Mysticism*, 334 n. 48.

132. Scholem, *Major Trends in Jewish Mysticism*, 7. See also, by the same author, "Mysticism and Society."

133. See "Religious Authority and Mysticism," ch. 1 of *On the Kabbalah: New Perspectives*.

134. Ibid., 11, 27–29, where Scholem identifies three auxiliary points for source identification. See the commentary by McGinn, *Foundations of Mysticism*, 335 n. 55.

135. See McGinn, *Foundations of Mysticism*, 336–37.

136. See the important article by Jonas, "Myth and Mysticism: A Study of Objectification and Interiorization in Religious Thought."

survey, Zaehner identifies three distinct varieties of mysticism: 1. An experience that tells you that you are everything and that everything is you—the natural mysticism that he calls "pan-in-henism." 2. Experiencing one's own soul as being the Absolute, and not experiencing the phenomenal world at all. 3. The normal Christian type of mystical experience in which the soul feels itself united with God through love.[137] McGinn observes that the most interesting recent comparative works on religious experience and mysticism tend to deal more with specific traditions than with the construction of general theories.[138]

Psychology, that continent opened up by Freud inside the human thought, has also turned its attention to religious experience and the accounts of the mystics. In doing so, its attitude has been more that of confrontation and suspicion than of properly positive support. Nevertheless, this criticism from psychology has often been beneficial to the study of religion and, within that, of mysticism itself. Although McGinn and other thinkers understand that the confrontation between mysticism and psychology is not a happy one, we cannot fail to recognize that many pathologies that had nothing to do with mysticism or even religion were brought to light thanks to Freudian theory.[139]

McGinn criticizes above all the importance given to the Freudian expression "oceanic feeling," to the point that intellectuals such the French novelist Romain Rolland defended it as constituting the essence of religion.[140] Although he severely criticizes religion (in *The Future of an Illusion*), Freud acknowledges, in his *Civilization and Its Discontents*, that transitory mystical experiences can have positive cathartic value.[141]

Jung, another great name in psychology, wrote little about mysticism, but his thinking greatly influenced the religious scholars of twentieth century. Erich Neumann, his disciple, holds a view of mysticism that is fully psychological: "For us mysticism is rather a fundamental category of human experience that, psychologically speaking, manifests itself wherever consciousness is not yet, or is no longer, centered around the ego."[142]

---

137. *Mysticism, Sacred and Profane*. See also McGinn, *Foundations of Mysticism*, 338 n. 70.

138. See McGinn, *Foundations of Mysticism*, 339 n. 79, where, for instance, he identifies the work of Anne Marie Schimmel on Islam.

139. See the criticism of McGinn, *Foundations of Mysticism*, 331.

140. Ibid., 332.

141. See ibid. See also what Michel de Certeau says about Freudian criticism in *mystique. Encyclopedia Universalis*, 2009.

142. See McGinn, *Foundations of Mysticism*, 332 n. 39.

Religious or Mystical Experience

Psychology—especially Freudian psychology—says that what happens in human religious experience is linked to more ancient, primitive and deeper experiences of our being, precisely those that configured our personality and our more specific personal structure. And these were the ones we received from our father and our mother.[143]

In the first moments of our existence, we do not yet have an I through which we may perceive our distance and difference from those around us. The illuminato, or purely religious person, is precisely one who has not completely accepted the distance that exists with respect to the first totality of the maternal world. This is the difference between religious and mystical experience. The mystics accept the alternation between presence and absence in relation to the totality of the Sacred. They accept the dialogue, the difference, the questioning, and the commitment resulting from that. But, unlike the mystics, the illuminati or charismatics aspire to dissolve themselves in the divine and eliminate their own I, as they are incapable of assuming their condition as a "separate being," which alone makes possible authentic encounter, dialogue and communication. "The charismatic loves the experience of love, but not the other." Many religious experiences run this risk.[144]

This risk can only be surmounted when the fusionist religious experience is penetrated by the intervention of the separation that will bring, to a nebulous and nameless totality, a form, a figure and a name. And there lies—we think—the difference between a simply religious experience and what can be called a mystical experience, or the experience of God. The God experienced here is thus—besides a source of joy in union—a requirement, a model, a challenge, and a life ideal. This God is the mobilizing source of an ethical commitment, of a project and ideal for the transformation of history.

But the experienced deity can also run a risk of great ambiguity, even if it becomes independent of the diffusiveness of a religious experience without a name or a face. If the first risk (of the charismatic or the illuminato) is that of the search for joyous sensations and fusions, the second risk would be that of sadistic normality, of sacrifice for the sake of sacrifice, of unredeemed guilt, of self-destruction and death. If the first is the religion of joyous fusion, without boundaries and Otherness, the second may turn out to be the religion of the norm and of a moralizing obsession, with neither space nor time for graciousness and joy.

Thus, granted that the first experiences of our lives constitute a real and fecund possibility for the experience of God to take root in us, it is also

---

143. See Freud, *The Future of an Illusion*.
144. See Domínguez Morano, *Orar depois de Freud*, 39–44.

possible that these experiences might initiate very serious deviations and deflections in our understanding of and communication with God. This is the basis of the radical ambiguity implied in any religious experience.

The rejection of religion may come, then, from several sources originating in this fundamental ambiguity:[145]

1. Rejection of a childish religion that resolves everything magically.

2. Rejection of the rigid heteronomy that generates the "myth of personal autonomy." This is the myth that during the Enlightenment was understood as the autonomy for each to find within himself or herself a proprietary law or *nomos*.

3. Rejection of a religious experience that for many may seem to be a danger to the maintenance of this autonomy.

4. Rejection of the symbolic, gracious, and contemplative dimensions of existence, based on the myth of technical reason.

5. Rejection that comes from the crisis of religious language, that is, the difficulty in experiencing—in reference to God—the feelings that others have. It is not as much a question of believing, as of experiencing in the same way.

6. Rejection of a God who may be seen as a rival, competitor, or adversary of the human being.

7. Rejection of a religious experience that history has proven to be capable of degenerating into destructive fanaticism or religious fundamentalism.

8. The absence of a collective project or utopia, and a supervalorization of the individual and of individualism, with the individual seen as the parameter for everything.

9. An allergy to commitment and the predominance of a religiosity opposed to any kind of institutionalization or any substantial concreteness.

McGinn is highly critical of the way psychology presumes to understand mysticism. According to him, the cold distance between empirical and transempirical epistemology is as pronounced now as it was at the beginning of the twentieth century. Nevertheless, he continues,

> even those who—like myself—are convinced that a purely empirical reading of mystical texts from a reductive psychological

---

145. Here we are following Domínguez Morano, *Orar depois de Freud*.

perspective has only an ambiguous contribution to make to the current study of mysticism, cannot but be surprised by the lack of conversation between psychological researchers and researchers involved in the study of the history and theory of the mystical traditions.

The conclusion of the historian is that both sides seem equally at fault for the failure of this conversation to take place.[146]

While recognizing that this vision of the contemporary history of religion and of religious experience is indispensable for any more rigorous reflection we might wish to undertake, it is important for us to take a step forward. More than about history and the schools of spirituality, or even about the systematic study of asceticism and mysticism as areas and disciplines of theology or spirituality, we want to talk about the search and thirst for experience that is present and visible in today's human beings. This thirst has always accompanied human beings in their historical journey, but we believe its current intensification has its roots in the so-called crisis of modernity, or in the advent of the fragmented postmodernity, as well as in the more or less hasty and anarchical movement to resacralize the same world in which modern reason hastily and unremittingly proclaimed its disenchantment and secularization.[147] That being the case, a contribution such as that of Jean Mouroux seems fundamental to this debate.

In the mid-twentieth century, in the decade of the 1950s, the French theologian Jean Mouroux came up with a reflection that attempted to bring to earth some concepts of Otto, Eliade, and other thinkers on religion, explicitly in the Christian sphere. In raising questions about the definition and conceptualization of the religious experience from a more theological Christian perspective, it is unavoidable that we refer to the seminal work of Mouroux. In 1952 he wrote a classic work on the Christian experience, in which he distinguished several degrees of profundity.[148] These diverse levels or degrees permit an approach to a conceptualization of religious experience, distinguishing it from what it is not.

Mouroux begins his reflection by citing the classic book of William James[149] in order to criticize it. His criticism takes the position that James seems unable to conceive of the reality of the religious experience except by omitting three elements: the institutional, the intellectual, and any precise

---

146. See McGinn, *Orar depois de Freud*, 343.

147. See on this the reflection that makes up the final part of Bingemer and Dos Santos Bartholo Jr.'s *Mística e política*, 287–88.

148. See Mouroux, *L'expérience chrétienne*.

149. See James, *The Varieties of Religious Experience*.

and definite relationship with God.[150] It would seem—in Mouroux's view—that James is only interested in the exaltation manifested in a religious experience, and not in the fellowship, which, according to the French theologian, is an integral element of that experience.[151] James would be running the risk—according to Mouroux—of developing an analysis of the religious experience focused only on the "emotive" or "emotional" aspects.

Understanding religion as a relationship with a Sacred Being as such, realized through adoration and love,[152] Mouroux highlights the value of the category of the integral and personal "relationship" in order to enable the religious experience as he understands it.[153] He then defines his understanding of experience—which is "when a person perceives himself or herself in relation to the world, to himself or herself, and to God," and concludes by defining experience as "the act by which a person perceives himself or herself."[154]

Mouroux also positions himself against William James' insistence on passivity as characteristic of the mystical religious experience. He remarks, "against any conception of the experience as pure passivity, let us say that what is experienced has to do with facts as well as circumstances."[155] In explaining the nuances that lead to passivity, his theory becomes clearer. He denounces the confusion between two kinds of passivity. There is a passivity that is like something suffered and endured under a power against which the human being is impotent to react in any way. And there is a passivity that is welcomed and consented to, and is therefore an active passivity.[156] To this passivity, after re-reading Mouroux, we would give the designation of theopathic passivity.

After this initial clarification, Mouroux distinguishes three possible levels in the structure of human experience. The empirical level designates the lived out experience, without repetition in critical reflection. With the experimental level one accedes to the provoked experience which coordinates its elements to produce science. The experiential level represents the most complete personal engagement and commitment. Those engaged at this level surrender themselves with their being and their having, with their

---

150. See Mouroux, L'expérience chrétienne, 14.

151. Ibid., 15.

152. Ibid., 17.

153. Ibid., 18.

154. Ibid., 21.

155. Ibid.

156. Ibid., 22. Several mystics expressed their experiences in this way, inventing, to that end, their own vocabulary. See Simone Weil, for instance, who talks of "action non agissante," and others.

reflection and their freedom. They give themselves to themselves in a singular meaning *vis á vis* the event, and this new sense can provide material for witness.[157]

"In this sense," says Mouroux, "*any authentic spiritual experience is of the experiential type.*"[158] Thus, born in what is simply lived out, experience progresses, in science, to the rational level, and in a privileged moment is elevated to the existential or meta-empirical ones. It is in this last that religious experience distinguishes itself.

Thus Mouroux defines the religious experience as "the act—or the set of acts—through which human beings perceive themselves in relation to God."[159] According to the author this is an integrating experience, encompassing all aspects of the person. It includes rather than excludes the intellectual component, since it has as a background the whole experience of a certain idea of God, which orients the attitude and specifies the relationship. It includes equally the intellectual, the voluntary or volitional, and the affective components.[160] It is an act of freedom and graciousness that permits and anchors the relationship between the human being and the holy Mystery that the human being calls God. It is indispensable—for it to occur—that human beings accept themselves in their situation as creatures, submitting themselves to and welcoming the greatness and holiness of God, committing their whole destiny and vocation to God, and surrendering themselves to God's service.

Mouroux further says that the religious experience is the experience of the Sacred (and while agreeing with Rudolf Otto's definition, he believes that his reflection has to be revisited and rethought). For him the Sacred is God seen only as God, as a Mystery that the human being can never fully fathom.[161] This is so because God is the wholly other and the Absolute Type of Being.[162] Therefore, Mouroux continues, in an affirmation that seems key to the understanding of religious experience, "all that we can say and experience of our similarity, of our kinship, of our proximity to God must be understood in the midst of a dissimilarity, of an Otherness, of a distance equally infinite."[163]

---

157. Ibid., 24.
158. Author's italics.
159. Ibid., 25.
160. Ibid.
161. Ibid., 27.
162. Ibid.
163. Ibid., 28.

Religious experience, then, occurring in a relationship with a being who has these characteristics, is equivalent to an "entry into eternity." But this mysterious entry, cautions the author, comes about in the midst of a reversion, since the act that establishes the relationship is equally and at the same time the act that receives it. I establish the relationship, but as someone who is established by another. Opening onself, seeking and giving oneself is equal to receiving and receiving oneself. "I give myself to God but as someone who is given to myself by God."[164]

According to Mouroux this experience is always mediated because it cannot be direct, since it involves the presence of an incomprehensible and non-manipulable God, who gives God's self through signs. "God is not given in the experience, but rather apprehended in it. And the sign through which God is apprehended is the religious act in itself."[165] The experience is the consciousness of this mediation, which establishes itself graciously, that is, a consciousness of God as the established and establishing term of the relationship. In the historical immanence of God's self-delivery, God allows God's self to be experienced as Transcendent.

> Since at the same moment that I establish Him, because I establish Him as transcendent, I am established by Him, and more established than establisher. I am wrenched out of myself, and this wrenching, which delivers me to God, at same time delivers to me God himself in his action.[166]

Therefore, as God is this non-manipulable and incomprehensible Mystery who nevertheless allows God's self to be experienced, it is impossible, according to Mouroux—who thus concludes his criticism of James—to enclose God in the order of feeling.[167]

Since God, by Christian parameters, is understood as love (See 1 John 4)—Mouroux continues in chapter 6, "L'expérience chrétienne dans la première épître de Saint Jean"[168]—the religious experience carries at its core an affective component. The act by which I pledge my destiny, and in which I completely fulfill my being by giving it to God, causes in me deep vibrations and awakes in me potentialities that I myself cannot produce, such as joy and praise. Mouroux concludes his reflection on the Christian

---

164. Ibid., 29. After Mouroux, other theologians said the same thing in different words. For instance, Karl Rahner, in his famous text "Ouvinte da Palavra," says that the human being is the patient, even when an agent (*Curso fundamental da fé*, 46).

165. Ibid., 31.

166. Ibid., 32.

167. Ibid., 35.

168. Ibid., 166–88.

religious experience by saying that its immediate principles are faith and love. According to him these are two aspects of the same grace. This love—agape—has a noetic function (to bring knowledge) and leads to a witness of love among brothers and sisters, to brotherly and sisterly charity.

Reflecting on the material provided by Mouroux, it follows that what in theology can be called religious experience, while opening a vast field for reflection, brings us a significant series of ambiguities that do not simplify the task of defining the concept. And these ambiguities begin with the reflection of Mouroux himself, as read today, after more than fifty years. Indeed, it seems to us that this contribution is extremely worthwhile. With the advances in research on mysticism, his work—which aims to center itself on religious experience—presents many of the characteristics seen today in mystical experience.

Mouroux is not yet aware of the great debate taking place today in the study of mysticism. Will it be an experience for just a few, or will all human beings have access to it once they respond to the vocation planted by God in their hearts since their creation? Mouroux appears inclined toward the first hypothesis, when he says at the beginning of chapter 2, "Sur la possibilité de l'expérience chrétienne," that mystical experience is reserved, and is not the call and common destiny of Christians. It is by definition, something new in relation to a simply fervent life.[169]

With such an affirmation, Mouroux is in line with a current of thinkers and students of mysticism that today is neither the main trend nor the most imposing one. The debate has continued since the publication of his book, which was invaluable for defining religious experience. It is taking place today more than ever, since the field of religion has suffered deep changes and presents a series of areas that are veiled rather than revealed, and even less explicit.

A great Brazilian philosopher, Father Henrique de Lima Vaz, may have made an important contribution to this debate. In 1975, in a memorable text,[170] Father Vaz conceptualized the experience of God—which in his thinking coincides with what we understand as the mystical experience—as an experience of plenitude, or of radical meaning. He thus distinguishes it from religious experience, which would be an experience of the Sacred but not necessarily a mystical one, or an experience of God. An experience of God would therefore be a totalizing experience, not limited to a single dimension of existence, but pervading it completely.

---

169. Ibid., 37.
170. See Vaz, "A experiência de Deus."

A second important text by Vaz on this theme dates from 1992. It was prepared for a seminar on "Mysticism and Politics" organized by the Centro João XXIII. This text was composed and presented as the main text of the seminar, and published later in the seminar's minutes.[171] In it he conceptualizes what he understands as mysticism in the Western Christian tradition, and also develops a typology to distinguish the different currents within this tradition.

His third text is a small book,[172] published by the Centro de Estudos Superiores da Companhia de Jesus in Belo Horizonte, Brazil. Here Vaz reworks the two previous texts, especially the second, giving them a more complete and polished form and presenting a convergence of the two main pursuits of his entire life, the experience of the Mystery of God and philosophical thought.

Vaz elaborates his thought in a moment when the field of religion is being redesigned, not only in Brazil but worldwide. With the theology of liberation, political discourse with its intra-historical utopias strongly penetrates religious discourse. The explicitly religious is often viewed suspiciously as alienation and subjectivism. The thirst for the Sacred and for the Mystery—appearing after their banishment was attempted by secularization and announced to the four winds by the masters of suspicion—denotes an apparently new emergence of values such as graciousness and prayer, and brings to the fore such criteria of verification as desire, feelings, and the rediscovery in a new dimension of the nature of the relationship of human beings with the planet.[173]

The concern raised by Vaz, which apparently still stands today, is that it is not at all clear that this almost ferocious search by our contemporaries for mystical experiences corresponds to a real search for a profound encounter through a disposition to be affected by the Otherness of the other. The search for more or less spiritual or mystical sensations does not necessarily imply a desire to open oneself to the experience of Otherness, and may not leave space for Otherness and the difference of the other to manifest themselves epiphanically, in all their freedom, inventing the relationship at every breath and step.

Vaz concludes his text on the future of mysticism by pointing out that Christian mysticism today is struggling with the question of its own identity. Sometimes it finds itself lost and fragmented in a sea of other religious experiences, which do not necessarily pass through the Otherness which, in its

---

171. See Vaz, "A experiência mística na tradição ocidental."
172. See Vaz, *Experiência mística e filosofia na tradição ocidental*.
173. See Bingemer, "Novos horizontes para a contemplação e a práxis," 288.

absolute freedom, reveals itself as Holiness, or as wholly other Otherness.[174] According to Vaz, God reveals God's self as the Radical Meaning of human life. If all religious experience is an experience of the Sacred, certainly mystical experience—understood as an experience whose major objective is union with God as mystery and grace—is an experience of Meaning that involves the whole person in a consciousness that apprehends (as Mouroux says), assimilates, and interprets the experience, and is not satisfied with the affective and cathartic sensation that it provokes.

If we too easily construe as mystical experience each and every search for spiritual sensation—which is sometimes achieved through artificial means rather than through a relationship that is uniquely inaugurated and deepened in graciousness, in listening, and in desire—we might betray the very conception of mysticism that has marked, to this day, all of Western tradition, and is at the heart of its identity as it has been and is understood.

Vaz concludes his most recent book on mysticism with a note of pessimism.[175] He observes that Western modernity put an end to mysticism as it had blossomed in the premodern period, unifying it with other sciences and borrowing language to express it, dispossessing it and robbing it of its identity.

Yet in a previous article, in 1992, from which this book originated, he presents a more optimistic perspective:

> Will the man of the twenty-first century know, once he has crossed the desert of nihilism, how to reinvent a new historical day, illuminated by the sun of Transcendence, and in which authentic mystical experience can blossom again, recognized as the most precious good of a civilization? I suppose that very few are asking this question today. But I find no other way to end this discussion except by formulating it with the secret hope that it will generate, in the womb of the history yet to come, a radiant yes.[176]

We venture to agree more with the earlier optimism than with the later pessimism of this thinker. At first sight this optimism appears to be delineated on the horizon of our contemporary history. Nevertheless, we

---

174. See the biblical meaning of Holy attributed to God: Holy is the separate, the different, that which cannot be added to anything or anybody, the wholly other. See the remarks of Armstrong in *A History of God*, 41: "The Hebrew *kaddosh* . . . has nothing to do with morality as such but means 'otherness,' a radical separation. The apparition of Yahweh on Mount Sinai had emphasized the immense gulf that had suddenly yawned between man and the divine world. Now the seraphs were crying: 'Yahweh is other! other! other!'" (Isa 3:6).

175. See *Experiência mística e filosofia na tradição ocidental*, 77–90.

176. See Vaz, *Experiência mística e filosofia na tradição ocidental*, 63.

also agree that only some human experiences (we are reminded of the memorable 1975 text of Vaz) are explicitly and consciously mystical and specifically experiences of God—situations in which one feels the revealing and salvific self-communication of God that invites one to make or renew a faith commitment. This does not mean, however, that God offers these experiences only to an elite and not to all human beings.

In speaking about these experiences, there is a special language often used to describe them, such as limit situations, limit experiences, mountain-top experiences, or in-depth experiences. It is also possible to identify these deeply felt experiences in the movement from death to life, from the absurd to the meaningful, and from hate or loneliness to love and community, or from pain to joy.

In discussing mystical experience as Christianity understands it, or the Christian experience of God, continues Vaz, we are dealing with the presence of Radical Meaning in a particular and historical existence, that of Jesus of Nazareth, spoken of through a conditional and historical word, the word of Revelation. The Word of God that accompanies God's people, leading them toward the fulfillment of the promise, develops a logic of its own in the experience of faith that it engenders in the history of this people. Thus the Incarnation of God in Jesus Christ, the culmination of this dynamic, is the full manifestation of Radical Meaning, manifested not only through a reality and its expression, but fully identified with it. It is in the vulnerable and mortal flesh of Jesus of Nazareth, and in His Spirit—that blows wherever it wants and pitches its tent in human flesh—that the experience of the unseen God will take place, and the logic of the Mystery, the logic of the ineffable, will finally be inaugurated.

From what we have reflected upon in this section, we see that the opening of the human spirit to the Absolute tends, through its own dynamism, toward an unattainable horizon—toward the fullness of being and of the good that mobilizes human intelligence and freedom, and is present in each cognitive or volitional act as a condition of its own possibility. This infinite horizon, toward which the human being is structurally turned, is the real God who is experienced as near and immediate, the foundation of the human hope to reach God.

Mystical Experience: Otherness and Relationship

Perhaps few concepts in philosophy and theology are as difficult to define precisely and adequately as is mysticism. Several authors and currents have

Religious or Mystical Experience

tried to do so, but without arriving at a conclusive agreement about the problem.

In this section of our work, we will try to see how three areas of knowledge—philosophy, psychology, and theology—understand and define the question of mysticism. Although the three areas are in dialogue with each other, and are interrelated, they undeniably have their own separate characteristics that shape their own specificity.[177]

In the area of philosophy, the book by William James, *The Varieties of Religious Experience* (cited above), is still a valid reference. James treats mysticism as incorporated into an all-encompassing theory of religion, an experience lived out by individuals. For him religion is a "state of faith." And without reducing religion to mysticism, he insists "that the personal religious experience has its roots and center in mystical states of consciousness."[178]

For James, mystical experience is something that happens between affection and thought. In his investigation of the "theoretical movement" of mystical states, he argues that these states promote an expansion of consciousness and allow the "surpassing of all the usual barriers between the individual and the Absolute."[179] Thus James goes beyond monistic belief, declaring it to be incorrect because it "collapses any vestige of distance between God and the individual, making impossible the partial separateness, freedom and agency necessary for moral action."[180] His preference is, therefore, for a "pluralistic mysticism."

McGinn, on the other hand, argues that the way James distinguishes between the affective state of mystical consciousness and the philosophical and theological concepts (which surpass beliefs) that are sometimes inserted into mystical consciousness, does little justice to the complex interactions between experience and interpretation on the one hand, and feelings and thought on the other. Mysticism, for James, is both cognitive and noncognitive, but one can never be certain how this comes about.

Another philosopher discussed by McGinn is the German Baron Friedrich von Hügel.[181] He defines religion as an interaction among the historical-institutional element related to the senses and memory (the Earthly principle), the analytical and speculative element related to reason

---

177. Here we follow the excellent analysis of this "state of the art," presented in the form of a survey by McGinn, the great North American historian of mysticism, in his book *The Foundations of Mysticism*, 265–343.

178. See McGinn, *Foundations of Mysticism*, 291–93.

179. See James, *Varieties of Religious Experience*, 329.

180. Ibid., 397–98.

181. His two-volume work *The Mystical Element of Religion* is an important reference on the literature on mysticism in the English language.

(the Pauline principle), and the intuitive-emotional element related to desire and action (the Johannine principle). Such conceptions are expressed by von Hügel as institutionalism, intellectualism and mysticism, and viewed as the three main elements of religion.

For von Hügel the highest mysticism is characterized by a love for and appreciation of creation, along with the need of the soul to transcend all special or ecstatic experiences in a mystical way. At the same time, the mystic must continually pay attention to contingent historical reality. Finally, the attention of the soul directed toward God and Christ is most intense only at the highest meditative states. Exclusive mysticism, according to von Hügel, was a dangerous temptation in the history of Christianity. The inclusive mysticism that he defends demonstrates that mystical religion and morality are closely allied, even almost identical in form. Both von Hügel and Troeltsch insist in that mysticism makes sense not in itself, but only as a component of a concrete religious life. According to them, no information exists of any person at all who was nothing but a mystic.[182]

As for the French literature on mysticism, McGinn's survey highlights the figure of the Jesuit Joseph Maréchal, who anticipated the so-called transcendental Thomism of Lonergan and Rahner. In his text "À propos du sentiment de présence chez les profanes et chez les mystiques,"[183] he reflects on mysticism not from the standpoint of a notion of union with God, but rather from that of psychological and philosophical research on the feeling of presence. He considers the *a priori* conditions for the possibility that an evaluation of the existence of the presence of God at the center of experience might also be a judgement of its reality.[184]

For Maréchal intelligence must be understood as fundamentally intuitive in its impulse and finality. "The affirmation of reality is, then, nothing more than the expression of the fundamental tendency of the mind toward unification in and with the Absolute."[185] It is thus evident what the mystical experience is for Maréchal, at least in its culmination: a direct, intuitive, unmediated contact, in this life, between intelligence and its objective, the Absolute. In his words, it is "the intuition of God as present, the feeling of the immediate presence of a Transcendent being."[186]

---

182. On this point we disagree with von Hügel, since it appears to us that the great contemplatives were persons whose mystical activity occupied their entire life space.

183. McGinn uses the English translation, "On the Feeling of Presence in Mystics and Non-mystics," in Maréchal, *A Maréchal Reader*.

184. See the famous work of Maréchal, *Etudes sur la psychologie des mistiques*.

185. Ibid., 1:101.

186. Ibid., 1:102–3.

According to McGinn, for this French Jesuit Christian mysticism is the *analogatum princeps* of all that can be said about mysticism as a whole. He suggests, but does not develop in detail, the argument that the philosophical study of mysticism involves an interaction among the three fundamental themes of metaphysics: God, the self, and the world around us.[187] From a comparative or descriptive point of view Maréchal offers a broad definition: "the mystical experience in any circumstance is superior to normality: it consists of something more direct, more intimate, and more rare." Mysticism, then, involves three elements: a religious doctrine, some unusual psychological facts, and a synthesis of the two, or "an interpretation of psychological facts as a function of doctrine."[188]

Maréchal—following an Augustinian model for a general discrimination of types of vision—distinguishes lower and higher states within mysticism. According to him, mysticism as a monotheistic Christian system has three clearly defined levels: 1. "integration of the ego and its objective content, under the preponderance of the idea of a personal God"; 2. "the transcendent revelation of God to the soul," often with the suspension of all other activities of the latter (this is the level of ecstasy, and is the special focus of a large part of Maréchal's research on Christianity); 3. "a kind of readjustment of the faculties of the soul" through which it reacquires contact with the creatures "under the immediate and perceptible influence of God, who is present and active in it."

As for ecstasy, which the author places at the second level, it is a synthesis of the empirical negativity characterized by the cessation of conceptual thinking (including consciousness of the dualism ego-not ego) and the transcendental positiveness in which the mind is immediately assimilated into God in the supreme intellectual intuition or union for which it was created.[189]

McGinn considers deplorable the fact that Maréchal never developed an analysis of the role of love in mysticism, but it appears to us that his basic philosophical position does not exclude this. At a certain point in his reflection, he insists in that reality constitutes not only an object to be known, but also a value to be *desired*—the Absolute—and the objective of any intellectual and volitional effort.[190] Does this not open the door to love as a category of knowledge of the mystical experience? We think so.

---

187. See McGinn, *Foundations of Mysticism*, 300, nn. 49 and 50.

188. See Maréchal, *Etudes sur la psychologie des mistiques*, vol. 2, 288.

189. All these reflections are found in *Etudes*, vol. 2.

190. See Maréchal, *Le point de depart de la metaphysique*, vol. 5, 305–13 and 344. The italicization of *desired* is ours.

Still in the area of French thought we find the name of Maurice Blondel, who proposes, in *L'Action*,[191] a new way to research the relationship between philosophy and Christianity. He starts with a critical reflection on the concrete active subject, in which he discerns both a *volonté voulante* (a dynamism common to any will) and a *volonté voulue* (the concrete in action). For Blondel, such a philosophy represents a desire for Transcendence, a demonstration of the need of humankind for contact with the supernatural in general, although this is not philosophical evidence that any form of supernatural revelation—such as Christianity—might indeed be an answer.

In truth, Blondel's answer is similar to that of Maréchal, although developed in a different direction. Mysticism is a prolongation of ordinary Christian life, and therefore all authentic human action points to mystical knowledge and, through it, to a beatific vision.[192] Connatural knowledge, which according to Blondel includes both the natural and the supernatural, is the point of contact.[193]

Blondel says that the deficiencies in all forms of human reason indicate that God can be known only through God's self-communication, which takes place in mystical knowledge. This knowledge, therefore, is not made less reasonable by the fact that it goes beyond all inferior modes of rationality. In conformity with the basic impulse of his philosophy, Blondel states that the natural dynamism of the intellect cries out for unitive mystical knowledge, even if the actual reception of the divine Mystery may remain a supernatural gift.[194] Citing John of the Cross, he summarizes the typical themes of the main traditions of Western Christian mysticism. He especially emphasizes that in the highest mystical states the extraordinary ecstatic experiences cease, because love and knowledge are unified there and subsumed within a harmonious life characterized by "a universal charity that reconciles and arranges hierarchically without confusion all the phases and degrees of human existence."[195] In this state the mystic "actively suffers and passively acts."[196]

Henri Bergson left his mark on the francophone world with a work in which he presents mysticism as the direct expression of an evolutionary

---

191. See *L'Action: Essai d'une critique de la vie et d'une science de la pratique*.

192. "Le problème de la mystique," "Qu'est-ce que la mystique? Quelques aspects historiques et philosophiques du problème." In *Cahiers de la nouvelle journée*, supplement no. 8, 1929, 18–19 and 44–45.

193. Ibid., 30–40.

194. Ibid., 52–53.

195. Ibid., 56.

196. Ibid., 62. How could one not be reminded here of Simone Weil's "action non agissante," or of Etty Hillesum's "mournful contentment"?

force at the heart of all reality. He describes this force as the *élan vital*. In this famous work, *Les deux sources de la morale et de la religion*, he distinguishes two interrelated forms of moral obligation: the morality of the law, based on societal pressures, and personal morality, based on attraction or on creative heroism. This corresponds to two basic types of religion: 1. static religion and 2. dynamic religion. Both are necessary for the *élan vital*, which leads life toward ever greater complexity and richness. The objective of mysticism is thus "the creative force that life manifests in itself."[197] Thus, as McGinn very accurately comments, Bergson—differently from von Hügel, who sees mysticism as one of the elements of concrete religions—made mysticism into the source and interior reality of all religion.[198]

The great Thomist philosopher Jacques Maritain was another thinker who reflected intensely on mysticism. In his book *Les degrés du savoir*[199] he distinguishes (artificially, according to McGinn) between 1) a negative theology that is purely an intellectual negation purporting to be mystical (of neo-platonic origin), and 2) a negative theology that issues from the connaturality of love and is thus an expression of true mystical experience.[200]

Maritain defines mystical experience as "an experiential knowledge of the profound things of God," approximating the definition attributed to Thomas Aquinas, *cognitio Dei experimentalis* or even "possession granted by the experience of the Absolute."[201] Maritain also uses another definition, and a happy one in our view, "fruitful experience of the Absolute."[202] According to Maritain's reading of John of the Cross, three things take place in the union called spiritual matrimony: we come to love God as God loves us because uncreated love becomes the agent of everything the soul does; the

---

197. See Bergson, *Le deux sources de la morale et la religion*: "Cet effort est de Dieu si ce n'est pas Dieu lui-même" (This force comes from God, if it is not God).

198. See McGinn, *Foundations of Mysticism*, 305.

199. See Maritain, *Distinguer pour unir: ou, Les degrés du savoir*.

200. See the criticism of McGinn, *Foundations of Mysticism*, 306–7: "The rigidity of the ardent Thomism of the French philosopher made it almost impossible for him to find any other philosophical system in agreement with his own intentions."

201. The brief definition of mysticism as *cognitio Dei experimentalis* is not expressly found in Thomas Aquinas' *Summa Theologiae*, but is offered by Gershom Scholem in his *Major Trends of Jewish Mysticism*, 4. Scholem cites the Aquinate in the work in German by Engelbert Krebs (*Grundfragen der kirchlichen Mystik dogmatischer erörtert und für das Leben gewertet* [Freiburg: Herder, 1921] 37), and does not check the citation with Thomas Aquinas' original (which is found in *STh* Ii. 2 quaestio 97, art 2 ad 2—answer to objection 2). Saint Thomas' expression is in the core of the question whether or not it is a sin to tempt God, and does not refer directly to mysticism.

202. See Maritain, "L'expérience mystique naturelle et le vide," in *Oeuvres Complètes* (1912–1939), 1125–58, cited by Vaz in *Mística e política*, 12 n. 4.

soul "gives God back to God"; and finally, the soul comes to participate in the true life of the Trinity.[203]

Yet McGinn rightly observes that Maritain's difficulty in dealing with the use of erotic language by the mystics—in spite of almost resentfully admitting it to be the most direct analogy to mystical love—is especially enigmatic for a thinker who gives such a central role to affective connaturality.[204]

Undoubtedly, however, the thinker who reflected the most and with the greatest originality on mysticism in the francophone world was Michel de Certeau.[205] This brilliant French Jesuit emphasized the point that mystical experience—besides being of profound significance in the personal life of the mystic—was necessarily a social phenomenon. As a historian and psychologist, he did not miss the fact that mysticism always reflects a socioreligious world as its background, while on the other hand it affects and even transforms the world through the creation of new types of discourse and the formation of new religious groups.[206]

In his article "Mystique," in the *Encyclopaedia Universalis*, Michel de Certeau says,

> Since the sixteenth and seventeenth centuries mysticism was no longer designated as a kind of "wisdom" elevated by the recognition of a Mystery already lived out and proclaimed in common beliefs, but as an experiential knowledge that slowly separated itself from traditional theology or from ecclesiastic institutions, and is characterized by the consciousness, acquired or received, of a fulfilling passivity in which the self is lost in God.[207]

Michel de Certeau insists that mystical experience could not be studied in itself, but only through mystical language and through the body of the mystic.[208]

Moving from France to the Anglo-Saxon world of the last forty years, McGinn presents a discussion of mysticism that centers on two questions: 1. What is the nature of the mystical experience? 2. What kind of knowledge

---

203. See Maritain, *Les degres du savoir*, 373–81.

204. Ibid., 7, 282–83. We agree with the criticism of McGinn (*Foundations of Mysticism*, 310 n. 115), although it seems to us that this problem affects many other commentators on Christian mysticism besides Maritain.

205. This evaluation of the original excellence of Michel de Certeau is ours, not McGinn's.

206. See to corroborate this point, the well-known works of Michel de Certeau: *L'ecriture de l'histoire*; "Historicites mystiques"; and his major work, *La Fable mystique. XVI–XVIIe Siècle.*

207. See Certeau, "Mystique," in *Encyclopaedia Universalis*, digital version, 2009.

208. See Certeau, *La fable mystique*, 12–15.

does it convey? Persistently searching for the nature of mystical experience, English and German philosophers tend to focus on the question whether all mystical experience, whatever its fundamental characteristics, is (yes or no) of the same nature—in other words, whether there is a nucleus common to all kinds of mysticism. In addition, they dwell on two other questions: 1. The question of typology. Are the various kinds of mysticism really distinct, or simply diverse manifestations of a single type of experience? 2. What is the relationship between experience and interpretation in the reports of the mystics? These questions are made more difficult by the insistence by so many mystics that their experience cannot really be communicated since it is, by definition, mystical and ineffable, and only capable of indirect communication through the paradoxical and analogical language that characterizes all thought and language about God.

Walter Terence Stace,[209] in opposition to comparativists such as Robert Zaehner, defends the universal or common nucleus of mysticism, even while admitting two distinct types of mystical experience (the introversive and the extroversive). The presupposition on which his argument is based is the importance of "as much as possible making a distinction between a mystical experience in itself and the conceptual interpretations that can be built upon it."[210] Stace distinguishes experience from interpretation, saying that any religiously distinctive term (God, Trinity, Christ, Buddha, Nirvana) is always subsequent interpretation, and that any term that is not distinctive (unity, undifferentiation, light, intimate spirit) is "uninterpreted description."[211]

Stace further says that mystical experience is neither subjective nor objective, but transsubjective, meaning that even if it is concordant in its universal manifestations—since it is the experience of an undifferentiated unity—it cannot be judged as internal or external to the harmony of the natural order.[212]

According to Stace, when mystics say their experiences are ineffable, what they really mean is that words cannot be used during the experience in itself, but that in a subsequent moment the memory of the experience of transsubjective unity allows the mystic to use words, whether metaphorically or literally, to describe what was experienced.[213] McGinn disagrees with Stace, arguing that mystics do not do philosophy, and, therefore, do not

---

209. See Stace, *Mysticism and Philosophy*.
210. Ibid., 31.
211. Ibid.
212. Ibid., 137–45.
213. Ibid., 295–306.

get involved in these conceptual discussions appropriate to philosophers. Moreover, he is suspicious of the possibility that Stace or any other philosopher can find words adequate to express the recollection of an experience of undifferentiated unity.[214]

After critically analyzing the philosophy of Stace, McGinn compares his contribution with those of other philosophers. Ninian Smart[215] differs from Stace regarding the characterization of the nucleus of mysticism and uses a subtler way to describe the relationship between experience and interpretation. William Wainright is basically preoccupied with the cognitive intention implied in the mystical experience. For him, the mystical experience is a unitary state, which is noetic but without specific empirical content. In his criticism, McGinn refers to the review of Wainright's work published in 1985.[216]

Also in the Anglo-Saxon world, Philip Almond develops a typology of mysticism consisting of five different models:[217]

1. All mystical experiences are equal. This, according to Almond, would be the model of James.[218]

2. The mystical experience is always the same, but their interpretations vary according to the religious and philosophical markers employed. Almond places the works of Evelyn Underhill, Sarvepalli Radhakrishnan, and Ninian Smart in this model.

3. A few types of mysticism transcend religious barriers, such as, for example, the reflections of Rudolf Otto and Robert Zaehner, and to a certain extent that of William Stace on religious experience and the divine as numinous, since these two types appear really to be fused into one.

4. According to Almond this category is implicit in only a few studies of mysticism. He says that there are as many forms of mystical experience as there are paradigmatic expressions, that is, expressions that refer to the central focus, objective, or nature of the experience.

5. Since, according to Almond, all these models fail to establish a link between experience and interpretation, he develops a fifth model

---

214. See McGinn, *Foundations of Mysticism*, 316.

215. Philosopher and historian of religion, and author of the entry "Mysticism, history of" in *Encyclopaedia of Philosophy*, as well as of several other titles and articles.

216. McGinn, Review of *Mysticism: A Study of Its Nature, Cognitive Value and Moral Implications*.

217. See Almond, *Mystical Experience and Religious Doctrine*.

218. McGinn disagrees with Almond on this point. See *Foundations of Mysticism*, 435 n. 184.

combining the insights of the second and fourth models with the recent work of Steven Katz, among others.[219]

In attempting to summarize, we could say that according to Almond there are many varieties of mystical experience, as many as the interpretations that they incorporate. A retrospective interpretation would take place following the experience, a reflexive one during it, and an incorporated one would precede and configure it.[220] However, he also argues that there are "higher" mystical experiences, which are—at least as limit situations—"without content" and outside of the subject-object dichotomy.

Steven Katz takes another direction. He holds that there is no unmediated experience. On the contrary, "all experience is processed, organized, and made available to others in extremely complex epistemological ways." According to him, Buddhists have Buddhist experiences, Jews have Jewish experiences, and Christians always have experiences related to Christ. He criticizes the interreligious and ecumenical eagerness to abolish the boundaries and differences among experiences.[221]

James Price, who is very critical of the intercultural vision of mysticism so predominant in Rudolf Otto, identifies, behind these typologies, sets of binary principles, which he describes as follows:

1. The distinction between the internal and external levels in human experience.
2. The assumption that mystical data must be understood
    a. as the object and content of consciousness, and
    b. as analyzable according to the metaphysical and doctrinal language used by the mystics.

In the end, under the influence of Lonergan, Price says that a divergence toward the inner horizon—which observes the operations of consciousness more than its object and content—is the necessary basis for an explanatory, and not merely a descriptive, account of mysticism.

Leaving the explicitly Anglo-Saxon contemporary world, McGinn turns to a great figure who writes in English but comes from the Netherlands, the Belgian philosopher of religion Luis Dupré—already cited in this book. His writings on mysticism are especially important in two areas: 1) the experience of the self in theistic mysticism, and 2) the role of mysticism

---

219. See Katz, *Mysticism and Philosophical Analysis*.

220. See Almond, *Mystical Experience and Religious Doctrine*, 162–63.

221. See Katz, "Language, Epistemology, and Mysticism," in Katz, *Mysticism and Philosophical Analysis*, 26–56.

in the modern secular world. On this point the author is perhaps a pioneer, having influenced a whole generation with his numerous writings on the living out of spirituality and on mysticism in a world that has lost its religious frame of reference.[222]

Dupré is a great expert on medieval mysticism, especially on the Rhenish and Flemish mystics, about whom he wrote many articles. According to him—in agreement with Eckhart and Ruysbroeck—the soul, in its self-consciousness, has available to it the appropriate basis for its identification with God. Dupré also engaged in research on the role of mysticism in modern secular society, where a direct experience of the sacred is in large part no longer available. He argues that the mystical sense of divine absence—like Eckhart's wilderness—provides a point of encounter between classical Christian mysticism and the uncultivated land of modern atheism. Even believers who "share, in fact if not in principle, in the practical atheism of their culture as a whole, have no other alternative than to give life to this negative experience and confront its feeling of the absence of God" in order to find the transcendent."[223] Only in this way can the modern believer overcome secular atheism and begin to discover and recognize "a transcendent dimension in a fundamental engagement with a world and human community at once totally autonomous and totally dependent."[224]

The last philosopher considered in McGinn's survey is Ewert Cousins, for whom the fundamental object of the study of mysticism continues to be the mystical experience. However, Cousins understands and affirms that the only approach to the experience as such is through the mystical text, whose penetration requires careful literary and historical study. The crucial stage in Cousins' method consists of a phenomenological analysis of mystical experience that explores the structures of consciousness through the cultivation of the faculty of empathy, through which "we can understand the way our consciousness enters the consciousness of the other and perceives reality from the perspective of the other's experience."[225]

McGinn's lucid and profound research appears to show that, in Western thought, reflection of a speculative nature on mysticism (which developed by way of philosophy into properly theological thought, based in its

---

222. Besides Dupré's numerous articles, see Dupré, *The Common Life*; Dupré, *Transcendent Selfhood*; Dupré, *The Other Dimension*; Dupré, *The Deeper Life*; Dupré, *Symbols of the Sacred*; Dupré and Saliers, *Christian Spirituality*; and Dupré and Wiseman, *Light from Light*. On the work of Dupré, see Casarella and Schner, *Christian Spirituality and the Culture of Modernity: The Thought of Louis Dupré*.

223. See Dupré, "Spiritual Life in a Secular Age."

224. Ibid., 31.

225. See Cousins, *Global Spirituality: Toward the Meeting of Mystical Paths*.

turn on scriptural data regarding the doctrine of Grace and spiritual life as elaborated by the Christian tradition) provided a solid ground for theology to engage in this field with its own instruments. Yet it is undeniable that even philosophers who were rigorously faithful to their epistemology had to accept that this reflection must be based on the agreement of witnesses about religious experiences recognized as authentic.[226]

It appears, therefore, that the definition of mysticism as *cognitio Dei experimentalis*, that is, as the knowledge of God through experience, remains as valid today as ever. If at any time mysticism can be approached by theology in a more intellectual and thoughtful way, this does not in any way eliminate the primary experiential level, which is fundamental to what is recognized and understood as mysticism—an experience of the Mystery of the wholly other, a knowledge of this other through experience. Since Christian theology is *intellectus fidei*—faith in search of its intelligence—it has often been accepted, throughout more than two thousand years of the history of Christianity, as a daring challenge, that of seeking to develop a rigorous reflection and articulate principles about something that fundamentally emerges from the experiential field—from the unutterable and the ineffable—such as mysticism.[227]

The word *mystical* first appeared in early Christianity, in the writings of Dionysius the Areopagite. But its use as a noun is more recent, dating from the beginning of the seventeenth century in France, as shown in the well-documented research of Michel de Certeau.[228]

In truth, more than a few difficulties were encountered in establishing the citizenship of mysticism within the theological domain, especially among the Protestants. This was demonstrated by McGinn, citing the definition by Albrecht Ritschl: "Mysticism is therefore the practice of neoplatonic metaphysics, and this is the theoretical norm of the supposed mystical delight in God. Consequently, the universal being who is seen as God, in whom the mystic wants to be dissolved, is a fraud."[229] And that of Adolph Harnack: "Mysticism as a rule is rationalism worked out in a fantastical way, and rationalism is faded mysticism."[230] McGinn criticizes Harnack's posi-

226. See Ladrière, "Approcio filosofico alla mística," 83.

227. See the remarks of Moioli on this issue: "Para definir la mística, se puede hablar de una experiencia religiosa particular de unidad-comunión-presencia, en donde lo que se 'sabe' es precisamente la realidad, el *dato* de esa unidad-comunión-presencia, y no una reflexión, una conceptualización, una racionalización del dato religioso vivido" ("Mística cristiana," 931, cited by Gamarra, *Teología espiritual*, 279 n. 64).

228. Certeau, "Mystique au XVIIe siècle: Le problème du language 'mystique,'" in Guillet, *L'homme devant Dieu*.

229. See McGinn, *Foundations of Mysticism*, 267.

230. Ibid., 268.

tion, affirming that it has the vulnerability of failing to explain how the Western mystical tradition initiated by Augustine is related to the Eastern one, whose major expression is found in the writings of Pseudo-Dionysius.[231]

Harnack, in his monumental multivolume work,[232] takes notice of the fact that in Christianity, since Methodius of Olympus in the third century, there has been an important current that values the interior and subjective dimension of the encounter with God. According to Harnack, this marked the irruption of the subjectivity of monastic mysticism into Christianity. This type of Eastern mysticism, "which bases its hope of redemption on the idea that the God-Logos continually unites himself anew with each individual so as to form a union," insufficiently explains the thinking of Harnack on the essence of Christianity. The notion of the birth of the Logos in the soul of the believer, the key component of what Eastern Christianity calls deification (*theosis*), is, for Harnack, implicit pantheism, and carries a magical vision of the sacraments.[233]

The position on mysticism of Paul Tillich, another Protestant thinker, was more complex and multicolored than that of other reformed theologians such as Barth and Brunner.[234] Throughout his life, Tillich maintained an interest in the question of mysticism, and devoted a major part of his work to reflection on the intuitive consciousness of the ultimate and definitive value of being, which is the basis of those philosophies that view religion as a "type of mystical experience."[235]

Ernst Troeltsch[236] had already claimed that mystical religion is based on the primacy of direct or mediated religious experience and therefore can be technically described as an independent religious philosophy, one that is present in several concrete religions. But McGinn observes that although Troeltsch's concept of a religious *a priori* gave an important role to mysticism, his failure to elaborate the concept left this role somewhat obscure. Troeltsch carries out a perceptive analysis of the reasons why the mystics found it easier to live within an ecclesiastic model than did the sectarians. But his reflection may have ended a little too soon. There may have been

---

231. Ibid.

232. See Harnack, *History of Dogma*.

233. Ibid., cited by McGinn, *Foundations of Mysticism*, 267 n. 14.

234. See ibid., 269.

235. See Tillich, *Systematic Theology*, vol. 1, 9. "The theological concepts of both idealists and naturalists are rooted in a 'mystical a priori,' an awareness of something that transcends the cleavage between subject and object" (ibid.).

236. See Troeltsch, *The Social Teaching of the Christian Churches*.

elements related to mystical religion other than the conscious insistence on the primacy of direct religious experience.[237]

Albert Schweitzer, another great Protestant biblical theologian, condemned—as did some of his peers and church brethren—the so-called identity mysticisms that emerged at the core of a negativist attitude toward life and the world. This great theologian, medical doctor, humanist and musician insists in his writings that an affirmation of life and the world could give birth to a true ethical mysticism, but only to the extent that it is based on what he calls "elemental thinking." This way of thinking, preoccupied with the basic questions of life, rests on a *Lebenschaung* (vision of life), which is the expression of the desire that precedes a *Weltanschaung* (worldview), the rational and scientific approach to an apprehension of the world. This mode of thought finds expression in Schweitzer's famous philosophy of "reverence for life." This rational, absolute and universal reverence for all forms of life forms the basis of an ethical mysticism involving the union of the human being with the infinite will.[238]

Schweitzer, like Paul, says that Jesus is eschatological in the expectation of the imminent end of the world, and holds that the hellenization of Christianity really began with Ignatius of Antioch and the Gospel of John. He defines mysticism as "the individual feeling himself, although externally in the midst of the earthly and the temporal, to belong to the supernatural and eternal."[239] In his negative evaluation of the mysticism of identification with God, Schweitzer's thinking concurs with the main current of continental Protestantism: "Mysticism purely of God remains a dead thing."[240] For the doctor of the African jungle, Paul was in a sense the last of the Christians, since his unified and integrated biography of Jesus was later fragmented among the several divisions of the religious proposal of Christianity, each one of them collecting and carrying with them their own fragments of what had previously been a seamless cloth."[241] In truth, Schweitzer—like almost all the continental Protestant theologians who reflected on mysticism—assumes that the so-called "mysticism of God"[242] always means identification with the divine, and is therefore, *ipso facto*, inconsistent with the Christian faith and its emphasis on the transcendental distinction between God and

---

237. See McGinn, *Foundations of Mysticism*, 271.

238. See Clark, *Ethical Mysticism of Albert Schweitzer*, esp. 62–67, cited by McGinn, *Foundations of Mysticism*, 271 n. 32.

239. See Schweitzer, *Mysticism of Paul the Apostle*, 1.

240. Ibid., 379.

241. Ibid., 395–96.

242. McGinn uses the expression "God-mysticism" (*Foundations of Christian Mysticism*, 272).

the human being. According to McGinn, the history of Christian mysticism suggests that this picture is too simple.[243] Nevertheless, the many accusations leveled against Christian spirituality as alienating and subjective may explain the reaction of historical Protestantism, which has a more ethical and practical configuration than that of Catholicism.

William Ralph Inge, English theologian and Dean of Saint Paul's Cathedral, says that true mysticism, based on the Johannine doctrine of the Logos, is defined as "the attempt to realize in thought and feeling the immanence of the temporal in the eternal, and of the eternal in the temporal."[244] In spite of his importance for theological reflection in the English language on mysticism, Inge has some serious limitations. These include his lack of understanding of negative or apophatic mysticism, which he calls "the greatest accident of Christian mysticism,"[245] as well as his failure to appreciate the role of the erotic element in Christian mysticism. According to McGinn, this imposes very severe limitations on his work, which is pioneering in other aspects.[246]

As do all scholars of mysticism, McGinn gives great prominence to the Anglican writer Evelyn Underhill, author of very important works on mysticism.[247] Underhill understood mysticism as "the expression of the innate tendency of the human spirit toward complete harmony with the transcendental order, whatever may be the theological formula by which this order is understood."[248] She identifies three symbolic models encountered by the mystics to produce reports of the experiences they lived through: the pilgrimage or search, the marriage of the soul, and the alchemical model of transformation.[249]

Another writer from the High Church of England, Kenneth Escort Kirk,[250] says that a true appreciation of the vision of God implies the absence of self-centered joy from the experience in itself (which he calls pan-hedonism, a term he takes from Henri Bremond). It is determined by the

---

243. Ibid.

244. See Inge, *Christian Mysticism*, 5.

245. Ibid., 115.

246. See McGinn, *Foundations of Mysticism*, 273. Georges Bataille himself observes that Christianity allowed other areas of human knowledge—psychology, for example—to appropriate sexual language that had already been used by the earliest Christian mystics. See the 1957 work of Bataille, *L'erotisme*.

247. See her reference work *Mysticism: A Study in the Nature and Development of Man's Spiritual Conscience*.

248. Ibid., xiv, cited by McGinn, *Foundations of Mysticism*, 274.

249. Underhill, *Mysticism*, 126–48.

250. See Kirk, *The Vision of God*.

priority of divine love and the active call to share this love with others. Kirk's conclusion is that

> the mystical experience is at the same time the most common and the greatest of human events. There is not a single one of us for whom this does not take place daily.... What Christianity offers with its presence and with the sacraments, the life of prayer and service, and its preaching on the Incarnate Son of God, is the vision itself in ever increasing plenitude.[251]

Whatever may be their individual differences, these three Anglicans (Inge, Underhill, and Kirk) agree that true mysticism always involves an affirmation of the goodness of the world and of the continuity between nature and spirit, as well as an acknowledgment that mystical life finds its true expression in active love of the neighbor. Their importance lies in the fact that they bring to the reflection on mysticism elements that conserve all its actuality, such as the lack of separation between the natural and the supernatural, as well as the ethical and practical element as the fruit of the experience of union with the divine Mystery.

The Catholic Edward Butler affirms in his work *Western Mysticism*[252] that "contemplation at its highest limit is identical to mystical experience and involves the claim of the mystics... to an experiential perception of the Being and Presence of God." Butler, according to McGinn, insisted that all Christians are "in some way" called to mystical contemplation, an affirmation that Catholicism continued to make and that reached its culmination in Karl Rahner in the twentieth century. However, according to Butler, "in some way" implies not all in the same way.

Perhaps the most notable of Butler's theological intuitions, according to McGinn, is the distinction between 1) the active "union of uniformity," as he calls it, with the will of God; and 2) the passive union that results from a direct conscious contact with God. This allows him to reintroduce a kind of double standard by which he argues that although all Christians are in some way called to mystical contemplation, only some of them are called to true contemplation and to more profound union.[253]

So far this journey demonstrates that the great discoveries—apparently so new—of twentieth century Christian mysticism, whether Catholic or Protestant, did not originate with the Second Vatican Council and modern secularization, which the Council tried to address in an absolutely original way. The Council Fathers, as well as the builders of ecumenism in

---

251. Ibid., 194.
252. Butler, *Western Mysticism*.
253. See McGinn, *Foundations of Mysticism*, 277, commenting on Butler.

the historical Protestant churches, walked on roads already strongly and deeply trod by their predecessors. Everything called up by the most recent historical studies of Christian mysticism led to the ecumenical and pastoral event of the Council like a river that finally arrives at the sea.

After Vatican II—and because of the anthropological Copernican turn that the Catholic Church brought to theology, influenced above all by Rahnerian thinking—the debates about mysticism in Catholic theology centered on two narrowly connected questions: 1) Is the call to mystical contemplation universally offered to all Christians, or is it a special grace available only to an elect few? 2) In what stage of the life of prayer does mystical contemplation properly begin? The second question touches a nerve in the theology of grace by raising the issue of the definition of Christian perfection.

In truth, the Council instigated a debate that was already going on in many segments of Catholicism, especially in Europe. In France, for instance, Augustin-François Poulain, SJ, and Auguste Saudreau disagree on these questions. The latter insists in that mystical contemplation is a normal objective of Christian life, toward which all are called whether or not they reach it in their lives, while the former takes different position.[254] For his part, the famous Thomist Dominican Reginald Garrigou-Lagrange, around the time of Jacques Maritain, said that there can be only one way to Christian perfection: that which begins with the supernatural gift of faith, advances through the activity of the gifts of the Holy Spirit, and finds its fulfillment in inspired contemplation.[255]

McGinn, however, says that these truly great figures do not exhaust the richness of the debate about mysticism in France and throughout Europe at the beginning of the twentieth century. He comes up with the names—although he does not dwell on them for long—of Maurice de La Taille, Adolphe Tanquerey, Joseph de Guibert, and Gabriele di Santa Maria Madalena.[256]

Turning to early twentieth-century Germany, the historian highlights the figure of the Benedictine monk Anselm Stolz (1900–1942), who lived and died before the Council but anticipated many of its intuitions.[257] Stolz argues that in order to understand the theology of mysticism one must begin with the Scriptures and study the thought of the great Eastern and Western fathers. Without denying the importance of Teresa of Avila and John of

---

254. See McGinn, *Foundations of Mysticism*, 278.

255. See the work of Garrigou-Lagrange, *Perfection chrétienne et contemplation selon S. Thomas d'Aquin et S. Jean de la Croix*.

256. The works of these theologians are carefully cited in McGinn, *Foundations of Mysticism*, 424 n. 79.

257. Ibid., 281.

the Cross, Stolz says that their visions conform with the teachings of Saint Thomas. Yet he unexpectedly reverses the order of authorities, positioning the church fathers rather than the sixteenth-century Spaniards as the first witnesses to the mystical experience in its plenitude. In so doing, and in calling up the early sources of Christianity, Stolz develops a theology of mysticism very close to that of the Eastern Orthodox Church as developed by figures such as Vladimir Lossky, among others.[258]

Among the topics considered by Stolz are 1) Paul's ecstatic experience of being lifted to the third heaven (according to the author, 2 Cor 12:1–5 is the starting point of the theology of mysticism, not Teresa's descriptions of the stages of prayer); and 2) scriptural themes such as being lifted to heaven, being in Christ, freedom from the power of the demon, and the restoration of the Adamic condition. Mystical prayer is seen by the author as a development of life in grace, essentially independent of feelings or psychological states. Stolz agrees with the definition of mysticism as an experience of God,[259] but the nucleus of this position is the claim that "mysticism, in its declared sense, is the transpsychological experience of being included in the stream of divine life that is given in the sacraments, and especially in the Eucharist."[260]

The questions raised by the work of Stolz—which, according to McGinn, challenge theological reflection on mysticism—are these:[261]

1. What distinguishes Christian mysticism—if it is possible to say that anything does—from Christian life in general? Stolz answers that mystical life is fundamentally nothing other than Christian life. In its restricted sense (the sense by which we name only some Christians as true mystics) it is the highest development of this root and foundation. McGinn then observes that Stolz differentiates between foundation (Christian life) and development (mystical life).

2. Is Christian mysticism different from the mysticism of other religions? Stolz's grounding of mysticism in the life of the church leads him to see Christian mysticism as in no way comparable to any other mysticism. In response to Protestants who say that mysticism is a diversion from

---

258. It must not be forgotten that one of the fundamental dispositions of the Council—taking a direction contrary to the tendency of theology to begin everything with Scholasticism—was a return to sources such as the Scriptures and the Greek and Latin patristics.

259. McGinn calls special attention to 151–52 of Stolz's *Theologie de la mystique*, where Stolz affirms the possibility of immediate knowledge of God.

260. See McGinn, *Foundations of Christian Mysticism*, 246.

261. See ibid., 282 nn. 88 and 89.

the true evangelical faith, Stolz affirms that since it is the essence of Christianity, true mysticism cannot be found in any other place.

Just as the historian has begun to demonstrate, the Catholic discussion about mysticism was more intense than ever in the first four decades of the twentieth century. The great turn came with the birth of the *nouvelle théologie* in France in the decade of 1940, and with the emergence of the transcendental Thomisms of Karl Rahner and Bernard Lonergan, which marked the official departure from the exclusive use of scholastic language and categories in the documents of Vatican II.

Lonergan wrote little about mysticism, but his project of reorganizing theology through the creation of a more adequate theological method, based on cognitive critical theory, was seen to offer significant new possibilities for mystical theology. Several current initiatives are exploring the implications of his method for the study of mysticism.[262]

The fundamental work of Lonergan, *Insight*,[263] focuses on intellectual conversion and sets religious conversion aside. But when this illustrious Canadian theologian considered the theological method in his work *Method in Theology*,[264] he could not avoid reflecting on how theology relates to faith, defined as knowledge born of the love experienced in religious conversion. Religious conversion is, then, for Lonergan, "to be in love with God" and "God's gift of love poured into our hearts" (Rom 5:5).

According to J. Randall Price (cited by McGinn[265]), in Lonergan's perspective the correct way to differentiate religion from mysticism rests on two points:

1. Religious consciousness is intentional insofar as it is oriented toward God as its objective, although it shares the mediated differentiations inherent in all intentional impulses.

2. Mystical consciousness, on the other hand, is a "mediated return to immediacy," in which an inter-subjective and vital relationship of union and experience between God and the human person takes place.

While the debate grew in intensity in the English- and German-speaking world, France played a less prominent role. The figure of Jean Daniélou

---

262. For example, the works of Johnston: *The Wounded Stag: Christian Mysticism Today*; *Mystical Theology: The Science of Love*; *The Inner Eye of Love*; *The Still Point: Reflections on Zen and Christian Mysticism*.

263. Lonergan, *Insight*.

264. Lonergan, *Method in Theology*.

265. See McGinn, *Foundations of Mysticism*, 284. McGinn uses here a manuscript by J. Price titled "Lonergan and the Foundations," 6–11, cited in ibid., n. 99.

stands out as a leader of the return to the Council's proclaimed sources, through his writings and with the creation of the collection *Sources Chrétiennes*. Side by side with Daniélou is the important Jesuit theologian Henri de Lubac, with many published writings, several of them tackling the question of mysticism. De Lubac argues that Christian mysticism, conceived as a deeper internalization of the Mystery of faith, is grounded in Scripture, in liturgy, and in the sacramental life of the church. Therefore, to be a mystic is almost synonymous with being a Christian. What is called mystical theology, then, must always be carefully distinguished from the non-Christian forms.[266] Louis Gardet, who worked intensely on Muslim and Christian mysticism, has a more positive vision than de Lubac. He distinguishes between the natural mysticism of immanence and the supernatural mysticism that takes the road of love and negation, but he finds both these forms present in Christianity and also at times in other religions.[267]

In the Catholic domain, the most significant contribution to mysticism in the twentieth century undeniably comes from the German Jesuit Karl Rahner, who is called—and rightly so in our view—the "Doctor mysticus" of that century.[268] The dogmatic key to his notion of mysticism lies in his differentiation between transcendental experience (i.e., the *a priori* openness of the subject to the ultimate Mystery) and supernatural experience, in which divine Transcendence no longer constitutes a remote and asymptotic objective of the dynamism of the human subject, but is communicated to the subject with proximity and immediacy.[269]

Rahner insists on the reciprocal unity (not the identity) between the experience of God and the experience of self, which is fulfilled in interpersonal relationships:

> ... the unity between the love of God and the love for the neighbor is conceivable only under the assumption that the experience of God and the experience of the self are only one thing.[270]

And Rahner also said,

> On the transcendental level as much as on the supernatural level (that is, God as question, God as answer), one must always

---

266. See de Lubac's preface to the work coordinated by Ravier, *La mystique et les mystiques*, 7–39.

267. See his work *La mystique*.

268. See Egan, "Translator's Foreword," in Rahner, *I Remember*, 3, cited by McGinn, *Foundations of Mysticism*, 286 n. 107.

269. See *Foundations of Christian Faith*.

270. See Rahner, "Experience of Self and Experience of God"; "The Experience of God Today."

have in mind the important difference between the experience in itself and its subsequent thematization or objectification in conscious reflection as a categorical mode of thought. Thematization can never capture the plenitude of the original experience, but the experience calls out for thematization in order to be communicated to others.[271]

For this reason Rahner speaks of mysticism in two ways:[272]

1. "There is a mysticism of everyday life, the discovery of God in everything," that is, the unthematized experience of Transcendence at the basis of all human activity.[273] Rahner's theology of Grace suggests that this experiential substrate always operates by grace in a uplifting way, the way in which God has already answered to the call that God placed in the heart of humankind—although this may not be evident from the standpoint of a psychological consideration of thematic knowledge of the acts in themselves.[274]

2. There are special mystical experiences, which Rahner admits can be found both inside and outside the boundaries of Christianity. As for the Christian faith, such experiences cannot be conceived as constituting any intermediary state between Grace and glory; they are rather a variety or modality of the experience of Grace in faith.[275] Although Rahner is firm in his opposition to any elitist vision that purports to find in mysticism a higher degree of Christian perfection beyond loving service to the neighbor, he speaks of the special mystical experience as a paradigmatic intensification, open to all, of the experience of God.[276]

Nevertheless, Rahner insists that whether mystical experience is truly the culmination of the normal development of the subject is a question for empirical psychology, rather than theology, to judge.[277] In his view some

---

271. See Rahner, "Experience of Transcendence from the Standpoint of Christian Dogmatics."

272. The bibliographical references that follow are provided by McGinn, *Foundations of Mysticism*, 286–89.

273. Rahner, *Practice of Faith*, 80–84.

274. Ibid., 75–77.

275. Ibid., 72–73.

276. See "Experience of Transcendence," 174–76. On the intensification of religious acts, See "Reflections on the Problem of Gradual Ascent to Christian Perfection," in *Theological Investigations*, vol. 3, 20–21.

277. Rahner, *Practice of Faith*, 77.

issues related to mysticism, such as the so-called "in-depth experiences," "altered states of consciousness," or the "experience of the suspension of faculties," essentially refer to natural phenomena, potentialities of the subject, whether or not uplifted by grace.[278] If such experiences are judged by psychology to be part of the subject's normal maturation process, then in a special sense mystical experience, thematized or not, is in its wholeness truly human and Christian. (Rahner's sympathy, according to McGinn, appears to align with this position, especially when he suggests, with his vision of Grace, that all in-depth experiences, inside or outside Christianity, are not only natural but are also empowered by grace.)[279]

For Rahner the Christ event is central to all mystical experience. The historical reality of Jesus, as communicated through the life of the church, is essential for all forms of salvific relationship with God. Our relationship with Jesus is unique, and in it an immediate relationship with God is conveyed through the mediation of the incarnate Savior. That is why this German Jesuit insists that "Christ is, in himself, the 'fecund model'" of a committed trust in the Mystery of our existence.[280]

According to McGinn, the Rahnerian theology of mysticism offers profound and original answers to some of the basic questions in the modern discussions of mysticism. To the question (at the root of many Protestant objections to mysticism) whether the mystical experience represents a higher level beyond the ordinary life of faith, his answer—theologically and perhaps psychologically—is no. As for the relationship between Christian and non-Christian mysticism, Rahner expands his famous thesis regarding the anonymous Christian to include a category that we can designate—using an expression coined by McGinn—as that of the anonymous Christian mystic.[281] In other words, he believes that some non-Christian forms of mysticism are true expressions of the special experience of the answer given by God in Jesus Christ, even if they are not explicitly conceptualized, named, and known as such.[282]

Besides Rahner, another great figure in the theological reflection on mysticism in the German language is that of the Swiss theologian Hans Urs

---

278. Rahner uses the German word *Versenkungserfahrungen* or *Versenkungsphanomene*, which McGinn prefers to translate as "in-depth experiences" rather than as "altered states of consciousness" or "experience of the suspension of faculties," as they are sometimes translated. See McGinn, *Foundations of Mysticism*, 287.

279. See the end of the text "Experience of Transcendence," where Rahner appears to accept the possibility of a natural mysticism.

280. Rahner, *Practice of Faith*, 61.

281. McGinn, *Foundations of Mysticism*, 288.

282. "Experience of Transcendence," 181–84.

von Balthasar. He starts by distinguishing between the objectivity of the mysticism found in the revelation of the Mystery of Christ, and the subjectivity expressed in the traditional definition of mysticism as *cognitio Dei experimentalis,* which must be found in the experience of the subject.

In the Balthasarian theology the thesis of the observed similarity between Christianity and non-Christian forms of mysticism is challenged by the theological antithesis which insists on their differentiation. Balthasar recognizes two types of antithesis: a) the Protestant version in which mysticism has nothing to do with the Christian faith, and b) the Catholic version, and the most frequent, in which Christian mysticism is the only true mysticism. His synthesis—introduced only in some of his essays—is an original version of the Catholic vision that judges the correctness of Christian forms of mysticism according to three criteria: 1) the biblical message, especially regarding the primacy of the divine initiative over human effort; 2) the emphasis on obedience over union as the ultimate religious value (Balthasar does not accept the mysticism of radical union as compatible with Christianity);[283] and 3) the uniqueness of the Incarnate Word as the expression of the unknowable God. These themes—all of them biblical—lead him to a relativization, if not a rejection, of the mysticism found in many classic Christian authors.[284]

Thus, a synthesis which can—according to Balthasar—provide the correct visions of mysticism within Christian life, follows these basic criteria: 1) the norm of the supremacy of reciprocal love for God and the neighbor; 2) the need for conformity with the model of Christ; and 3) the insistence on the unknowability of God in and through God's manifestation in the Word made flesh.[285]

McGinn observes that all these three criteria can be positively compared with Rahner's vision of mysticism, in spite of the suspicion that the Swiss theologian always showed regarding the place of mysticism inside Christianity. Balthasar—closer to Stolz and Schweitzer—insists that the only true mysticism is Christian mysticism.[286]

From what we have seen, then, there is a certain consensus—not a unanimity—in the Catholic domain regarding mysticism in the twentieth century. Mysticism is not a special higher or elitist form of Christian perfection, but rather one of the requirements of a life of faith in itself.

---

283. See McGinn, *Foundations of Mysticism,* 289 n. 135, citing *The Glory of the Lord,* vol. 1, 138.

284. Ibid., n. 136, citing Balthasar, *Grundfragen,* 57–65.

285. Ibid., n. 137.

286. See ibid., 290.

Nevertheless, there is no common agreement or consensus on how this requirement must be understood and, above all, lived out and practiced.[287] More recently, Catholic theologians have expanded the historical scope of the investigation into Christian mysticism and attempted in several ways to reformulate the traditional questions in the light of the post-scholastic era made official by the Second Vatican Council.[288]

In this regard, one cannot fail to cite some Catholic theologians of Mediterranean Europe (Spain and Italy) who have more recently published valuable reflections on mysticism. Whether they agree or disagree with what has been said by francophone, Germanic, and above all anglophone academia, these reflections should be mentioned here. In Italy, among our contemporaries, we highlight two names: the priest Franco Asti and the Carmelite Luigi Borriello.[289]

Luiggi Borriello is an Italian Carmelite, professor of theology in Rome and consultant in several Vatican congregations. He wrote a number of works on mysticism, and served as co-director of the *Dictionary of Mysticism* of the Vatican Publishing House. But we especially want to refer here to his recent work *Esperienza mística e teologia mística*.[290] For Father Borriello, mysticism is not a secondary aspect of theology, and it is important to make clear what Christian mysticism is at a moment when we see all religions interested in the subject.

Another important point in Borriello's reflection is that he resists any reference to the mystics as illuminati or as persons distanced from reality, because for him mysticism, of all that exists, is at once the most rooted in the world and the most uplifting: it is union with God.

He explains this in *Esperienza mistica e teologia mistica*, a book that is part of a series called Experiência e Fenomenologia Mística, which he directed jointly with the scholar Maria Rosario del Genio. For Borriello, mysticism is the place of the Mystery, and in his book he distinguishes between the mysticism of closed eyes and the mysticism of open eyes.[291] Even if mystical experience takes place in a reserved and silent place, what it says is for everyone. In this sense, for Borriello, every human being is called to holiness and to mystical experience. And this experience, in turn, is an unmistakable invitation to witness.

287. Ibid.

288. McGinn's work, in several volumes, is an attempt in this direction. (See the bibliography at the end of this volume.)

289. See Borriello, *Esperienza mistica e teologia mistica*; Asti, *Spiritualità e mistica*.

290. The book has a prologue by archbishop Luis Ladaria Ferrer, secretary of the Congregation for the Doctrine of Faith.

291. See *Esperienza mistica e teologia mistica*.

He further emphasizes—differently from other contemporary authors—the importance of ascetism, affirming that it has an illuminating reciprocal relationship with mysticism.[292] Likewise, in line with other authors cited here, especially with reference to Dionysius, he considers mysticism a theopathic experience, one of passivity, because in it the human being submits to the divine.[293]

Yet, throughout his book, Boriello emphasizes the fact that the experience of God has as its center of attention not the mystical subject or the experience in itself, but the manifested presence of God, of whom the subject assumes consciousness. In this he agrees with McGinn who, at the end of his survey, defines the mystical experience as a consciousness of the immediate presence of God.[294]

The prominent figure in Spain is the philosopher of religion and theologian Juan Martín Velasco. He has a PhD in philosophy from Louvain and since 1970 has been a professor of phenomenology of the history of religion at the Pontifical University of Salamanca. Father Velasco has published numerous books and articles analyzing the religious phenomenon in modern and postmodern society,[295] as well as philosophical essays on religion.[296] More recently, however, his work and publications have increasingly focused on mysticism, a theme that has been the subject of his research and has resulted in lively and important studies.[297]

Velasco states,

> relying, above all, on the texts of the Christian mystics, although aware that our affirmations also find support among Muslim and Jewish mystics, we can offer, as the center and sum of the mystical experience, the affirmation that in it the subject lives in the mediated immediateness of loving contact, the most

---

292. Ibid.

293. Ibid.

294. Ibid., 126–28, citing the book by McGinn that we have been using here.

295. *Cambio socio-cultural y cristianismo hoy* (1980); *Increencia y evangelización* (1988); *El malestar religioso de nuestra cultura* (1993); *Mundo en crisis, fe en crisis* (1996); *Ser cristiano en una cultura posmoderna* (1996); *Utopía y esperanza cristiana* (1997); *Metamorfosis de lo sagrado y futuro del cristianismo* (1998); *La transmisión de la fe en la sociedad contemporánea* (2002).

296. *Hacia una filosofía de la religión cristiana* (1970); *Filosofía de la religión* (with J. G. Caffarena [1973]); *La religión en nuestro mundo* (1978); *El hombre y la religión* (2002); *Introducción a la fenomenología de la religión* (2006).

297. *La experiencia cristiana de Dios* (1995); *El fenómeno místico* (1999); *A experiência de Deus* (2001); *La interioridad: un paradigma emergente* (edited by D. Aleixandre et al., 2004); *La experiencia mística* (2004); *Mística y humanismo* (2007).

intimate union with the very reality of God as present in the profoundest depth of the subject's being.[298]

Like other authors discussed above, Velasco works out his own typology of mystical experience. He identifies three nonnegotiable elements that must be present in the mystical experience:

1. The intimate union with God as the content and goal of the experience.
2. Its condition as an immediate experience in the mediation of the soul and the vestige left in it by the presence of God.
3. Love as the way and means of the union.[299]

The author argues, like McGinn, Dupré, and others whom he knows and cites,[300] that union is the most frequent form for expressing the mystical experience in its highest degree. The other categories—ecstasy, contemplation, vision of God, deification, theopathic state, etc.—are important, but none of them is as crucial as that of union.[301]

It is not only with Christian or even monotheistic mysticism that this Spanish philosopher and theologian is concerned. His books consider, in depth and with close attention, nonreligious, secular, or natural mysticism, as well as pluralistic mysticism—which carries elements from several traditions—and mystical elements from other great traditions, among them Buddhism.[302]

We cannot close this cast of students and thinkers without mentioning the recently departed scholar of religions and mysticism, Raimon Panikkar. He was born in Barcelona on November 3, 1918, of a Catholic Catalan mother and a father who was Hindu by birth and religion. Thus, since his childhood, he was able to adopt, cultivate, and elaborate diverse traditions, in which he never felt himself to be a stranger. He published more than fifty books, mostly in Catalan, Spanish, Italian, and English, which were translated into French, German, Chinese, Portuguese, Czech, Dutch, and Tamil.

---

298. *El fenómeno místico*, 30–31.

299. Ibid., 31.

300. Ibid., 27.

301. Ibid. The author extensively and profoundly elaborates the issue of mystical union in his book *El fenómeno místico*, especially in ch. 3, "La estructura del fenómeno místico," sections 5 ("Rasgos característicos de la experiencia mística") and 6 ("El núcleo originário de la fenomenologia de la mística").

302. See especially *El fenómeno místico* and *Mística y humanismo*. Besides Velasco, there are other contemporary students of mysticism who also adopt this multireligious, interreligious, and even transreligious approach.

He himself translated, over the course of ten years, an anthology of one thousand pages of the Vedas.[303]

For thirty years he kept in contact with India, which he visited for the first time in 1954. "I left as a Christian, discovered myself a Hindu, and returned as a Buddhist, without ceasing to be a Christian," he said. Raimon Panikkar is not a conventional thinker. On the contrary, he rejects many conventions, schemes and prejudices. His intellectual formation between East and West allows him to reflect, in his work, on the ongoing conversation among diverse traditions, ideologies and beliefs. His solid understanding of Western philosophical traditions and his exceptional knowledge of Eastern philosophical and spiritual traditions, endow him with absolutely unique conditions and a capacity for interreligious dialogue.

In his reflections on religious and mystical experience in the West and the East, Panikkar portrays this pilgrimage as symbolic of life. The pilgrimage must be not only external but also internal.

After this journey through the philosophy and theology of the twentieth century, we must attempt a provisional summary that will allow us to proceed with our conceptualization of what mystical experience is. Based on the consensus identified in the historiography of the concept, we can affirm without a shadow of doubt that whatever can be said about mysticism must come by way of experience.[304] It is not a matter of a theory of the Other, and much less of a well-articulated and rigorous discourse on the Other. All that there is of discourse and theory here emerges and becomes intelligible from the standpoint of an experience.

Starting from this premise, we understand as mystical experience what philosophy and theology mutually agree to be its definition: a consciousness of the divine presence, perceived as immediate, in an attitude of passivity, and lived out prior to any analysis and conceptual formulation. It has to do with the concrete life of the human being, who faces, thanks to something he or she does not control or manipulate, a Mystery or a mysterious and irresistible Grace that reveals itself as personal Otherness and proceeds lovingly, in graciously proposing and bringing about a fellowship that would be impossible according to human criteria, one that only Grace can freely offer.[305]

---

303. See also *The Experience of God*; *De la mística*.

304. See Vaz, "A experiência mística na tradição ocidental," in Vaz, *Experiência mística e filosofia*, 7–21.

305. See *Diccionário de las religiones*, s.v. "experiencia cristiana y experiencia religiosa." See also Moltmann, *Trinity and the Kingdom*, 4; L. Boff, *Experimentar Deus hoje*, especially the chapter by Vaz; Velasco, *A experiencia cristã de Deus*; Gelabert, *Valoración cristiana de la experiencia*, in addition to other sources provided in this book.

This experience—not to mention all the categories that appear with greater vigor and more consensus in the other authors we have looked at (such as ineffability, immediacy, and passivity, among others)—is fundamentally a relationship experience. That being so, it presumes Otherness and the difference of the other, and cannot be reduced to an unresolved symbiosis or a desire for fusion, as might be the case with some supposedly religious experiences.[306] In this sense—of a relational experience—and only in the light of this primary fact, can one speak of the noetic dimension of mysticism, that is, that the mystical experience is a an experience of knowledge.[307] Mysticism is indeed knowledge, but knowledge that comes from experience and into which intelligence and intellect enter, not to apprehend and interpret the experience as an abstraction, but to grasp what the subject at the center of the experiential act feels.[308] And this feeling implies an Otherness and a relationship.

In the mystical event, which unfolds between the human being and the divine being, one therefore finds not only the subject who knows—the I or the self—but also the other—the you or even the he or she, who by their Otherness and difference move the I toward a journey of knowledge with no previously traveled ways and without any assurances other than what can be provided by a progressive adventure of discovery of something or someone other than I. This someone who is not I is also not an it (a reified

---

306. See the remarks on the danger of this ultimate situation in Domínguez Morano, *Orar depois de Freud*; "El Dios imaginado": "En realidad, en esa situación no se desea Dios, se desea tan sólo la experiencia misma de la relación con lo que, como Dios, se imagina. Se pretende además,mantener uma presencia ininterrumpida, una permanencia constante del gozo de la fusión. Y en esa permanente aspiración a fundirse con una totalidad de corte materno, hay una incapacidad para asumir la ausencia del otro, la distancia inevitable que nos constituye como 'seres sparados.' Dios queda reducido a la condición de fuente de placer y de consuelo. Nos encontramos así con la pasión mística que pretende ignorar cualquier limitación en su aspiración a fundirse con la totalidad. Sólo quiere saber del deseo, deseo de fusión, de inmersión en un todo en el que pretende perderse. La fe se convierte entonces en una vana ilusión en el sentido más estrictamente freudiano del término: pura quimera, realización de deseos infantiles, cuando no, puro delírio."

307. See the biblical sense of *knowing*, which is inseparable from *loving*. Moltmann, *Trinity and the Kingdom*, 9.

308. See the words of Saint Thomas Aquinas on this: "Non intellectus intelligit sed homo per intellectum." This means that concrete human beings in their intentional polyvalence are the subjects of the act of opening themselves to their object, a movement that characterizes the experience. In opening themselves, they are able to welcome the being in the analogical richness of its absolute universality. *Summa Theologiae* 1a., q. 72, a. 2 ad 1m, cited by Vaz, "Mística e política," 10. See also Vaz, *Antropologia filosófica*, vol. 2, 37 n. 8.

thing)³⁰⁹ but someone who approaches me, who speaks to me, and to whom I respond—another subject whose difference imposes itself on me as an epiphany,³¹⁰ or a revelation.

In the case of mysticism, this relationality with the difference of the other receives differentiated dimensions insofar as it puts into the process and movement of the relationship a partner of absolute dimensions, for whom the human being is of no concern, and with whom the human being cannot even think of maintaining a symmetric relationship or one based on need rather than desire.³¹¹ It is an other whose mysterious profile is designed especially in limit situations of existence, and radically transforms the lives of those involved in the experience.³¹²

The relationship with the Transcendent Divine Other, who generates a unique kind of knowledge, is therefore integral to the mystical experience per se. And in the case of Christian mysticism, there is an anthropological component at the center of the identity of this other, this Otherness, since the experienced God made God's self flesh and showed a human face. Therefore nothing that comes from the mystical experience can deviate, abstract or even distract from that which constitutes the humanity of the human being. It is paradoxically in the deepest proximity and similarity with the human that the God of the Christian revelation shows God's difference and absolutely transcendent Otherness.³¹³ Even more than in other times, Christian mysticism nowadays is challenged to rediscover its place and ways, and to see the human as the necessary way to the divine. It must ask itself: what are the ways that will show us the differences that are emerging today with vigorous questioning, when speaking of the human? And more: how can these ways lead to the fulfilling experience of union with God or knowledge of God through experience?

The Experience of God: Mystery and Grace

> Man—whether or not he wants to expressly affirm it, whether he wants to repress this truth or let it surface—finds himself always exposed, in his spiritual existence, to a Sacred Mystery

309. See Buber, *I and Thou.*

310. See Levinas and his whole discourse on Otherness. See especially the work *Autrement qu'être ou au-delà de l'essence.*

311. See my remarks on this in Bingemer, *Alteridade e vulnerabilidade*, especially in ch. 4, "Experiência de Deus. Possibilidade de um perfil?"

312. See Vaz, "Mística e política," 11–12.

313. See Henry, *L'incarnation.*

which constitutes the foundation of his existence. This Mystery is the most primitive, the most evident, but for this reason it is also the most hidden and ignored; a Mystery that speaks while keeping silent, that "is there" while, being absent, it reduces our own boundaries. And all this because, as an indescribable and unexpressed horizon, it unceasingly encompasses and sustains the small circle of our cognitive and active everyday experience, the knowledge of reality and the act of freedom. We call it God.[314]

The source of every experience of the fundamental and holy Mystery finds a common denominator in seduced desire, in the fascination and irresistible attraction to the Mystery of this other, whose beauty and difference involve, seduce, and incite passion, and who provokes an uncontrollable urge for closeness, embrace, and union.[315] This is not an intellectual experience, but an affective one that speaks to the heart. The Mystery of this other whom we call God doesn't offer contents to be apprehended regarding God's person, but reveals God's self to those who approach God as a Mystery of Love. This is how God wants to be known and experienced.[316]

Theologically, the Mystery encompasses the idea of the communication of God with humankind and of an initiation of the human being into God's designs, action, and being. According to the New Testament, the Mystery conjoins within it two apparently opposite polarities: the Mystery is both hidden and manifested, occurring in time while introducing eternity into this same time, inaugurating inside history a new time, a *kairos*.[317] For the Christian faith, the place where this Mystery attains its plenitude and is manifested in full glory is in Jesus Christ. He is the mediator of the Mystery, who reveals to human beings the call to fellowship with God and leads them to enter into that fellowship.[318]

Fully revealed in Christ, the Mystery is known and lived out by the community that believes in it and follows it. Therefore the Mystery implies mysticism. It produces in the faithful a light and a force which inspire and

---

314. Rahner, "The Need for a 'Short Formula' of Christian Faith," in *Theological Investigations*.

315. The French dictionary *Petit Robert* defines *seduction* and *desire*, respectively, as "action to seduce (divert from the way), to corrupt, to pull, but also to attract, to charm, to fascinate"; "that which arouses consciousness of a tendency toward any known or imaginary object."

316. This can be said of all religions. But here we will be mostly dealing with Judeo-Christian religious experience.

317. See Édouard Jeauneau, *Encyclopædia Universalis*, accessed April 19, 2016. Online: http://www.universalis.fr/encyclopedie/mystere/. "mystère": "for each person knowledge of the Mystery implies a before and an after."

318. Ibid.

involve them beyond all measure. Furthermore, it stirs within them gratitude, recognition, and effective love, following the example of Jesus Christ and in fellowship with him. This is not first and foremost an uncommon event. It is an action of the Spirit of God who transforms human beings on the inside by bringing Jesus Christ into their lives, grounding and deepening them in love.[319]

In Christian terms, the category of Mystery is not applicable to merely cultic practices such as those of other religions of Antiquity. The Mystery reaches its fulfillment and plenitude in Christ and in the church in which he is incorporated. This being so, the Mystery graciously attracts human beings with a seductive power that has, indeed, an erotic component, but above all an agapic one. Agape means, above all, gracious love. The mystery of love and grace is useless and ineffective to human eyes, but fundamental for the life that does not die and is fulfilled—the greatest desire of the human heart.

The mystery is not an excuse for failing to look attentively at reality. In the perspective of the mystery, this world is not idyllic, perfect, complete and reconciled, as many discourses would portray it. We are thinking particularly of those affected by the optimism born of the progress and conquests of modernity, as opposed to those replete with legitimate questioning regarding ecological, racial, ethnic and gender issues, or regarding deplorable injustices. The involvement in temporal and earthly realities is specific to each person who is touched by this Mystery, and can happen in different ways depending on the configuration of the person's experience.

It is in the midst of this world that the human being touched by the Mystery is called to live out what we call the experience of God, and to discover the fact, at once so great and so simple, that God is a Mystery who wishes to be revealed, a God who reveals God's self, and even more, who allows God's self to be experienced. And this experience is not unilateral (the human being experiences God), but takes two directions (God allows God's self to be experienced by the human being who seeks and experiences God). Thus, while allowing the human being to feel the taste and flavor of the divine life, God enters into the mortal and contingent human reality—in history and in the experience of a project of Covenant and love. This is the Mystery of Grace and truth whose allure brings about the fellowship that results in a plentiful life.

As with Mystery, the word "grace" is of vital significance for the understanding of what constitutes the experience of God in the Judeo-Christian tradition. The reality that the word Grace expresses is of central importance in human life and in the history of theology. This is a word that could

---

319. Ibid.

confront the diffuse and unexplained feeling of culpability and anxiety common to all human beings, with the purpose of freeing them from it by dissipating it.[320] To human beings torn between their lives and their ideals, between their behavior and the dictates of the society where they live, Grace provides an unexpected verdict that reverses the logical order of things and allows those receiving it to begin their lives over as not guilty. If mediation between God and the human being must travel a long road between human imperfection and divine perfection, Grace is an act that shortens this distance and eliminates all that separates heaven from earth, thus allowing those who welcome it a new existence starting from a miraculously renewed blank page.[321]

In secular Greek, the word *charis* means grace. It originally meant that which shines, that which gladdens. Several other classical meanings derive from this: the charm of beauty or the act of joy and pleasure; favor or benevolence; acknowledgment or gratitude; and reward. The Scriptures combine Greek with Hebrew, and understand grace as a concrete and effective action that allows human beings to live fully, regardless of what they have or have not done in their lives. Grace is par excellence the act of divine mercy. The person who is the object of such grace, this divine favor, is called to welcome and fully enjoy it.

The only thing that can follow this experience of God—as a Mystery who comes in grace, the fruit of the full and radical gift of this same God—for those who radically and profoundly feel it in their being, is the total offering of their lives, their unique and most precious blessing, in spiritual and joyful worship of God. After a total divine surrender, the only possible response is a corresponding and equally total surrender by the human being.

It is important to see how this total desire and surrender are configured in the life of each person. Depending on the kind of life or the space in which it takes place, each person must carry out his or her offering of life with different emphases and tendencies.

Since New Testament times, Christians have been persons who live between time and eternity—or better said, who experience in their flesh and in their lives the eternity that crosses historical time, elaborating it and shaping it. They are, therefore, living eschatological beings, citizens at once of an Absolute future and of the heavenly city. For this reason they are foreigners in this world, in which they always find themselves exiled and out of place. Yet, in this ambiguous condition they experience the sublime paradox that this earth, which is not their definitive homeland, was given to them by

---

320. See Casalis, "Grace," in *Encyclopaedia Universalis*.
321. Ibid.

God as a gift and a mission: as a realm to be administered, as a work to be completed, as plentifulness to be brought to fruition.[322]

The proposal of Christian mysticism today must therefore be made in the midst of a history which is essentially that of the emancipation of humankind from the patriarchal and authoritarian conceptions of life and society. In this context, to propose Christian mysticism as the discipleship of Jesus is tantamount to proposing an experience of God as Father. And that implies a filial life of obedience and loving dependence, which acknowledges paternal heteronomy as the source and compass of life. If this is true and inevitable, what can be done about the belief that the idea of the paternity of God is anachronistic?[323] Would it not be a hopeless task to speak of God the Father to human beings for whom paternity has no value and is even associated with negative ideas?

In truth, it seems to me that it is time for us to ask ourselves—especially when we speak of spirituality as an experience of God—if true emancipation is not what the prodigal son discovered when he returned to the father's house, to the home where, because of the love that reigned there, the prevailing order was neither domination nor anarchical freedom.[324]

Ours is a generation of all kinds of emancipation, and at same time a generation of fatherless children both in the heavenly and earthly sense. This empty space left by the father's absence provides an opening in the most advanced societies for the growth of its byproduct, such as the structurally anarchical and chaotic sects.[325] The absence of the father in basic institutions such as the family reverberates in the political structure with the advance of totalitarian systems and of charismatic figures with no base of support. In these developments there is, at a symbolic level, a clearly perceptible yearning for the paternal attributes of the judge, protector, provider etc.

If, on the one hand, modern criticism of paternity as oppressive authority may be pertinent and positive, on the other hand the disappearance of the father certainly leaves an unfillable void in the minds and hearts of our contemporaries. In a certain sense it is true that today's parents no longer know how to be teachers. They no longer know what they should teach, or to whom. This reminds us of the gospel text in which Jesus himself distinguishes earthly paternity from the paternity of God: "And call no one your father on earth, for you have one Father—the one in heaven. Nor

---

322. Ibid.
323. See Daly, *Beyond God the Father*, among others.
324. See Visser 't Hooft, *La paternité de Dieu dans un monde émancipé*.
325. See Bingemer, *Alteridade e vulnerabilidade*.

are you to be called instructors, for you have one instructor, the Messiah" (Matt 23:9–10).

From a theological and spiritual standpoint, to surpass or even eliminate the Father today must mean to recover the most authentic sense of the paternity of God, beyond all symbolic and liturgic referential weakness, along antiauthoritarian lines, and especially taking into consideration the general uneasiness of a culture that lives in short circuit with its own radical foundations.

Instead of killing the Father, the experience of God teaches us today that we must resurrect the father from the numerous deaths—some of them necessary—of his symbolic and social history. Death and resurrection, besides being the coordinates of our daily lives, are the two cardinal concepts of our culture in its Judeo-Christian roots. They are also the deepest and most constitutive characteristics of all Christian mysticism. The current generation is asked to follow a cultural and spiritual direction opposite to that taken by the theoretical and social destructuring of paternity. It is asked to take a spiritual path where the surpassing of heteronomy by autonomy can have only one name: theonomy. And it is asked—as in the famous gospel story of the prodigal son—to stand up and walk to meet the father anew.

This could be an encounter no longer characterized by authoritarianism and oppression, but by the natural vulnerability of love.

The Christian Experience of God: Incarnation and Vulnerability

The word *mystical* is found neither in the New Testament nor in the Apostolic Fathers. It probably first appeared sometime during the third century. Moreover, the figure of Jesus presented in the Gospels, especially in the Synoptic Gospels, corresponds more with that of a prophet of the kingdom of God than with that of a visionary. The Synoptics seem to accentuate the moral conditions and virtues that prepare the way for the coming of the kingdom. The same vision of God is attributed, in the Sermon on the Mount, to the pure of heart.

For this reason quite a few authors exclude mystical experience from Christian sources and attribute the appearance of mysticism to external influences, especially Gnosticism and Neoplatonism, as was the case for Judaism. Similarly, some interpretations of the history of mysticism contrast an introspective psychological mysticism coming especially from the sixteenth-century Spanish mystics with the objective, scriptural, eucharistic mysticism of ancient times.[326]

However, if the Old and New Testaments are sources of revelation for Christians, it is possible that one may find in either one of them the roots of Christian mysticism, of the Christian experience of God. From very early on the people of Israel understood the primacy of the mystical experience, insofar as they were coming to understand their identity as directly related to their experience of their God's love for them. The prayer by which the just and pious Israelites expressed their fundamental declaration of faith opens with God's love as that which will make possible the knowledge, love, and timelessness of the law.[327]

The love of God is what opens the ears of the people and of each of their children, who repeat several times a day, "Hear, O Israel: The LORD is our God, the LORD alone. You shall love the LORD your God with all your heart, and with all your soul, and with all your might" (Deut 6:4–5). God, the God of Israel, is a God who loves and wants to be loved with all the humanity of the human being, and is therefore a God who can and should not only be feared but also loved—an affirmation that would never have been ventured before Deuteronomy.[328]

This love is expressed by the person's total commitment, evoked in the triple formulation "with all your heart, and with all your soul, and with all your might." In many other passages this petition for love is affirmed and reaffirmed, sometimes in a double rather than a triple formulation (10:12; 30:6: "with all your heart and with all your soul").

In still other passages of this book, so fundamental for understanding the experience of the people, one finds other words about love that delineate the relationship of this people with their God. They are: "seek the LORD your God" (4:29); "to serve the LORD your God" (10:12); "to observe these statutes and ordinances" (26:16); "obey him with all your heart and with all your soul" (30:2); "turn to the LORD your God" (30:2–10). With these different expressions the biblical author evokes the infinite concrete forms that love for God can and should take, while evoking as well the love of God for the people who were chosen and especially beloved by God.

The experience of the love of God is dynamic and radical, and perpetually in motion. And those who bond with God become part of this irreversible movement. It is not something that can be acquired once and for all, but something one must constantly seek, live out, hear and obey, and to which

---

326. See Velasco, *El fenomeno místico*, 211 n. 79.
327. See Bingemer, "Amar a Dios sobre todas las cosas: una invitación a todos."
328. See note c in *Traduction Oecumenique de la Bible* (TOB), French edition.

one must return if any distancing occurs. It is something that requires all one's heart, all one's soul, and all one's might, without any dimension of the person excluded or less insistently or forcefully called.

If one can say anything about the people of Israel—not forgetting, even for a moment, that they are the people of the law—it is that they are the people of love. And this love shapes their existence, their way and their life project. The love of God is the criterion by which the stature of each person, and of the people as a whole, will be measured.

The model leader whom the people recognize as such must be someone who "loves the Lord," such as the just and wise King Solomon (1 Kgs 3:3). Similarly, in several passages of the Old Testament one finds different metaphors signifying the love of the Lord, accentuating those interventions where God reveals more intensely God's presence (as in Ps 119:97–165, "Oh, how I love your law!" or in the words that 1 Chr 29:3 puts in the mouth of King David: "I have a treasure of my own of gold and silver, and because of my devotion to the house of my God I give it to the house of my God").

The book of Psalms is punctuated with exclamations of the intense love through which the psalmist praises his God, to whom he gives diverse names to express affection, adoration, and worship: my Strength, my Refuge, my Rock, my Shield, etc.

The whole experience of loving and being loved that characterizes the way of the people of Israel, as well as the unmistakable and exclusive requirements of this love, were shown early on to be more than a matter of affection and feelings. This love of God has a very real and concrete dimension that demands practice as a demonstration of faithfulness to God's person—the practice of justice and righteousness for all, but especially for those who are most deprived of strength, voice, and privilege: the orphan, the poor, the widow, the stranger.

This way of loving God is the subject of the book of Leviticus. It proclaims the Law of Holiness, a set of precepts that have as a common denominator the holiness of God, which must shine through all the acts and circumstances in the life of the people who are consecrated (*qadosh*) to the holy (*qadosh*) God. The law is summarized in the precept: You shall love your neighbor as yourself (Lev 19:18).[329] The *ethos* of the love of God above all things arises as a primordial requirement revealed in the Face of the Other, of the neighbor, toward whom the people must practice the love that is graciously given in order to be pleasurably experienced.

The commandment to love one's neighbor as oneself (Lev 19:18), combined with the commandment to love God with one's whole heart, soul, and

---

329. See note 1 of *Traduction Oecumenique de la Bible* (TOB) on Lev 19:1.

might (Deut 6:5), was retrieved by Jesus to express the essence of the law of Moses (see Matt 22:37-39).

Revealing the God of Abraham, Isaac, and Jacob as his Father, who demands to be loved without conditions or restrictions, Jesus proposes something similar to his disciples. The Sermon on the Mount (Matt 5:43-47)—the Magna Carta of the project of the kingdom of God—brings new color to the way Jesus' disciples should love.

The configuration given by Jesus to his teaching about love is unique. He does not simply interpret the Old Testament as did the scholars and savants of his time, but goes beyond them. He says something new based only on his own authority (see Mark 1:22-27ff.; Matt 5:21-22, 27-28ff.): "You have heard that it was said to those of ancient times . . . But I say to you . . ." This then is a word that adds to or goes beyond what "was said to those of ancient times" by God.

The "but I say to you" of Jesus is to be understood as the definitive word of God. Unlike the prophets, who would punctuate their discourses with explicit references to the God of Israel, such as "thus says the Lord" or "the Word of Yahweh," to make it very clear in whose name they were speaking, Jesus does not distinguish his own words from the words of God. On the contrary, he understands himself and is understood as God's mouthpiece, as God's own voice.

What is proposed to Christians, then, is active conduct: to tolerate and countenance everything, to actively and dynamically love all human beings, including those who do them harm. The principle here (vv. 43-44) is to go beyond loving the neighbor as was pronounced in the Old Testament to those of ancient times. According to the law, this still preserves a restrictive meaning, and the mention of the enemy expresses the antithesis suggested by its initial phrase (v. 44): "love your enemies."

But what kind of love is this? Certainly it has nothing in common with a spontaneous tenderness based in affinity, which would be impossible in this case. The Greek term to express this love, the verb *agapán*, shows that this feeling derives from a desire not compelled by the self-restraint required of human beings in dealing with their enemies. Moreover, it is necessary for us to leave the purely psychological field, since Christian love—or charity—must be practiced in the form of active goodness and must result in concrete beneficial effects.

This teaching, thanks to a technical word—enemy—generalizes to include any situation in which Christians are maltreated, even running the risk of death, because of their faith. This is confirmed by the contrast drawn (v. 47) between the brother or sister and the enemy. Here, the enemy in question is neither the personal adversary within the religious community, nor the enemy of the nation in a political or military sense, but the persecutor of the faith, the enemy of the messianic community formed by the early Christians.

The insistent motivation of the evangelist to uphold such love and such a requirement is to be sought beyond the world of creatures. The motive that can sustain such behavior is found in the imitation of God, in the desire to act as God's children. And this desire rests in the central and vital experience of being infinitely loved by this God, in spite of all one's sin and unfaithfulness. Experiencing themselves as loved in this way, human beings can imitate God. They can love without measure and without restriction of any kind.

For Jesus of Nazareth, according to the Gospel of Matthew, humans become children of God the moment they begin to live out the practice of love toward their enemies, in imitation of this God whose grace and benefits are shared among all human beings, without distinction. The proof of being a child of God is in faithfulness and obedience. Such conformity to the divine had already been expressed in Judaic ethics as the imitation of divine behavior, in line with the conviction that the human being is the image of God.[330]

Therefore, according to Matthew's interpretation of Jesus' teaching, Christians must go beyond loving the neighbor as themselves, beyond the justice of the scribes and pharisees. They must go beyond the sinful categories mentioned by the writer. God, by sovereign example, personally calls them to surpass themselves constantly and without limit: "Be perfect, therefore, as your heavenly Father is perfect" (v. 48). And God gives them the conditions for this in allowing them to experience God's infinite and boundless love.

Jesus, the Son of God, drives his disciples to unsuspected limits. He doesn't put forward simply the skill to live in this world, but rather a positive obligation, a universal ministry of love. In this he goes far beyond the duty of forgiveness. His requirement to love one's enemies includes this, but goes further, rejecting whatever remains of condescension even in forgiveness. Further, Jesus calls his disciples to forget in order to think only about generous self-giving, without any resentment or hidden intention.[331]

It is simply a matter of love, without strategic thinking aimed at maintaining a utilitarian peace at the service of ecclesiastical policies, and without using benevolence as a propaganda tool for conversion. It is therefore, without a doubt, a love that is more divine than human.[332] It would indeed

---

330. See Lev 19:2: "You shall be holy, for I the Lord your God am holy."

331. See Bingemer, *Violência e religião*.

332. See Saint Bonaventure, *Vita mystica* II, 39, in *Mystical Opuscula*. See also Bingemer, "Jesus Cristo e a prática da não violência."

be inhuman in the case of those without the courage to believe in the first commandment—to love God above all things—and therefore unable to lose themselves in order to gain Christ (Phil 3:8) or to reach, with him, through him, and in him, a semblance of the divine. It would be not only inhuman, but impossible, if the requirement for this behavior were not grounded in the primordial experience of being a beloved child of God—the experience of learning to love in the discipleship of Jesus Christ, the Beloved Son who loved until his death on the cross—and if at each step the experience of being inhabited by the Holy Spirit were not felt, the love between the Father and the Son that makes possible the expression in the world of the same love that from all eternity animates and configures the Trinitarian fellowship.[333]

The proposal of Jesus to his disciples invites them to have no hesitation and to set no limits when it comes to love. One must love above all else, because that is the way God loves. It is in the person of Jesus, the perfect synthesis of the human and the divine, that his followers recognize that this love is possible for human beings who are inhabited by the Spirit of God. At the end of the Gospel of John, the One who is near the Passion says to his followers, as a testament: "I give you a new commandment, that you love one another. Just as I have loved you, you also should love one another. By this everyone will know that you are my disciples, if you have love for one another" (John 13:34-35).[334]

Biblical revelation, therefore, sees in the human experience of the encounter with the Unconditional, historically revealed and only God, the foundation of the universal normativeness of the divine *ethos*.[335] Christian faith affirms that the experience of the encounter with God in Jesus Christ is an experience of a radical sense of being. It is a foundational theonomy of personal liberty and responsibility, an experiential rooting of the person in the Unconditional and the Absolute with a unique name and a loving face, assuring at once both freedom and limits.[336]

The term used in the New Testament for this love of God is *agape*, usually translated as love. The intention was to signify a concept of love for which the more common Greek words such as *eros*, *filia*, or *storgé* seemed neither adequate nor appropriate. In agape/love the emphasis is on

---

333. See Bingemer and Feller, *Deus Trindade: a vida no coração do mundo*. And by the same authors, *Deus Trindade: Graça que habita em nós*.

334. Fraternal love between persons, generated and made possible by Jesus Himself, is the sign *par excellence* of the presence of the love of God in the life of human beings.

335. See Küng, *Proyecto de una ética mundial*, 75.

336. See Mathon, "Sainteté," 704. See also Festugière. *La sainteté*, a work, as we observed in a previous note, comparing the Greek hero, the savant, and the Christian saint.

disinterested and oblatory generosity—without any extraneous interest or the possibility of joy and satisfaction other than love itself—and on the willingness to move away from oneself and toward the other. The non-profaning Otherness is the starting point for this self-offering, which has its roots in a self-giving God. This self-revealing God is thus perceived, experienced and adored as actually being love. This is expressed with obfuscating clarity in the first epistle of John: "Whoever does not love does not know God, for God is love" (1 John 4:8).

The condition for the effective possibility of loving God above all things is found in God's own self. The God who demands to be so loved, loves the creation and humankind unconditionally and before all things. The New Testament texts proclaim this more than effective truth with the most affective exclamations:

> For God so loved the world that he gave his only Son (John 3:16).

> If God is for us, who is against us? He who did not withhold his own Son, but gave him up for all of us, will he not with him also give us everything else? . . . Who will separate us from the love of Christ? . . . In all these things we are more than conquerors through him who loved us . . . [Nothing] will be able to separate us from the love of God in Christ Jesus our Lord. (Rom 8:31–39)

For this same reason the first letter of John states, "We love because he first loved us" (4:19). And loved us without restrictions, without conditions. Therefore, the loving dynamics into which God brings us must also be free of any restriction or condition. It cannot be subordinated to any other realm or priority. It is above all things.

It is true that the thoughts, words and works of human beings often bear no trace of faithfulness to the revelation of the agape-God in Jesus of Nazareth, which radicalizes and clarifies the revelation of the God of Abraham, Isaac, and Jacob. But this does not extinguish the Light which illuminates life and guides it into the ineffable experience of being enlightened by the love of this God. For this is the same Light that, according to the prologue of the Gospel of John, shines in the darkness and is not overcome by it (John 1:5).

This light which has shone since all eternity became in history a heard, experienced and obeyed word, as expressed in the first commandment of the Old Testament: "Hear, O Israel: The Lord is our God, the Lord alone. You shall love the Lord your God with all your heart, and with all your soul, and with all your might" (Deut 6:4–5). Romano Guardini reminds us of this simple truth: A saint is one to whom God has conceded the Grace to take this commandment with perfect seriousness and "understand it in its profundity and do everything to fulfill it."[337]

Now, at the beginning of a new millennium, to love continues to be the great challenge. And loving God above all things is the form which this love takes when lived out in the light of the Christian faith. The call to holiness must appear more than ever, for the man and woman of the twenty-first century, as a radical and demanding call to love above all things, against the tide of a society which glorifies the easiness of immediacy and seeks a short cut to an illusory happiness.

Theology—a second language trying to articulate this call at the heart of post-modern society—is not the entire revelation, but a contingent and limited interpretation of it. Theology is an explanation of the faith which, for its part, is a practical, experiential, and rational adherence to what was revealed by God to the people of Israel and in Jesus of Nazareth. Nobody but the glorified *Kyrios* (the Lord) has a total and global vision of the revelation. Therefore, all revelation must be criticized and judged by the figure of Jesus Christ, in contemplation and pursuit of his person, message and praxis. Human discourse is constantly being summoned to judgement by the Word of God. It serves as a critical theory of society, as socioanalytical mediation, as analysis of ecclesiastic conjuncture, but not in a complete way.

Differently from other religions, Christianity never equated its ideal of holiness with the attainment of mystical states. Neither did it encourage such pursuits for their own sake. Yet, if we look into its origins, we will find there a strong religious experience, indeed a mystical experience. It was unmistakably a mystical impulse that propelled what was initially seen as a movement within the synagogues, but which went on to acquire universal dimensions. Surely the mystical profundity of the new path proposed by Jesus of Nazareth, and illuminated by his death and resurrection, greatly determined its later development.[338]

The mystical quality of the life of Jesus is clearly stated in the gospels, but—according to Dupré—it is mainly in the Fourth Gospel, a late arrival written at the end of the first century, that one finds its full expression.[339]

---

337. See Guardini, "Der Heilige in unserer Welt," 419.

338. There are, today, theologians who raise the issue whether it is appropriate to call Christianity a religion. They argue that Jesus was a Jew and did not intend to launch a religion different from his own. Therefore, his teachings, life, and practice should be seen as a way, as a proposal for life, but not as a religion. See the interesting reflection by Moingt, *L'homme qui venait de Dieu*, and by the same author, *Dieu qui vient à l'homme*, vol. 1.

339. See Dupré, "Mysticism," 251.

In this Gospel, the two main currents of Christian mysticism have their sources: 1) in the theology of the divine image, which calls Christians to conform (with Christ who is to be adored as God, and through Him, with God), and 2) in the theology that presents intimacy with God as related, in universal ways, with love.[340]

Paul's letters—written even before the Gospel, and portraying the birth of the first Christian communities—elaborate the idea of the life in the Spirit (2 Cor 3:18). The principal gift of the Spirit, according to Paul, consists in *gnosis*, that insight which takes one to the core of the Mystery of Christ and enables the believer to understand the Scriptures in a more profound and revealed way. This insight, which goes to the core of the Scriptures' hidden meaning, leads to the Alexandrine interpretation of the mystical subject, discussed in what follows.[341]

When Christianity began to elaborate its theological discourse, achieving a more or less successful marriage between Hebrew anthropology and Greek philosophy, the thought of Plotinus represented an important source for much of the ideological apparatus of a Christian theology of the image. The central insight of this philosopher is at the same time the source of his mystical fertility, namely, the immanence of the One throughout the lower hypostasis. For him the mystical-intellectual process consists in a return to the ever-present One, a principle beyond the grasp of intelligible forms. A crucial role in this process is played out by the notion of the image, so important in primitive Christian mysticism. For Plotinus, each emanation reflects the previous one in the form of an image. Even the world—although fully immersed in the substance of an image which allows no further emanation—reflects the soul and the mind. Clearly, in this context, an image is more than an external copy. The union with the One in Plotinus' thought was called ecstatic, but, as Dupré correctly says, the term "instatic" might have been more appropriate to describe a movement of interiorization and simplification.[342]

The other name highlighted by Dupré is that of Origen, a major figure in the early centuries of the life of the church, who compares spiritual life to the exodus of the Jews through the desert, out of Egypt. Leaving behind the vices of the heathen idols, the soul crosses the Red Sea through a new baptism of conversion. It passes by the bitter waters of temptation and of the distorted utopian visions, until, wholly purified and enlightened, it reaches Terah, the place of union with God. His commentary represents the first

---

340. Ibid.
341. Ibid.
342. Ibid., 252.

articulation of a theology of the image. The soul is an image of God because it shelters the primal image of God, which is the divine Word. Just as this word is an image of Father through its presence before the Father, the soul is an image through the presence of the word which lives in it, that is, through its (at least partial) identity with it. This entire mystical process consists in a conversion into an image, a conversion into an ever greater identity with the intimate Word. The privileged position that Origen gives to love is the element which distinguishes his theology from Neoplatonic philosophy.

Gregory of Nyssa describes the mystical life as a process of *gnosis* initiated by a divine Eros, which results in the fulfillment of the soul's natural desire for God, of whom it carries the image. Although related since the beginning to God, the soul's mystical ascension is a slow and painful process which ends in an obscure absence of knowledge—the mystical night of love. This theology of darkness, or negative theology, was developed to its extreme limit by a mysterious Syrian who wrote in Greek and introduced himself as the Dionysius converted by Paul at the Areopagus. He was a neoplatonic as no other Christian theologian ever dared to be, and he identified God as the unnamable One. Through constant negation, the soul goes beyond the created world which bars the mind from reaching its ultimate destiny. The mystical theology of Dionysius is more ecstatic than introspective in its conception, in that the soul can fulfill its vocation of union with God only by losing itself in the recesses of the divine Super-Essence. In this he differs from Western mysticism, which he profoundly influenced.

In the fourth century, Augustine described the divine image in psychological terms, referring to the three powers of the soul—memory, intelligence and will—to explain his perception of the experience of God. God remains present to the soul both as its origin and as its supreme goal. God's presence in this interior realm invites the soul to turn inward and to convert ecstatic similarity into ecstatic union. It then gradually becomes united with God.

For Meister Eckhart God is being, in the strict sense that only God is. For Eckhart the creature does not exist. God is wholly immanent in the creature as its own essence, although totally transcending it as the only being. Only the unlimited self-expression of God in God's eternal Word (the Son) is God's perfect image. For its part, the mind fully actualizes this immanence. Rather than presence, Eckhart talks of identity: the being of the soul is generated in an eternal now with (in truth, within) the divine word. The spiritual soul does not prepare a place for God, since God is the very place where God works.[343]

---

343. Ibid., 253.

Religious or Mystical Experience

The mysticism of the image cannot go further than Eckhart took it. Because of the temerity of his affirmations about the human relationship with God, this great Dominican had problems with the church. The identity which he so powerfully affirmed excluded any positive consideration of the difference. A reading of his works shows that some questions remained unanswered. Should the difference of the creature remain without any spiritual meaning? Is it no more than the circle of nothingness drawn around God's own being? Are even the Trinitarian distinctions in God, pursued for centuries by theology with such difficulty and tenacity, destined to be superceded in a permanent repose in the unnamed unity?[344]

These questions—a legacy of Eckhart and Rhenish mysticism—were the ones that confronted the late mystics of the Rhine and the Netherlands, such as Ruusbroec and Hadewijch of Antwerp, among others. Also for Ruusbroec, the soul must move within the unnamed unity of God. But this divine wilderness is not a final resting place. The very being of God, as the Mystery of the Trinity reveals, is dynamic, never resting and never permanently withdrawing into God's own darkness. God's silence is filled with the revealing Word and with the life-giving Spirit. And for Ruusbroec God also lives in darkness. In its union with God, the soul participates in the internal and intimate movements of God.[345]

Unlike Eckhart, Ruusbroec includes in his mysticism of the image a mysticism of the creation. Finitude in itself, even if different, is never separated from the divine image. Thus, his theory of contemplation culminates in the ideal of a rhythmic balance between withdrawing into the inner life and coming forth for the practice of charity.[346]

Towards the end of the Middle Ages, the mysticism of the image gave way to a more personal and private mysticism of love. At a certain time during the twelfth century, Christian piety underwent a fundamental change. Its approach to God became more human and affective. Of course, love had always been an essential element of mysticism. But now it became the totality. Christian mysticism appears to corroborate the New Testament definition par excellence of God: God is love (1 John 4). If it is love, then it can only be experienced in love, says the logic of mysticism—which is not rational logic, but the invention of a new logic.

William of Saint-Thierry, in his influential works, presents two currents of contemplation and affection, that of the identity-image and that

---

344. Ibid.
345. Ibid., 254.
346. See, besides the article cited, which we are referring to here, the book by Dupré himself, *The Common Life: The Origins of Trinitarian Mysticism and Its Developments by Jan Ruusbroec.*

of loving similarity. The understanding of the thinking being becomes the contemplation of the loving being.[347] Ruusbroec brought both tendencies into a powerful synthesis in his "Spiritual Marriage."[348] Along the same lines, Bernard of Clairvaux, in a famous sermon on the Song of Solomon, defines the unity of the spirit with God as the result of "a competition of desires, rather than of a union of essences."

The transitional quality of ecstatic love, its submission to the psychic rhythm of the soul, and its affinity with human Eros, all announce the advent of a different type of spirituality. The Mystery of the divine incarnation reaches here a more universal level of meaning, as if Christians suddenly understood how precious the creation must be to God, so much so that God became flesh.[349]

In this sense, still in the twelfth century, Francis of Assisi taught his contemporaries to look at nature in a different way. But the discovery of the presence of God in creation received a systematic treatment only when Bonaventure, one of Francis' followers, provided a demonstration of it in his *Itinerarium mentis in Deum*.[350] Now the Christocentric orientation of the new spirituality moved to the humanity of Christ, the perfect man, so intimately and perfectly united with God that, from here on, human love could never divert the soul from the love of God.

Thus the presence of God was found by Christian mysticism within rather than beyond the creation. It was not by coincidence that many mystics of love became saints—persons who through heroic virtue learned to love without possessiveness, in total self-giving and devotion to God, within historical time and space and the circumstances of their lives. All mysticism demands bodily and mental purity. But for those for whom the love of God passes through the creation, the purifying process proves to be especially exact and precise. It is also more demanding, even compared with the hardness of reality. Yet, once the experience and the true mystical state have begun, spiritual men and women tend to cease or reduce this arduous asceticism and active self-mortification, and no longer feel called to achieve so much austerity or such heavy penitence.[351]

John of the Cross, one of the most articulate mystics of love, describes the whole spiritual process as a progressive purification, as a "dark night"

---

347. See Tracy, *Triniarian Theology and Spirituality: Retrieving William of St. Thierry for Contemporary Theology*.

348. See Dupré, *The Common Life*.

349. See Dupré, "Mysticism," 255.

350. Apostolado da Oração, Braga, 2000.

351. See Dupré, "Mysticism," 255.

in two great stages—a passive and an active stage—and in two dimensions of the soul—that of the senses and that of the spirit. The process starts with the senses, goes on to the understanding, and ends in the total darkness of the union with God, called the night of the spirit.[352] The followers of this tradition tend to equate the beginning of the mystical life with the state of passive prayer, which happens after the active purification of the senses and excludes the ability to meditate as well as the capacity to produce anything at all. They all emphasize the need for total passivity in relation to the divine operation, attributing the action entirely to God, and to the human being only loving and humble consent.

With this emphasis on total passivity, the prayer of quietness (experienced and practiced by Teresa of Avila, Miguel de Molinos and Jeanne Guyon) was controversial and questioned. The question was whether the quietness was obtained through human effort or freely infused by God. Fénelon, the spiritual director of Mme. Guyon, brought the dispute to the question of pure love: the only love worthy of a spiritual person is that which loves God exclusively for God's self.

The purgative way is followed by the illuminating way. This is the moment when everything is illuminated and the experience sees with clarity the things that God reveals to it. Yet the illumination which normally follows the period of purgation should not be taken as a succession of new insights. John of the Cross distinguishes concrete visions from those known as spiritual apprehensions. Among the latter he finds the more direct expressions of the experienced presence of God. This Carmelite mystic equates such intellectual visions with the revelations of the being of God, in the naked understanding of the soul which has reached the state of union, and with the spiritual feelings that emerge. In such states, the illumination in fact becomes union.[353]

According to Teresa of Avila, what characterizes the final stage of mystical love—whether defined as cognitive or affective—is its permanence. It is what she refers to as matrimony. Here the distinction between the similarity of the mysticism of love and the identity of the mysticism of the image ceases to exist, even in the terminology. In the highest union of love, intentional intermediation is surrendered to the substantial presence. The tendency of similarity toward unity appears and resplendently shines.[354]

---

352. See St. John of the Cross, *Ascent of Mount Carmel, The Spiritual Canticle,* and others.
353. See Dupré, "Mysticism," 256.
354. Ibid.

The expression "experience of faith" often appears in religious topics and among the different theoreticians who are phenomenologists of religion, including psychologists, philosophers of religion, and theologians (such as James, Lohfink, etc.).[355] The experience of faith can take on a genitive objective case, as in the case of an experience which has faith as its object. But faith is more than an affirmation of truth. More than mere belief, it affirms the truth of some propositions based on the authority of those who convey them. It is an attitude which involves, according to Saint Thomas, "a transmutation of the soul" and provokes a restructuring of all dimensions of the person around a new center of existence discovered and recognized by the theological attitude. Thus, faith generates a movement of the whole person, who takes on a new way of being, of giving attention, and of consciously and lovingly living out the new relationship with God made possible by the theological attitude.[356]

Since faith is a theological attitude with God as its boundary, the experience of faith is, at its core, an experience of God. Thus faith, as Saint Thomas says, does not end in propositions but in the purpose to which it addresses them. The human being unites with God through faith, and the experience becomes, without abolishing the distance between the believer and God, an insuperably obscure experience of God. For faith, animated and vivified by love, possesses a light which grants to all believers the capacity to discern the things of God, while love and charity bring to them the capacity to accomplish a kind of affective contact with God.[357]

There is, therefore, an initial mystical dimension of faith and charity which is a real experience of God at the level of the fervent Christian life. The true mystical experience, then, is engraved in this Christian life, which—since it contains the experience of faith—is already endowed with the germ of mysticism and can advance and grow toward its coronation.[358]

One characteristic of Christian mysticism is its constant regulation of, and reference to, the experience of the Mystery, as the content of this experience. Such a characteristic is more clearly visible in the more original forms of Christian mysticism represented in the New Testament texts and in the writings of the Holy Fathers. However, it was obfuscated by the influence of Neoplatonism—especially the mystical theology of the Pseudo-Dionysius—on the mediaeval and modern mystics. More recently, the regulation of the experience of the Mystery found its proponents in theologians such as

---

355. See Velasco, *El fenómeno místico*, 284.
356. Ibid., 285 n. 38.
357. Ibid., 41 and 43.
358. Ibid., 287.

Balthasar, Bouyer, and de Lubac, who used it to combat the risk of psychologizing Christian mysticism supposedly brought about by some phenomenological—and especially psychological—interpretations of the mystical experience in the early twentieth century. Henri de Lubac says, "Mysticism constantly interiorizes the Mystery, owes its life to it, and brings it to life. . . . Without the Mystery received by the believer, mysticism is degraded."[359]

This presence and prevalence of doctrinal content concerning the mystic's way of life is common in all forms of authentic religious mysticism. What really constitutes the originality of the Christian mystical experience is the particular configuration of this experienced Mystery. The Christian Mystery is, in first place, the personal God of a monotheistic and prophetic tradition. It is also the Mystery of the Incarnate God—Jesus Christ, in whom we have access to the Father in the Spirit. And, thirdly, it is the Mystery that—by virtue of the incarnation and the continuation of the Old Testament revelation of God—unveils itself in human history while guiding it to its eschatological end. Furthermore, it is the Mystery to which human beings adhere by faith as the only way for them to respond. And, finally, it is the Mystery which gathers the believers into the fellowship of the church as the seed of the kingdom of God, the end point of history.[360]

Thus, according to De Lubac, the Christian mystical experience lies in the logic of the life of faith. The Christian mystical experience is a fruit of faith. It is not a deepening of the experience itself, but rather a deepening of faith. It is not an attempt at evasion of reality through interiority, but is rather Christianity itself.[361] Its originality lies in the particular adherence to God which Christians call faith, hope and charity. The emphasis on faith, according to De Lubac is that "faith is a promise of experience" (quoting Saint Bernard). "Detached from mysticism, the mystery is externalized and runs the risk of being lost in pure formula."[362]

Mysticism always moves in the interior of faith, and can never pretend to supersede it. Mystical experience achieves, at its level, the same harmony of apparently contrary aspects which constitutes the originality of the Christian faith. As in the case of faith, Christian mysticism is related to the Mystery, emerging from its manifestation in obscurity, and living in its presence which is never completely disclosed. And this relationship is not achieved by a mere prolongation of the unfathomable interiority of subject. It requires reference to the revelation, to the Word with which the Mystery

---

359. Ibid., 217 n. 98.
360. Ibid., n. 218.
361. Ibid., n. 99.
362. Ibid., n. 219.

awakes the profundity of the human being and sends it to that always unattainable beyond, which resounds in the depth of the subject and in the word that arouses it.

Velasco says that the experience, rather than being described through individual autobiographical narratives, constantly refers back to the paradigmatic scriptural models based on the journey of the elected people, such as the exodus, Moses' ascension to Mount Sinai, the entry into the cloud, etc. We believe that one does not exclude the other. On the one hand, it is true that Christian mystical experience always finds its reference in the pilgrimage of the people of Israel and in that of Jesus of Nazareth. But this does not preclude the fact that each mystical itinerary is original and unrepeatable, or that each mystic has something new to say about humankind's experience of faith. Indeed, the Christian mystics always narrate their experiences with the Christian Mystery as their background.[363]

The connection between mysticism and the Mystery for the Christian mystics clearly appears in other facts. We point to the lively personalized and personalizing configuration of the experience of the Christian mystics as an echo and subjective reverberation of the eminently personal character of the configuration of the content of this experience, which is offered by the Christian faith and its representation of the Mystery of God—the only God, the creator of the world and the guide of history, revealed in the New Testament, who as Father, by the action of the Son, conveyed the Spirit to us.[364]

This new factor shines unequivocally in the ineluctable christological dimension of every kind of Christian mysticism. Although in the state of union the mystic may seem to transcend all ways, forms, and determinations of the human knowledge of God (including those present in the propositions in which faith expresses its obscure knowledge of the Trinitarian Mystery, and, more concretely, in the determinations and forms which carry the knowledge and representation of the humanity of Christ), Jesus remains the reference for these Christian mystics for living out and describing their experience, including their highest states of union and loving transformation.[365] The narrative of the life of Jesus, the contemplation of his Mystery and the experiences lived out by his followers form the solid nucleus of Christian mysticism.

---

363. Ibid., 220.
364. Ibid., 221.
365. Ibid., n. 108.

Narrating the Experience: The Gateway to Discourse and Praxis

The prime source for the content of the mystical experience is the witness of the mystics themselves. They are the first and most important theoreticians of their experience and the most competent to reflect upon it. The biography of the believer, the mystic, is, therefore, the condition for the possibility of a theological reading of the mystical experience and its message in today's world.[366]

If the affirmations we are making come from the Christian faith, then there is much more reason for the truth of what we said above. Many contemporary theologians insist on the importance of moving from overly speculative theological thinking to a theological narrative, in which the revealed Mysteries can be stated, narrated and reflected upon.[367] There is also a growing emphasis in current theological circles on the importance of producing a theology based on accounts and examples of the witnesses' lives, rather than only on texts.[368] The connection between faith and praxis in following Jesus implies that this cannot be replaced by pure reflection or theoretical investigation. Up to a certain point, theology is obliged to think from the perspective of the following of Jesus, and can only be called theology when this following defines the place of reflection, and also when the reflection is itself the practice of an existential commitment and of this following.[369]

When this is the case, to read about the lives of the mystics is to read about the revelation of God, the One who writes with the Spirit in the body and life of the mystic. Saint Paul clearly says this in 2 Cor 3:3, when he affirms, "and you show that you are a letter of Christ, prepared by us, written not with ink but with the Spirit of the living God, not on tablets of stone but on tablets of human hearts." Thus, theological reflection is not concerned with God as an external object, but with a personal God who enters human thought in the ecstasies of a believing existence.[370]

---

366. See the precious little book of Schneider, *Teología como biografía*, esp. 22.

367. See, for instance, the works by Joseph Moingt (*L'homme qui venait de Dieu* and *Dieu qui vient à l'homme,* among others). See also Johann Baptist Metz, *Memoria Passionis*, as well as Jon Sobrino, with the whole perspective of his theology, "no de textos sino de testigos" (not from texts but rather from witnesses).

368. This could also find support in the *Evangelii Nuntiandi* of Pope Paul VI, no. 41, on the need to have witnesses so that the modern human being may believe.

369. See Schneider, *Teología como biografía*, 24.

370. Ibid., n. 16.

As Gustavo Gutiérrez properly says, "What comes afterwards is the theology, not the theologian."[371] In this context the theologian must be someone who is committed to, and a mouthpiece for, the witnesses whose lives he or she narrates. Sometimes this kind of commitment implies risks and dangers, and always—as Gutiérrez says, citing Isaiah and Saint Paul— the death of wisdom and understanding: "I will destroy the wisdom of the wise, and the discernment of the discerning I will thwart" (1 Cor 1:19). For this reason it can be said that to speak of a first and a second moment in the making of theology is not simply an issue of theological method. It is a question of lifestyle, of a way to live out the faith itself. Ultimately, it is a problem of spirituality: "Our methodology is our spirituality."[372]

From this perspective theological reflection derives from mystical and spiritual experiences and from their visibility in the world and history. The theologian's task, then, is to pay profound attention to the action of God in human lives, to organize what is gleaned from attentive observations of these lives, and to integrate them into a space where they can question Christian life, ecclesiastic life, and theological thought. Furthermore, theologians are not called to write hagiography, that is, to present an account of spiritual experiences. Rather, they are invited to take these experiences into serious consideration for the purpose of posing the question to themselves. And to others, as well.[373]

The reason for this is brilliantly and clearly presented in the affirmation by Karl Rahner that "human beings are the a priori transcendental of the Revelation and the faith, while Christianity is their historical a posteriori."[374] Theological knowledge is not something to be conveyed first and only through concepts, but rather through the following of Jesus—in the biographies and thought of men and women who make of love, as understood in the Gospel, their experience and the meaning of their existence, announcing it through their own lives and often through their own deaths as well. Their experience of faith confers upon theology a precious and original narrative-practical feature.[375]

We are convinced that each and all of these mystical lives develop a theology which can be shattered and separated while continuing to be true and precise, because in the fragment that is human life the divine totality is present and Self-communicating, through word and silence, through

---

371. Gutiérrez, *A força histórica dos pobres*.
372. Ibid., 75.
373. See Schneider, *Teología como biografía*, 26.
374. See Rahner, *Curso fundamental da fé*, 75.
375. As Metz says in *Faith in History and Society*.

presence and absence. And those who experience it can do no less than give witness to that which is stronger than they are, and in which they can find meaning for their lives and the life of the world.

It is important to remember here the contribution of Melchior Cano, who said that one of the *loci theologici* is the authority of the saints, because "the meaning of all the saints is the meaning of the Holy Spirit itself."[376] While aware of the need to distinguish between holiness and mysticism, we believe that the same can be said of the mystics. (Not all mystics are holy, in that not everyone is aware of his or her vocation for the mystical life, and not all who are aware of it respond fully, but may do so in a weak and partial way.) Mysticism is not a matter of morality, as wisely pointed out by Simone Weil.[377] It is rather an irruption of God into human history, providing answers to historical challenges and conferring upon these experiences and actions a normative meaning for the whole community of believers.

This is why we find it important to emphasize and value the twentieth century mystics. The so-called Godless century is not without the presence of God. But perhaps this presence takes place and makes itself visible in a different way. The medieval and modern worlds, at their beginnings, each formed a Christian culture and civilization. In a Godless century, in a secular era where the traces and footprints of God are almost invisible and religion appears to assume a nebulous and vacuous form, mystical experiences continue to happen in strong and unexpected ways. But with syntheses which differ from those of previous times.

The mystics are no longer found mainly inside the cloisters or in the religious orders.[378] We can find them in the factories, the midst of the noisy and stressful rhythm of machines and industry. Or in the streets with the poorest and those left behind by the so-called progress. Or in the prisons, due to their activity and commitment considered dangerous by the established authorities. Or in the hell of labor camps and gulags of all kinds. In other words, in very secular situations.

Why do we call them mystics rather than just political activists, good and honest persons committed to the most important struggles of

376. Cano, *De locis theologicis, Liber VII: De sanctorum auctoritate*, 63.

377. See the work of Simone Weil, *Attente de Dieu*, 81. "Aujourd'hui ce n'est rien encore que d'être un saint, il faut la sainteté que le moment présent exige, une sainteté nouvelle, elle aussi sans précédent" (Today to be a saint is nothing; we need the holiness that the current moment requires, a new holiness, one that is also without precedent).

378. We say "mainly" because mystical life obviously still goes on, and is very much alive, in the convents. See, for example, Thomas Merton, whose marvelous experience caught the attention of all of Western culture, with his commitment to political struggles and his pioneering of one of the most important topics of Christian theology today, the dialogue between East and West. And all of this from his Trappist monastery.

humankind? Although the objectives are often the same, and the same struggles can be carried out by believers of any tradition or by nonbelievers, the signature of the mystical experience is love, the intimate and loving relationship that these persons maintain with God. As well as its consequences and fruits. The consciousness of this love which moves and transforms lives is the reason they are there and in no other place, in spite of their own fragility, weakness, and indignity. Their lives and words are precious material for theological reading and thinking. And perhaps they will also provide a way to help our contemporaries rediscover the meaning of life they are thirsting for, and which they will certainly not find in frenetic consumerism or in superficial and volatile sensations, and even less in ephemeral, weak and provisional affective relationships.

In the midst of current and common circumstances, the mystics reinvent everyday life by being active subjects of their own history and by creating a new alphabet to express what constitutes the primary motive in their lives. Even when talking about the everyday trivialities of people and of the world, they are always talking about the things of God.[379] When they speak of the Mystery that they contemplate and that fills them with love, strength, and courage, the mystics are talking of those things that one does not need to know first in order to love them, but rather to love in order to know, in a movement that comprehends truth only through love. Many thinkers and persons of faith of our time have reflected on how difficult it is to find meaningful words to express these things of God for the ears of our contemporaries:

> There are times when speeches and texts are no longer enough to make the necessary truth comprehensible to all. In such times the mystic's actions and sorrows must create a new alphabet to unveil once again the secret of truth. Ours is a time such as this.[380]

Or we could remember the words of Pope Paul VI in the encyclical *Evangelii Nuntiandi*: "People today do not listen to their teachers. They listen to witnesses. And when they do listen to teachers, it is because they are witnesses."[381] This invention of a new alphabet for the loving narrative—which flows from and brims over the experience of the Mystery—collides with the customary norms of expression of the language, whose *ratio*, emancipated from the logic of the heart, articulates and makes pronounce-

---

379. Simone Weil said that to know if a person loved God, one had to pay attention not to the way he or she spoke of God, but rather to the way he or she spoke of the world.

380. See Baumgarten, *Ein aus 45 jaehriger Erfahrung geschoepfter Beitrag zur Kirchenfrage*, vol. 1, cited by Nigg, *Heilige im Alltag*, 32.

381. Paul VI, *Evangelii Nuntiandi*, no. 41.

ments about the real. And usually its pronouncements are replete with consequences for a world in crisis, when discernment is a primary need.

These mystics are deeply immersed in the world where they live and witness. In other words, they recognize the authentic value of the real and the profane. They are aware of the fact that this acknowledgment implies that they not succumb to logic of secularism, nor decline to be "a figure of the logic of graciousness."[382] These are attitudes that demand acceptance without reservation of all the risks carried by that gesture of crazy love, the Incarnation. This is precisely what the mystics do through their presence in this world as a sign of "that One who submits neither to being manipulated, appropriated, nor exchanged for whatever it might be."[383]

This is the way it has always been in the history of religions, and especially in the history of Christianity. While this history has often been read and narrated by a negativist mentality as the history of sin, it can also be presented as the history of the revelation of the Holy Mystery, and of the response to this Mystery in consenting to enter into a radical relationship of love and surrender, a relationship of holiness. Whether officially recognized or not, this experience as narrated today encounters an enormous thirst for Transcendence by men and women who have experienced the fall of the utopias, who have seen what appeared solid evaporate in a frustrating culture of sensations.

As friends of God and friends of life, contemporary mystics deserve to have their life stories presented from the standpoint of their own experience. These stories show us the possibility, in a Godless century, of an exemplary life of heteronomous autonomy, lived out in the primacy of the divine and human Otherness.

Furthermore, these mystics and their narratives represent a dangerous and subversive memory, one which does not allow the narrative of the Mystery—which is near to Grace and which self-communicates with any creature in this world—to lose its questioning strength and its salvific potentiality.

The biographies of these lives, lived out in a profound alliance with the Mystery, say what cannot be said, speak of the ineffable, and narrate what cannot be narrated. In so doing they give witness that they are more than one science among others. They are the theory of a praxis whose fruit is an art—the art of living.[384] An art which simply through its exercise unveils in the world and in history the access to the Mystery of God.

382. See Valadier, *Igreja e modernidade*, 87.
383. Ibid., 120.
384. Ibid. The author uses the expression *ars vivendi*.

4

Mystical Biographies and Theological Narrative

AFTER SEEING IN THE previous chapter how mystical experience is characterized, and after examining it throughout the history of Western thought in order to look more deeply and accurately into its precise conceptualization, we will concentrate here on the issue of the language which governs the mystical narrative.

The fact that those who experience God deeply feel the need—or are urged by others—to register in writing the states of their souls and the content of their experiences, demonstrates that the mystical narrative is essential for the understanding of this phenomenon and the mystical experience as a whole. Moreover, such narratives raise questions and provide a challenge for theology when called to take the issue as the object of its thinking.

Therefore, in this chapter we shall consider several aspects of the interface among theology, the biography of the believer, and the mystical narrative, in order to perceive their intersections and reflect on how they question and enrich the interpretation of faith.

A Theology of Texts or of Witnesses?

In juridical terms, a *witness* is a person who has seen or heard of an important event and can provide information and details about it. A witness is, therefore, someone who narrates an experience he or she was part of and lived through, and who has it engraved in memory.

The term *witness* also refers to the deposition of this person who saw, heard, experienced and memorized the event, which is presented at court for the purpose of ensuring its validity. It is therefore a subjective experience that was opened to the public domain in bring about justice or to reestablish

Mystical Biographies and Theological Narrative

the order that may have been disrupted, or even to show the way to those affected or those who may benefit from the narrative.

The word *witness* is fundamental in the history of Christianity. Faith in Jesus Christ, in whom the community recognized the Word made flesh and who revealed the merciful Father, was transmitted through the ages by stories and texts which attested to his existence, his deeds and his words. But even before that it was also transmitted by witnesses, persons who were indeed living texts in whose flesh the Holy Spirit wrote—not with ink but with the holy breath of the Spirit—the foundations of the new law of love.

Not seldom was this faith transmitted through written texts by witnesses who carried them engraved in the fragility of their human hearts, expanded by the experience of the living God whom no one could see without dying, and now incarnate in human mortality. A few of them, at the beginning, were eyewitnesses who saw and believed the deeds and words of Jesus of Nazareth, whom they came to call Lord and Christ. Today, from the distance of the twenty-first century, many of us are auditory witnesses who hear of and believe in the announcement of the good news of the Gospel narrated through his church. Or we are witnesses who live out such a powerful experience of the presence of the Risen Jesus Christ in our own persons that we cannot remain silent, and must communicate what we are living through to others. We are irresistibly called to be servants of God's Word, which is alive and effective and cannot be contained, but goes on being revealed in human flesh as it was in Jesus of Nazareth.[1]

With full secularization and the unstable ways of postmodernity, historical Christianity is living through a deep crisis in its official institutions, norms and formulations. This is a time in which we, as persons of faith, are called to "wake up from the dogmatic dream from which Kant wanted to free us."[2] And this awakening leads us to the realization that there are two ways to do theology: one, the traditional way from the texts of Scripture; and the other from the witnesses who narrate their experience of God, converting into flesh the concepts and categories that the texts elaborate and interpret. Both are in permanent hermeneutic circulation. Yet today, perhaps more than in other times, the theology which emerges from testimonial narratives is listened to more, due to its charismatic questioning for human beings who are struggling between the crisis of modernity and enlightenment reason, as well as the disintegration of so-called postmodernity.[3]

---

1. See Heb 4:12.
2. See Sobrino, *No Salvation Outside the Poor*, 13.
3. Here we adopt the concept as presented by Bauman in the several books that we have cited.

Doing theology based on the narratives of witnesses brings with it an increase in credibility, since they are the ones who hold more profoundly the knowledge of the Mystery of God as revealed in Jesus Christ, and bring about its presence in the midst of the world through their bodies and lives. Therefore our choice for this book, and especially in this chapter, is to concentrate on witnesses rather than on texts as the basis for the possibility of the experience of God by the contemporary human being.

A witness is someone who is torn apart in flesh and spirit.

> Torn apart first within himself, between the supreme witness at the highest point of his being and the lamentable individual whose life he assumes all day long. Torn apart still by the abyss which separates the truth about which he bears witness from the world which does not want to receive his message.[4]

According to Jean Philippe Pierron, the autonomous and glorious human beings exalted by modernity were crushed by the totalitarian ideologies—Nazism, Communism and their byproducts—who wanted to change them radically and collectively. In their place emerged in society humiliated humans, apparently subservient to the implacable need for a new destiny, no longer confident either in their capacity for initiative or in their power to innovate in freedom whatever they might wish. Subjugated to the globalization of the economy, to the laws of the market, to the dictatorship of consumerism, efficacy, beauty, pleasure and so much else, they find little room to maneuver in seeking to rediscover the way to their identity and their intrinsic dignity.[5]

The author places the witness between the exalted and the humiliated human being, and calls him or her the frail human being. This applies to those who have lucidly renounced their dreams of omnipotence without abdicating their identity and their capacity for initiative. And the irreplaceable originality and value of these witnesses lies in the fact that their testimony—that which they cannot cease offering to their world and their contemporaries, and even to the history of humankind as a whole—inseparably and concretely ties together their narrative and their way of being and existing, thus mobilizing all human capabilities, whether for words, attitudes or resistance.[6]

Thus the witnesses are always inconvenient, embarrassing and disturbing, because they bring into play something radical and excessive—the

---

4. See Adamov, "Printemps 1940," in Rilke, *Avertissement: le livre de la pauvreté et de la mort* (trans. Adamov), 7, cited in an epigraph in Pierron, *Le passage de temoin*, 9.

5. See Pierron, *Le passage de temoin*, 16.

6. Ibid., 17.

Mystery as the foundation of the human condition as such, which rejects any attempt to reduce, insult or diminish it. The witnesses are those who have experienced the Absolute and turned this experience into the guiding principle of their lives. In this way the witnesses and their narrative infiltrate, so to speak, the world's volatility and ephemerality, making of the truth their biography—the history of their lives—and showing the courage to invent a new logic and a new language to express the Absolute and the truth for which humankind has an unquenchable thirst.

Witnesses are unavoidably vulnerable persons who are exposed and delivered to the world and to others in total availability. Par excellence relational, they attest to things which as human beings they have seen, heard, and touched with their own hands, and which constitute a fundamental experience in their lives. Such experiences, however, were not given to them to be lived out for themselves, but to be humbly and generously shared with others. A witness is the image of a mediator among conflicts, bringing forth from them apparently difficult dialogues. A witness is also the figure of someone at the service of the Absolute and the truth, and a hostage of the other in voluntary self-abdication, losing himself or herself in the Otherness that questions the witness while claiming him or her as mediator.[7] They testify through themselves rather than of themselves. Witnesses are carriers of a truth which cannot be reduced to a mere opinion. Where an opinion is objective and subjectively contingent, witnesses attest to a truth which might not be objectively verifiable and sufficient, although subjectively it is indeed so. This endows their witnessing with some normativeness, since they tie the destiny of the truth to their own destiny.[8]

Witnesses can be assimilated into what the history of ideas calls the hero, a category that—along with those of the saint and the wise person—serves to classify the moral attitudes required of the human condition.[9] Heroes put themselves at the service of a cause which surpasses them and leads them to surpass themselves. They distinguish themselves by their strength of soul and energy of character, as well as by the greatness and nobility present in their choice of concerns.[10]

Who are our heroes in today's world? Who are the persons and figures to whom we look with admiration, feeling that they have something important to tell us and teach us? In ancient times, the saint, the savant, and

---

7. See the magnificent reflection by Levinas, *Autrement qu'être ou au-delà de l'essence*.

8. Pierron, *Le passage de temoin*, 23.

9. See Bareau et al., "Sainteté," in *Encyclopaedia Universalis*. See also Festugière, *La sainteté*.

10. Ibid.

the hero were the paradigmatic figures whose example any human being wanted to follow. Nowadays, soccer players and movie stars have taken their place, especially regarding their millionaire's salaries and their sex life.[11] Anti-values are thus introduced, which, instead of constructively mobilizing what is most noble in human beings and giving them hope, reinforce their state of lethargic consumerism or incurable depression.

It seems to us that a change of heroes is urgent. And given the thirst for Transcendence experienced today in spite of the crisis of culture and civilization we are going through, the contemporary mystics could be these other heroes—different, discrete, and humble—who are found where nobody would like to be, who go where nobody wants to go, and who burn with a flame which never goes out. They are fragile and immoderate men and women who are willing and ready to die for the truth that they experience, and eager to witness among their contemporaries.

One need not enter the confinement of the cloisters to look for them, as they are not to be found exclusively there. On the contrary, we meet them in the streets, in the big cities, at the margins of the world and in the basements of humanity, in difficult and—according to our aesthetic sensibilities—ugly places, or in dangerous places which make us tremble with fear.

The witnesses of the Mystery, which has seduced and involved them and with which they have consented to enter into intimate communion, testify to all that they have seen, heard, touched and learned there, using their knowledge, which is another name for the word *love*.[12] After achieving mystical union, the heroes and heroines of the divine intimacy proceed gently and joyfully toward the risk and danger of witnessing in the public square. The ardor of their zeal irresistibly impels them toward the encounter with others, amidst threats, conflicts and often violent death.

The etymological history of the word *witness* reveals something important about its content and identity. This history is inseparable from that of *martyrdom*, which has always been understood as witness to the point of bloodshed. In Greek the word *witness* is translated as *martyr* (not so much in the juridical as in its anthropological sense).

---

11. See the TV program *Big Brother*, which originated in Holland and is showing in several countries. It features a group of persons who live in a house for several days and are filmed in their most private intimacies by TV cameras. Each week one of them is chosen to be expelled from the house. The media makes public, without any shame, the most intimate secrets of these persons, their lives, their habits, their desires. Those who remain until the end are called "the heroes." They receive a fat sum of money as well as lucrative contracts as actors and actresses.

12. In the Bible, *knowing* is inseparable from loving. It is an inclusive word, employed in reference to sexual relations. The husband *knows* his spouse in the intimacy of their bedroom, etc. (See Gen 4:1, 17, 25, among many other texts).

Martus comes from *mrtu*, the root of *mermera*: anxiety, concern, worry. It is also the root of *mermerizo*: to be busy, full of responsibilities. The underlying Indo-European root is *smer* (*mer*), which means to reflect, to think, to recollect, to be careful, to be worried, to be reminded. *Smrti* in Sanskrit means that which is remembered, entrusted to memory, that is, to tradition.

> Thus, according to the etymology and history of the word, one arrives at the following description: *marturia*, witness, is the act or result of witnessing, that is, of testifying, of relying upon a conviction that in itself is burdensome, about which we worry, which we recollect, and which causes us anxiety and anguish.[13]

Although mystics in a strict sense are not always martyrs, they are those who, within history, consent to the self-expression of the divine and the affirmation of the meaning of life with and in their bodies, words, and lives. They are those who, at the risk of a painful internal laceration, maintain themselves between the truth they carry and the world which rejects them, and between the greatness of what they have experienced and their own fragility and weakness.

The love which feeds their ardor is the love of God, who is life, and who can be found and experienced today wherever men and women are suffering any kind of constraint and need, or are crushed by depression and longing for a light of hope to assure them that life has meaning. Mystics do not understand their experience as purely subjective, but rather as a dynamism which compels them to inspire and bring forth newness and creativity to human life and human reality. Thus the obligatory synthesis of contemporary mysticism lies in its conscious and explicit connection with ethics. Anchored in their experience of the loving Mystery of God, the mystics confront the great ethical challenges of their time and place.

Mysticism and Ethics: An Indissoluble Alliance

We understand ethics as the area of philosophy responsible for the investigation of the principles that motivate, distort, discipline or guide human behavior, reflecting a consideration of the essential nature of the norms, values, prescriptions and exhortations present in any social reality. Within the field of philosophy, ethics—as related to rationalist and metaphysical doctrines—undertakes the study of the ultimate or ideal goals, and in some

---

13. See Pierron, *Le passage de temoin*, 21, quoting Pannikar, "Temoignage et dialogue," in Castelli, *Le témoignage*, 373.

cases transcendent ones, which orient human action toward maximum harmony, universality, excellence or perfectibility—implying the overcoming of thoughtless passions and desires. On a more colloquial level, ethics would be the set of rules and precepts of the value system and moral order of an individual, social group, or society.[14]

In our research into the etymology of the word *ethics* we find its origin in the Greek word *ethos*, which means "way of being, character, custom."[15] In later philosophy, the Latin noun *ethica* means "ethics, or natural morality . . . the area of philosophy that studies the 'moral.'"[16] For its part, *moral* is a Latin word which has its etymological roots in customs (*mor, mores*). It signifies a set of values, such as honesty, goodness, virtue, etc., universally considered to guide the social relations and conduct of human beings. It is, therefore, the set of rules, precepts, etc., characteristic of a particular social group which establishes and defends them. In philosophy, the word applies to each one of the variable systems of laws and values encompassed by ethics as an autonomous discipline, which are characterized as organizing the life of multiple human communities by differentiating among and defining behaviors that are proscribed, ill-advised, permitted, or exemplary. It is the part of philosophy that studies human behavior in the light of the values and prescriptions that regulate the life of societies.[17] Etymologically, *moral* comes from the Latin *moralis*, as translated by Cicero from the Greek *ta ethica*.

Both terms—*ethics* and *moral*—designate that which has to do with customs, character, and human attitudes in general, and in particular to the rules of behavior and their justification. Although there is no general agreement on this point, it appears that the Latin term (*moral*) is used in the analysis of concrete moral phenomena, while the Greek (*ethics*) is applied to the fundamental problematic of morality as a whole, and to the study of basic concepts such as good and evil, obligation, duty, etc.[18]

After the events of the Second World War, both philosophy and theology were compelled to rethink their discourse. And this could no longer be done by way of the great metaphysical principles. They were, rather, obliged to proceed through ethics and through the responsibility toward the other who shares the human condition. The contribution of Hans Jonas, in

---

14. *Dicionário Houaiss*, electronic dictionary, 2007.

15. See *et(o)-*; f. hist. sXV *etica*, sXV *ethica*, sXV *eetica*.

16. From the Greek adjective *éthikós*, fem. sing. *Éthikê*, "ethical, related to morality," noun, plural neuter *tà éthicá*, "treatise on morality, ethics," linked with the Greek.

17. *Dicionário Houaiss*, electronic dictionary, 2007.

18. See E. Weil, "Morale," in *Encyclopaedia Universalis*, numerical version, 2009.

particular, is fundamental here. In his book *The Imperative of Responsibility*, he affirms,

> The paradox of our situation consists in that we must recover the lost dignity from the standpoint of fear, the positive from the standpoint of the representation of the negative: respect for what man has been and for what he is, recoiling in horror before that which he could become, a possibility which looks at us fixedly from the perspective of a future that foresees the thought.[19]

Post-Auschwitz thought cannot proceed in the same way as before.

That is how the Lithuanian Jewish philosopher Emmanuel Levinas thought, as well. During his whole life he pursued one and only one objective—to demonstrate why ethics, which finds its origin in the primordial experience of responsibility for the other, should be recognized as the "first philosophy," worthy of that name. According to Jonas, it was the Nazi horror that led Levinas to question certain grounds underlying Western philosophy, which is attracted to the "Self" and the "Totality" more than to the "other" and the "Infinite." Thus a phenomenology centered on the epiphany of the Face of the Other joins the metaphysical desire for the wholly other.[20] This explains why Levinas inspires not only philosophy, but also theology.

According to the phenomenology of Levinas, the experience of the Absolute and the Mystery—that is, mysticism—necessarily passes through the epiphany of the very real and concrete questioning of the Face of the Other, which confronts me with the existential question to which the only possible answer is not found in the Cartesian *cogito*, but in the humble and available accusative, Here-I-am! This is a privileged possibility of a way to approach and meet the Wholly other, in the direction impelled by my desire.

The main characteristic of contemporary mysticism is, therefore, its indissoluble connection with ethics and all that derives from it: transformative action in the world, political commitment, dialogue with other religious experiences, and alliance with a conflictive and suffering world. This is a constitutive element of its synthesis and a powerful criterion for its authenticity. It is in part a matter of a just reaction against the subjectivist intimacy which for a long time defined mysticism, divorcing it even from theology itself, and leaving mysticism reduced to a handful of minor devotions, losing its speculative backbone along with its connection to theology. It is also

---

19. See Jonas, *O princípio responsabilidade*, 10. See also Trémolières, "Le principe responsabilité," in *Encyclopaedia Universalis*. English version: "The imperative of responsibility in search of an ethics for the techological age," Chicago, University of Chicago Press, 1985.

20. See Greisch, "Lévinas, Emmanuel," in *Encyclopaedia Universalis*.

reduced to purely inner experiences, without the necessary impact on the world of the polis—or even on reality itself—and exposed to the danger of alienation and regressiveness. For its part, theology runs the risk of becoming pure rationality, dry and arid, and unable to inspire the Christian life.

In the 1960s historical Christianity, especially Catholicism, underwent a truly Copernican turn with the Second Vatican Council. Among its numberless contributions to the living of the Christian faith in a world wounded by two world wars and suffering situations of extreme injustice and helplessness, the Council raised some fundamental points which turned the eyes of the community of believers toward the positiveness of earthly realities, the need to dialogue with other Christian denominations and other religions, and the urgent necessity to struggle against injustice and racial violence. This produced a Christianity in action, engaged with reality and committed to transforming it.

That explains why many people are alarmed by what is happening today, fifty years after the Council, in the return of mysticism to the theological proscenium. These anxieties are based on the possibility that this return may represent an abandonment of the priority of a commitment deeply rooted in history, proposed by a praxis transformative of reality.[21] The fear is of the danger that alienation will return to haunt a Christianity disenchanted by seeing around it the loss of its paradigms—including its political ones—and tired of being defeated on this same ground.[22]

Nevertheless, we believe that—contrary to these fears—the linkage of mysticism with ethics, with politics, and with transformative action is possible and necessary. We further believe that both polarities may simultaneously have a place once they find their precise point of intersection. A social and political praxis of justice inspired by a universal ethic can even provide the space and nourishment for an authentic mystical experience.

It is well known that the theme of a mysticism of action, of a spirituality strictly connected to a transformative commitment involving the polis—and therefore closely related to the topic of mysticism and politics—has been present in Liberation Theology since its beginnings, when it emerged and developed in Latin America with the pioneering book, now a classic,

---

21. See liberation theology and its criticism of the regressive alienation of a certain type of spirituality.

22. See Libânio, "Mística e missão so professor." See also Libânio, "Cenários da Igreja," where one finds explicitly stated, "It is verified that the crisis of militancy is a fact. There is a shift from militancy to mysticism. Those who in the decade of the 1960s and 1970s were engaged in revolutionary movements, disillusioned, turn to religious offerings."

by Gustavo Gutierrez, in the early 1970s.[23] But it was present even before that, in the action, thought, and words of many men and women, clergy and laity, Catholics and Protestants, who were awakened by the experience of the Spirit of God to the indisputable need to not separate mysticism from ethics, or the experience of God from the practice of justice.

Albert Schweitzer, the great Protestant theologian and biblical scholar, is one of them. His theology strongly embodies the kind of liberalism that understands the essence of the Christian message as a reflection on the person and teachings of Jesus. What inspires all his thought and action, and is the foundation of his personal ethics, is respect for life, which can be practiced in relation to all.[24]

This great theologian, doctor, and humanist insists in his writings that the affirmation of life and of the world can give birth to a true ethical mysticism.[25] This way of thinking finds its expression in Schweitzer's famous philosophy of reverence for life. This rational, absolute, and universal reverence for all forms of life is the basis of an ethical mysticism of union with the infinite will of God.[26]

Schweitzer tries to make explicit the indissoluble connection between mysticism and ethics, between union with God and a commitment to reality, to the extent that he defines mysticism as "the individual feeling himself—although externally in the midst of the earthly and the temporal—as belonging to the supernatural and the eternal."[27] Schweitzer negatively evaluates the mysticism of identity with God, saying that "a mysticism purely of God remains a dead thing."[28] For him the so-called "mysticism of God"[29] always means identity with the divine in the experience of union, and therefore is *ipso facto* inconsistent with the Christian faith as regards the obligatory transcendental distinction which must be made between God

---

23. See Gutiérrez, *Teologia da libertação*. See also Casaldáliga and Vigil, *Espiritualidade da libertação*, especially the section "Constantes da espiritualidade da libertação," 228ff.

24. See Encrevé, "Schweitzer, Albert," in *Encyclopaedia Universalis*.

25. Ibid., 271, where he says that this could happen, but only to the extent to which the affirmation is based on what he calls "the elemental thought." This way of thinking, concerned with the basic questions of life, rests on the *Lebenschaung* (vision of life), the expression of the desire that precedes the *Weltanschaung* (vision of the world), the scientific and rational approximation of an apprehension of the world.

26. See Clark, *Ethical Mysticism of Albert Schweitzer*, esp. 62–67, cited by McGinn, *Foundations of Mysticism*, 271 n. 32.

27. Schweitzer, *Mysticism of Paul the Apostle*, 1.

28. McGinn, *Foundations of Mysticism*, 379.

29. McGinn uses the expression "God-mysticism" (ibid., 272).

and the human.[30] Yet, the many accusations against Christian spirituality as being alienating and subjectivist could explain this reaction of historic Protestantism, which is more ethical and practical than Catholicism.

The French Catholic philosopher Maurice Blondel, in his work *L'Action*, seconds Schweitzer's uneasiness, in a certain way. He holds that persons pass away, but their acts persist. Thus, although limited by historical time, human beings enjoy eternity even here, in the midst of history, as well as the perpetual renewal of the duration of time. They benefit from universality at the same time that they live out the singularity of their personal lives. Through action they are connected with the whole of humankind, while the execution of this action is inaccessible in its uniqueness and singularity. Blondel especially highlights "the great works of science, of art or of virtue, which surpass individual consciousness and belong to all."[31]

Thus, for Blondel, action is an experience of the divine in the world. Human beings aspire to be God, and—contrary to sin, which makes them wish to be God without or against God—are called to be for God and with God. This choice operates through action, which is, according to Blondel, where the cosmic and spiritual vocation of humankind is accomplished.[32] A rereading of Blondel nowadays, in the course of the reflection we are undertaking here, allows us to conclude that the mystical experience can—and effectively does—maximally inspire and fortify this action, which leads the theological and spiritual vocation of all human beings to fulfillment. Therefore, mysticism cannot remain hidden or ignored, but rather must overflow into the specific action which has its source in open and available passivity, illuminated by the divine, in order to make itself into a humane and humanizing ethics and practice.

The French Jesuit Michel de Certeau, for his part, affirms that mystics are led by each of their experiences to a deeper and more radical level, which also goes beyond their strongest moments. The unity that attracts them inward also propels them outward in the direction of still unpredictable stages for which they or other persons will generate or invent the vocabulary, with an eye to a language which belongs to no one but which they feel called to pronounce in the midst of the world. Others will complete their fragmented speech, which nevertheless remains indispensable because it is unique and original. Mystical language is, therefore, necessarily social, since anyone illuminated by Grace is reintroduced to the group, transported to the future,

---

30. Ibid. According to McGinn, the history of Christian mysticism suggests that this image is too simple.

31. See *L'Action*, 1:237. See also Blondel et al., *Qu'est-ce que la mystique? Quelques aspects historiques et philosophiques du probleme*.

32. Blondel, *L'Action*, 1:237.

written into a story which must be told to others, and must—inseparably—open up to and make room for others.[33]

Michel de Certeau goes on to affirm that the transitions from personal to social life represent a return to the sources, since they not only manifest the truth and authenticity of the mystical experience but also revert to the sociocultural situation which preceded them and made them possible. The extraordinariness of the mystical experience lies, to a great extent, in the discovery of meaning in the midst of the anonymity of actual facts.[34]

Thus, according to de Certeau, spiritual perception develops in a corporeal way,[35] within a mental, linguistic and sociocultural organization which precedes and determines it, giving it form before any explicit consciousness. The mystics receive from reality a way to express it, even if the mystical excess, the wound, and the opening to meaning—which Derrida calls the hyperbolic moment—shatter the limits of the historical and cultural structure.[36] In an analogous manner they are called to give back to reality—in the form of concrete, compassionate and transformative behavior—that which they received from it in support of their experience of fellowship with the Absolute Mystery.

The German Jesuit Karl Rahner made a decisive contribution to the return of transformative ethics and its practice to a central place in contemporary theology. Living in the middle of the twentieth century, his major concern was to help the people of his time to believe. For that reason he was against what he considered the vulgarity of a world from which God had been exiled. He engaged in a dialogue with nonbelievers, anchored in two principles. The first was to highlight the fundamental human experience common to both sides of the dialogue. This would function as the platform of understanding from which the exchange of arguments would proceed. The second was to acknowledge where each interlocutor stood. The believer feels and thinks as a believer; the nonbeliever feels and thinks as a nonbeliever.

In Rahnerian theology, theologians—in elaborating their discourse—are deeply committed to their experience of God. Theological discourse, therefore, comes from the faith of its author and addresses the faith of the reader. As a person of faith, Rahner addresses himself to the human beings of his day with the intention of helping them to believe and to respond to the challenges of the world they are living in. He speaks from a deep interior

---

33. See Certeau, "Mystique," in *Encyclopaedia Universalis*.
34. Ibid.
35. The application of this word to de Certeau's thought is ours.
36. See Certeau, "Mystique," in *Encyclopaedia Universalis*.

experience and in that sense he produces a mystical theology, yet one which does not, in any way or at any time, lose sight of the concrete challenges of his epoch and his moment.

Catholic theology owes to Rahner the achievement of the so-called anthropocentric turn which, so to speak, established what is known today as bottom-up theology. Instead of a theology that comes from above, from transcendental principles and affirmations of God's attributes and the truths of faith, his theology begins from the bottom—from the human being who is the hearer of the Word, the *a priori* transcendental of the Revelation and of faith. For Rahner, theology is not an end in itself. He says of himself, "I always did theology keeping in view the preaching, the pastoral."[37] Paradoxically, he was very speculative and at the same time concerned with ethical challenges and desirous of conveying a faith that would provide a response to them.

Karl Rahner believes it is not necessary to raise the question of God in the abstract. His intention is to formulate it starting with human beings as such. It is from there that the credibility of the Christian proposal must be verified. He tries to maintain a strict link between the essence of the human being and the essence of Christianity. The former questions the latter, and the latter must be prepared to respond. On the one hand, human beings bring with them a question which they never cease to confront: the question of what they themselves deeply and truly are. All beings embody this question, or even better, all human beings are this question. On the other hand, one must think about what Christianity fundamentally has to say in answer to such a question. Through his formal and fundamental theology, Karl Rahner called all of theology to a new and fecund task and proposed a new basis for its self-understanding. With the deepening of existential logic and ethics, he made an important contribution to basic morality. His work is a concrete demonstration that in thinking about faith one has to take into account on the one hand its interior experience, and on the other the demands and problems of the modern world, while trying to ensure that theological activity is always at the service of the coming of Jesus Christ, the Incarnate Word, for an encounter with the men and women of today and of all times.

Rahner gives great importance to inner experience, as can be seen in his innumerable writings on spirituality and mysticism, among them *Encounters with Silence*;[38] *The Need and the Blessing of Prayer*;[39] *Mary, Mother*

---

37. See Rahner and Metz, *The Courage to Pray*.
38. Rahner, *Encounters with Silence*.
39. Rahner, *The Need and the Blessing of Prayer*.

of the Lord;⁴⁰ *The Mystical Way in Everyday Life*;⁴¹ and numerous articles published in the journal *Geist und Leben*. He also publicly acknowledges, without hesitation, that he learned the essentials of his theology in his experience with the Spiritual Exercises of Saint Ignatius, which remained the matrix of his theological thought throughout his whole life. Thus he understood that all mysticism must yield fruits in the reality where it occurs and is located. At the core of Rahner's theology lies the conviction that high theology must take seriously small things and concrete life. And here one finds evidence of the ethical concerns of this German theologian. His theology interweaves mystics and ethics in a fertile way, in order to be intelligible to contemporaneity.

Johann Baptist Metz is one of the most brilliant disciples of Rahner and the founder of the school of thought known as political theology, which strongly influenced Latin American liberation theology. At a certain moment in his journey Metz turned away from the transcendental theology of his master Rahner in order to elaborate a fundamentally practical alternative. In his works he makes frequent reference to his own experience. Thus it is easier to understand his thought in depth, since, as he himself says, "not even the theme 'God' exempts the theologian from his biography."[42]

During the Second World War, Metz fought as a young soldier. Near the end of the conflict he was sent to serve in several villages. When he arrived at their barracks he found all his comrades dead, killed in a most violent way. He could not muffle the cries of ethical perplexity this aroused.

> Nowadays my prayers are laced by that cry. And my theological work is marked by a special sensitivity to the so-called theodicy question, the questioning of God in view of the incomprehensible stories of suffering in the world, which must without doubt be "his" world. . . . Since then, for me, questions for clarification have arisen, addressed to God, to the God of Abraham, Isaac, and Jacob, to the God of Jesus; questions in search of explanations for which a language is available, but no answers. And thus I have been appropriating them in the form of prayers.[43]

It is Metz who says that one must be a mystic with eyes open to the world in order to perceive its challenges and feel its sufferings and conflicts.[44] In one of his last works, *Memoria Passionis*, he searches for ways to

---

40. Rahner, *Mary, Mother of the Lord*.
41. Rahner, *The Mystical Way in Everyday Life*.
42. Quote from http://protagonistas.blog.com/2010/08/13/johann-baptist-metz/.
43. See Metz, *Memoria Passionis*.
44. Metz, *El clamor de la tierra*, 26.

answer the following question: in view of the innocent victims of injustice in an environment of globalization and pluralism, is there in the diversity of religions and cultures irrevocably recognized today a criterion of understanding and fellowship binding on everyone, and therefore capable of being acknowledged as true? For Metz, the key words for finding the answer are, on the one hand, the subversive memory of the victims that makes them once again active in history, and on the other, *compassio*.[45]

It is with this *attitude-concept* that he tries to express the need for Christianity to abandon its threatening self-privatization. *Compassio* is not approval from above or from the outside, but the perception of the suffering of the stranger, in which one is ethically obliged to participate. For this compassion the categoric imperative is: "Stop, listen and look."[46]

Compassion is the capacity to partake of the suffering of others. Indeed, the most terrible suffering is not so much suffering in itself, but loneliness in suffering. Metz attempts to elaborate the *memoria passionis* as a basic category for a theology of the public square. It is a matter of remembering the suffering of others, a public recollection of the suffering of the stranger which is incorporated for public use in such a way that it leaves its imprint there. Compassion comes, therefore, from the universality of the experience of suffering. From there, according to Metz, the need emerges for a new political theology that would make a vigorous contribution toward a church of *compassio* in which the *memoria passionis* would function as a provocative recollection in the foundation of a new ethics.

This *memoria passionis*—the foundation of a new ethics—comes from the open-eyed mysticism taught and lived out by Jesus as he confronted the suffering of strangers and human pain. It is this spirit of compassion which takes hold of contemporary mystics and gives them the courage to go out and face the political, social, and cultural conflicts of today's world. Thus, in order to assert its authenticity as an experience of God, mysticism submits to an authority which is both demanding and accessible to all persons, that is, to the authority of those who suffer, and above all of those who suffer unjustly and guiltlessly. This would be the inner authority of a global *ethos*, of a worldwide morality, which would mobilize all persons irrespective of any ideology or persuasion, and consequently could not be set aside or relativized by any culture, religion or church. Any true mysticism today, especially after Auschwitz, cannot avoid being inspired by this *ethos*. And a politics inspired by this *ethos* would be more than and different from a sheer executor

---

45. Ibid.
46. Ibid.

of the law of the market, of technology, and of their obvious oppression in our time of globalization. It would certainly be more humanizing.

That political theology made explicit in postwar Europe—and was conceptualized in Latin American Liberation Theology beginning in the 1970s—was already, and still is, lived out by many in their spiritual lives and experiences, and expressed in their praxis. We are referring here to phenomena such as the European worker priests of the 1950s, and to persons like Madeleine Delbrel, the apostle of the streets of Paris, and Simone Weil, the agnostic philosopher who in the decade of 1930s, before the horrors of the Second World War, found God and Jesus Christ in the course of her physically grueling factory work. And to many others who were then already living out and narrating what theology would later articulately and rigorously elaborate.

The Christian spiritual experience is born from the encounter with the Lord in the face of the poor, the unhappy, the suffering. The resulting practice takes as its only objective the construction of the kingdom of God. It is a practice that, besides originating in the most authentic mystical experience, further develops this experience, nourishes it and makes it grow, by making it present in the world—in a conflict-stricken world, ridden with all kinds of injustice.

It is therefore possible to state that mysticism may find its origin and environment in the questions raised by the poverty and pain of the other, and by the compassion that it arouses. All this activity is not only ethical but also mystical—or better said, it is mystical because it is ethical and vice-versa, since in the biblical Revelation and in Christianity these two are not separate.

We begin by finding the foundations in God, who in the Revelation to the people of Israel appears as the active and effective Word, who does what God says and makes things happen, who acts in human beings and in reality, and who unceasingly works in the creation with the sole intention of bringing it back into a fellowship of love. We continue with the Incarnate Word, Jesus of Nazareth, who affirms in the Gospel, "My Father is still working, and I also am working" (John 5:17). The God of the Christian faith is Someone who never ceases to work and act. And God's praxis is addressed to the human being, who in turn actively receives and cooperates with this divine practice that happens in the midst of the world.

If all human praxis corresponded to or resulted from divine praxis, then social and political praxis would not deviate from this principle. Like any human praxis, political praxis—under some criteria—certainly can be, and effectively often is, the Mystery of an exodus from oneself which is also an ecstasy, that is, an immersion in the other, in the suffering and the disfigured reality of the other—identifying with this reality, participating in it, and communing with it in order to denounce it and make possible its transformation. If, on the one hand, the ecstasies of the mystics recognized by official religion are not highlighted (and rightly so) as the most important criteria for recognizing the authenticity of their experiences, on the other hand their concrete works—the fruits which accompany or follow such ecstasies—surely denote their authenticity to a greater or lesser degree.

The life of the mystics is, therefore, a permanent exodus—and based on what we just affirmed, an ecstasy—toward the Otherness of God who inspires and fills them with joy and delight, and toward the Otherness of the neighbors, whom they serve more and more under the inspiration of this same God. The experience of union with God which characterizes mysticism is, therefore, far from being a cost-free benefit of the delights and marvels of contemplating the eternal Mysteries. It is rather, and above all, a matter of being sent into the world and assuming responsibility for those who, from the heart of a disfigured and unjust reality, clamor for justice and compassion. Since the word *mysticism* finds its roots in another word—Mystery—and since mystical experience means, in sum, an experience of intimacy with the Mystery, it is a matter not only of the Mystery of Otherness which shines from the depth of reality while at same time transcending it, but also of a Mystery of responsibility in which each is responsible for the others. They experience in the flesh the consequences and weight of an evil which they do not practice, and are graciously made partners in the economy of a redemption which is neither invented nor presided over by them.

If mysticism is union with the divine Mystery, for Christianity and for many other religions, certainly this divine Mystery is not found outside the realities of this world. On the contrary, it is by immersing ourselves more deeply in all things that we can find the mystery of our Creation, the Transcendence that we desire and for which we thirst, and which surpasses us while at the same time coming near, from the heart of reality.

It is here that mysticism, ethics and politics show more clearly the possibility of their intersection. If God, the greatest subject of mysticism, allows God's self to be found in all things, and if in the world—in this world as it is—one can experience God's ineffable presence, then human action in this world is definitively consecrated and is an integral part of the sphere of the Sacred and the divine. And this is so even within its profane and secular condition, without abdicating or escaping from it.

The God who acts and works in the world is both the condition for the possibility of human praxis, and its springboard. Experienced as Mystery, this God will engender in human beings an action which is no longer theirs, but is indissolubly interwoven in one sole move with the action of God.

To encounter God is thus to encounter at the same time the world and the others, and the contemplation of God is synonymous with bringing about, in the midst of all the problems and ambiguities of reality, the will and the project of God.

It remains for us to ask what comes first, or if one thing is a consequence of the other. Is it necessary, in order for mysticism and contemplation to be granted value and to be accepted as a topic of the first magnitude, that all that makes up the world of doing and acting, of transformative efficacy, of conscious and articulate intervention in reality, should lose their appeal and credibility? In other words, must one renounce politics or the politician in order to enter deeply into the world of mysticism? Or, vice-versa, in order to choose a life in the polis, in the world, in the secular city, is it necessary to turn one's back on mysticism, condemning it to become the subject of just a few specialists, the inhabitants of cloisters and monasteries or other explicitly contemplative religious communities?[47]

Not if one takes seriously what the mystic Paul of Tarsus says in the early days of Christianity: "and you show that you are a letter of Christ, prepared by us, written not with ink but with the Spirit of the living God, not on tablets of stone but on tablets of human hearts" (2 Cor 3:3). The God of the Christian faith is someone who works. This God is a Spirit who keeps on hewing and sculpting in the reality of the creature a new genesis: the genesis of the new creation.[48]

This praxis is addressed to human beings. It is addressed to those who, to the best of their strength and possibility, at once passively receive the divine praxis and actively cooperate with it—with this unceasing work that aims to redirect all things toward the desired and dreamed of fellowship with the Creator. Thus, in light of the Christian theology, all human praxis is a result of the praxis of God—and not simply as a reflex. It is the divine praxis happening within the world and reality through the mediation of human flesh. Political praxis is no exception to this rule.

Today, as always, the experience of the relationship with God and even of union with this God in the face of the poor—the experience of suffering with the one who suffers injustice and oppression—continues to be for mysticism, especially in the Judeo Christian tradition, a favored way to the encounter with the One who "did not regard equality with God as something to be exploited, but emptied himself, taking the form of a slave, being born in human likeness . . . obedient to the point of death—even death on

---

47. See our reflection on this question in Bingemer and Bartholo Jr., *Mística e política*, 287ff.

48. See Tresmontant's beautiful reflection on this in *La mística cristiana y el porvenir del hombre*, especially the chapter "La finalidad de la creación," 46 ff.

a cross" (Phil 2:6–8). Taking upon oneself the weight and pain of reality in the other's stead, in solidarity with the other, is not only an ascetic and voluntary effort but also a mystical experience, one of the deepest and most authentic experiences of God.

This was certainly the north star that guided the compass of many mystics' lives in the twentieth century. They were never found resting in the fruits of their loving encounter with the divinity, or silent before the suffering of the other. They suffered the consequences. They carried on untiringly until their deaths. The same ones who humbled themselves and went into seclusion in order to enter into fellowship with God (who in loving proximity narrated God's Mysteries to them), also went out to meet the poor, confronted dangers and made an offering of their lives in situations of suffering, such as in the Second World War and the final solution of Hitler's Nazism, or in chronic situations where suffering had become a habit for public opinion, as the abandonment of the homeless, the rootlessness of migrants, and the inhumane routine of workers in modern factories.

From all we have said thus far, only feebly and lightly touching its unmeasurable greatness, a deep and central conviction remains: the Christian mystical experience is an experience of Otherness—an Otherness in which anthropology and theology are indissolubly united. It is therefore an experience which does not immobilize those in contemplation, but leads them to close their eyes just to open them again, and to mobilize their bodies for service to the poor and indigent.

It is not an experience of the transcendent pure and simple, nor of something which dislocates human beings from the ground of their reality and moves them toward a supernatural level or a nirvana—situated in an unknown space—where one might go in search of sensations, expecting the cessation of all worries linked to the reality and concreteness of human life.

Especially in Christianity, the mystical experience is an experience of an incarnate God. Outside of this central and absolutely necessary basis, there is no Christianity.[49] Without incarnation there is no possibility for God to assume all things from within and to live out history step by step, in a way, so to speak, contrary to God's eternity. Without incarnation there is no cross, no redemption, no Salvation, and, therefore, no covenant between the flesh and the Spirit.[50]

---

49. See "Encarnación," in Poupard, *Diccionario de las religiones*. The meaning of the word *incarnation* is "to enter into the flesh."

50. See the warning about this in the document *Orationis formas* ("Letter to the Bishops on Some Aspects of Christian Meditation"), issued by the Congregation for the Doctrine of the Faith in 1989.

This is certainly the major contribution—even to spirituality in general terms—that Christian mysticism has to make today, in these times of resacralization as well as of the search for Transcendence and new paradigms. Nothing which is human is alien to Christian mysticism. And no new discovery or new emphasis regarding humanity can threaten it, but will, on the contrary, feed it, nourish it and bring it more in line with the dream of God the Father, Son, and Holy Spirit, who desires to christify and renew everything and everyone through God's sanctifying praxis which presides over history and labors within the flesh of the world.

Any attempt to escape from this, is, on the contrary, a temptation by which mysticism would lose the distinguishing characteristics inherent in its personality, in its Trinitarian configuration, and in its historical and incarnative dynamics. To confess with voice and heart that the Word became flesh, and that the Spirit was poured out upon all flesh, implies a search for an experience of union with the God who decided to communicate in this way with humankind—through the flesh in which it is possible for one to experience God. And this flesh is the flesh of the others who suffer oppression and injustice, and whose faces reveal the God who has forever been their defender and advocate. To integrate the flesh of the other into the most ineffable experience of the divine love is the greatest challenge that, now and forever, confronts Christian mysticism. Mystics who at the same time are witnesses in the heart of secularity do not allow us to forget this fundamental fact.

A Mysticism of Open Eyes and Listening Ears

All mystics, irrespective of their gender, time, or place, can be defined as persons deeply in love with God. The divine entered their lives with the force and violence of a tremendous passion and took them over entirely, subduing them with the imperative of God's love. In their relation with God they experienced joy and pain, absence and presence, each one of them in his or her own and original style. But all, without exception, were certain that they were dealing with the deepest and holiest Mystery, with the One to whom the religions have tried to give a name, but who always escapes any human attempt at circumscription or capture.

The mystical experience is, without doubt, an experience of God, by definition and in faithfulness to what the etymology of the word—derived from the term *mystery*—signifies. Theology may drink at the fountain of the narratives of the mystics from all times and places, in order to know better the God of their faith. Even if these "lovers of God"[51] may not be or claim to be academic theologians, it is undeniable that in their writings one finds a great deal of theology in the fullest and most strict sense of the word.

This is what Karl Rahner says regarding Saint Ignatius and his *Spiritual Exercises*.[52] And it is also what we say regarding the contributions made to Christology by Saint Teresa of Avila and Saint John of the Cross, and regarding the elaborations of the church fathers—many if not all of them mystics—based on their experiences with the Holy Trinity.[53] And regarding so many others as well.

The same can be said about contemporary mystics. In their writings, especially the more autobiographical ones where they describe their experiences, we can perceive the delineation of a divine face which helps theology today to more pertinently elaborate its discourse.

These contemporary mystics, who have lived out the theopathic experience of passivity configured by divine love and union with the Mystery, are appropriate mediators to say, today, who God is, and to announce God in the midst of a secular world which seems to have lost the language for speaking of God. Since they are, as mystics, witnesses of the Absolute whom they have experienced in their own lives, their testimony is a form of mediation through which the divine tries to speak and self-express today.[54] The theologian Johann Baptist Metz, illustrious disciple of Karl Rahner and founder of the Catholic theology of politics, uses the expression "mysticism of open eyes" to speak of the cry of the earth and of the union between the biblically inspired experience of God and the intense perception of the suffering of the other.[55] According to him, "The biblically inspired experience of God is not a mysticism of closed eyes, but rather a mysticism of open eyes; it is not a perception related only to ourselves without an intensified perception of the suffering of the other."[56]

Surely Metz is referring here to the etymology of the word *mysticism*, which comes from the Greek verb *muo*: "to shut, to be quiet, to close one's mouth or eyes." He goes further, affirming that the mysticism of the

51. See Meroz. "La vie des amants de Dieu."

52. See Rahner, *Élements dynamiques dans l'Église*. See also Rahner's remarks on the influence of the *Spiritual Exercises* of Saint Ignatius on his own theology in *I Remember*.

53. See the theology of the Holy Spirit, which had its beginnings in the theology of the Cappadocian Fathers, the monks Basil of Caesarea and Gregory of Nyssa, who, based on their spiritual experiences, helped the Council of Constantinople arrive at the final definition of the Third Person of the Trinity.

54. See Pierron, *Le passage de temoin*, 30.

55. See Metz, *El clamor de la tierra*, 26.

56. Ibid.

Judeo-Christian tradition is an open-eyed mysticism. Thus, mysticism consists not so much in having extraordinary visions as in having a new vision of all of reality, and discovering God as one's ultimate truth, that is, as one's living, active, and always new foundation.

The closed-eyed mystic lives out, with unusual depth and consciousness, the endless journey of encounter with God, which everyone begins on the first day of life. Leaving God's hands to enter the space and time of life in the world is not a farewell, but rather the beginning of a new encounter without limits. We close our eyes in order to experience an inner life filled with the inexhaustible Mystery of a God turned toward us. This mysticism was thoroughly reflected upon and developed in all its phases by great masters of spiritual life, such as Saint Teresa of Jesus and Saint John of the Cross.

On the other hand, the open-eyed mystics direct their gaze toward all of reality, because they know that the ultimate dimension of everything real is inhabited by someone, namely, by God. They relate themselves to the world with attention to the signs of the God who fills all creation with unceasing action and endless fascinating creativity. The passion of their lives is to observe contemplatively. They never tire of contemplating life because through it they seek the face of God. They immerse themselves in human situations, whether afflicted or happy, searching for the active presence of the God who provides life and freedom. Scholasticism and classic theology had already affirmed that mysticism is *fides occulata*, a faith endowed with eyes, an enlightened faith since it can see reality in the light of God.[57]

Both types of mysticism—the open-eyed and the closed-eyed—are found in the history of the church. There are abundant examples of both in the Bible and the tradition. In the Old Testament the prophets have open-eyed visions and ecstasies, as in the case of the prophet Balaam.[58] His eyes looked out from the perspective of God. Although contracted by the king to curse the Jewish people, when he contemplated them in their reality he saw that they were replete with the blessings of the Most High and announced for them a future of peace and abundance. This is someone who beheld God with open eyes, closely scrutinizing history, inspired by what he felt in his heart and what flowed out to him through his eyes.[59] Thus the gaze by which he saw the people was intrinsic to his experience of God.

In this act of seeing, in this opening of the eyes, what is discerned is the fullness of the human and the created as the place of revelation by the invisible God. Thus, Christian mysticism, if it contemplates God, can only do so

---

57. See Panikkar, *De la mística*, 53.
58. See Num 24.
59. See González Buelta, *Orar en un mundo roto*.

by way of the Otherness of the Other. The face of the Other, of the neighbor, is the only way for the contemplated God not to be a deceptive projection, that is, an alienating fantasy that dismisses the reality which clamors for justice.

In this way the biblical God, since the beginnings of the trajectory of the people of Israel, has revealed God's self as the *go'el*, the defender, the mouthpiece of the orphan, the widow, the stranger, the poor, and of all who have no one who speaks for them. Mysticism and ethics have since then been forever reunited in the biblical faith. And there is no possibility of practicing one without the other. For God speaks through the mouth of the prophets, saying that God's mouth vomits out the sacrifices of fat young bulls which are offered at the expense of the exploitation of the poor and of injustices furtively committed in sumptuous palaces. Or accusing those who fast and worship God while, at the same time, selling the poor for a pair of sandals.[60]

In the New Testament, Jesus of Nazareth, in whom the early community recognized the Christ of God, took the golden rule to its ultimate consequences. In the midst of his relationship of love and filial trust for the Father, Jesus opened his eyes and saw around him the rejected, the poor, the sinner, and the sick. In other words, the least of all the categories did not escape his compassionate gaze, by which he was able to see and feel in a new way. As he recreated his gaze, he recreated at the same time the lives of the people upon whom he laid his eyes, and they, seeing themselves reflected in these eyes as in a mirror of life, rediscovered themselves as sons and daughters, brothers and sisters, and human beings, with new dignity. A true gaze at reality must, therefore, be capable of taking the measure of the victims of evil, injustice, and violence in this world: the poor, the sick, the unhappy, the marginalized. Herein lies the proof of the conversion—of love for God and respect for the other, and the desire to serve both—which is the heart of true mysticism.[61]

And the Gospel of Matthew, in chapter 25, says that the value of human life is not measured against the first, the most wealthy, and/or the most famous, as is commonly thought. The measure is rather the value and attention afforded the last and the least. It is here that the mystical gaze is sharpened, and now perceives the Mystery that in the eschatological judgment will be seen with absolute clearness: "Lord, when was it that we saw you?" "Just as you did it to one of the least of these who are members of my family, you did it to me."[62]

60. See Isa 1:11–13; Amos 6:4; Jer 6:20; 7:21; Hos 8:13, among others.
61. See Marty, "Sentir et goûter," 294.
62. See González Buelta, *Orar en un mundo roto*.

Spirituality, or mysticism, therefore embodies an alert, vigilant, and open-eyed attitude toward seeing, reading, and understanding reality, and transforming it according to the Spirit of God. It is a concrete way to live out the gospel as moved by the Spirit—precisely the way to live before the Lord and in solidarity with all persons, especially the most oppressed and the poorest.[63]

Thus was the gaze of the prophets and of Jesus of Nazareth. Thus also— it seems to us—is the gaze of the mystics who today, in the total wilderness of secularity, look for the footprints of God in the caverns of history. They advance into the Mystery of an encounter with God where they are purged of their impurities and insufficiencies, thus entering further and further into the intimacy of the endless loving union. What they contemplate as they close their eyes and immerse themselves in their inner life through prayer, allows them to see, with a transfigured gaze, a reality purified from prejudice and discrimination.[64] For is there anyone who, not enjoying the intimacy and knowledge of the Lord with closed eyes, could meet the Lord with eyes open to a reality which at each step appears to deny its own existence?

While evil brutally imposes itself with the propagation of violence, treason, and bloodshed, dominating the front pages of the newspapers and the news on the Internet and television, God's action in the world is humble and discrete. It can be detected only by the open, attentive, and purified senses of those who see beauty where the naked eye sees only destruction and wickedness, and who can decipher the inverted signs of the Mystery of love, which appears as the inverse of Itself.[65]

For the contemplative gaze of the mystic, no reality is profane, since God is present in every reality, loving it and freeing it from within, with infinite discretion. Perceiving this presence, assuming consciousness of it and experiencing it as love, the mystic reveals it to others and joins its liberating action.[66]

The open-eyed mystics are not blind to reality. They respect it as it is, in its tenderness or its painful callousness. But they know that it is loved by God, and for this reason they stand before any space, situation, or person, seeking the transparency, translucence, and luminosity which they believe to come from the experience of God. They contemplate the world with the eyes of love, since only love makes visible what is not apparent, like the Servant of Yahweh who "had no form or majesty that we should look at him,"

---

63. Ibid., 107ff.
64. See ibid.
65. See González Buelta, *Ver o parecer*.
66. Ibid.

but was the place of sorrow where Salvation was engendered in the one who took upon himself our pain and infirmities.[67]

Before the pain and harshness of reality, the open-eyed mystics see that which is not apparent, committing themselves to that seed of life which seems suffocated by death and destruction. And this fills them with a hope which appears to the world as senseless and dangerous. From the inner illumination given to them when, with closed eyes, they diligently and lovingly sought contact with the Mystery of their God's love in seclusion and silent prayer, they now with open eyes see everything differently, with a new lucidity regarding the translucence of the real, pregnant with life and hope.[68]

The primordial source for the topic of the mystical experience is, therefore, the witness of the mystics themselves. They are the first and most important theoreticians of their own experience. The believer's biography is the condition for the possibility of a theological reading of the mystical experience and its message to today's world. And this is true to the extent that the biographies of the believers and the concrete configuration of their lives—coming from the event of God in their lives and from the narrative they make of it—manifest themselves as a history of Salvation, a concrete exegesis of the faith.[69]

More and more, many contemporary theologians affirm the importance of a transition from a rigidly speculative theology to a narrative theology, where revealed mysteries can be narrated and simply reflected upon.[70] Currently, there is also a growing emphasis on the importance of a theology based not simply on texts, but also on witnesses.[71] The connection of faith with the praxis of the discipleship of Jesus implies that this way of proceeding cannot be replaced by mere theoretical reflections or any kind of research. Theology, up to a point, is obliged to think from the perspective of the discipleship of Jesus, calling itself theology only when such discipleship defines the appropriate place for reflection, and when reflection is the practice of the existential commitment of such discipleship.[72]

---

67. See Isaiah 52–53.

68. González Buelta, *Caminar sobre las aguas*.

69. See Michael Schneider's precious little book *Teología como biografía*, esp. 22.

70. See, for example, the works of Joseph Moingt: *L'homme qui venait de Dieu* and *Dieu qui vient a l'homme*, vols. 1 and 2, among others. See also Metz, *Memoria Passionis*. The same reflection is found in Jon Sobrino, from the perspective of his theology "no de textos sino de testigos" (not of texts but of witnesses).

71. This is also supported by *Evangelii Nuntiandi*, par. 41, where Pope Paul VI says that nowadays people no longer have masters, but only witnesses. And that if men and women listen to a master it is because he or she is a witness as well.

72. Ibid., 24.

When this happens, reading about the lives of the mystics will be tantamount to reading about the revelation of God, whose Spirit writes in their bodies and in their lives. Theological thought, therefore, does not deal with God as an external object. It is God in person who enters and communicates with human thought in the ecstasies of an existence informed and inspired by faith.[73]

Mysticism and Deinstitutionalization

Throughout two thousand years of history, Christianity has had to deal with the question of the conflict between charisma and institution. Almost all Christian mystics had difficulty with the ecclesiastic institution and overcame it in different ways.[74] But, today, in full postmodernity, when secularization is an irreversible fact and the theocentric world (in which the language of institutional religion was configured as both the center and the expression of knowledge) has been definitively left behind, there is a process of withdrawal from the ecclesiastic institution which reaches all spheres of Christian life. The mystical experience does not escape it.

It is well known that, beyond the reaffirmations allowed by the language of the return of religion or of the Sacred, what is happening before our eyes is a change in the definition of religion. On the one hand, the politics today is not limited to the state, which demonstrates that neutrality regarding the separation of church and state is insufficient to delineate the relationship between religion and politics. On the other hand, there is a visible deinstitutionalization of religion, as evident in the proliferation of informal churches, movements, and groups no longer tied to the protocols of ecclesiastical authorization or sanctions, as well as a diffusion and dissemination of the religious beyond the frontiers regulated by religious institutions. All this emerges in the wake of a weariness with politics and institutionalized religion. And it occasions an embrace of the diffuse or mystical religiosity which characterizes the contemporary environment, and often results in businesses using self-help stress-reduction therapy as motivational inspiration for the most diverse groups. It is common for us to see sociopolitical militants seeking the support or solace of religiosity to renew their utopian energies, or even resorting to religious practices as a substitute for political action.[75]

73. Ibid., n. 16.

74. See the examples of Saint Ignatius of Loyola, who on four different occasions was in the hands of the Inquisition; of Saint Teresa of Ávila, who was under the strict vigilance of the theologians and spiritual leaders of her time; and of Saint John of the Cross, who was incarcerated by his own colleagues, etc.

75. See Burity, "Religião e política na fronteira."

The religious or spiritual experiences of individuals are in large part characterized by the significant religious autonomy of actors who circulate throughout the existing diverse groups. They construct their own religiosity, as a kind of handicraft (a personal arrangement of errant religiosity or spirituality, of diffuse religions, of a holistic individual model, and of coexisting paradigms), through a process of increasing de-traditionalization of religion and deinstitutionalization of religious identity. There is a growing subjectivization of religion and a radicalization of religious plurality. This tends to transcend the institutional dimension, and to be configured above all in conformity with the individual consciousness. And the argumentation behind it leads to a privatization of the religious experience. The divine would be inside each one of us, with no need for an institutional presence. One would simply have to develop it.

We are, therefore, confronting a scene centered around the search for self-improvement and self-fulfillment, in a constant experimentation that embodies individual ways to the spiritual dimension as well as to the psychic, the corporal, and the intuitive, while trying to characterize itself as a holistic search. It is an overlapping of therapeutics and spirituality, where the ultimate truth is constructed and orchestrated by the subject, as an experimenter par excellence.[76]

We are seeing a process of privatization of religious beliefs and a pluralization of the faith, called by a diversity of designations such as religious liberalization,[77] diffuse religion,[78] flexible-fluctuating religiosity or religious identity,[79] new mystical-esoteric sensibility, nonreligious sacredness, new syncretic religiosity,[80] heterodox nebulosity,[81] mystical-esoteric nebulosity and diffuse creeds,[82] multivalent nebulosity of the New Era, and diversity in the forms of adherence.[83]

We are therefore confronting a process of deinstitutionalization of the historical religions and of de-traditionalization of religiosity, with an emphasis on the present, on experimentation, on the individual, and on a break with the notion of representation. This de-traditionalization tends to

---

76. See Siqueira, "Pluralidade e trânsito religioso na atualidade."
77. See Pace, "Religião e globalizaçao."
78. See Cipriani, *La religione diffusa*.
79. See Hervieu-Léger, *La religion pour mémoire*.
80. See Mardones, *Para comprender las nuevas formas de la religión*.
81. See Maitre, "Les deux côtés du miroir."
82. Champion, "La nébuleuse mystique-esotérique."
83. See Sanchis, "O campo religioso contemporâneo no Brasil."

be associated with a post-Christianity, and especially with a post-Catholicism.[84] The movement of religious deinstitutionalization, of the trivialization of religious boundaries, and of the break with the monopoly or hegemony of Catholicism, is accompanied by an ever stronger process of formation of a religious pluralism.

This state of things is reflected in mysticism, as well. One of the characteristics that contemporary mysticism carries with it is a tendency toward deinstitutionalization, or autonomy in relation to ecclesiastic institutions and authority. The process of secularization developing in the West with the crisis of Enlightenment reason and the emergence of an era of emptiness and fragmentation—called postmodernity, late modernity, or hypermodernity by some thinkers[85]—makes its consequences felt in the form and expression of the spiritual experience, which presents itself in a new way. It is freer and less institutionalized, more open to plurality, and in dialogue not only with atheism and agnosticism—the fruits of secularization[86]—but also with other religious traditions.[87]

On the other hand, the mystics, the men and women who live out a profound and visceral experience of God, are no longer withdrawn from the world, or into the silence of the monastery. On the contrary, they can be seen in the streets, "in the heart of the masses," as active participants in the great challenges of our time, involved in very secular issues while inspired by their spiritual experience.[88] Many, if not almost all, of these mystics have been very critical of the institutional church, although never doubting the Christian matrix of their own experience. Almost all of them have had real

---

84. Ibid.

85. Such as Vattimo, Braudel, and Lipovetsky.

86. Cf., for instance, the beautiful book by Comte-Sponville, L'esprit de l'athéisme, among others.

87. Cf., for instance, the entire work of Massignon, and especially *Parole donnée*; see also Le Saux, *La montée au fond du coeur*.

88. See Raïssa Maritain, a philosopher who, together with her husband and her sister, created a community of prayer in their house, where they received the whole French intellectual circle of the 1930s. See Maritain, *Oeuvres Complètes*. Madeleine Delbrêl left her job as a laborer in order to be involved with the street people. See Delbrêl, *Oeuvres Complètes*. Dorothy Day was a mystic and a militant in the streets of New York; see her autobiography, *The Long Loneliness*. Etty Hillesum, a young lawyer whose mystical experience led her to the Westerbrok transit camp to "help God save my people and to be a balm for all wounds"; see Hillesum, *Une vie bouleversée*. Even Thomas Merton, a Trapist monk—an exception that proves the rule—was an original and unexpected kind of monk who in his regular writings for the press dealt with questions very current for his country, the United States, and who was a pioneer in the dialogue with Buddhist monastic life. See *The Seven Storey Mountain*. See also Bertelli, *Mística e compaixão*.

difficulties with their own institutions and have made their way, so to speak, at the margins.[89]

This fundamental tension between experience and the institution is not new. The use of the category *experience* was always problematic in modern Catholic theology, due as much to the notorious difficulty in making it precise as to the fact that the word *experience* is always taken as code for psychological impulses or subjective conscious states, described at the expense of doctrinal clarity.[90] On the other hand, today we observe the claim, especially on the part of contemporary Catholic theology, that failing to take experience into account is a risk that may leave theology reduced to an abstract ahistorical discourse, with no blood in its veins. Any effort to close the gap between theology and spirituality will be in line with a serious attempt to reestablish the mystical and religious experience as a category capable of inspiring a theology that is more inclusive, more multicolored, and therefore more vital and more profound.[91]

Throughout the history of Christianity the great spiritual masters established clear criteria to verify whether an experience is an authentic experience of God or is, on the contrary, a deceptive fallacy or a deranged psychological phenomenon. Thus, Saint John of the Cross speaks of three kinds of blindness that may impede the soul from reaching the end of the road leading to the encounter and union with God. Such blindness may come as much from a bad spiritual director as from the soul itself.[92] In the same way, Saint Ignatius of Loyola, in his *Spiritual Exercises*, gives to those who engage in the exercises some sets of rules appropriate to each of its phases, with warnings of the risk of deceit by the bad spirit even when it has the "appearance of good."[93]

This also has an impact on the gaze that is projected from the outside on mysticism and on the profound and transformative spiritual experiences of contemporary men and women. No longer can this be the only or the principal criterion for the evaluation of the greater or lesser adherence of these persons to the institutions they belong to, or to any institution. It is

---

89. Cf., for example, the Italian Ignazio Silone (see Danese, *Ignazio Silone: Percorsi di una conscienza inquieta*), or Emmanuel Mounier himself, in *Le personnalisme*; *L'engagement de la foi*.

90. See McDonnell, "Spirit and Experience in Bernard of Clairvaux," cited by Cunningham, "Authority and Religious Experience," 9.

91. See the famous article by Balthasar, "Theology and Sanctity," in *The Word Made Flesh*.

92. See John of the Cross, "Llama de amor viva."

93. See *Spiritual Exercises* by Saint Ignatius of Loyola. See also all rules for discernment of spirits for the first and the second week of the *Exercises*.

no longer binding or imperative that the experience of God occur inside the boundaries of an institution. For it is undeniable that one can find experiences with all the characteristics of a mystical experience outside the institution or at its margin, or even unknown by it. In other words, it is not obligatory or necessary for mystics to have problems with the institution and insuperable criticisms of it—as was the case with Simone Weil, among others.[94] It is possible that they may not have even thought of belonging to an institutionalized religion—as was true, for instance, of Etty Hillesum.

In this case, the criterion for discerning if their experiences are authentic is exclusively their fecundity, that is, the fruits of their experience in their environment and among other persons. From a subjective Christian viewpoint, the prototype for the evaluation of the mystical experience would be the list of fruits found in the writings of Paul: peace, joy, patience—signs of the presence of the Spirit of God in the human flesh. Moving to an objective standpoint, we see a widening of the criteria. The fruits which issue from the life of the mystic must be oriented toward support and protection of life, service to others, and ever increasing simplicity and self-denial.

One of the characteristics of contemporary mysticism is, therefore, the existence of a sensibility which seeks a direct experience with the Mystery of ultimate Reality. This seems to run through all religions and religious confessions. This search for direct experience no longer presents clear institutional contours, but on the contrary shows a transreligious tendency, in which the desired contact is achieved at the deepest profundity, with the ultimate secret of reality—which we call God, and which scholars of religion identify as the common denominator, the nucleus, of all religions.[95]

The symptom is identified by observers and scholars as a clear and undeniable dissatisfaction with the predominant institutionalized religiosity. Thus begins a more personal and experiential search for the divine.[96] The risk of this step, once taken, is undoubtedly the superficiality that may prevail when human beings choose a free spiritual flight, independent of anything that would regulate and control them, refusing to be guided by an institution.

On the other hand one has to recognize an extremely positive aspect here: the corroboration of God's freedom, which does not allow itself to be imprisoned by any institution, code, or system, religious or not. The spirituality of our epoch did not wait for reform of the churches or religious institutions before carrying out its own search. And even less for the blessing of

---

94. See Bingemer, "Simone Weil et Albert Camus."
95. See Duquoc, *L'unique Christ*, 125.
96. See Heisig, *Diálogos a una pulgada del suelo*, 246ff.

the academy. Our contemporaries intermingled vocabularies, concepts and symbols from every provenance and citizenship without asking for permission from academicians and churchmen.[97]

Looking at this phenomenon from the point of view of Christianity, we see that it means the definitive disappearance of so-called Christendom, that grandiose sociopolitical and religious system, constructed over many centuries, which made its mark on many generations. But this does not mean the end of Christianity. On the contrary, contemporary mysticism, with its greater or lesser degree of deinstitutionalization, could be a powerful factor for conversion to this same Christianity.

As understood by some theologians, this is a rare opportunity for Christianity to rediscover the mystical codes of faith, and, in doing so, to place at the center of the faith the experience of the God of Jesus, rather than the dogmatic and moral proposals of the institution. In this way, contemporary Christianity will really be seeking its most fundamental identifying nucleus, the center of the Christian faith, where God is communicated to us through the power of the Holy Spirit.[98]

Contemporary mysticism helps Christians today—and can help them more tomorrow—in the secular and plural world we live in, to say "I believe," based on a personal experience of God, although limited and therefore almost impossible to conceptualize. An impersonal faith without deep inner roots cannot easily avoid the risk of being reduced to a set of beliefs, to a knowledge that is well organized but not supported or nourished by spiritual experience—to a house built on sand rather than on rock.[99]

On the other hand, a faith which clearly rediscovers its mystical codes will not pretend to be an exclusive alternative to the doctrinal dimension. Nor can it fall into a shallow subjectivism. It is only at the heart of a spiritual experience that the truths of faith can illuminate from the inside, with flavor, meaning, vitality and fertility. Thus, mysticism is not the letter that kills, but the spirit that enlivens.[100]

Writing as Resistance and Witness

The three monotheist religions—Judaism, Christianity and Islam—are usually called the religions of the book. And, to a certain extent, this designation

---

97. See Mardones, *La tranformación de la religión*, 201–2.
98. See Carozzo, "Mysticism and the Crisis of Religous Institutions," 24.
99. See Matt 7:24–27.
100. See Carozzo, "Mysticism and the Crisis of Religous Institutions."

is fairly accurate.[101] Indeed, the three Abrahamic religions—unlike the religions of the Far East, for instance—understand their Sacred texts not as classical or even Sacred, but as Scripture, which in some way participates in what is construed as God's self-revelation.

Some contemporary Jewish thinkers propose that a relationship between the oral and the written Torah can be found either in a revelatory event understood as an encounter—in the opinion of Martin Buber[102]—or in the foundational revelatory events that occurred on Mount Sinai and during the Exodus. Later the biblical texts would be interpreted as witness or testaments to the foundational revelatory events—such as the delivery of the law on Mount Sinai—but not as the Revelation itself.[103]

In fact, Christian theology, with its heritage of Greek logocentrism, obscured rather than clarified the role of the written word and its self-understanding. It set up far too radical a difference between written and oral traditions, advocating the preponderance of the latter in view of the possibility of the real and concrete presence of the speaker and the listener. This theoretical model of a real presence through the spoken and reflective word constitutes a major part of most Greco-Christian models of autocommunication. These models are independent of external influences such as those of similar derivatives which are merely related to the technical character of writing.[104]

In the history of Christianity the written text has been of the utmost importance, not only as a reference where the narrative of God can be found, but also as a testimonial to the living out of the Christian faith in several moments of history, opening access to the life of the Spirit and of Grace to persons of flesh and blood. Among these writings, those of the mystics—often biographical—have special importance.

The very idea that a person writing about his or her life is doing something important seems evident enough. Subjects who narrate their own story are impressed on us with strength and conviction. And along with subjectivity comes naturalness, sincerity, intimacy, and the singularity of situation and vocation. These are the values which engender and organize the autobiographical literary genre as experience and proposition: "The pursuit until death of a foreseen, desired and never accomplished unity."[105] In its origin and in its innocence, autobiography refuses to accept the difference among three apparently irreconcilable terms, which it meanwhile

---

101. See Tracy, "Writing." In *Critical Terms for Religious Studies. Credo reference.*
102. See Buber, *I and Thou.*
103. See Tracy, "Writing."
104. Ibid.
105. See Mounier, *Le personnalisme.*

unites: *auto* (I) + *bio* (life) + *graphy* (writing, my writing, my hand, and therefore I).[106] Thus, autobiography as a literary genre is called a rhetoric of the I.

Autobiographical or personal writing, in a certain way, exposes the intimacy of the subject. And this happens as epiphany. Far from reinforcing a separation between the public and the private, some autobiographies, memoirs, or confessions bear the testimony of subjects who are active in the public space.

If we enter the domain of mysticism, we find an element which further valorizes autobiographical writing. The affirmation of the primacy of personal interiority in human life is inconceivable outside of, or far from, the divine gaze that grounds the subject and delves into his or her intimacy. Neither can it be conceived outside of the Word with its invitation to a direct dialogue. Throughout the history of Christianity we find precious examples of this Christianity in the first person, which became models of a rhetoric of the I, gathering together, in one exercise, introspection and spirituality, research and confession.[107]

The decision to undertake the writing of a mystical autobiography in order to register the experience of God and the interior movements of the Spirit in human life, is always accompanied by an acknowledgment that the closest of everything that is close to myself, this profound I which I discover in myself, is also the most distant; that the most personal is also the most incommunicable. In perfect coherence with the experience of an *absconditus* God, who is simultaneously, and without contradiction, the revealed God, the mystical ego must therefore inscribe itself in a narrative and leave the ecstasy behind, in order to be committed to the realization of the writing, in a glorious and at the same time impossible attempt to explain the ineffable which it has experienced.

All mystical autobiographies are writings instigated by another. And they must pass through the testimony of a conversion that legitimizes them. The mystics who write them are obliged to cut a path through the discursive norms the institution, therefore submitting themselves to a perpetual rewriting of their singular and only colloquy with God through the narratives already completed, which are those of the deeds of Christ and the life of the saints.

Perhaps the most prototypical mystical autobiography in the history of Christianity is the *Confessions* of Saint Augustine. This great Doctor of the Church did not intend to entrust the knowledge of himself to anyone other

---

106. See Oster, "Autobiographie," *Encyclopaedia Universalis*, numerical version, 2009.
107. Ibid.

than God, "whose gaze sees as naked the abyss of human conscience."[108] And before this all-encompassing divine gaze, which scrutinizes everything, Augustine writes, with the purpose of retracing the events of his life and expecting the appearance of the Word through his writing, "Thus through him I may lay hold upon him in whom I am also laid hold upon; and I may be gathered up from my old way of life to follow that One and to forget that which is behind, no longer stretched out but now pulled together again . . ."[109]

Thus, the mystic's writing does not refer only to a social body of language, but takes as scripture the letter and the symbol of the body. The mystic receives from his or her own body the law, the place, and the limit of his or her experience. The transcription onto paper, through writing, of what is written in the body, is a second act in relation to the scripture already written in his or her person and corporality. Friar Philoxenus of Mabbug, cited by Michel de Certeau, said, "the sensible is the cause of the conceptual; the body is the cause of the soul and precedes it in the intellect."[110]

It is worthy of note that mystics of all times, especially those belonging to the Judeo-Christian tradition, wrote diaries, letters, confessions and other autobiographical texts. They were moved to do so by an inner impulse they felt, whether under the encouragement of a director or confessor, or of someone who perceived their personal mystical vocation and advised them to write their experiences, in order to achieve self-understanding, to pursue their inner spiritual process, and to provide witness and pedagogy to others.[111]

There is another aspect of the mystics' writing that is no less worthy of note: the resistance that is present in the process of writing. Often, when facing limit-situations, apparently insuperable difficulties, extremely grim and distressing perplexities, risks, dangers, or dreadful and threatening torments, the mystics write. They write to live. They write in order not to lose

108. Augustine, *Confessions*, bk. 10, ch. 2.

109. Ibid., bk. 11, ch. 29. [Translator's note: the English here is taken from Augustine, *Confessions and Enchiridion*, trans. and ed. Albert C. Outler (1955).]

110. See Certeau, "Mystique," in *Encyclopaedia Universalis*.

111. As in the case of Saint Teresa of Ávila, who had problems with the Inquisition while writing *Libro de la Vida (The Book of Her Life)*. Yet her spiritual director, Father Gracián, ordered her to write another book: "And thus I ordered her to write this book on the Mansions, asking her, in order to better persuade her, to discuss this as well with Doctor Velásquez, who had sometimes confessed her. He also ordered her to do it" (Gracián's notes in Antonio de San Joaquin, *Año teresiano*, vol. 7 [1758], 149). Saint Ignatius wrote his *Spiritual Exercises* from the perspective of his own experience, hoping he could be of service to others. There he systematizes what he had experienced, offering a methodology for finding the will of God for one's own life.

the thread of the Spirit's voice in their interior. They write to resist resiliently, without losing the capacity to love, to be thankful, or to worship in the midst of tribulation. As the philosopher and theologian Emil Fackenheim said, in reflecting on the Holocaust, this is a matter of spiritual resistance present in the victim's determination to survive the dehumanization and destruction coming down upon him or her.[112]

In her book about four Jewish women who found in writing a means of resistance to the evil that was exterminating their people during the Shoah,[113] Rachel Feldhay Brenner penetrates the personal, ethical, and religious dilemmas of these four personalities and explains how their writing developed and responded, in a certain way, to the acute crises in their personal lives and in their surrounding world.[114]

In writing about the state of their souls and about what they lived through in those circumstances, these four women, according to Brenner, accomplished an impressive hermeneutical work regarding the Holocaust. They combined feminist, philosophical, ethical, literary, and theological interdisciplinary and transdisciplinary insights. Thus they made patent and inseparable the connections among writing, resistance, and commitment to life in the face of an evil that posed as Absolute and before which they constructed an ethics—and, we will add, a mysticism—of compassion.[115]

In truth, in all the genocides that humanity, under the evil of empire, has managed to invent, those who consciously and actively suffered persecution and extermination have, through their writing, reversed their position as victims to that of witnesses, and deeply so. The extermination intended to eliminate them from the world is transformed into an opportunity for them to be present, as never before, in this same world, through conscious, resistant, and testimonial writing.

Of these four women, three of them—Edith Stein, Etty Hillesum, and Simone Weil—had experienced a profound encounter with God and can be called mystics. Their witness at this time and place, besides being historical and hermeneutical, received the sacred stamp of divine inspiration. They

---

112. See Fackenheim, *To Mend the World*, 248, cited by Brenner, *Writing as Resistance*, 4. Fackenheim cites the impressive witness of Pelagia Lewinska: "She 'perceived the motivational principle' of the Nazi plan which condemned her and the other companions 'to die in our own filth, to drown in mud, in our own excrement,' and felt herself 'compelled to live . . . as a human being'" (ibid., 217).

113. Brenner, *Writing as Resistance: Four Women Confronting the Holocaust*.

114. See the endorsement of Brenner's book by Anne Carver Rose. Online: http://www.psupress.org/books/titles/0-271-01623-X.html.

115. See the endorsement of Brenner's book by Alan L. Berger. See web page cited in previous note.

are scriptures from the Spirit of God in the midst of the flesh of the world, and into the density of history. Like them, many other men and women were witnesses whose struggle, nobility, commitment, and ideals came to us thanks to the written word.[116]

In the writings of the contemporary mystics, exposed in great measure to this kind of situation, one often finds the text in this dimension. In the twentieth century, the Jewish or Christian mystics who lived through the horrors of war, injustice, and all manner of violence wrote of their experiences as they suffered the persecutions and torments lavished upon them by the historical moment.[117]

Today, in the twenty-first century, the mystics continue narrating their profound experiences, which may serve as inspiration to their contemporaries. We owe to the miracle of writing the fact that we can drink from the fountain of their experiences and delve into the richness of their inner world. Writing has fixed on paper that which cannot be fixed and is always dynamic, because it flows from the fountain of living water which is the experience of God.

Theology as Biography

For the human being, each biological moment is always a biographical event.[118] Consciousness of the meaning of a human being's existence requires an orientation to life of constant awareness regarding the threat of inevitable death. It is because I know that I am going to die that questions about the meaning and value of my life are more forcefully presented to me. From this comes my need to witness, at least through my autobiographical narrative, which humbly relates my experiences of intimacy with God, my

---

116. Moving from the Holocaust to another twentieth-century genocide, the one perpetrated in El Salvador, we can find witnesses such as Monsignor Romero, bishop of San Salvador. While denouncing injustices and risking his life for love of the poor and the victims of a harsh war—until he was killed by the machine of this same war—he wrote letters, sermons, and personal notes that helped him resist the threats that tried to paralyze him, and that after his death were, and still are, precious testimony and a source of theological reflection for future generations. The lives and writings of four American women, three religious and one layperson—Maura Clarke, Dorothy Kazel, Ita Ford, and Jean Donovan—are likewise eloquent testimonials of persons who chose to remain in the midst of the conflict for love of the people, for whom they gave their lives. See on Monsignor Romero: Romero, *Homilías*, vols. 1 and 2; on the four women, see Noone and Glavac, *Compañeras en el camino*, among many other works.

117. See previous note.

118. See Pierron, *Le passage de témoin*, 246. What the author says about the witness, we apply here to the mystic, believing the application to be pertinent.

learning of God's Mystery, and how such experiences have transformed me into a witness of God's love.

The Absolute which the mystics experience—and which makes their biography paradigmatic and exemplary—brings with it the imperative of being witnessed and attested to. What is radical in mysticism is that the life of the mystic is uninterruptedly related to an Absolute.[119] Mystics understand themselves as definitively affected by the Absolute Other, the wholly Other, who is God. And for this reason the passiveness of their theopathic experience, gently configured by God, persists in their activity of witnessing, of which an important part is an account of their experience and its concrete effects in life. Although the biographical account of the mystic is written in the first person, the I is not the triumphal I of fanaticism but, on the contrary, an I affected by the other. To the extent that God affects him or her, there is written in the person of the mystic an open vulnerability by which the Otherness of the other, of the neighbor, of the brother or sister, constantly affects him or her as well.

When narrating his or her biography and God's action in it, the mystic attests, "I experienced," "I felt," "I believe it is true, because I saw it, heard it, and touched it with my hands." And the ultimate legitimization of what is said will be found in the biography of the speaker. The seriousness of the testimony in the narrative comes from the fact that the sincerity of the witness is implicated.[120]

For this reason it is not enough for the mystic just to tell what happened. The narrative takes on a form of expression which does what it says. It is efficient, performative, and makes things happen. As such, the testimony of the mystic who narrates his or her own biography calls on theology to make use of this narrative in elaborating its discourse.

The rediscovery of biography as a theological resource was concomitant with the development of contemporary narrative theology. Besides the many important theologians who have made more or less successful attempts in this direction,[121] there is still a reflection being developed in the area of theological ethics. We are referring, for instance, to the work of McClendon,[122] in which the author, speaking from the context of an ethics of "characters-in-community," affirms that "theology must be at least

---

119. Ibid., 258.

120. Ibid., 35.

121. We are referring here to previously cited theologians such as Metz, Schneider, and von Balthasar, among others. All of them have been cited above.

122. McClendon, *Biography as Theology: How Life Stories Can Remake Today's Theology*.

biography."[123] He further adds that if the effort to do theology from the standpoint of credible biographies of real persons succeeds in inducing us to reform our own theology, making it more authentic, more faithful to the sources, more adequate to our times, then the effort will be validated, and "*Biography at its best will be theology.*"[124]

According to McClendon, the lives of significant persons can illuminate systematic theology, because they will eloquently say "what in the doctrine must be stressed, and what may for their part be laid aside."[125] For, he continues, "if there were no such lives we should be imperiously urged to acknowledge that this doctrine had lost its power; if in the future there should be no more such lives, we should then have to make that concession." McClendon works with the category of atonement.[126] This brings him to view these prototypical lives, these "exemplars of the doctrine of the cross," as the guiding thread of his work.[127]

This argument is similar to that of Schneider,[128] who says that "the lived and exemplary theology of these theological existences develops an 'experimental dogmatic' which leads to bearing witness to the faith not on the basis of concepts, but on the basis of one's own life."[129] For his part, Izuzquiza puts together a combination of methods, constructing a methodology which unites biographical-narrative aspects with others which are more systematic. In fact, he proposes making explicit the theological characteristics of the interpreter instead of relying only on the narrative.[130] According to him, it is necessary to make evident the lenses that the interpreter—the theologian—uses in reading about the life of the witness (in our case, the mystic).[131]

Theological thought is not concerned with God as an external object, but rather intends to demonstrate that, in truth, it is God who imposes God's self on human thought, in the ecstasy of a believing existence, and in its exodus toward others in the practice of charity. The systematic knowledge of the truths of the faith is not something to be conveyed primarily and

123. Ibid., 22.
124. Ibid.
125. Ibid., 80.
126. Ibid.
127. Ibid.
128. Schneider, *Teología como biografía*, 19.
129. Ibid.
130. See Izuzquiza, *Rooted in Jesus Christ*, 90.

131. Ibid. Izuzquiza develops this methodology with the case of Dorothy Day, emphasizing the politics lived out by her in the Catholic Worker movement and applying it to the contemporary situation. See ibid., 90–110.

uniquely through concepts, but rather through the event of discipleship, that is, through men and women for whom the Gospel is their experience, made known with and through their own lives. This experience of faith thus confers upon theology a practical-narrative feature that is indispensable to its consistency and communicability.[132]

Throughout the history of Christianity there were always men and women who contributed to the doctrine largely from the standpoint of their narrative of a particular way of living the faith. In the life witness of these theological existences one finds a profound and consistent theology. Although the particularity of the mystics' biographical accounts embodies and demonstrates their full awareness of the particularity and singularity of their experiences, as well as of their fragmentary nature, with no claim to totality or universality, it is equally certain that they translate the image of faith into their concrete lives without thereby losing sight of the totality. Indeed, their narrative makes possible a perspective through which one can glimpse such a totality, which thus shines in the individual, in the personal, in the singular and in the particular.[133]

Each one of these biographies reveals the totality of the Mystery in a fragmentary and partial way, but without distorting the perspective of totality which has belonged to the Mystery from the beginning. For in fact each and every one of these theological existences—marvels of the Spirit of God in history—develops a theology which, in spite of its incompleteness and fragmentation, is precise; given that in this fragment which is his or her life, the narrator—through words, silences, and gaps in discourse—resembles what he or she is portraying or testifying about. The narrator thus becomes, according to the French semiologist Roland Barthes,[134] a logothete, a founder or creator of language.

Furthermore, the mystical account, understood as theological biography, gives back to theology its true status: that of a peregrine discourse, a way, a *theologia viatorum*, rather than a closed construction or system.[135] This is so because it does not admit of a rushed and superficial systematization. The believing community is called to turn their eyes to this narrative, verifying its status as either a theological phenomenon or a theology in person, through writings often in the first person, and through many others

---

132. See Metz, *Faith in History and Society*.

133. See Schneider, *Teología como biografía*, 19.

134. See Barthes, *Sade, Fourier, Loyola*, in which he calls Saint Ignatius a "logothete," a creator of language.

135. On this point, see Schneider, *Teología como biografía*, 29, where he says that theology should learn from liturgy: the celebration of the church year always represents the same totality, but with a continually new individuality.

Mystical Biographies and Theological Narrative

narrated by third persons who may be narrators, interpreters, hermeneuts, theologians, and so on.

Yes, the lives of these persons, their biographies, are like a kind of mystagogy, an orientation, an itinerary for a journey toward the Mystery of God. And for Christian theology these biographies of theological existences are truly nothing less than a continuation of the root-biography, which is the life, the deeds, and the words of Jesus of Nazareth, the Incarnate Word of God. Following—explicitly or anonymously—the One who is the New Adam, grounding their lives in him or in the way proposed by him, enouncing his discourse about God and his theology with an internal surrendering of their own lives, the mystics, who are simultaneously and inseparably witnesses, prove themselves to be true masters. They can really teach who God is, what God's Mystery consists of, and how God's person can bring meaning to human life in this world.

The experience of God, which overflows into discipleship and witnessing, therefore has its origins in the one who is the Authentic Theologian: Jesus Christ. He is the true and only exegete of the Father, who can translate and interpret, in a language understandable to human beings, the original discourse of God about God's self—which is, in short, theology.[136] He did this in his mortal and vital incarnate kenosis on the Cross. Once the silence of death put an end to his words, the Holy Spirit, the same one given to him by the Father, poured over all flesh the interpretation of his incarnation, life, death and resurrection. And thus he made into participants in the biography of this one whom the community recognized as Lord and Christ, all those who believed in him and resolved to follow him wherever he went.

Among them are the mystics of yesterday and today, who are living examples of the truth that the experience of God, which overflows into witnessing and loving practice, is the biographical exegesis of the life of Jesus of Nazareth.[137] The true and only mystical biography, therefore, is that of Jesus. His is the prototypical biography which inspires all the others and on which all the others depend.[138]

---

136. See 1 John 1:1–3ff.: "We declare to you what was from the beginning, what we have heard, what we have seen with our eyes, what we have looked at and touched with our hands, concerning the word of life—this life was revealed, and we have seen it and testify to it, and declare to you the eternal life that was with the Father and was revealed to us—we declare to you what we have seen and heard so that you also may have fellowship with us; and truly our fellowship is with the Father and with his Son Jesus Christ."

137. See Schneider, *Teología como biografía*, 42.

138. We are obviously speaking here from a Christian perspective. We are fully aware that there are great non-Christian mystics. We mean no disrespect and have no intention to impose Christianity as the only mystical way.

The way of faith consists, therefore, in living according to the biography of Jesus and in translating the message of the incarnation into an experience of God. And here the humanity of God in Jesus is real and constitutive of the Logos, the visible sacrament of the invisible God, thus making it possible for any experience of God, any mystical experience, to remain happily involved in the sacrament of a human experience, of a human biography. From the Christian point of view, any experience of God is therefore a participation in the experience of Jesus Christ.

One of the characteristics of the Christian experience of God is the alternation between silence and the word. Simone Weil, a twentieth-century mystic, called these two moments the "nuptial chamber" and the "public square." That which is heard and possessed in the silence and in the resonant loneliness of the union with God carries at its core the imperative of being transformed into words for communication to others. The verbalization of the experience of God is an indication of its true and genuine character, making this experience unique and different from all the others. Although they use language to speak of what they have experienced, the mystics do not take possession of it because they constantly struggle, in an apophatic tension, between an inner imperative to speak of what they have experienced and the ineffability of an experience which shatters the limits of language. The mystical language experiences simultaneously "the incapacity to express what was lived out and the power of language, hostility toward language and joy in it, the persistence of silence and the exuberance of a powerful eloquence."[139]

However, this biographical narrative takes the form not only of written words but also of acts which write the divine narrative in the world and in history. God's mark is imprinted on human beings, sending them to the neighbor, to the Other. From this perspective, then, to have an experience of God means more than to joyfully receive God in prayer. It means, as well, to make God visible and perceptible in the world. Thus the mystics reproduce in themselves the sending of the Son by the Father. "Thus, those who have the experience of God are drawn to the heart of the dissimilarity and of the difference, also inherent in God, of the incarnation, of the kenosis and of the cross, in the heart of the experience of 'identity in alienation' and of 'identity in the neighbor.'"[140] Unceasingly questioned by the Otherness of the other, the mystic, who has experienced a loving union with the divine, is configured

---

139. See Haas, *Sermo mysticus*, cited by Schneider, *Teología como biografía*, 51.
140. Ibid.

by this divine in the sacrament of the brother or sister, to whom the mystic is sent to be eucharistically eaten and drunk for the life of the world.[141]

Theology has, therefore, a fundamentally narrative orientation, rather than a speculative one. Instead of formulating the vital content of the faith in a conceptual and dogmatic system, it appears far more fruitful for contemporary theology to disclose it in a narrative form, returning to the concept later for the task of interpretation. Telling and listening to biographies is today among the practices most fundamentally related to the meaning and implications of being a Christian. This is also true of the fact that the believers can and do have the right to tell the story of their lives in Grace and in faith, or to make their biographies available for reading and interpretation by others. All of this elevates narration and historicity to the category of an existential principle of the faith community itself.

The consequence of this is that each theoretical system in the community and in the ecclesiastic institution is obliged to assume biography as a keyword, that is, as an inalienable and necessary component of its own being. In an epoch such as ours, of sudden transformations and deeply painful experiences, the narrative as a point of departure acquires a very special significance. As in all times, the newness of the experience of faith can only be identified in narrative terms. The anonymous character of the suffering caused by the injustice and violence lived out in the contemporary world stumbles upon insufficiency when analyzed conceptually in speculative argumentation. It is essential to confront it through narrative.[142] The contemporary mystics help us in this arduous endeavor.

Theology as Loving Narrative

The human being, besides being relational, intersubjective and dialogical, is a historical being. The history into which he or she is inserted is, therefore, always the history of a community, a supra-individual history. It is a joining together of universal events as the determination and work of the

---

141. See the desires of many contemporary mystics in this regard. Etty Hillesum, in her diary on the eve of being taken to Auschwitz: "I have broken my body like bread and shared it out among men. And why not, they were hungry and had gone without for so long" (*Letters and Diaries*, 549). Or Simone Weil, in the eucharistic prayer at the beginning of the book *La connaissance surnaturelle*: "Father, in the name of Christ grant me . . . that this love may be a totally consuming flame of love of God and through God. That all be plucked from me, consumed by God, transformed into the substance of Christ and given as food to the unfortunate ones who are deprived of all kinds of nutrition in their body and their soul."

142. See Schneider, *Teología como biografía*, 61.

human being. But how is it possible for human words to speak of God inside history? How can God be related to history, if God transcends history? Is God not the atemporal and eternal unmoved mover? And isn't history the domain of the provisional, the contingent, and decay? Furthermore, isn't history the domain of conflict, struggle, and ambiguity? How can God, who is the transparent and Absolute Truth, reveal God's self in the midst of the shadows and pain of time and space?[143]

The Judeo-Christian tradition tells us that the revelation certainly takes place through nature, that is, through the creation, the seen and contemplated world that enchants us with its beauty and reveals the presence of the artist who conceived it. But above all it happens inside history, which, together with the creation, is the space in which the people of Israel and the first Christian community perceived, in a privileged way, the presence and action of God.

For the Christian, a fundamental conviction is that God—besides revealing God's self in the creation and being found in and through nature—revealed and reveals God's self in history. One need not leave history to hear God, find God, and receive God's revelation. It is in concrete history that we can hear God's Word and understand what it has to tell us. Thus, Christian revelation, besides being a cosmic revelation (making itself known in the world, in creation, and in nature), is a historical revelation.[144]

The fact that a God communicates with men and women, speaking to them in the midst of history, was the great contribution of the people of Israel to the religious journey of humankind. This people perceived that the events which took place in their history of captivity and liberation—their struggle to settle in a land, their need for political organization, etc.—were not isolated or unrelated instances, nor did they have to do only with the immediacy of each moment. Rather, these events carried at their core a greater meaning which need to be very attentively listened to and observed, because one finds there God's self in person.[145]

The Judeo-Christian revelation as presented in the Bible constantly shows us that its writers were concerned much less with concepts and ideas than with accounts, narratives, and genealogies, that is, with literary genres which emphasize historical time as an essential category. Thus they highlight the fundamental principle of the faith, that God reveals God's self in the invisible fluidity of time, in the midst—not outside—of history. In

---

143. See Rahner, "The History of Salvation and Revelation," in *Foundations of Christian Faith*, 138–75.

144. Ibid.

145. Ibid. See also Libânio, *Teologia da revelação*, 283–306; see especially "Revelação e história: reflexão introdutória."

experiencing communication with God and listening to God's Word in the midst of historical events, and later interpreting this experience, the people were configuring the historical and salvific project which God desired.

Although the people of Israel initially identified their God as a God tied to a space, to the land inhabited by God's worshipers, this conception was progressively dismissed during the Babylonian captivity, when the Israelites came to understand, with great suffering and pain, that they had lost their land, but not their God. They understood that their God was independent of the implications of space, and was no less God in the land of Canaan than in cruel Babylonia. And yes, it was possible to sing God's song and praise God in a foreign land.[146]

From that moment, it became clear that the territorial gods were *baalim*, idols, created by human fantasy, and inferior to human beings. They were not like the God of Abraham, Isaac and Jacob. While the deities of other peoples were associated with places and things, the God of Israel was more and more understood as the God of events which should be narrated, and whose narration was therefore fundamentally dynamic. Increasingly, this strengthened the power of God's Transcendence.

Consequently, the first thing sanctified in the religious history of God's people was a moment in time: the Sabbath. It was the day in which God rested, and in which all of Israel was called to rest as well.[147] Although regularly celebrated, the Shabbat did not correspond to any natural cycle, be it of the moon, the stars, the sun, or the human body. Its recurrence was a way to observe the passing of time, rather than a celebration of a circular repetitive cycle. It was a celebration whose essence consisted in finding fulfillment not in doing things or moving in space, but in existing.[148] It had to do with a moment, a point in time that is a describable interval, to be narrated again and again. In the same way, God is the One who, within time, reveals God's face to the people, unveiling God's identity to them—an identity that, as with time but even more so, is not fixed but moves and goes forward.

And there is a reason for this. Just as human beings cannot grasp time as they do other things and other dimensions of life, they learn that God is always greater than our desire and our tendency to circumscribe and capture God. God is a being in constant motion and able to involve us in God's movement. "In him we live and move and have our being."[149] Peren-

---

146. See Bingemer and Feller, *Deus Trindade: a vida no coração do mundo*, ch. 3.

147. See the beautiful reflection on the Sabbath as the ultimate point of creation in Moltmann, *God in Creation*.

148. Ibid.

149. See Acts 17:28.

nially on the move, always on the road, the people of Abraham developed a teleological vision of the world and of the human being. It is a vision that constantly looks toward the future and the desired end. In this perennial journey they encounter the Transcendence of God, who is present in the midst of historical change, and is never immobilized.

Never prisoners of a vicious circle of perpetual return, and contrary to the religions which adopt cyclical visions of the world—which incessantly return to the natural cycles, to the seasons of the year, to the reproductive cycles of humans and animals—the people of the Bible met their God in the dynamic and incessant movement of time and lived on looking forward, sustained by hope. At the beginning of their journey their hope had a shorter horizon, which widened as they came to understand that human mediation could not fully reveal the divine (as it could a king or any human figure). Therefore the plenitude of God's revelation must be deferred, and expected in the course of history with the arrival of the Messiah, who would then inaugurate a new time, not subject to decay, in which the promises would be fulfilled.

Christianity holds that this plenitude arrived with Jesus of Nazareth, in whom the community recognized the Christ of God, the expected Messiah. But this does not mean that with Christianity the centrality of time disappeared. On the contrary, it marked the beginning of a new type of narrative, the narrative of the life, words, and deeds of Jesus of Nazareth, under the impulse of his Holy Spirit, poured over all flesh. Thus, Christianity is fully coherent with the Judaic revelation, while at the same time introducing into it a radical newness, since the expected Messiah, whom it proclaims to have arrived, makes history turn on its hinges and inaugurates a qualitative *novum* inside historical time.

The *locus* where God is revealed is in time, in history. For this reason the favored form of expression through which human beings articulate their discourse on the God of their faith preferably should not be conceptual theology, but narrative theology. Today an important tendency in Christian theology, whether Catholic or Protestant, aims to retake the centrality of narrative in articulating its discourse, since the excessive space occupied by the absolute dominion of abstract concepts has excluded some of the theological treatises on the life of the community and the people.

No longer configured as narrative, but as creeds, philosophical elaborations, and ideas, theology constructed an image of God where impassiveness gained ground at the expense of movement, while timelessness was imposed on historical revelation, and discourse was crystalized into concepts which had little or nothing to do with the biblical revelation of God.

Mystical Biographies and Theological Narrative

Throughout history, Christian philosophers such as Blaise Pascal have observed that the God of the Bible is the God of Abraham, Isaac, and Jacob, "not of philosophers and scholars."[150] "This is true in the sense that the biblical faith is, to the perplexity and scandalization of many thinkers, of a fundamentally historical character. Its doctrines are realities and historical events, not abstract values or ideas that exist in a timelessness realm."[151]

The experience of the people of the Bible is paradigmatic for us. Certain clearly historical events in the history of Israel point beyond themselves, that is, to a divine disposition and providence. For this reason they should time and again be narrated, related, and repeated, so that the people may believe and pass on what they hear to future generations.[152]

Yet, we don't have the totality of history. We assume the totality in the form of anticipation and expectation, and the action inspired by it. History does not run according to the laws of necessity. It is contingent and provisional, made by human beings, and is conditioned by a freedom which is also human.

But what does it mean, then, to hold that God presides over history, and at the same time to see in this history the same conditionalities, partialities, and provisionalities which our limitations bring to it? If everything were absurd, our own existence would also be absurd, and no longer would we be able to live even for a single instant. Meaning is not only the goal of human life but also its foundation and presupposition. Fragmentarily, we experience the meaning which refers us to Meaning. We see only some of its signs and signals, which represent history and point us to the passage of God, its Lord, who through it opens the way for us.

The Christian faith accompanies this passage of God into history. It does so through a Scripture which is always trying to decipher and interpret it; through a word to be listened to and always retransmitted to new and other interlocutors; through a historically situated event which never ceases to be recast in our history; through the horizon of the end of times; and through an ethical task of humanization to be carried out in the secularity of history with all people of goodwill. Thus, the Christian faith, which is faith in God's revelation, escapes the fascination with the Sacred out of which other religions are born, and transcends the rites and observances where they seek their practice and fulfillment. But it weaves into the texture

---

150. See Pascal, in his intense spiritual experience, later called "the night of Pascal" (la nuit de Pascal): *Pensees*.

151. Quote from http://www.cafeteologico.com.br/br/index.php?option=com_content&task=view&id=127&Itemid=11.

152. See Ricoeur, "Hermeneutique de l'idée de révélation."

of history, with narrative and hermeneutics, the fabric of the revelation, in perpetual dialogue with the faith of humankind.

This can only happen when this faith is thought of as an occurrence, an experience which takes place in the midst of time; as a gaze, a perspective for reading and interpreting this history; and as a study guide which permits the understanding of history from the standpoint of God's gaze. No historical event, even the most somber and negative, can escape this rule, if it is to be theologically read.

Here, then, is an important objective for the Christian faith in the contemporary world: to recover the narrative of God which generates the faith, and—no less important—to recover the narrative of the witnesses who wove this history with their experience, their commitment, their testimony, and their blood. It is here, we believe, that one must recognize the importance of the narratives of the mystics who experienced the presence of God in a strong and palpable way, and left their narratives as a legacy to future generations.

The mystics are persons who experience in their lives the event of the presence of God, who talks to them and teaches them while inviting them to participate intimately in God. The locution which the mystic hears in his or her interior may take the form of words, touches, or emotions. However, when closely followed, the process of this divine locution will be more and more perceived by those who receive it as a coherent narrative, a writing which the Spirit of God carries out in their interior, and which transforms their lives. In the words of Ulpiano Vásquez Moro, it is a theography, a set of marks and tracks that God leaves in our hearts in communicating God's self in love.[153] From this writing, the mystics can read what God teaches them—as the teacher teaches a pupil, in the words of, for example, Ignatius of Loyola—and later they transmit it to others through oral or written narrative.[154]

This writing is always a loving narrative, a locution marked by love. The proof of this is in the language used by the mystics to describe their experiences, in which images of the affective and even the sexual world are very present. In the case of Christian mysticism, the loving relationship acquires even more pronounced hues and shades, because the environment where the mystical experience takes place is that of the Incarnation. There, the experienced and loved God became flesh and showed a human face.[155]

153. See Moro, *Orientação espiritual: Mistagogia e teografia*.

154. See *Autobiografia*, no. 17.

155. See Saint Teresa of Ávila and her immense devotion "to the humanity of Jesus." Indeed, for Teresa, Christian life is a personal relationship with Jesus that culminates in union with Him through grace, love, and imitation. This explains the importance she

For this reason Christian mystics of all times have used words taken from the vocabulary of sexuality and erotic love to describe the state of their souls and to narrate their experiences.[156] Bodily pleasure and pain—even if faint and insufficient—are the channels through which they seek to communicate their ineffable experience, of which they are protagonists by Grace rather than by their own effort.

Mystical love, ineffable and indescribable, therefore cannot deviate or be isolated from that which constitutes the humanity of the human being. Paradoxically, it is in the profoundest similarity with the human being that the God of the Christian revelation shows God's difference and absolutely transcendent Otherness. Mysticism takes place in the area of anthropological structure where being-in-itself becomes being-for-others, which is the truth about being. That is why the mysterious and profound experience of love, which occurs in the secrecy of the heart with repercussions on affectivity and corporality, necessarily emerges in humble and loving service to the other, especially the poor and the needy. In their faces the mystic finds, again and again, in the profoundest intimacy, the presence of the experienced and loved God.

In truth, what is offered here, in the process of loving knowledge between the Transcendent God and the finite creature, is a process of New Creation.[157] Those who experience intimacy with the Mystery of God in this way, and accept the transformation of their lives by this Mystery, are completely recreated. They begin to experience themselves as new and as having just come from the hands of the Creator. This is, constitutively and inseparably, an experience of love, one which carries in itself the process of a new birth. It includes an entirely paradoxical dimension of birth and of coming into the world—pain and joy, beauty and suffering, concealment and revelation, gracious amazement and the practice of humble and disinterested service to others. The One whose self is thus experienced is the Creator of all things. In self-revealing to the creatures, and having them participate in the most intimate Mysteries of the Creator's life and being, the Creator realizes in them a new creation. For this reason the mystical process

---

attributes to meditation on the Passion and to the Eucharist as the presence of Christ in the church, for the life of each believer and as the heart of the liturgy (See *Libro de la Vida* 33:5).

156. Even a mystic as truly discreet as Simone Weil uses the expression "nuptial chamber" to signify the relationship that the "friends of God" have with the Lord (See *Attente de Dieu*, 59). Thus in her *Notebooks*, written in London near the end of her life, she speaks in erotic terms of "the soul that lay with God" (See *Cahiers*).

157. See Tresmontant, *La mystique chretienne et l'avenir de l'homme*.

is inseparably and paradoxically both pleasurable and painful, without ceasing to be loving.[158]

The loving pleasure thus experienced takes place in the flesh, with its vulnerability, mortality and finitude. And it constitutes the experience of a love that is greater than everything that exists. It provokes seduction and fascination, but at the same time pain for what is absent, for what is missing, for incompleteness. It provokes a nostalgia brought about by the sense of not being able to consummate a foreseen union, and of constantly having to feel the poverty of one's limitations. It provokes the joy—although in the midst of tribulation[159]—of seeing oneself as a grain of sown wheat which will yield something new to be enjoyed by others. The light that shines supreme may hide itself, disappearing at any moment, leaving the soul alone and abandoned to the inclemency of aridity and desolation. But when it shines once again, it finds that same soul stronger, more mature, and ready to enter into a more solid and enduring stage of love.[160]

This is why the mystics sing their love in paradoxes, as did Saint John of the Cross (1542–91) in speaking of "a pleasant burn and delicious wound."[161] Saint Augustine (354–430) declared, "I tasted You, and now I hunger for You. You touched me softly, and I burned for your peace. The more I possess You the more I search for You."[162] In our times, Edith Stein (1891–1942) said, "I am happy for everything. We can only acquire the science of the Cross by experiencing the Cross until the end; . . . I repeat in my heart: *ave*, oh cross, the only hope."[163]

In the same way that the New Creation made itself present in Jesus Christ through the Easter transmission of suffering and pain, so too in any experience of the great Western Christian mystics one will find this paradoxical mark of the Cross and Resurrection—fulfillment laced by absence, pleasure threatened by dark night, love stronger than death—which has passed through the sieve of the Passion and finally found serenity by the

---

158. Ibid., 90–95.

159. See the paradoxical expressions that the same mystics use to express their states of spirit. See, for instance, Etty Hillesum saying she is in a state of "mournful contentment," or Simone Weil saying that every time she thought of the Passion of Christ, she committed the sin of envy (See *Attente de Dieu*, 81).

160. See the stages that classical theology distinguished in the mystical itinerary: the purgative, the illuminative, and the unitive. See what Saint John of the Cross explains in *The Ascent of Mount Carmel* regarding the several "purgations" that the spiritual life carries with it: active or passive, of the senses or of the spirit.

161. See Saint John of the Cross and the poem "Living Flame of Love."

162. See Augustine, *Confessions*, 10.27.38.

163. See Letter 330 in Stein, *Self-Portrait in Letters*, 341.

light of the Resurrection, the apex of the revelation of the Incarnate Word. The experience of contemplation and union with God revealed here is a mixture of pleasure and pain, of light which vanquishes the darkness, of plenitude and serenity which triumph over pain and mortality.

All of this, which we see in the mystics of the Spanish *siglo de oro* or in other earlier ones—such as Saint Augustine, for example—continues to be true of the mystics of the twentieth century. These words of Simone Weil confirm what we are saying:

> When the authentic friends of God—as was Master Eckart, according to my feelings—repeat words which they heard in secret, in the midst of the silence, during the union of love, and they are not in accord with the Church's teachings, it is simply because the language of the public square is not that of the nuptial chamber.[164]

A return to the accounts of the mystics—as the church of the Second Vatican Council proclaimed in returning to the texts of the Holy Fathers—can renew theology by recovering it as narrative. And as loving narrative of erotic and agapic love which is transformed into *caritas*, into service and oblation toward others, especially in their pain and suffering.

Mysticism and the Desire for Fellowship with Human Pain

One of the great criticisms and suspicions of mysticism is the risk that it may be alienating, that it may facilitate evasion of the harshness of reality, providing those who go through this experience with an escape valve by which to avoid adherence to the opacity of history, with its pain and suffering.

It seems to us that, on the contrary, all the contemplative currents in the history of humankind, all the schools of meditation and contemplation, are places where one learns to see and hear, and even more, to refine one's vision and hearing so as to be able to grasp the real in all its amplitude and profundity.

This hearing and seeing is related not only to one's inner life, or to one's desires and spiritual feelings, but also to the clamors of reality, to the suffering of the neighbor, and to the painful reality of the world. In other words, mysticism, rather than providing an escape from suffering and death, from problems and conflicts, leads to an immersion in them, and a compassionate embracing of them, with a deep desire for solidarity and fellowship.[165]

164. See *Attente de Dieu*, 59.
165. See Mardones, *La tranformación de la religión*, 210.

The mystical revolution—taking place in the interior, in the intimacy of the human heart—is not antagonistic to political commitment, to incarnation into reality, as it has often been accused of being. On the contrary, it has been observed in recent decades, in many parts of the world, that many of those who found themselves engaged in a militancy that has lost connection with their prayerful and celebrative motivations, ended up abandoning their militancy because it has lost the meaning for which they were struggling.[166]

Mysticism, on the contrary, leads people to confront themselves and their tremendous loneliness. It challenges the evasive consumerist society which maintains a lively configuration of spectacle and superficiality. It compels human beings to face themselves holistically, including the shadier dimensions of their personalities, and to become aware of their human capacity to confront and integrate these dimensions.[167]

The authentic mystical experience is, in truth, a bulwark and a guarantee in the face of the anthropological reductionism which proliferates in a light consumerist culture. It confronts and contradicts this reductionism with a real and consistent critique of society as conceived and structured today. It is, indeed, a countercultural experience and way of life. The most tangible witness of this is the recurring evidence that contemporary mystics, far from being alienated persons who escape from the world and take refuge in a stratosphere of sensual and cathartic gratifications, are deeply committed to the struggles and problems of their time. And they feel the call to proceed in this way as coming from the experience of God, which opens their sensibilities and makes them vulnerable to it.

The writings of the contemporary mystics, therefore, demonstrate that they do not run away from the conflict and suffering of which their environment and historical moment are full. On the contrary, they feel as their own, and very near to their bodies and their hearts, all the postmodern discussions concerning "death and dying, innocent suffering, limit experiences, radical Otherness and, positively, the Good beyond Being."[168] Furthermore, they take these painful realities upon themselves and into the interior of their bodies and lives.

David Tracy, just quoted above, refers to the French philosopher and mystic Simone Weil in thinking of the consciousness of God's presence

---

166. On this theme see Andrade, "Encantos e desencantos: militância do cristão em tempos de crise"; "A crise da modernidade e as possibilidades de uma nova militância cristã."

167. Mardones, *La tranformación de la religión*, 211.

168. See Tracy, "Afterword," 242.

Mystical Biographies and Theological Narrative

as inseparable from the historical consciousness of innocent suffering.[169] Further, he notes that she suggests—although only implicitly—that one can begin a mystical process with a sense of the tragedy of undeserved suffering. This sense of tragedy, in Simone's life, was never separate from compassion or from the desire for fellowship and participation, as the whole course of her life shows.[170]

The mystical experience in our times, therefore, can often begin with apophatic moments of suffering and the cross, which are experienced in the face of evil and of unjust and innocent suffering, only later to evolve into the "yes" that—according to Karl Barth on his deathbed, cited by Tracy—is the final word of a Christian to every great no.[171] The yes that the contemporary mystics speak to God—who calls them and inhabits them, causing them to experience God's love—begins for many of them where theodicy often faces a perplexity, and where great and brilliant men such as Albert Camus found no response other than indignation and atheism: the suffering of the others, the innocent and unjust suffering which they desire to embrace with passion and compassion.

Far from being a painful masochism, this desire—which is a criterion for the verification of the authenticity of contemporary mysticism—opens the door, from the depth of the human condition, to a vital remembrance (a reminiscing in the heart), which keeps alive, in the subjective inner life and in objective history, the subversive memory of all the suffering of many generations, besides carrying in the body the marks of this suffering, and not wishing to be separated from it.[172]

Simone Weil, even in her early youth—already in the philosophy class of her teacher, Alain, at the Sorbonne—wrote that the saint is distinguished by not wishing to be separated from the pain and suffering of his or her contemporaries, but rather to be a full participant in it.[173] Like other Christian mystics, she considered holiness to be a transmutation as profound as that of the Eucharist, where one must consent to a spiritual death in order to be

---

169. Ibid. See the remarks of Simone Weil in "L'amour de Dieu et le malheur," in Weil, *Attente de Dieu*. See also the admirable text "L'Illiade ou le poeme de la force," in Weil, *Oeuvres*, 540.

170. See also Bingemer, "Simone Weil. Une mystique pour Le XXeme siecle." See also my book *Simone Weil: una mística en los límites*.

171. See Tracy, "Afterword," 243.

172. Once again we cite Simone Weil because it seems to us that she best expresses what we said above: "The saint inclines toward perfection less by seeking integrity than by loving God (or the divine) in the ardor of a faith that leads to total devotion and to self-forgetfulness" (*La connaissance surnaturelle*, 325).

173. See the remarks on Simone Weil by the Dominican Father Perrin, her spiritual interlocutor: "For those who truly love, compassion is a torment" (*Attente de Dieu*, 9).

totally transformed into Christ. "Total humility is consent to death, which makes of us an inert nothing. Saints are those who while still alive consent to death."[174]

The great Swiss theologian Hans Urs von Balthasar boldly affirms that God's revelation—and therefore the experience of God—has a special affinity not only with God's acts but also with God's incomprehensibility, which is strictly related to pain and suffering.

> One can never sufficiently emphasize that this exegesis of God has absolutely no parameter in any of the other human religions. Here, God exposes to human sight his most profound being in suffering—a suffering which, furthermore, freely assumes an alien guilt—while the remaining ways leading from the human being to God are ways of overcoming pain, of seeking the "blessed life," of the desire to never again be exposed to contingency and tribulation.[175]

The desire to commune with the pain and suffering of the stranger is therefore, according to Balthasar, a special gift of the mystic. And this suffering can assume several forms: poverty, disgrace, persecution, extermination, discomfort, illness, deprivation of freedom, torture, and any depressing and painful human situation burdened with the weight of negativity and clamoring for relief, solidarity and redemption. And this desire, which results in compassionate and loving practice, is a sign, inside the world, of the mystic's Christification, which is configured in Christ—and therefore in God—to the extent that it is carried out inwardly by the same Spirit that the Father gave to the Son. In the desire to commune with the pain of the other, it is God who, in the person of the mystic, goes to meet human pain. In this way, the mystic passes from the loving nuptial chamber to the public square, where human destinies are at play, and suffers the pain and conflicts of a humankind not yet reconciled.[176]

The revelation, from which the mystic receives direct communication, unveils above all the heart of God.[177] The mystic receives and interprets it, usually with the help of another person who is spiritually trusted. And, in accord with the interpretation which can be gleaned from this divine in-

---

174. *La connaissance surnaturelle*, 325: "L'humilité totale, c'est le consentement à la mort, qui fait de nous du néant inerte. Les saints sont ceux qui encore vivants ont réellement consenti à la mort."

175. See Balthasar, "Gott ist sein eigener Exeget," 11, cited by Schneider, *Teologia como biographia*, 64 n. 58.

176. See Weil, *Attente de Dieu*, 59.

177. See Schneider, *Teologia como biographia*, 65.

spiration, the mystic carries it into practice. Thus his or her attitude is not simply one of submission and respect for a will which is taken to be an intrinsic and severe law. The whole person of the mystic is invited, and even more, convened to be transformed by the pain of the other into the language and practice of effective and concrete love.

Levinas—although he never says he is speaking of mystical experience—makes similar affirmations, radically deepening what constitutes the human condition. With impressively radical words, he conceives of the human subject as a hostage to others and their suffering: "The hostage is the only culprit, since upon him has fallen all the guilt, and he can do nothing but carry on, suffer, give and atone."[178] In realizing that, this same hostage assumes a messianic configuration. And again Levinas states,

> The Messiah is the righteous one who suffers, who took upon himself the suffering of the others . . . The fact that he did not evade the burden imposed by the suffering of the others defines his own ipseity. All persons are Messiahs . . . The I, as I, taking upon itself all the suffering of the world, designates itself as totally alone in this role. To designate itself in this way, not evading the moment to respond before the call is heard, is precisely what it is to be I. The I is that one who promoted himself to assume all the responsibility for the world . . . And here is why he can take upon himself all of the suffering of everyone: he cannot call himself "I" except to extent to which he already took upon himself this suffering . . . And, concretely, this means that each one must act as if they were the Messiah. Messianism is not the certainty of the coming of a man who will stop history. It is my power to bear the suffering of all. It is the instant when I recognize this power and my universal responsibility.[179]

What Levinas expounds in terms of ethics—which according to him is the true and only philosophy—Christianity recognizes in the entire history of its mystics. For the mystic, this language that speaks of the desire to assume the pain of the other, and this loving praxis of effectively deciding to do it, are—and will always be—surpassed in essence by the Cross of Jesus Christ. In becoming incarnate, God suffers a passion, a kenosis, a diminution which is not limited just to the moment of the incarnation, but also takes place when the ineffable must be fixed in writing, must be born in a particular situation,[180] and must be expressed through the words, deeds, attitudes and choices which will mark a life and determine a future.

178. See Levinas, *Autrement qu'être ou au-delà de l'essence*.
179. Levinas, *Difficile liberté*, 120.
180. See the material proposed by Saint Ignatius of Loyola for contemplation

If Christian mysticism is a configuration in Christ, if it is a Christic process, then the criterion for verifying the truth of the encounter and union with God is gauged by its capacity to assume and integrate the pain of this world—the pain of those whom the Gospel calls the last, the least, and the lost, and who in the parable of the last judgement are the hungry, the thirsty, the naked, the strangers, and the prisoners. In other words, by its desire and capacity to construct a human life worthy of this name, for all persons who inhabit this earth. And God teaches, in the intimacy of the nuptial chamber and in the profanity of the public square, that it is God, personally, who is there suffering hunger, thirst, nakedness, and captivity. The mystics, who yearns for union with God, who loves them and whom they love, cannot desire anything other than to be placed in the same situation as the beloved, always a situation of extreme fragility and absolute vulnerability, where God reveals God's power from the standpoint of the impotence of love.[181]

---

regarding the gospel scene of the birth of Jesus, in *Exercícios espirituais*: "[116] 3° puncto. El 3°: mirar y considerar lo que hacen, así como es el caminar y trabajar, para que el Señor sea nascido en summa pobreza, y a cabo de tantos trabajos, de hambre, de sed, de calor y de frío, de injurias y afrentas, para morir en cruz; y todo esto por mí; después reflitiendo sacar algún provecho spiritual."

181. Once again, it is Simone Weil who finds the right words to express such a profound experience: "When a mother, wife or bride knows that the one she loves is prey to anxiety and that she can neither help him nor join him, she would at least like to bear equivalent suffering, in order to be less separate from him, to lighten such a heavy burden of impotent compassion. The one who loves Christ and imagines him on the cross must feel similar relief when assaulted by disgrace" (*Pensées sans ordre concernant l'amour de Dieu*, 101).

— 5 —

Stories and Experiences of Love

BIOGRAPHIES ARE LIVING AND concrete narratives of personal existences—even the mystical ones. And above all the mystical ones, given the background laid out in the previous chapter. In this final chapter we want to put forward some concrete examples of all that we have reflected upon. To that end we present three biographies in which one finds in abundance what we have so far tried to convey.

These are the biographies of two women and a man. Two lay persons and a priest. A mother, and two childless young adults. Two Catholics and a Jew. Two of them young, and the other a woman who has arrived at the end of her days, and would die at an advanced age. Three learned and cultured human beings living in the same century, in different countries of the northern hemisphere—the United States, Holland, and Belgium. All of them under the full impact of the Second World War, the Holocaust, the Great Depression of the United States, the Cold War, the 1968 revolution, the Second Vatican Council, the Vietnam War, and all the great events which configured the profile of the last century. They are three persons who confided to the pages of their diaries, or their writings, the transformative work that the mystical experience had been carrying out in their bodies and their lives.

They share two passions, which are really just one: a passion for God and a passion for the world. All of them passionately and insatiably sought God, and were rewarded with a profound encounter that gave them the most definitive experience of their lives. They all heard and obeyed the call to turn their eyes toward the pain of the world and to embrace it in order to redeem it. We will put forward a summarized version of their biographies, in the belief that they can help bring to our reflection a stamp of reality and concreteness as we come to the conclusion of this book.

Dorothy Day: A Revolution of the Heart[1]

The greatest challenge of the day is: how to bring about a revolution of the heart, a revolution which has to start with each one of us.

Dorothy Day was born in New York, in 1897. She spent most of her childhood in Chicago, where she studied for two years at the Illinois University at Urbana-Champagne, before returning to New York with her family in 1916.

Upon returning to New York, she found work as a reporter for the newspaper *The Call*, the only socialist periodical in the city. Afterwards she worked for the magazine *The Masses*, which opposed the involvement of the United States in the First World War and was closed in September, 1917. In November of that same year, Dorothy Day was sent to jail as one of forty protesters who rallied in front of the White House against the denial of the right to vote for women. In detention they were brutally treated, and they responded with a hunger strike. Eventually they were freed as the result of a presidential order.

In New York Dorothy had a very agitated and bohemian life. An affair with an impetuous womanizing journalist, Lionel Moise, resulted in pregnancy and an abortion. Dorothy never wrote explicitly about this painful experience, but narrated it in the third person in the pages of the novel *The Eleventh Virgin*, in 1924. Instead of Dorothy and Lionel, the characters are called June and Dick. If she had narrated factually what she recounted as fiction, the story would have been as follows:

> I fell in love with a newspaperman named Lionel Moise. I got pregnant. He said that if I had the baby, he would leave me. I wanted the baby but I wanted Lionel more. So I had the abortion and I lost them both....
>
> I hobbled down the darkened stairwell of the Upper East Side flat in New York City. My steps were unsteady. My left arm held the banister tightly. My right arm clutched my abdomen. It was burning in pain. I walked out onto the street alone in the dark. It was in September of 1919. I was twenty-one years old and I had just aborted my baby.
>
> Lionel, my boyfriend, promised to pick me up at the flat after it was all over. I waited in pain from nine a.m. to ten p.m. but he never came. When I got home to his apartment I found only a note. He said he had left for a new job and, regarding my

---

1. On the life of Dorothy Day as told by herself, see the following works: *The Long Loneliness*; *House of Hospitality*; *On Pilgrimage: The Sixties*; *The Duty of Delight*; *By Little and By Little*; *From Union Square to Rome*; *Loaves and Fishes*. There is also a vast bibliography about her.

abortion, that I was only one of God knows how many millions of women who go through the same thing. Don't build up any hopes. It is best, in fact, that you forget me.[2]

A scholar of the life and mysticism of Dorothy Day—Stephen Krupa—suggests that the restless and irresponsible Lionel Moise was a replica of his very emotionally distant father, and that the abortion was Dorothy's attempt to hold on to him at all costs.[3]

After that, Dorothy—still traumatized by what had happened—married a literary publicist, Barkeley Tobey, in a civil ceremony. She took a long trip to Europe with him. A year after they returned, aware that she didn't love him, she left him and went to Chicago for some months to try to revive the failed romance with Lionel Moise.[4]

It was after this that she found a more mature love, with whom she led a life of greater emotional and affective stability. He was a botanist named Forster Batterham. She entered into another civil marriage with him. They lived in Staten Island, beside the sea. With Forster, Dorothy learned to love nature, and they had a daughter. Her conversion to Catholicism followed the birth of her daughter. And her own baptism was followed by the breakup of her marriage, as her husband didn't accept her religious choice.

---

2. See Lynch, "Dorothy Day's Pro-Life Memories." See also *The Eleventh Virgin*, Part 3, ch. 4, where Dorothy writes, "It was not a baby that she wanted. She wanted more of Dick. And she would lose Dick altogether unless she went to a doctor immediately and said nothing at all to him about it.

"It was four months later. June lay on a single cot bed in the home of Dr. Jane Pringle, a six-room flat in a huge apartment house on the Upper East Side. Pretty soon it would all be over with. It ought not to take but a few hours more the doctor had said. Just to lie there and endure. Three hours seemed an eternity, but the minutes sped by very fast. One pain every three minutes. How fast they came! It seemed that the moments of respite could be counted in seconds. The pain came in a huge wave and she lay there writhing and tortured under it. Just when she thought she could endure it no longer, the wave passed and she could gather up her strength to endure the next one.

"The door of the little hall bedroom where June lay was closed. Just before nine o'clock she heard the doctor's small boy stamp past on his way to school. It was because of him that Dr. Pringle accepted such patients as she. She had lost her husband when he was a baby and her practice brought in very little money. Occasionally she took the case of a friend or the friend of a friend she told June.

"The small boy was gone and now her door was open to the silent flat. Dr. Pringle was gone too to make several morning calls. She would be home at noon to see how June was and to make lunch for her son. Until then, June had the flat to herself. She could lie there and groan. It helped a great deal to groan every now and then. After twelve she must keep very quiet for the small boy would be back then."

3. See Krupa, "Celebrating Dorothy Day."

4. Ibid.

Soon afterwards she established contact with Peter Maurin, the great companion and partner of her spiritual life and apostolic work. In him, Dorothy Day found a Christian and reformer with whom she experienced a fellowship of mind and feeling. In 1933, they launched together the Catholic Worker's Movement, which published an influential newspaper that quickly reached a circulation of more than a thousand copies. It also set up a number of houses to shelter and give assistance to the homeless. The United States was suffering the consequences of the Great Depression which followed the 1929 crash of the New York stock market. There were many people without homes or money for food. The shelters were a great help in that situation.

Dorothy Day was certainly a revolutionary, but a revolutionary consistent with the revolution of the heart which she desired and praised. She was certainly a mystic, but a mystic out of the ordinary. In the 1960s she was appreciated and praised by leaders of the counterculture such as Abbie Hoffman, who called her "the first hippie," a description that she liked and approved. She wrote passionately about women's rights during the 1910s, but disagreed with the sexual revolution of the 1960s, having observed and experienced in her own flesh, in the 1920s, its devastating effects.

This was someone who managed to combine a progressive attitude toward the defense of human, social and economic rights with a very orthodox and traditional sense of Catholic morality and piety. Yet, her devotion and obedience to the church were neither blind nor uncritical. For example, she publicly condemned the Spanish phalangist leader Francisco Franco during the Spanish Civil War, thus incurring the opposition of many American Catholics, lay and clergy. And she had to change the name of her newspaper (*The Catholic Worker*), "ostensibly because the word *Catholic* implies an official church connection when such was not the case."[5] Her principal struggle was for justice and peace. For this she lived and died. Her earthly pilgrimage ended on November 29, 1980, at the Maryhouse in New York, where she died amidst the poor.

What strikes one most in attempting a theological reading of Dorothy Day's biography is the enormous sensibility of this woman, who is apparently no different from so many others. Here is someone who loved and was loved, who dreamed about a home and children, who worked and made a living with her own effort and toil. This trait of extreme sensibility is what first jumps out at the reader when Dorothy Day talks about herself. She is someone whose potentialities are all open and vigilant—someone who allows herself to be deeply touched and affected by the surrounding world

---

5. See Coles, *Dorothy Day*, 81.

and by other persons, and who is therefore open to be deeply touched by God, to whom, at the right moment, she was to deliver her whole life.

Corporal Sensibility

Dorothy Day was always a very feminine woman and conscious of her own body. More than once during her youth she fell deeply in love. She liked to be with persons of the opposite sex, she liked affection, she liked to love and be loved. The proximity of another person's flesh pleased her. For this reason her extreme corporal sensibility felt very diminished and assaulted in her first serious relationship, with Lionel Moise, and with the consequent abortion which was carried out in the hope of securing his companionship.

The subsequent failure of the relationship and the indelible mark that the abortion left on the physicality of such a sensitive woman were determinative of her human and spiritual evolution. In this episode of Dorothy Day's life we can palpably experience the affirmation of Saint Paul that "where sin increased, grace abounded all the more."[6]

Her amorous relationship with Forster Batterham brought about a very beautiful and positive moment in her life. There was a syntony between the two of them not very common among most couples: "We fished together, we walked every day for miles, we collected and studied together, and an entire new world opened up to me little by little. We did not talk much, but 'lived together' in the fullest sense of the phrase."[7]

What marked a definitive Copernican turn in Dorothy's Day life, making her the apostle of the poorest, the defender of the voiceless, the champion of peace and justice, came about through her extreme feminine corporal sensibility. But what was decisively the most gratifying human and corporal experience of her life was maternity. As a consequence of the abortion she underwent years before her relationship with Forster, she feared that the damage to her womb from the surgery to remove the fetus would make any future conception impossible. She believed that she would never become pregnant with another child. She thought that the abortion had made her sterile, and this deeply distressed her. "For a long time I had thought I could not bear a child, and the longing in my heart for a baby had been growing," she says in her autobiography. "My home, I felt, was not a home without one."[8]

From her union with Forster Batterham, Dorothy once again became pregnant, and this she considered nothing less than a miracle. In July of

6. Rom 5:20.
7. *The Long Loneliness*, 114.
8. Ibid., 136.

1927 she experienced the happiest day of her life with the birth of Tamar Theresa. This birth was the culmination of the happiness she had found in her relationship with Forster, and was at the same time a definitive call to see God as the center of her life: "No human creature could receive or contain so vast a flood of love and joy as I often felt after the birth of my child. With this came the need to worship, to adore."[9]

Her ideology—all that she had up until then—generated inside her a great conflict between the call of God and the renouncements that such a call demanded of her. She remembered the authors she had read, and their criticism of religion:

> "Christianity," Bakunin said, "is precisely the religion par excellence, because it exhibits, and manifests, to the fullest extent, the very nature and essence of every religious system, which is the impoverishment, enslavement, and annihilation of humanity for the benefit of divinity." I certainly believed this, but I wanted to be poor, chaste and obedient. I wanted to die in order to live, to put off the old man and put on Christ. . . . Why should not Forster be jealous?[10]

God's call prevailed over everything else and Dorothy found nothing better to do with the immense gratitude that filled her heart than to baptize her daughter in the Catholic Church.

> I did not want my child to flounder as I had often floundered. I wanted to believe, and I wanted my child to believe, and if belonging to a Church would give her so inestimable a grace as faith in God, and the companionable love of the Saints, then the thing to do was to have her baptized a Catholic.[11]

Tamar Theresa was baptized before her mother. Dorothy was not baptized until December 28 of the year of her daughter's birth, after a harsh and painful definitive separation from Forster, undoubtedly due to the religious abyss that opened between the two of them and deepened after Tamar Theresa's birth. Her decision to baptize her daughter and to accept the Catholic faith herself came at an enormous personal cost to Dorothy. It resulted in the end of her union with the man she loved and the loss of several friends and companions.[12]

---

9. Ibid., 139.
10. Ibid., 149.
11. Ibid., 142.

12. See the love letters she continued to write to Forster after the separation, in Day, *All the Way to Heaven*.

After a long and painful waiting period she decided that she had to ask for the same baptism she had requested for her daughter, even though it meant a definitive break with Forster. She knew that the break was coming and that it would bring a great deal of suffering, as she loved the father of her child as much as before, or even more. Her descriptions of her amorous contacts with him show us the truth and depth of that love:

> Fall nights we read a great deal. Sometimes he went out to dig bait if there were a low tide and the moon was up. He stayed out late on the pier fishing, and came in smelling of seaweed and salt air; getting into bed, cold with the chill November air, he held me close to him in silence. I loved him in every way, as a wife, as a mother even. I loved him for all he knew and pitied him for all he didn't know. I loved him for all the odds and ends I had to fish out of his sweater pockets and for the sand and shells he brought with his fishing. I loved his lean cold body as he got into bed smelling of the sea, and I loved his integrity and stubborn pride.[13]

In fact, even after the separation from Forster, Dorothy wrote him letters that testified to the love she always held for him, even though the strength of her Catholic vocation—unleashed explicitly by her daughter's birth—had brought her to that definitive separation, since in facing a choice between God and the man she loved, she understood that she had to choose God.[14]

In the letters that the independent Dorothy wrote to Forster Batterham after the separation, she confessed her love and tried to explain the reasons for her conversion, and she capitulated to the desire to ask him to come back to her. She begged him humbly and insistently, but without success. Then one day she realized that the separation was final, and wrote him a last and admirable letter in which she let out all the love and longing that her woman's body felt for this man who had been her definitive and irreplaceable companion:

> Sex is not at all taboo with me except outside of marriage. I am as free and unsuppressed as I ever was about it. I think the human body a beautiful thing, and the joys that a healthy body have are perfectly legitimate joys. I see no immediate difference between enjoying sex and enjoying a symphony concert, but sex having such a part in life, as producing children, has been restricted as society and the Church have felt best for the children. I believe that in breaking these laws one is letting the flesh get an upper hand over the spirit, so I do not want to break these

---

13. *The Long Loneliness*, 148.
14. Ibid.

laws. St. Augustine says, "If bodies please thee, praise God on occasion of them." And I feel no sorrow for all the joys we have had in the past together. . . .

You think all this is only hard on you. But I am suffering too. The ache in my heart is intolerable at times, and sometimes for days I can feel your lips upon me, waking and sleeping. It is because I love you so much that I want you to marry me. I want to be in your arms every night, as I used to be, and be with you always. I always loved you more than you did me. That is why I made up with you so many times, and went after you after we had had some quarrel. We always differed on principle, and now that I am getting older I cannot any longer always give way to you just because flesh has such power over me. . . .

. . . It all is hopeless of course, tho it has often seemed to me a simple thing. Imaginatively I can understand your hatred and rebellion against my beliefs and I can't blame you. I have really given up hope now, so I won't try to persuade you any more.[15]

But even this did not mean the end of the relationship between this man and this woman who loved each other so much. Throughout the years they remained in contact with each other because of Tamar. There would be friendly notes, exchanges of gifts, and hospital visits. In Dorothy's final years, Forster constantly called her. He was present at her funeral in 1980, and later at a memorial Mass at Saint Patrick's Cathedral.[16]

To be the owner of a feminine body inhabited by desires, which trembled with pleasure under the caress of the beloved man; a body which conceived, gave birth to and nourished the beloved daughter who was from then on the light of her life; a body which must now face loneliness and the burden of struggling as a lay woman and single mother in a society which discriminates against women, and in a church still very much marked by machismo—this was to be the stamp of Dorothy's destiny from then on. But this same body would vibrate with compassion and solidarity for all the poor and unhappy men and women who were to cross her path and cause her to experience as her own the pain of the world and of humankind.

Through the experience of maternity, Dorothy allowed all her potential for love to flow toward all those who crossed her path bent under the weight of poverty and need. She also passionately embraced causes such as pacifism and nonviolence, which made her feel responsible for the maternal care of suffering humankind. All this was given to her by God, who demanded of

---

15. Day, *All the Way to Heaven*, 61–63. The date on the letter is 1935; therefore Tamar was already eight years old.

16. See Ellsberg, "Dorothy in Love."

her the supreme sacrifice of her love but also rewarded her a hundredfold, as stated in the Gospel.[17] In reply to a priest who criticized her for speaking of personalism and community without being married, she thought to herself:

> But I am a woman of family. I have had a husband and home life—I have a daughter . . . How can I let anyone put over on me the idea that I am a single person? I am a mother, and the mother of a very large family at that. Being a mother is fulfillment, it is surrender to others, it is Love and therefore of course it is suffering.[18]

This didn't mean that renouncing the beloved man had not always been supremely difficult. She herself said so in the mature years of her life:

> A woman does not feel whole without a man. And for a woman who had known the joys of marriage, yes, it was hard. It was years before I awakened without that longing for a face pressed against my breast, an arm about my shoulder. The sense of loss was there. It was a price I had paid. I was Abraham who had sacrificed Isaac. And yet I had Isaac. I had Tamar.[19]

Aesthetic Sensibility

Even as a young person in Chicago, her city, Dorothy's personality already showed contemplative traits. Walking through the poorer and more desolate neighborhoods, she was able to find unsuspected beauty where ordinarily one would only find desolation and deprivation. One of her biographers, Jim Forest, observed:

> She had a gift for finding beauty in the midst of urban desolation. Drab streets were transformed by pungent odors: geranium and tomato plants, garlic, olive oil, roasting coffee, bread and rolls in bakery ovens. "Here," she said, "was enough beauty to satisfy me."[20]

Eventually, during the years with Forster Batterham in Staten Island, this aesthetic sensibility was opened to the mysteries and revelations of nature. As she herself confesses, while her tendencies and tastes were extremely

---

17. See *The Long Loneliness*, 111; the reference is to Mark 10:28–31.
18. *The Long Loneliness*, 236.
19. Ibid.
20. Forest, *Love Is the Measure*.

urban,[21] she learned under the guiding hand of her beloved companion to discover the beauty that existed far from the grey periphery of the great metropolitan areas—in the sunrise and sunset, in the tumult of the sea, in plants and animals, in seashells and mollusks, with which the landscape was prodigal.

It is true that all the beauty of the creation did not come to her without the centrality of the human being who was present there. Forster's presence and her love for him were certainly the lens through which Dorothy was able to read the new world of creation she had discovered. And in him and through him she was able to see the presence of God as its origin, as making its existence possible.[22]

Dorothy Day was also, since her early childhood, deeply passionate about the vital art of literature. Her reading during her childhood and youth had a great deal of influence on her life after her conversion. Avid reading of the great European authors—such as the Russians Fyodor Dostoevsky and Leon Tolstoy, the French writers Georges Bernanos, François Mauriac, and even the less well-known Huysmans, the English writer Charles Dickens, and the Americans Upton Sinclair and Jack London, among others—formed her imagination and her rich aesthetic sensibility.

Because she was someone who could not live without writing—which is perhaps the best definition of a writer—Dorothy always deeply assimilated her readings, which so affected her throughout her life and helped to configure what came to be her mysticism and her private theology, her reading of the world through the gospel. The way she had of comparing her literary readings with biblical ones,[23] or with the stories of the great mystics,[24] shows a refined sensibility regarding literary creation which, furthermore, was pedagogical in describing the way she immersed herself, more and more radically, in her option of love and service to the poor.[25]

In a brilliant article, June O'Connor analyses four aspects of the Christian conversion of Dorothy Day: the affective, the cognitive, the moral and the religious.[26] In her analysis of the cognitive aspect, the author calls attention to the literary angle. The influence of the Russian writers shaped Dorothy's imagination, especially Dostoievsky, but also Leon Tolstoy, whose

---

21. *The Long Loneliness.*

22. Ibid.

23. See the prison narratives in *The Long Loneliness.*

24. She was a reader of Saint Teresa of Ávila, Saint Thérèse of Lisieux, Saint John of the Cross, and Simone Weil. See Miller, *All Is Grace.*

25. See Brady, "Dorothy Day: A Love of Fiction and Her Love of the Poor."

26. O'Connor, "Dorothy Day's Christian Conversion."

non-institutional vision of Christianity had a particular attraction for her. These factors were, at least in part, responsible for her freedom in facing the ecclesiastic institution, with which she rarely had moments of total harmony.[27]

At the same time, O'Connor calls attention to the fact that the works of other writers, such as Kropotkin, Upton Sinclair, and Jack London, encouraged and supported Dorothy's empathy with the poor.[28] But O'Connor affirms that the conversion she calls cognitive was complete only after Dorothy Day's decisive encounter with Peter Maurin. He "offered her an informed historical and theological vision of her recently embraced tradition of faith, which she only then made hers."[29]

Under the guidance of Peter Maurin, Dorothy read new works in which the social thinking of the church was an obligatory presence. Thomas Aquinas, Jacques Maritain, Hilaire Belloc, G. K. Chesterton, Eric Gill, and Vincent McNabb, among others, became her customary readings. First captivated by the vision of Maurin, and then making her own cognitive synthesis, Dorothy Day was able to give definitive shape to her vocation, centered around two great loves: God and the poor.[30]

Social Sensibility

Dorothy Day's sensibility was always profoundly touched by the economic and social injustice she saw around her. Her wounded sensibility led her to a response which was not just rational or intellectual, like those of so many other thinkers of her time.[31] It reflected, rather, a passionately loving proximity to those affected by this state of things, with whom she would progressively identify herself, to the extent that she walked under the gaze of God. As we have seen, literature played a role in this process.

While still in Chicago during her adolescence, Dorothy began to read books which moved her social consciousness and her sense of justice. Upton Sinclair's novel *The Jungle* greatly inspired her. Unlike the books on social injustice by authors such as Charles Dickens and Victor Hugo—whom she read abundantly—this was a story set in her own time, and not in Europe but in

27. Ibid., 165.
28. Ibid. See also Brady, "Dorothy Day," on the same theme, affirming furthermore that an education for the true option for the poor should, following the example of Dorothy Day, include literary texts.
29. Ibid., 166.
30. Ibid.
31. We refer here to Simone Weil and Egide van Broeckhoven, among others.

her own Chicago, in its livestock pens and slaughterhouses. Sinclair's hero was a Lithuanian immigrant, the only member of his family not completely destroyed by misery and injustice. Eventually he commits himself to the struggle for a just social order and becomes a member of the Socialist Party.[32]

Sinclair touched Dorothy's heart with this book. She took long walks through the poor neighborhoods of Chicago's South Side. This marked the beginning of a lifelong attraction to the areas that many people avoided, precisely because she wished to be closer to the poor. "I walked for miles ... exploring interminable gray streets, fascinating in their dreary sameness, past tavern after tavern, where I envisaged such scenes as that of the Polish wedding party in Sinclair's story."[33]

When she was just fifteen years old, she already looked at the world with open eyes and a vulnerable heart which many of us could envy. Reflecting on the lives of the people in those oppressed neighborhoods, victims of injustice and poverty—although rich in many other ways—she had a vivid sense of what she would become, a kind of premonition of her own vocation as inseparable from the life of God's favored ones, the poor. "From then on my life was to be linked to theirs, their interests were to be mine; I had received a call, a vocation, a direction to my life."[34]

This feeling of identification, this sensibility and this yearning for a loving proximity to the poor grew as her Christian mysticism and vocation grew. Of her first experience in prison as a young adult, she said: "When I first wrote of these experiences I wrote even more strongly of my identification with those around me. I was that mother whose child had been raped and slain. I was the mother who had borne the monster who had done it. I was even that monster, feeling in my own breast every abomination."[35]

All this says a lot about her sense of belonging, which is one of the identifying signs of her mysticism: to feel completely at home in the midst of the least of the earth, and to feel that her place was wherever the poor were found. There she must be and remain, because it was there that God wanted her to be, and where she felt more lovingly united with God.

Dorothy Day's social sensibility had features extremely relevant to the current moment. Her level of consciousness was ahead of her time. Her love for the poor never showed any assistencialist or alienating tendencies. It was always very clear to her that it was necessary to be with the poor, but constantly struggling against poverty. For her, assistencialist charity was

32. Forest, "The Living Legacy of Dorothy Day."
33. *The Long Loneliness*, 40.
34. Ibid., 37.
35. Ibid., 78.

never sufficient. It was not enough to assist the victims of social injustice. One must also, and inseparably, work to attack and destroy the causes of social disorder.

This thought came to her constantly, as she contemplated those miserable conditions and even the resources made available by the government and by the church to remedy them. For instance, she discovered that there were day nurseries where working mothers could leave their children. "But," she asked, "why didn't fathers get money enough to take care of their families so that mothers would not have to go out to work?"[36]

Her sensibility felt deeply touched, awakened, and challenged by questions such as these. And her response was clearly inspired by the gospel, and was not purely intellectual or materialistic. "Where," she asked, "were the saints to try to change the social order, not just to minister to the slaves but to do away with slavery?"[37]

Issues such as justice and the transformation of social structures—considered by the church of her youth as alien to the search for individual salvation through spiritual growth, seen as separate from responsibility for the organization of the world—had always preoccupied her. It is not enough to fight against the effects of poverty. Poverty is an evil and must be extirpated. For this, society must be transformed from its roots. These reflections show that Dorothy Day, in living out her mysticism, received from God an inspiration and knowledge which put her ahead of the most advanced Catholic thought of her time.

These reflections, which are multiplied throughout all her writings, show her to be a pioneer of the movements that emerged shortly thereafter in the church. For instance, the consciousness of social sin and of the need for structural solutions instead of simple palliatives is very present in Liberation Theology, which erupted forcefully in the Latin American church of the 1970s. Beyond her acute criticism, with clear Marxist elements, Dorothy Day always had a deep sense of the Grace of God and of gratitude for God's love as the source of all the good that human beings are capable of practicing in this world. Her social sensibility was inseparable from her immense spiritual sensibility.

Spiritual Sensibility

It must be said that Dorothy Day had a deep spiritual sensibility even before her conversion and baptism in the Catholic Church. Her stories of how she

36. Ibid., 70.
37. Ibid.

felt an inner urge to praise God, in which she affirmed that worship is the deepest and the most beautiful act that a human being can perform, are very moving.[38]

What Dorothy Day really desired was to bring about a revolution of the heart. Furthermore, she believed that the only true revolution is born in a converted heart, touched by divine grace. That was her experience, and it was the only experience she considered worth communicating to those who approached her.

In the Catholic Worker Movement, Dorothy lived a life of fidelity to the revelation recorded in the Scriptures, practicing voluntary and radical poverty[39] and dedicating herself to works of mercy and to the struggle for justice and peace. Her pacifism is one of the strongest characteristics of her mysticism and her militancy. She wrote important texts denouncing every kind of war and violence as radically contrary to the gospel.[40] It can be said that she radically lived out and practiced what Pope Paul VI so strongly expressed in his 1974 encyclical *Populorum Progressio*: that justice and peace go hand in hand.[41]

Many of the positions that she embraced, risking her physical integrity and her life, were prophetic and revolutionary, but they always emanated from the heart of the gospel and from the examples of saints such as Saint Francis of Assisi and Saint Thérèse of Lisieux.[42] Throughout her long life Dorothy Day was militant and an activist, but always found her source in the gospel of Jesus.

She understood her action as the fruit of God's action in her interior. This is why, in her mature years, she engaged in many spiritual retreats, and emphasized the importance of both daily prayer and sacramental living for the consistent growth of a Christian life. Passionate about the project of the kingdom of God as announced and proposed by Jesus of Nazareth, Dorothy Day was, since the beginning of her conversion, increasingly and

---

38. See Forest, "Dorothy Day Servant of God."

39. She wore clothes donated to the poor whom she attended, sometimes belonging to sick paupers who died in public hospitals. See her own comment on the smell that remains in such clothes, in Miller, *All Is Grace*, 104.

40. See the numerous texts in the *Catholic Worker*, besides other more voluminous essays, letters, and other writings. See the complete collection at http://www.marquette.edu/library/archives.

41. See *Populorum Progressio*, especially no. 32.

42. On the identification of Dorothy Day with Thérèse of Lisieux, See Casarella, "Sisters in Doing the Truth." See also the book on Therèsè written by Dorothy herself: *Therese*.

profoundly conscious of the need to first live out this justice and this peace in her heart, before trying to communicate it to others.

In her book *From Union Square to Rome*, addressed to her brothers and sisters who were communist in belief and praxis—from whom she later separated because of her conversion, but to whom she always felt very close—she writes beautiful words. It is quite surprising to see her courage in defending the primacy of the spiritual over the material:

> I felt this despair when I lay there in jail for fifteen days, contemplating the fundamental misery of human existence, a misery which would remain even if social justice were achieved and a state of utopia prevailed. For you cannot pace the floor of a barred cell, or lie on your back on a hard cot watching a gleam of sunlight travel slowly, oh, so slowly, across the room, without coming to the realization that until the heart and soul of humankind is changed, there is no hope of happiness for us.[43]

Etty Hillesum: A Transfigured Holocaust[44]

> What a strange story it really is, my story: the girl who could not kneel. Or its variation: the girl who learned to pray.
>
> We should be willing to act as balm for all wounds.

In presenting the surprising biography of Etty Hillesum, one must be vigilant against the current inclination to liken her to Edith Stein or to see her as an adult Anne Frank. Likewise, one must guard against the tendency to appropriate as Christian Etty's life and person.[45] Whatever the research about her may have discovered regarding her openness to the truth, whatever her origin and wherever she might be found, Etty Hillesum lived and died as a Jew. Nothing like a religious conversion to Christianity happened in her life. There are no indications of conventional forms of worship or methods of

---

43. Day, *From Union Square to Rome*, 156.

44. See Hillesum, Etty: *The Letters and Diaries of Etty Hillesum, 1941–1943*. (The French version, *Une vie bouleversée, suivi de Lettres de Westerbork*, was used for the original Portuguese version of the current book.)

45. She is certainly not a Christian mystic, but we can safely affirm that she is a mystic. In truth, it is hard to identify Etty Hillesum from the standpoint of religious affiliation. She is not a practicing Jew. Yet she has a great sense of belonging to the Jewish people, as her own life demonstrates. On the other hand, her mysticism unfolds in a climate of absolute freedom before a God who seduces her, conquers her, and takes complete possession of her. It is a *wild* mysticism, of anonymous affiliation, which can be read from any point of view, including the Christian one.

prayer in her biography. She was a Jew who had a profound encounter with God, and from then on chose her own way.[46] Yet it is undeniable that she very frequently read the New Testament, the Gospels, and Saint Augustine.

Like many other European Jews of the first half of the twentieth century, Esther (Etty) lived in a country characterized by a Christian culture. She was born on January 15, 1914, in Middelburg, Holland, where her father, Louis Hillesum, taught classical languages. Her mother, Rebecca Bernstein, was a Russian Jew. In 1924 the family moved to Deventer, where Louis Hillesum assumed the position of director of the Municipal Gymnasium. Esther, or Etty, was the eldest of three children.

Etty left her father's school in 1932. She obtained her first university degree in law at the University of Amsterdam, after which she enrolled in the college of Slavic languages. Eventually, after the beginning of the Second World War, she became interested in psychology and fully immersed herself in its study.

When she moved to Amsterdam to pursue her university education, Etty went to live in the house of Han Wegerif, a sixty-two-year-old widower, with whom she developed a very intimate relationship.[47] She supported herself with a job similar to that of a housekeeper, and also as a language teacher. She taught Russian, the language of her mother. Her diaries recount the reactions of a group which met frequently in Wegerif's house to the growing restrictions imposed on the Jews—an integral part of the project of extermination taking place in that historical moment, of which many of them would be victims. Like others, Etty was not initially aware of what was happening, but became more and more conscious of that reality. In her diary Etty tells of her conflicted feelings regarding her relationship with Wegerif, whom she refers to as "Papa Han," and by whom she became pregnant—a pregnancy which later ended in miscarriage.

Much more important than her encounter with Han Wegerif was her relationship with Julius Spier, the "S." in her diaries and the guru of a group that met to talk, play music, discuss literature, and support each other in those hard times of war.[48] Spier studied with Jung and is known as the founder of psychochirology, the study and classification of the palm prints of the hand. He was the father of two children, but was divorced from his gentile spouse. He had a highly charismatic personality, almost magi-

---

46. See Downey, "A Balm for All Wounds: The Spiritual Legacy of Etty Hillesum."

47. See a brief biographical note regarding Han Wegerif in Hillesum, *Une vie bouleversée*, 946 n. 41.

48. See the biographical details on Julius Spier in numerous notes by the editor of *Une vie bouleversée*: 943 nn. 33 and 35; 945 n. 36; 951 n. 61 (concerning his first wife, from whom he was divorced).

cal. He read palms and made his interpretations with extraordinary charm and clarity, arousing an incredible fascination among the women of his entourage. Etty felt absolutely seduced by this man and became his assistant, intellectual partner, and lover.

Her passionate love for S—who was a man of faith—helped her develop an enormous religious sensibility, which gave her writings a ubiquitous spiritual, even mystical, character. It was S. who taught her to pronounce God's name without constraint, and who also invited her to undertake the journey into the depths of human intimacy and loneliness, where God's presence is awakened and emerges into consciousness. Etty moved toward an ever more intense and consistent conversation with the God she discovered in living out a great human love. And as she devoted herself more frequently and more deeply to prayer, she began to feel graced by very strong experiences.

All this was interrupted, however, when at the height of the persecution of the Jews she took a job as typist for the Jewish Council, which was charged with mediation between the Nazis and the Jews. The Council had been established by the Nazis, with the illusion on the part of the persecuted Jews that through mediation and negotiation, it might be possible for some of them to be spared the worst of fates. But that entity soon turned out to be a weapon in Nazi hands.

After just two weeks with the Council, Etty voluntarily decided to go to the Westerbork camp as a social worker. It was a freely chosen interruption of her life that even offered the opportunity to escape, if she wanted to. Her diaries show that she was convinced that she would be faithful to herself only if she did not abandon those who were in danger—her suffering people—and only if she used her energy to bring life to the life of others, to be a balm for their wounds. The very near future would show that she was not exempt from the fortunes of the people to whom she belonged.

She arrived at Westerbork just when the deportations to Auschwitz were beginning. For more than one hundred thousand Jews, Westerbork was the last stop before Auschwitz-Bierkenau, the dreadful extermination camp in Poland. Between August of 1942 and September of 1943, Etty Hillesum—then twenty-eight years old—used her time making entries in her diary, writing letters, and taking care of the sick in the camp hospital. During this period she traveled to Amsterdam twelve times with official permission, carrying letters, securing the provision of medication for the sick, and bringing back messages. But she had to stay in bed during most of her time in the city, as she was sick and suffering several discomforts. Her health, which had always been fragile, visibly resented the restricted nutritional regime, the prohibition against using transport, and the necessity to take long on walks on foot as the situation required. The last part of her diary was written in Amsterdam, after her first month in Westerbork, and describes the tempestuous sickness and death of Julius Spier. Etty was with him in his last moments, along with her friend Tide (Henny Tidemann). The blow of her beloved man's death was lived out by her with serenity and as part of the pain of that moment. Afterwards she went back to Westerbork, but returned to Amsterdam once again to be hospitalized. Finally, in early June of 1943, she left Amsterdam and went to Westerbork for the last time.

Many details of Etty's personality are fascinating. A young, beautiful, and refined woman, greatly attractive to men, she had even at a young age many boyfriends and a legion of admirers. Extremely intelligent and cultured, with a command of several languages—Dutch, German, French, English, and Russian—she had a deep knowledge of Russian and German literature and was especially passionate about Rilke and Dostoievsky. Refined in her taste, she had a special love for flowers and for well kept, comfortable environments, and she surrounded herself with this refinement and good taste. At the same time she was open to others, and made friends very easily. She dreamed of being a writer and of traveling all over the world, of learning other languages and of becoming familiar with other cultures. Her diaries reflect a preoccupation with perfecting her own writing style, which reached a notable level of growth in the final stages of her life. One of her friends, who was part of her most intimate circle, says that "Etty was like a fairy. She spoke with us and immediately made us relinquish banality."[49]

But it is her nobility of soul and her deep and luminous experience of God which most calls our attention here. In her prime at twenty-nine years of age, and facing the certainty of the final interruption of her life—an enormously frightening situation for anyone—Etty assumed a fully heroic, courageous, and generous attitude. She confronted with extreme courage, and with serene acceptance, her deportation from Westerbork and her anticipated extermination by the Nazis. She ardently desired to give of herself, to offer herself to others, to share her life so that those suffering so much around her could see their suffering relieved and their hunger satiated. On November 30, 1943, the balm which was the life of Etty Hillesum was spilled in the gas chambers and crematory ovens of Auschwitz, in solidarity with her own people and millions of other human beings. And this young life was voluntarily given for all wounds, even those of the persecutors.

Etty Hillesum's wild and hard to define mysticism has some extremely distinctive points which merit emphasis and comment.

---

49. See Dutter, *Etty Hillesum, une voix dans la nuit*.

The Integration of Eros and Agape

Etty was a young, beautiful, and very sensual woman. She was fully aware of her body and of her sexual hunger and thirst. She was very feminine and also extremely independent and free in her choices. Etty lived out deeply the multiple and varied relations she experienced with persons of the opposite sex, even when they resulted in continuous conflicts—as in the case of the widower and older man, Han Wegerif. Or when they produced a super-abundance of intense passion, as in the case of Julius Spier.

Regarding Spier, one can see in her diaries that Etty experienced the whole range of feelings which inwardly move a woman who is deeply in love and not fully confident in the man she loves. Spier's amorous liaisons were not exclusively lavished upon her—the psychological seducer had several captive women at his feet. Many of them were charmed by this older man with clear eyes, gentle hands, and a sensual mouth.[50] And he generously responded to the various passions he aroused, getting emotionally involved with several of his clients and fans. In spite of this, Spier wanted to marry Hertha Levi, a German Jew like himself, who had managed to emigrate to London where she was then living and writing to him frequently. He had promised to marry her some day, and maintained an attitude toward her which he regarded as fidelity, in spite of his many affairs with other women. Etty was very jealous of this woman who was the fiancée of her lover, and contemptuously called her his "little friend" (*Freundin*, in German).[51]

But this does not mean that Etty's enormous and intense capacity for love was confined to the erotic level. The rather uncontrolled and possessive libido of her young years was nothing but the immense fortress of an unquenchable desire, a call to a life of self-giving[52] Like all women of her age, Etty dreamed of sharing her life with a companion who would support and love her, and with whom she could build a future and participate in dreams and projects: ". . . I am able to acknowledge that I am really a very serious person who does not like to make light of love. What I really want is a man for life, and to build something together with him."[53] The desire to share all this love, which she feels in abundance, will come true, but not exactly through marriage and motherhood.

---

50. See the numerous and almost obsessive comments in Etty's diary about Spier's mouth. One can see that he aroused in her an ardent attraction. See the comments on this by Dutter, *Etty Hillesum*.

51. Concerning Hertha Levi, See the editor's note in *Une vie bouleversée*, 951 n. 61.

52. Ducrocq, "Etty Hillesum, une vie bouleversante." The author ends her comment on Etty's last moments with "Etty can now allow herself to be touched by everything."

53. Hillesum, *Etty: The Letters and Diaries*, 33.

One can observe, in reading her diaries, how this intelligent, beautiful, and brilliant young Jewish woman was capable of passing from the immediate pleasures of life to the greatest sacrifices for love and solidarity with her people—all with joy, gratitude, and a deep spiritual consciousness, without any vestige of bitterness. She was capable of finding beauty in the mortal desolation of the concentration camp, and went singing with her family to Auschwitz, appreciating in the midst of the horror of the final solution, of which she was a victim, the beautiful elements of nature such as the flowing water and the perfume of flowers. She managed to feel herself rich and graced, even when forced to confront and bear an unavoidable and unjust death.

Spier was, without doubt, the person who served as the catalyst for her radical spiritual liberation in the midst of the extremely painful restrictions and the sickening confinement she would have to bear. Etty's affective depth was aroused and explored in her relationship with S. He was at once her lover and mystagogue, since he opened her to a relationship with God, who in the end became her only interlocutor. Through him she came to see how suffering, once accepted, does not diminish but rather strengthens life qualitatively. The love between them was at once erotic and contemplative. Spier guided her in her search for what was essential, intensified by the urgency brought about by her consciousness of the cruel destiny reserved for the Jews. It was he who taught her to speak of God without shame, and to talk with God without interruption. It can be seen in her diary and letters that, while the external world surrounding her narrowed (with restrictions, rationing, prisons, deportations and all kinds of suffering), her inner life was infinitely enlarged and widened (through prayer, discipline, self-knowledge, and an ever increasing love for others and for God).

It was also Spier who pointed out to Etty the place where the real battle of life takes place. Faced with the certainty that what the Nazis wanted was the total destruction of the Jews, Etty saw that the demons who inhabit people's inner lives were real forces against which one needed to fight. Spier did not descend to the depths of this deadly fire. He sickened and died before he could be deported. By the time of his death, Etty's mysticism had already taken its full form. It was manifested not in denying historical reality and facts, but in entering the peaks and valleys of reality and transforming them both with a practice illuminated by the profound mysticism which she lived out.

It seems to us that the turning point in Etty Hillesum's spiritual journey was reached on April 30, 1942, when she made the decision to marry Spier so that she could accompany him if he were deported.[54] At that time

---

54. Hillesum, *Une vie bouleversée*, 500–507, at the end of the sixth notebook of the diaries.

she said to herself, to the lawyer she consulted on the practical possibility of her gesture (who warned her of the risks of such an initiative), and to her diary: "Yes, I know, we find ourselves simply with a destiny in place of a life."[55] In those pages, which close the sixth notebook of her diary, Etty develops profound reflections concerning her process of growth during that year, in which she came to know Spier more deeply. She felt mature enough to assume a destiny and all that it entailed: leaving the safety of old Han's protection to embrace a rootless life, cut off from both the past and the future.[56]

With very feminine words, Etty compares this process and its termination with a pregnancy: "Something had matured in me during the past few months, it was there, and all I had to do was to accept it. Then I knew that I would bind my life to his, in a pretend marriage, just to be with him. One day, I would surrender him unharmed to his girlfriend."[57] Etty desired the radicality of a fellowship born of love. Such a fellowship meant sharing the anxiety and pain of the man she loved, sacrificing her personal happiness and her future.

That desire not to be separated from the man she loved, and her wish to give her life for him, would not be fulfilled. Spier would die before Etty could accompany him in the flight that would free him. The destiny for which God had matured Etty Hillesum's heart of flesh, however, was larger than Spier and would bring her to all her people. Etty received Spier's death with resignation. Death was for her the great Mystery of life, to be glimpsed in anticipation, received and revered.[58] She wrote that the eventuality of death was integrated into her life. And she continued, with full dignity:

> My life has, so to speak, been extended by death, by my looking death in the eye and accepting it, by accepting destruction as part of life and no longer wasting my energies on fear of death or the refusal to acknowledge its inevitability. It sounds paradoxical: by excluding death from our life we cannot live a full life, and by admitting death into our life we enlarge and enrich it.[59]

The entry in her diary on the occasion of Spier's death is like a great doxology: "I love people so terribly, because in every human being I love something of You."[60] In loving S. passionately, spontaneously, and honestly,

55. Ibid., 504.

56. Ibid.

57. Hillesum, *Interrupted Life*, 131. ("Girlfriend" was the German *freundin* or "little friend" in the original.)

58. Hillesum, *Une vie bouleversée*, 168.

59. Hillesum, *Interrupted Life*, 155.

60. Hillesum, *Etty: The Letters and Diaries*, 514.

she was loving God, or the One she knew as being God. Eros was not kept exclusively for the beloved "you," but rather became an inclusive love without ceasing to be particular and singular—that of a woman who loves a man in the full meaning of this feeling. After Spier's death she wrote of him, "You were the mediator between God and me, and now you, the mediator, have gone, and my path leads straight to God. . . . And I shall be the mediator for any other soul I can reach."[61]

The destiny for which Etty feels herself maturing was later understood by her as a common fate.[62] She writes, after noting that the day was a very hard one, "We must learn to shoulder our 'common fate.'"[63] The destiny for which Etty Hillesum became mature through the love of Spier and, above all, through the infinite and unconditional love of God, was the destiny of her people, in which she participated without reservation, seeing clearly that there was no place to think of her own individuality while a whole people—her people—was being massacred:

> Everyone who seeks to save himself must surely realize that if he does not go another must take his place. As if it really mattered which of us goes. Ours is now a common destiny, and that is something we must not forget. A very hard day. But I keep finding myself in prayer. And that is something I shall always be able to do, even in the smallest space: pray. And that part of our common destiny that I must shoulder myself; I strap it tightly and firmly to my back, it becomes part of me as I walk through the streets even now.[64]

Etty's love was transfigured into pure agape, into gracious and generous oblation. And this is the love that she will pour over the deported of Westerbork and Auschwitz until the time of her death.

A Thousand-Year-Old Soul and a Long Spiritual Heritage

Etty felt that on her way to meet a hard and painful destiny, her inner life grew beyond her dreams. From the moment she began to experience an intense inner and spiritual life and to observe the motions in her soul, she perceived the wealth she had there. On October 10, 1942, she wrote that the age of the soul is different from that recorded in the registry of births

---

61. Ibid., 516.
62. Ibid., 484.
63. Ibid.
64. Ibid.

and deaths: "One can also be born with a thousand-year-old soul . . ."[65] Spier himself said, when they spoke of the age difference between them (twenty-eight and fifty-five years), "Who can tell whether your soul is not much older than mine?"[66]

Besides this, she felt that she belonged to a long spiritual tradition, that she was one of numerous heirs to a great spiritual patrimony, and promised God and herself that she would "be its faithful guardian" and would share it "as best I can."[67] On July 4, 1942, she wrote,

> A hint of eternity steals through my smallest daily activities and perceptions. I am not alone in my tiredness or sickness or fears, but at one with millions of others from many centuries, and it is all part of life, and yet life is beautiful and meaningful too.[68]

Such were, undoubtedly, her soul and her spiritual tradition, and in these characteristics is found her wisdom "forged out of fire and rock crystal."[69] Her wisdom is full of honesty and the capacity to see the truth in all its nakedness, to support it and carry it without finding in it any discernable comfort. This thousand-year-old soul is like a vast space in which there is room for everything. In observing the gradual transformation of this person and her impressive realization of the divine inhabitation, we are not turning our backs on the historical facts that fell upon her, and to which she responded. The dichotomy of the inner/outer world appears completely alien and distant to this woman who knew the reality she was living through and, above all, expected it and took it upon herself with love and full joy. "Yes, we carry everything within us, God and Heaven and Hell and Earth and Life and Death and all of history."[70]

Besides the Psalms and the Gospels, cited several times in her diary, Saint Augustine, especially the *Confessions*, was among Etty's habitual religious readings. Fascinated by the vivid personality of the bishop of Hippo, she comments, "He is so austere and so fervent. And so full of simple devotion in his love letters to God"—which is what she calls the *Confessions*.[71]

---

65. Ibid., 548.
66. Ibid.
67. Hillesum, *Une vie bouleversée*, 722, entry for September 18, 1942.
68. Hillesum, *Etty: The Letters and Diaries*, 466. See also Remy, "Etty Hillesum et Saint Augustin"; Pleshoyano, "L'heritage spiritual d'Etty Hillesum."
69. Hillesum, *Etty: The Letters and Diaries*, 549.
70. Ibid., 463.
71. Ibid., 546. See also the editor's note in *Une vie bouleversée*, 756.

She adds, "Truly those are the only love letters one ought to write: love letters to God."[72]

Once she learned to deeply pray, to speak directly to God, to tell God of her inner being, Etty Hillesum felt inside herself a deep attraction to the life of prayer, so much so that several times a day she felt an ardent and almost unrestrained desire to withdraw to her room to be sheltered and alone with God. Furthermore, certain monastic hues can be identified in her mystical experience which show that her contemplative vocation was radical and real. In response to a friend who told her that she could not live alone, without a husband and children, she said to herself: "Yes, I could live like that, I might even be able to put up with a bare cell, kneeling for years on a hard floor, and there would still be great and burgeoning life in me, everything that life could offer would be in me."[73]

Her experience of God was completely free, making it difficult to identify it either institutionally or traditionally. In truth, the tradition Etty inherited was the mystical tradition—which belongs to all of humankind—from the time she discovered herself to be finite but inhabited by the Infinite. The words with which she describes the feeling of the presence of God, who lives in her, are truly impressive. For example, she says in the entry of September 16, 1942, "Sometimes, when I least expect it, someone suddenly kneels down in some corner of my being. When I'm out walking or just talking to people. And that someone, the one who kneels down, is myself."[74]

A Thinking Heart and a Balm for Wounds

Whether writing from Amsterdam or from the camp itself, Westerbork is the obsessive subject of Etty's diaries and letters. In her diaries one first sees the journey of a young Jewish woman deeply in love with someone who helps her and allows her to stand on her own two feet, and to speak the name of God without constraint. This speech develops within an uninterrupted dialogue which grows into an ever more involving and ardent passion in Etty's life. It became the "thinking heart of these barracks … the thinking heart of a whole concentration camp."[75]

Etty Hillesum's soul, more than one thousand years old and heir to a long and precious spiritual tradition, found its highest expression at

72. Hillesum, *Etty: The Letters and Diaries*, 546.
73. Ibid., 371.
74. Ibid., 516.
75. Ibid., 543, entry for September 15, 1942, at the beginning of the eleventh and final notebook.

Westerbork.⁷⁶ She unconditionally put herself at the service of her people. And in spite of this, her desire increased incessantly in a manner reminiscent of canonized saints such as Saint Thérèse of the Child Jesus and Edith Stein, as well as of contemporary and heterodox mystics such as Simone Weil. The similarity between the desires of the young Jew Etty and the young Carmelite Thérèse Martin is quite evident. Westerbork was scarcely enough for her. It was a microcosm from which her compassionate heart and her desire to give reached the limits of the universe. On October 2, 1942 Etty writes,

> I want to be sent to every one of the camps that lie scattered all over Europe, I want to be at every front, I don't ever want to be what they call "safe," I want to be there, I want to fraternize with all my so-called enemies, I want to understand what is happening, and share my knowledge with as many as I can possibly reach—and I can, if You will only let me get healthy, oh Lord!⁷⁷

And she continues, in the words of Saint Paul in 1 Cor 13, "And what good is it all if I have not love?"⁷⁸

---

76. Hillesum, *Une vie bouleversée*, 728 and 733.

77. Hillesum, *Etty: The Letters and Diaries*, 541.

78. Ibid. Saint Thérèse had written very similar words in her diary a century earlier: "My ardent desire for myself was an authentic martyrdom. I went, then, to the letters of Saint Paul to see if I could find a response. My eyes fell by chance on chapters twelve and thirteen of the First Epistle to the Corinthians. In the first of these, I read that not everyone can be at once apostles, prophets, doctors, and that the Church consists of several members; the eyes cannot at the same time be hands. A clear response, no doubt, but not able to satisfy my desire and give me peace. I persevered in reading without discouragement and found this sublime phrase: 'Strive for the greater gifts. And I will show you a still more excellent way' (1 Cor 12:31). The Apostle makes clear that the best gifts are nothing without charity, and this charity is the most excellent way which surely leads to God. At last I found rest.

In considering the mystical body of the Church, I did not find myself in any one of the members listed by Saint Paul, but, on the contrary, I wanted to see myself in all of them. Charity gave me the axis of my vocation. I understood that the Church has a body composed of various members and that in this body the necessary and noblest member cannot be absent: I understood that the Church has a heart, and this heart is inflamed with love. I understood that the members of the Church are impelled to act by a unique love, such that if it is extinguished, the apostles would no longer proclaim the Gospel, the martyrs would no longer shed their blood. I perceived and acknowledged that love includes in itself all vocations, that love is all, embraces all times and places, in a word, love is eternal.

Then, delirious with joy, I exclaimed: Oh Jesus, my love, I finally found my vocation: my vocation is love. Yes, I found my place in the Church, you gave me this place, my God. In the heart of the Church, my mother, I will be love, and in this way I will be everything, and my desire will be fulfilled." Thérèse de Lisieux, *Story of a Soul*, 58–59.

Spiritually free as always, she did not hesitate to use words that, even more than Christian, are eucharistic—but are they not the patrimony of all humankind?—to express her desires at the end of her last diary entry, dated October 13, 1942: "I have broken my body like bread and shared it.... And why not, they were hungry and had gone without for so long."[79] She concludes her diary with the words: "We should be willing to act as a balm for all wounds."[80] From then on she only wrote some letters to friends who had remained behind. She devoted herself to showering the love which filled her heart upon all who were suffering in the camp, and later during their transport to Auschwitz and in the extermination camp itself.

As the inner life of Etty Hillesum grew, revealing and manifesting this God with whom she entered into an uninterrupted dialogue, one can witness in her writings the gradual overcoming of her inclination to find comfort and relief in illusions, fantasies, satisfactions, and immediate sensations as she proceeds toward the eternal ideals or truths taught her by God through the mediation of the hardest reality. From time to time she tells God that the lessons are hard to learn, and that she wants to be a good pupil of what God teaches her in her heart, things she never dreamed of learning: "Your lessons are hard, my God, let me be your good and patient pupil."[81] She feels herself inserted deeply into the hard reality which she must live out, profoundly relating to concrete and particular facts, to individual persons, and to encounters and events. She gradually accepts her extremely limited situation in life, and this acceptance transforms her. This progressive self-acceptance develops to such a degree that she perceives dwelling within herself another—God—whose presence allows her to live out this transformative process. Bathed by the Grace of this other, she looks upon life with resolve and recognizes that one must accept things as they are. And she asks God to let her accept the sufferings sent to her by God, not those she chooses.[82]

Etty Hillesum refused to remain in a mood of disappointment and despair regarding her own life and that of others. As an intelligent person and a writer aware of reality, she turned her attention to those responsible for the

---

79. Hillesum, *Etty: The Letters and Diaries*, 549. One cannot avoid comparing Etty Hillesum's experience with that of another twentieth-century mystic, also Jewish: Simone Weil. In London, unable to cross into occupied France, Weil wrote what has been called "the terrible prayer," in which she says, "Father, in the name of Christ, grant me this ..." And what she asked for, and what was granted, was that nothing of hers should remain, but all should be completely distributed to others.

80. Ibid., 550.

81. Hillesum, *Une vie bouleversée*, 722.

82. Hillesum, *Etty: The Letters and Diaries*, 538.

destruction of herself and her people, and with acute discernment described their cowardice and temerity masquerading as bravery and power. The fact that she accepted what was happening around her did not mean that she painted it in illusory colors. On the contrary, she nipped the illusions in the bud. She saw clearly through the self-deception through which the Nazis were blinded by the madness of an insane dictator and system. It was the Nazis themselves who were imprisoned by barbed wire fences. Not their prisoners.

In this young woman there was a complete absence of artificial posturing or a deceptive vision of things. Her vision developed amidst the most grotesque and dehumanizing circumstances. And in this painful and negative scenario she clearly saw that the Germans planned the systematic extermination of her people. Yet she held that "if there were only one decent German, then . . . because of that one decent German it is wrong to pour hatred over an entire people."[83] And "despite all the suffering and injustice I cannot hate others."[84]

Her vision of human nature can properly be described as radically altruistic. In spite of the darkness and disintegration around her, she believed that it is always possible to find meaning and beauty. "Even if we are consigned to hell, let us go there as gracefully as we can."[85] If we accept our own nature and things as they really are, we can have confidence in the trustworthiness of life and death in their own terms.

A Suffering to Be Embraced and Never Forgotten or Rejected

Etty poured out her life in the service of others and in sacrifice to them, and in the desire to die in solidarity with the victims. She knew that those around her, whether victims or oppressors, did not accept the facts of their existence, reneged on their destiny, and betrayed the beauty and meaning of life. She did not blame God for the disintegration and destruction of her people, but rather human beings. Looking reality in the face, and knowing what was in store for her and her family, she tirelessly insisted that meaning and beauty can be found even in the worst situations.

Above all, she felt at one with the share of suffering reserved for her people at that historical moment, from which she did not wish to be either

---

83. Ibid., 18. See also *Une vie bouleversée*, 648. Here, upon hearing a friend tell of a noble gesture by a German soldier, Etty says that all should pray for him.

84. Ibid., 259.

85. Ibid., 460–61.

excluded or released. She confided her feelings to her diary a year before her departure to Auschwitz:

> During our walk ... I also knew that a time would come when there would be nothing like that and all our walks would end in some barracks. I knew this while we were walking, knew it would be true not only for myself but also for all the others, and I accepted that too.[86]

In Etty's vision of the human being, suffering is a central theme, and this she learned to embrace when she embraced S. "Through suffering I have learned that we must share our love with the whole of creation."[87] "Suffering is an art. It is possible to suffer with dignity or without. But suffering, like death, is part of life."[88] In her life, Etty learned the art of suffering, which fostered compassion born of a fragile, trembling, but thinking heart, faced with of the enormity of her people's suffering.

Facing the muddiness and the unending deportations from Westerbork to Auschwitz, she wrote: "I am in a strange state of mournful contentment."[89] "There is room for everything in a single life. For belief in God and for a miserable end. . . . It is a question of living life from minute to minute and taking suffering into the bargain."[90] Struggling not to flee from the reality presented to her, she emotionally implores God: "I shall have to learn this lesson, too, and it will be the most difficult of all: 'Oh God, to bear the suffering you have imposed on me and not just the suffering I have chosen for myself.'"[91]

Etty Hillesum saw her own soul as a battlefield on which the great dramas of history were disputed: "I feel like a small battlefield, in which the problems, or some of the problems, of our time are being fought out. All one can hope to do is to keep oneself humbly available, to allow oneself to be a battlefield."[92]

Her dignity before the suffering yet to come is expressed in estimable and impressive words: "Of course, it is our complete destruction they want! But let us bear it with grace."[93] In the midst of her terrible suffering and

---

86. Ibid., 466.
87. Ibid., 442.
88. Hillesum, *Une vie bouleversée*, 641.
89. Hillesum, *Etty: The Letters and Diaries*, 611, letter to Han Wegerif and others.
90. Ibid., 460.
91. Ibid., 538, entry for October 2, 1942.
92. Ibid., 63.
93. Ibid., 542.

that of the acquaintances she comes to know every minute of every day, she feels deeply loved.

A Compulsion to Kneel

Two focal points help us understand Etty's relationship with God: her compulsion to kneel and the content of her more intriguing prayers. She herself says that hers is the story of a girl who learned to kneel, and thus learned to pray.[94] Even more than her reading (of the Gospel of Matthew, of Saint Augustine, or of Rilke), having to kneel to learn to pray—not a common feature of prayer in the Judaic tradition—was evidence of her relationship with God. From time to time her diary tells of occasions in her gradual adoption of the kneeling position for prayer: in the bathroom; on a cocoanut fiber carpet; in the corner of a room, near a window, and walking in the street, among many other situations. She suggests that the act of kneeling is more intimate than the intimacies of her sexual and love life.[95] And this posture is the sign of her surrender, of her consent to the Mystery which irresistibly takes possession of her person.[96]

Her growing consciousness that she can pray in any place—whether behind a barbed wire fence or in a room in Amsterdam—is very instructive. As she grows in the awareness that she can pray wherever she goes, she describes her desire to inwardly kneel, a kind of internal posture that she assumed regularly and with increasing frequency. She knelt before God, who is the Saint of Israel, although she does not call God by this name. This was an inner prostration without words or images, in the depth of her soul, before the One who must there be experienced, discerned, thanked, and praised. Etty's body, so sensitive and open to everything, felt the desire to kneel as a true and complete reconfiguration of her whole person, as she described it on April 3, 1942:

> A desire to kneel down sometimes pulses through my body, or rather it is as if my body had been meant and made for the act of kneeling. Sometimes, in moments of deep gratitude, kneeling down becomes an overwhelming urge . . . a gesture embedded in my body, needing to be expressed.[97]

---

94. Ibid., 547.

95. Ibid: "That is my most intimate gesture, more intimate even than being with a man."

96. See the comments of Bériault, *Etty Hillesum*, 80–81.

97. Hillesum, *Etty: The Letters and Diaries*, 320.

This gesture would be of great comfort to her in the difficult days she knows she must face. She writes on October 10 of the same year,

> When the turmoil becomes too great and I am completely at my wits end, then I still have folded hands and bended knee. A posture that is not handed down from generation to generation with us Jews. I have had to learn it the hard way. It is my most precious inheritance from the man whose name I have almost forgotten but whose best part has become a constituent of my own life.[98]

This God before whom Etty Hillesum kneels is not the God of conventional theology. In some of her most inspired and inspirational prayers, Etty promises to take care of God, to protect the place where God lives within her. God is seen as unable to do anything about the circumstances and sufferings she is living through, or about the fate of the Jews. God cannot help her, so she will help God. "I shall merely try to help God as best I can, and if I succeed in doing that, then I shall be of use to others as well."[99]

God is not accountable to us for historical events. We are accountable to God for the ways in which we have betrayed the divine gift and God's presence in it. Etty lived with an undeniable sense of God's proximity. The great and only Holy Mystery, present in the heart of all creation and active in history, must be protected and cared for in the depths of the soul, because it is fragile and crushes no one under the weight of its omnipotence. Etty's most significant insight relates to the vulnerability of divine life. Yet she feels the presence of this fragile God as loving protection over her. The more the clutches of the Nazis close around her future and destiny, the more she feels protected and caressed in God's loving arms. "I don't feel in anybody's clutches; I feel safe in God's arms."[100]

"And if God does not help me to go on," she says, "then I shall have to help God."[101] The vulnerability of this God—of this God who needs help and is nevertheless her only interlocutor in the midst of the hell in which she lives—is the hinge that keeps together the several ambiguities and paradoxes of her interrupted life, the vital center of the ardent love and strength that bursts from her like fire.

---

98. Ibid., 547.
99. Ibid., 485.
100. Ibid., 487.
101. Ibid., 484.

A Lily of the Field in the Midst of the Darkness of Evil

At a certain moment very near the end of her life, on September 22, 1942, Etty Hillesum expressed a wish: "I would love to be like the lilies of the field. Someone who managed to read this age correctly would surely have learned just this: to be like a lily of the field."[102] Etty is certainly referring to Matthew 6, in which Jesus teaches the disciples the gospel's secret to freedom: to be like the lilies of the field, which neither toil nor spin, but have a beauty and splendor greater than that of Solomon in all his glory; or like the birds of the air, which neither sow nor reap, yet are fed by their heavenly Father. Jesus' conclusion is logical: if God so clothes the flowers of the field, and so feeds the birds of the air, then how will God treat the human being, God's most beloved creature?

Etty knows this secret, because none other than her God revealed it to her. It is enough to allow oneself to be, and to trust in the infinite goodness of God, who may not respond to all our requests but who fulfills all God's promises in us.[103] The fulfillment of these promises can be seen in the fact that God accompanies and supports humankind in the midst of trials and tribulations, so that the darkness will not vanquish the light.[104]

Etty trusts this weak and impotent God, who suffers with the victim instead of annihilating the executioner. She knows there is little that God "can do about our circumstances, about our lives."[105] More and more she allows herself to be taken over by the love of this God. For this she understands that she has to put aside big words and grandiloquent attitudes. "We have to become as simple and as wordless as the growing corn or the falling rain. We must just *be*."[106]

Etty's big black eyes were closed at Auschwitz in August 1943. But her words and witness still endure today. Her writings are among the most profound readings and interpretations ever made of that time of darkness and banality initiated by the evil in action that was the Nazi genocide in Europe. From her pen, on July 27, 1942—when, already certain of the fate in store for her, she began to prepare her knapsack to take to Westerbork—came this declaration: "And yet there must be someone to live through it all and bear

---

102. Ibid., 526.

103. See the similarity between Etty's prayer and that of the Protestant Christian Dietrich Bonhoeffer, who wrote it in prison before being hanged by the Nazis: "Prayers in Time of Distress," *Letters and Papers from Prison*, 142–43.

104. See Bériault, *Etty Hillesum*, 120.

105. Hillesum, *Etty: The Letters and Diaries*, 488, entry for July 12, 1942.

106. Ibid., 483, entry for July 9, 1942.

witness to the fact that God lived, even in these times. And why should I not be that witness?"[107]

Etty Hillesum's witness reverberates ever more eloquently today in the ears of our contemporaries. As a mystic of the twentieth century, she teaches us more and more to care for the God discovered within each of us, to enable us to face the difficulties presented by reality, and to compassionately take the pain of others upon our fragile shoulders and make it our own, and help God to redeem it.[108]

Egide van Broeckhoven:[109] Intimacy with God and with the Poor

> Love is only happy when it ventures into unexplored territory. God is the land we have not yet explored: our own inner life; for He is the ultimate Interior, the unfathomable Depth. Lord, teach me to discover in every man the unexplored territory which is Yourself. In order to venture into unexplored territory, one must leave behind the lands he knows.
>
> The place where we find God, the burning bush, is the world of today carrying in its heart all these friendships, this ardent love: this is the place where we find God.

Egide was an obscure young Jesuit, a worker priest whose tragic death in Brussels, on December 28, 1967, did not go unnoticed by the Belgian press of that time. Those who knew him were aware that his work in the factory and his brutal death were the culmination of a passionate search for God. His fidelity to this search led him, not to the silent seclusion of the Carthusian order to which he had felt attracted since his early years, but toward the burning bush of the great city, in a poor neighborhood near the railroad station, inhabited by foreign workers.[110]

Egide van Broeckhoven was born in Antwerp on December 22, 1933. His mother died a few days after his birth, on December 28 of the same year. He was educated by adoptive parents in Schilde, his aunt and uncle, for whom he always held enormous affection and gratitude. He went to

---

107. Ibid., 506.

108. Hillesum, *Une vie bouleversée*, 666 and 703.

109. We basically follow Egide's diary, published in French under the title *Journal spirituel d'un jésuite en usine*. The title in the original Flemish is *Dagboek van de vriendschap* (1971). In Portuguese there is an abbreviated version of the diary with the title *Diário da amizade* (São Paulo: Loyola, 1978).

110. See *Journal spirituel*, 7.

secondary school at the Saint Francis Xavier College in Antwerp. On September 7, 1950, he entered the Jesuit novitiate in Tronchiennes, Belgium. After two years as a novice, he continued with classical studies for three years. From 1955 to 1958 he studied philosophy at a Jesuit educational institution in Louvain, and from 1958 to 1960 he pursued university studies. After obtaining a master's degree in classical philology in July, 1959, he requested and obtained permission to take a course in the mathematical and physical sciences, but failed his examinations in 1960.

From 1960 to 1961 he was sent by his superiors to teach Latin at the Saint John Berchmans College in Brussels, and from 1961 to 1965 he studied theology at the Jesuit seminary in Heverlee-Louvain. He was ordained as a priest on August 8, 1964. The key period in Egide's short life was from August 1965 to December 1967. During that time he labored as a worker priest in Anderlecht, Brussels, in four different factories, interrupted from September to December 1966 by a spiritual retreat, his third probation, in Tronchiennes.[111] On December 28, 1967, he was killed in an industrial accident and died right there, in the factory. He was thirty-four years old.

The available material about his personal life and his mysticism is scarce. There are only his diary and a few articles in journals specializing in theology or spirituality. Nevertheless, the spiritual narrative of this young Jesuit attracted the attention of theologians such as Hans Urs von Balthasar[112] for the authenticity and quality of his experience of God, which he presented at a crucial moment in the twentieth century. At this time, after the Second Vatican Council, Catholic religious life was going through profound changes, raising suspicions in the church hierarchy of secularization and disparagement of its identity.

The diary covers only the last ten years of Egide's life. It begins in April 1958 and continues until the eve of his death. It is basically what its title indicates: a spiritual diary, in which the author records what he calls "his lights, his desires, and his experiences"—in other words, the movements of the Spirit of God within him, the divine call to which he feels compelled to respond.

---

111. The third probation is the last stage in the formative life of a Jesuit, which lasts for about fifteen years. It is a period of six months in which the Jesuit—usually already ordained as a priest and having been involved in pastoral work for several years—undertakes once again the complete *Spiritual Exercises* for thirty days, studies the Constitutions of the Society, engages in pastoral experiences in hospitals and peoples' communities, etc. At the end of this period he is at last prepared to take the perpetual and solemn final vows of his profession in the Society of Jesus.

112. See the commentary by Balthasar below.

The central theme of this diary—and, we dare say, of Egide's life—is friendship. Friendship with God and, inseparably, friendship with people, together in a harmonious and vital whole. Egide lives out the action of God within himself, amid his ongoing activities: studies, an active apostolate, everyday life, and above all friendship, meetings, and contacts with all those who cross his path. There appears in his diary an endless parade of names and faces, a complete list of which would take several pages, although he writes only their first names and often only their initials. Through these people Egide meets the God of his love, and for this he constantly gives thanks.

The unity of Egide's life was, therefore, brought about by the intimate conjunction of three realities: his experience of God, his experience of friendship, and his apostolic work. Since his intention (made explicit in his diary) was to write a book on friendship,[113] his notes are not uncoordinated, but are organized by the author with the expectation that this project would come to light. On the eve of his death he was occupied with planning for this book, which was never to be written.

Attracted since his youth to the monastical and contemplative life, at the age of sixteen Egide paradoxically joined the Society of Jesus, an eminently active and apostolic order, with a calling to be present at the frontiers of modernity. There, not succumbing to the continuous pull arriving in his soul from the Carthusian way of life, Egide came to feel perfectly in harmony with the Jesuit apostolic and contemplative life in action, and to occupy himself constantly with understanding and living out his whole life as a conscious participant in God's Trinitarian movements as an extension of the incarnation of God in this world. This was without doubt a result of the formation he had received as a novice in the Society, but was also due to his assiduous reading of mystics such as John of the Cross, then of the Flemish mystics Hadewijch and Ruusbroec, and finally of Teilhard de Chardin.

Egide had received, and he lived out, the gift of assimilating deeply the brilliant intuitions of the great mystics, and of applying them to ordinary life without losing their Transcendent emphasis. In concrete and everyday reality, in casual encounters with person after person, with his factory co-workers and with his neighbors, Egide was humbly aware of being—as he, moved to tears, called himself—"a Teilhard of friendship,"[114] showing his friends, men and women, that the same infinite depths that the great

---

113. See *Journal spirituel*, entry for December 29, 1963.
114. Ibid., 16.

Teilhard discovered in cosmic reality are neither less intensely present nor less real in every tie of friendship.[115]

In this obscure, short, but extremely intense life, there are noteworthy elements that we think can throw light on the search for God by our contemporaries today.

Intimacy with God: From the Carthusian Order to the Society of Jesus and the Factory

It was precisely his fidelity to the search for God, which never ceased to disquiet and move him intimately, that led this young mystic not to the silent Carthusian retreat—as had been his wish since his earliest youth and as he had felt called since the beginning of his religious vocation—but to the Society of Jesus, a missionary order par excellence, characterized by obedience and the availability to go to any place or situation where one might be sent by the Holy Spirit through the mediation of the religious superiors.

In living in the Society, Egide attests that he is accomplishing the will of God, given that his intense and ardent mystical life continues to grow uninterruptedly, in spite of his having to go through long periods of purification and dark nights of the soul. In entering the Society of Jesus, Egide had to make a real choice: to renounce a life of pure contemplation in order to embrace a kind of life which, once effectively chosen, still seemed to him difficult to reconcile with what he believed to be Ignatian spirituality.

While in the Society of Jesus, Egide felt nostalgic for the radically contemplative Carthusian vocation. Statements he heard during his formative years, such as "Our mysticism rests upon our apostolate," made him feel inside that the truth was just the opposite: "I do not believe I can be an apostle who lives a life of prayer on the side; I can only be a man of prayer and a contemplative, led by his contemplation toward an ever more intense apostolate."[116] But his loving heart was always attentive and open to divine inspiration. Egide understood that the sacrifice demanded of him at that moment was not simply to renounce the contemplative life, but to decide to live it in an explicit and radical way, in union with "the Trinitarian love which comes to meet all men." As his commentator and biographer Georges Neefs says, "Egide renounces the operation in his life of a movement of introspection in God and in his Transcendence, in order to insert himself into

---

115. Ibid.

116. Ibid., 117; *Journal de l'amitié*, 52. See the exegesis of this fundamental text of Egide in Neefs, "Portrait d'un 'contemplatif dans l'action,'" 105.

the exiting movement through which the Trinitarian and transcendent God manifests his immanence in this world."[117]

During his formative years Egide lived out this great love, which attracted him irresistibly to ever more profound prayer and to friendship and relations with his fellow Jesuits. He experienced, in its deepest dimension, the attraction of God, more intimate than himself, but also—and we almost could say above all—at the ultimate depth of the others. For instance, in his diary we find numerous allusions to a deep friendship of many years with a fellow Jesuit. In the narrative he relates that this experience is always and only the mystical invasion of friendship and the progressive discovery of the streams of divine love on which this friendship carries him.[118]

When he later felt called to walk toward the burning bush of the great metropolis, in a poor neighborhood near the train station where foreign immigrants lived, he did not vacillate and used all means to respond to this call.[119] There, among the poor, identifying with them, living out a deep friendship for them, Egide passed the last moments of his existence.

Intimacy with Others: Friendship

Throughout Egide's spiritual diary, friendship appears as a key concept. The unity of the life of this young religious is found in the intimate conjunction of three realities: his passionate and loving experience of God, his experience of friendship, and his apostolic work. Since he intended—as he himself explained—to write a book on friendship,[120] his notes are not confused and jumbled, but rather organized by the author himself with the hope that this work will come to light and be of help to others. Until the day before his death we can find him occupied in organizing his future book, which would never be finished.

Through this life story breathes the fresh air of a holiness born of friendship with God and with others, so much so that Hans Urs von Balthasar himself praised the work of the young Egide as the most authentic

---

117. Neefs, "Portrait d'un 'contemplatif dans l'action,'" 105.
118. Ibid., 106.
119. See *Journal spirituel*, 7.
120. See *Journal spirituel*, entry for December 29, 1963.

Stories and Experiences of Love

he had ever seen.[121] Marcel Legaut said of him: "The church needs men like this in order to become young."[122]

Concerning friendship with God and human life, which he saw as a creation of God, Egide recorded some extremely inspired testimonials in his diary, beginning in his early youth:

> The friend is like a house made of diamond: within there shines a bright light of great beauty. But one cannot get in without breaking down the outer wall: this is a painful operation also for him who breaks it down, for he wounds himself as well. But once the wall is down, the light inside, like a red flame, shines with a new brightness. He will break down several walls, one after the other, and he will wound himself more and more deeply. But he does not act like one who casually breaks a beautiful vase and then walks away without caring in the least. His wounds grow deeper and deeper, until he comes to the last wall; he already senses the light through it, and it seems to him that if he breaks through the wall, the light will go out. And yet he must break down this last wall too: this is the price he has to pay in order to find the deepest, most intimate center of the friend, the divine Trinity. My friend is like the tender dawn of the eternal love of God. All the happiness of heaven consists in this love.[123]

Egide—always graced with deep and sensitive experiences of God—therefore felt called to a new ecstasy. He felt called to pass from the ecstasy of intimacy with God to the ecstasy of relationship with the other, his neighbor, his brother, his friend. In the Society of Jesus, without setting aside the continuous inner calls which would bring him nearer to the Carthusian life, he was inwardly led through pastures known to God, although not to himself. Submissively and lucidly he allowed himself to be led.

The chastity to which he was committed by the religious vows which consecrated him played an important role in the mysticism of friendship that Egide lived out and deepened throughout his life. In order to come closer to people, he understood that an abstinence from Eros—which is not only restriction, but transfiguration—makes a great deal of sense. For him

---

121. Ibid., 15. Balthasar, in a letter of April 20, 1971, addressed to Georges Neefs, says, "I cannot point out to you in detail the reason for my interest, but the general impression is of an authenticity of such perfect accuracy and lucidity, that in the murky waters of the theological and spiritual journalism of the current time, one feels immediately touched." Neefs, "Portrait d'un 'contemplatif dans l'action.'"

122. Cited in *Journal spirituel*, 15.

123. Ibid., 23.

the path of chastity passes through friendship with God and with the human being.[124] And this friendship has very particular characteristics:

> It seeks what is deepest in the other person and is ready to sacrifice anything, just to reach this depth. Friendship seeks the other inasmuch as he is in God, inasmuch as his inner life dwells in the Inner Life of God. In this way, friendship is hidden in the mystery of love which is God.[125]

Clearly, Egide was not naive. He knew that human beings are called by God with all the manifestations of their humanity, including erotism, which is a model for our desire for God.[126] From the slow purification of human Eros, which seeks to become ever more free in order to be able to deliver itself more fully to God and to others, is born the divine Eros, which is like a torrent of grace. But it always demands self-denial and sacrifices. As Egide himself says in his diary: "He who seeks God must be ready even to lose Love. On this expedition one is alone; the seeker for God ventures far beyond all human love."[127]

Yet he knew—and more than that, he experienced, as can be understood from his words—that human sexuality is not foreign to any intimate and devoted relationship which can develop among persons, even if its objective is only to love, glorify, and serve God. Egide was not afraid to walk into a greater union with God through human reality with all its consequences, utilizing to that end the very strengths of his libido, instead of setting them aside:

> For one who lives in chastity, he may well allow himself, in the Eros which takes him to the most intimate depths of a person, an attraction of a sexual kind, on condition that he does not turn in upon himself; for then the sexual element is lived out in itself, and not in a movement of Eros which transcends sexual reality . . . thus he could exert a function of attraction toward the person, without confining himself to an inferior intimacy; in confining himself, he abandons precisely the intimacy of the person himself, in favor of an intimacy which remains beneath the profound dynamism which links it to God.[128]

---

124. See the comment of Meroz in "La vie des amants de Dieu," 45.
125. *Journal spirituel*, 37.
126. See Meroz, "La vie des amants de Dieu," 46, citing Saint John Climacus.
127. *Journal spirituel*, 31.
128. Ibid., 82–83.

Stories and Experiences of Love

Undoubtedly due to his formation in the novitiate of the Society of Jesus, but also thanks to his asiduous reading of the mystics, Egide grew in perfect harmony with the apostolic life of the Jesuits. Just as the founder, Ignatius of Loyola, had wanted for the members of the Society, Egide was truly a contemplative in action, constantly heedful of offering and giving his whole life—through a conscious participation in the movements of the Trinitarian life of God—as an extension of the Mystery of the Incarnation of God in this world.[129]

The liberty of the mystic coexisted in him perfectly well with the obedience and observance of the Jesuit, as he himself says in some beautiful passages in his diary:

> My God, if I cannot call you a friend, then I am left with nothing else. I do not wish to find strength in anything other than having looked at you. Many religious neglect the rules and prescriptions under the pretext that they are trivial, not considering them from the point of view which would allow them to appreciate their real value and their relativity: the point of view of everyone who has a personal and intimate love of God, lived out in an adult and ineffable way.[130]
>
> The aim of the apostolate is to bring people closer to God; in order to bring them closer to God one must be much closer to them; in order to be close to someone, one must be close to God.[131]

The appeal of the cloistered life returned repeatedly to Egide, but little by little he grew in the discovery of the contemplative dimension of Ignatian spirituality within the religious order where he chose to live. And this helped him to definitively choose the space in his life where the Lord called him to live out his love. He writes, at the end of a retreat,

> I saw once again with great clarity the extent to which all my vocational problems find a basic solution in the very essence of the Jesuit vocation: total availability and complete surrender to the will of God, opening ourselves to the purely religious spaces where God can reach us. These spaces are the same ones where the Carthusian finds God, but the form they take is not fixed in a definite configuration; it follows the movements of the Holy

---

129. See all the writings of Saint Ignatius, especially the Constitutions of the Society of Jesus.
130. *Journal spirituel*, 102.
131. Ibid., 106.

Spirit in everything, like a friend ready to follow his friend anywhere, without himself deciding where to go.[132]

The Burning Bush in the Factory: A New Intimacy

As he matured and reconciled himself with his Jesuit calling, Egide grew toward the plenitude of his vocation, characterized by a mysticism of incarnation. Neefs, in the article we have cited, shows that the Grace of the call felt by Egide to reach out to the poorest had been sustained by the charisma of the order itself, since the foundation of the Society. He cites a reflection by Father Nadal on prayer and the apostolate that perfectly and harmoniously applies to the life of the young Flemish Jesuit: "The birth of Christ is the source of an impulse of Grace (the starting point or a 'work') where the prayer of the Society is nourished, and where all the Society's ministries begin."[133]

To be a friend of the poor in order to be friend of all—this is what drove Egide to "descend to meet God" in another burning bush: the life of the poor foreign immigrants in the hard reality of factory workers in Brussels.[134] In his diary he explains his decision as follows:

> Our first duty is not to proclaim the history of salvation sent by God, but first of all to be a bit of that history ourselves. The Church should become in us the tangible reality of God's love for the concrete world of today. Now the only way we can really reach these poor people who are such strangers to the Church, and the only way to love them, is to become like one of them (just as Christ Himself the first of all gave us an example); therefore we must go to work like them, be of no account like them, defended by no one just as they are. . . . This is what motivated Christ to become the least of all men; otherwise, the little ones would never have come to really love Him.[135]

Egide discovered the essence of what would become the heart of his missionary vocation as a Jesuit: an apostolate among the most forgotten and oppressed of human beings.

---

132. *Journal spirituel*, 67–68.

133. *Mon. Hist. S.J., Epist. P. Nadal*, vol. 4, 692, cited by Neefs, "Portrait d'un 'contemplatif dans l'action,'" 107.

134. See Rambla, *Dios, la amistad y los pobres*, 166.

135. *Journal spirituel*, 342–43; *Journal de l'amitié*, 153–54.

> God has led me to understand that my desire to live completely for Him is not to be satisfied in the solitude and renunciation of a Carthusian monastery, but in the decision to go toward those men who are farthest from Him: this seems to be the environment for the contemplative life in which God wishes to place me. And there it seems, in discerning the action of the Spirit in me, that my vocation as a "contemplative in action" is to be found; this touches the central point of what God wanted to make me understand in calling me.[136]

To live out the gospel and the compassion of Jesus Christ for all the poor and suffering, for all the multitudes who are without a pastor, without guidance, and without friendship, was thus what brought Egide to fully immerse himself in the life of the workers. There he further deepened his friendship with God and with the poor, who were then, more then ever, his companions. He himself affirmed: "God tells me: 'Now it is necessary to love without raising more questions. No longer to look to me in any way, but to love, completely free of oneself, which means in a state of love.'"[137] And further: "God was very close to me and wanted to be close, and to remain close in order to encourage me, comfort me, and strengthen me with his Presence. He insisted a second time: no more making a problem of the apostolate; it is enough to love."[138]

Intimacy Configured by Love

During his hard work at the factory, Egide was confronted by the reprimands of the bosses for not having disclosed to them that he was a priest, and he suffered more than one accident, which seriously affected his hands. He received dismissals, humiliations, etc. But in the midst of this hard reality he continued deeply and joyfully living out the experience of friendship: "The place where I meet God, the burning bush, and the world of today with all these friendships in its heart, and this ardent love: this is the place where I meet God."[139]

When he felt the confirmation of the call to a life among the workers, Egide said,

---

136. *Journal spirituel*, 50–51.
137. Ibid., 83.
138. Ibid., 70–71.
139. Ibid., 85.

> Another motive which urged me to take up this life was a great desire for God; and God, I believed, could be found only in the reality of the world of today, preferably among the poorest of the poor. He cannot be found in artificial situations; He is wherever the world is in need of saving; He is certainly there and He lives in the friendship we give one another, but especially in the friendship we receive from the people we go to live with.[140]

A life of such radical kenosis, humiliation, and commitment was a great challenge for Egide. The sacrifices that this new condition of life asked of him were very hard because they were very real. It is impressive how humbly and lovingly Egide perceived and accepted all the hardships waiting for him at the factory. He was aware that whoever has received so much love from God must in turn give more.

> I have had to realize, not without a long and lively struggle, a truth which keeps becoming clearer to me: God has given me, more than he has given others, a great deal of experience with love. God is calling me into the unexplored depths of love where only I will be able to enter, deeper than my friends . . . but not without them; ultimately, God will bring us all together. . . I need to understand how God is calling me farther than my brothers, in order to fulfill my vocation and my mission completely. Then God alone will be my Rock, the Spirit my sole strength, and His Son the first and last Word. God is calling me into a land of loneliness and death, the only place where fulfillment and the encounter with life are found.[141]

Going to the factory, in the midst of the gray and concrete desolation found on the outskirts of the great cities, surrounded by violence, poverty, and exhaustion, as well as facing hard realities, Egide ended his life with death in an industrial accident—a solitary death with no witnesses. He felt in his body and expressed the terrible difficulty he experienced in living and working in such a dechristianized, hopeless, "exhausting and brutish" environment.[142] These words bring to mind the factory diary of another twentieth century mystic, Simone Weil, who said that exhaustion from the work prevented her from thinking, and she felt that if she gave in to this tendency, she might end up not thinking at all.[143] However, with words full of

---

140. *Journal spirituel*, 322-23; *Journal de l'amitié*, 153-54.

141. *Journal de l'amitié*, 77-78.

142. *Journal*, 375-76; *Journal de l'amitié*, 145.

143. See her factory diary in *Oeuvres Completes*, 24, cited by Pétrement, *Vie de Simone Weil*, vol. 2, 22 n. 2.

light and hope, Egide says: "This very concrete dechristianized environment ... is the environment in which I am to live as a contemplative (Carthusian, Trappist). The leap I have to take in order to live in this environment is for me like the leap involved in entering a Carthusian or Trappist monastery: abandon everything, risk everything, sell everything—for God."[144]

The choice to go to the factory, to meet the poor, at last coincided for Egide with his reconciliation to his life as a Jesuit. In the entries of July 1962, he discovers that "Iñigo [Ignatius] pursues and claims him." He finally surrenders completely to the Ignatian vocation:

> The detachment of the Jesuit is, from a certain point of view, more radical and purer than the detachment of the Carthusian: the latter seeks fulfillment in his own detachment, while the Jesuit detaches himself with a view to service, without an explicit preoccupation with fulfillment. . . which does not prevent his detachment from receiving a response of love which fulfills him in the same way.[145]

Egide cries with joy and consolation in meditating on the beauty of his vocation, which comes to him "like an announcement of spring."[146]

In explaining why he decided to move from the life of a professor, or of a spiritual educator in the monastery—toward which his Jesuit mission naturally led him—to go to the factory, and why he feels happy with this life, Egide says:

> Because I have become, very concretely, a friend to all these poor people, these workers, these "little guys" who feel abandoned by the Church and by their pastors; because I have established bonds of friendship with the poorest among them, Muslims, Greek Orthodox, people uprooted from their own traditions—with those nine workers fired last week; and because, through my friendship with these men, I feel united concretely to the whole mass of the poor, the "little guys," the dechristianized; and since this concrete and total friendship is, in my estimation and in my case, the only authentic way—sometimes painful but always very comforting—by which the kingdom of God is growing in this world today: I cannot, I must not go back on my decision to become a worker-priest.[147]

---

144. *Journal spirituel*, 375–76.
145. Ibid., 133–40.
146. Ibid.
147. Ibid., 363.

Egide's path as a mystic, as an intimate friend and lover of God, brought him to understand that he would not find the greatest love in the refuge of the cloister, but rather in the world with all its agitation and conflict, there where men and women, the children of secularization, turn away from God because they have no one to speak to them as a witness to the infinite love which God revealed in God's Son Jesus.[148]

Reproducing in his body and life, and also in his death, the kenotic itinerary of Jesus of Nazareth, the Incarnate Word of God, "who did not regard equality with God as something to be exploited, but emptied himself ... obedient to the point of death—even death on a cross,"[149] Egide narrated with his life what great theologians such as Karl Rahner—also a Jesuit— elaborated as a reflection on the joy of the world: the modern cloister of the contemplative, which was conceived by Ignatius of Loyola at the dawn of modernity, but which God wants to provide to all creatures who open themselves to this experience.[150]

In order to belong only to God one need not run away from the world, even a world from which God appears to be absent. On the contrary, one must immerse oneself more and more in this world, reaching out to all who are lost, hungry, and exiled from comfort and hope. Being with them completely, living their lives, suffering their pain and dying their death—this is the way one marks history with the affirmation that God is love. To follow the itinerary of Jesus, even without explicitly naming it, in the basements and underworlds of the great modern cities, is to live the greatest love. Egide, the young priest dead at thirty-four years of age, continued to teach this to the new generations. And in his wake, the theology of the twentieth century tended more and more toward the option for the poor as the heart of the Gospel.

Many priests, friars, and nuns in Africa, Asia, and Latin America did what Egide did. And many from the First World, from the wealthy continents of Europe and North America, left their prosperous societies to spend their lives among the poor in developing countries. The infinite creativity of the Holy Spirit produced many other Egides, who also experienced the profound and total intimacy with God in the heart of the underworld of the poor.

Another Jesuit, a contemporary of Egide—a Spanish national who spent his whole life in the Caribbean, between the Dominican Republic and Cuba—lived out the same experience and described, with other words, what Egide had already experienced in the 1960s. In his book *Bajar al encuentro*

---

148. See Rambla, *Dios, la amistad y los pobres*, 163ff.
149. See Phil 2:5–11.
150. See Rahner, *La mistica ignaciana de la alegria del mundo*, 313–30.

de Dios,[151] based on his living for five years in the lower class neighborhood of Guachupita, on the outskirts of the capital of the Dominican Republic, Benjamin González Buelta, SJ, writes,

> The religious life created spaces of silence and art to aid the contemplation. We remember cloisters that took years to build, with big blocks of stone on the floor, graceful columns, faces of angels at the top. The signs of faith came to meet the contemplative in niches and on walls. In the marginal neighborhoods we find narrow and irregular little streets where garbage decomposes until the next rain cleans everything... Here also solidarities and fortitude are woven through the lives of those who survive. These are our cloisters. Each person is a temple of God. But it was always easy for man to silence the statues with flowers and lights.[152]

On Christmas Day, 1967, a few days before his death, Egide wrote in his diary, "Giving my life totally and losing it for this world in its most concrete reality."[153] And on the 27th: "Rediscovery of my desires to encounter and reach men in depth,"[154] and "Great consolation meditating on the loss of everything for God (leaving your native land etc.) which is realized in losing your life for the world ('follow me')."[155]

On the 28th an industrial accident took the life of the young worker priest who had discovered in the underworld of the poor, in the modern factory, the burning bush where God speaks to today's world.

Like Jesus Christ, Egide lost his life in a modern crucifixion in the factory, where the machine pulverizes the human being. There he lived and gave testimony to his vocation as a friend of God and a friend of life.

---

151. See González Buelta, *Bajar al encuentro de Dios*.
152. Ibid., 14.
153. *Journal spirituel*, 377.
154. Ibid., 378.
155. Ibid., 363.

Conclusion

AFTER THIS LONG JOURNEY, during which we have tried to understand our epoch and the situation of religion in it, we find that we are living in a moment when the culture is going through deep mutations, when religion is confronting diverse postures, from indifference to atheism. We have seen that experience is, in this situation, the way par excellence for communication and the transmission of values to disenchanted human beings who are thirsty for the Transcendence and Spirit which will give meaning to their lives

We have tried to carefully delineate the concept of experience, and then to apply it theologically to religion. This analysis led us to the mystical experience, which all thinkers, scholars, and believers consider the culmination of the life of faith. This experience of union with God, often accused of alienating the human being, shows itself, on the contrary, to be very fertile and pregnant with value and hope. It is capable of fascinating and seducing the disoriented creature who is swimming in choppy postmodern waters, confronted by an infinity of proposals for self-help and various spiritualities, some of them very superficial.

The whole reflection which we have tried to do (especially as based on the life stories we analyzed) brings us now, at the end of the road, to some conclusions. We do not intend to exhaust the topic, but to modestly point out some clues by which the reflection can continue.

Today's mysticism—above all Christian mysticism—is a countercultural path where the humanization of human beings and the experience which gives meaning to their lives take a direction opposite to that of the society where they live, and to what it conveys as a proposal for happiness.

In a culture of seduced pleasure and sensations, the mystical experience turns away from the self and allows one to be affected by others in their difference, their Otherness and their needs. This path to the encounter with the Otherness of the other's face implies a deep and radical detachment and a rigorous asceticism. It implies choosing the stranger's pain as one's own. It implies being a space where pain can find shelter, and a balm for the wounds of those who cry and moan, just as Etty Hillesum wished to be. Seduced by God, the mystics, defenseless and without a way back, embark upon an adventure in which this seduction leads them to lose themselves in radical communion with the pain of the other, suffered by choice in their own flesh.

In a consumerist culture, propaganda ensures that maximum happiness consists in having more and more, and in promptly discarding all that one has—from things to persons—while always increasing the volatility and speed of the frenetic swallowing of goods and values. Facing this, the mystical experience offers giving, surrendering, and caring for the other, especially for those most deprived of support, those who find themselves unhappy and abandoned. The more deeply the mystics enter into the experience of the Mystery of God, the more they feel called to divest themselves, to cast aside their security, their possessions, and their power, in order to find meaning for their lives in giving while retaining nothing for themselves, and in the poverty which finds peace less in not possessing anything than in tireless and uninterrupted self-giving.

In a culture that proclaims freedom as autonomy, accountable to no one and ruled by its most immediate desires, while cultivating an arrogance of power even at the cost of what belongs to others by right and in fact, the mystical experience is, par excellence, receptive and passive and, above all, aware of its impotence. It is a theopathic experience, which welcomes and receives what is given to it, suffering in itself the presence and action of God but unable to do anything to bring it about. Mysticism thus commends humility and passivity, the action without agency which, according to Simone Weil, is the primordial disposition of every human being. In a culture where power is glorified, the mystical experience teaches that human beings are patient, even as agents, because they are incapable of producing anything at all by themselves, since they are unable to give to themselves the being which makes them exist and which configures their identity.

In a culture where the highest inspiration is to avidly devour everything that is presented, consuming without digesting and immediately moving on to something else, to another person, and so on, the mystical experience teaches that human fulfillment lies in the desire to give of oneself, to dispossess oneself while surrendering oneself to be consumed by the needs of others, to serve them in all their needs, to give of oneself and to eucharistically share oneself with them as nutrition for all.

In a culture which divides society between winners and losers, which teaches that one must pursue success in everything, all the time and by all means, even if in doing so one must eliminate the others, ignoring their desires and needs, the mystical experience teaches that the greatest Grace one can receive is to lose one's own life for the love of others, especially for the neediest: the poor, the unhappy, the helpless, the homeless, the persecuted, and the victims of all kinds of injustice and violence. The mystical experience does not lead to profitable investments, but rather to giving one's own life so that others may have that life which pours abundantly from their union with the Mystery. In a culture where we are taught to profit by commanding others, the mystical experience teaches me to be a hostage to others, a hostage to the face of the other which turns towards me and establishes me as a subject. Instead of "I think," "I can," "I do," "I wish," the speech of the mystic is declined in the accusative and can only utter with immense gratitude, "Here I am!"

In an unjust culture, where resources are distributed according to selfish and totalitarian manipulation by some to the detriment of others, where the well-being of some is achieved at the price of the progressive and systematic impoverishment of many, the mystical experience teaches one to practice justice and to live according its parameters—not a retributive justice which gives to each what is deserved, but rather, in imitation of God, a restorative justice which gives to others what they need in order to live. And for this justice to be done, the mystics pay the price with their own persons, exposing and risking their lives so that others may have more life, and abundantly so. In a culture where injustice reigns, the mystical experience teaches one not to wish to be on the side of the conquerors but rather on the side of the defeated, and not to wish to enjoy the benefits of progress while so many are left without access to them. It teaches solidarity with the victims of injustice, sharing their condition and suffering the same injustice in one's own flesh.

In a culture where violence rules and every day produces fatalities by the hour, the mystical experience teaches that the only place to be is with the victims, because any other option would strengthen the position of the torturers and executioners. Union with the loving Mystery, which configures their whole lives, gives to the mystics the strength to confront violence without repaying it in kind, without the vengeance and aggression which equalizes all in the same hatred and in the same destruction. On the contrary, those who have experienced the powerful and loving presence of God as the holy Mystery, who have felt loved, forgiven and comforted by this presence, will go through such violence and take upon themselves its consequences, in the endeavor to construct a peace which is not simply the absence of wars, but the active and redeeming love which restores and renews everything on the face of the Earth.

The mystics, whether inside or outside the church and religious institutions, whether radically committed to them or at their margins, teach us that the experience of the Mystery of God in the midst of the world leads to an ardent passion for this same world, and to ceaseless work for its redemption and transformation. Whatever their life situation, their social condition, or their intellectual capacity, contemporary mystics return to the nuptial chamber where the experience of love occurs in its plenitude and delight, in order to fully immerse themselves in the disfigured reality of the world in which they live, seeking to configure it according to the heart of the God whose Face was mercifully revealed to them, and who made them participants in God's life.

Appendix
Translator's Note Regarding Sources and Footnotes for Chapter 5

WE ATTEMPTED TO FIND published English translations for the quotes from the three mystics featured in this chapter, and where relevant we adjusted the footnotes to reflect those sources.

This applies only to chapter 5. It applies only to quotes from the mystics themselves (Dorothy Day, Etty Hillesum, and Egide van Broeckhoven), except where specifically noted. Quotes from other writers (except where noted) were translated directly from the Portuguese into English.

Any changes are to the content of the footnotes only. The location in the text remains unchanged.

Dorothy Day

We used an edition of *The Long Loneliness* that is different from the editions referenced in footnote 1 and in the bibliography. We did not change the references in the footnotes, assuming the wording would be the same as in the referenced editions (*The Long Loneliness: The Autobiography of the Legendary Catholic Social Activist* [New York: Harper & Row, 1952]).

In the few cases where we did not find the quotes in this edition, we used sources as noted below in each specific case.

For quotes from other writings, we indicate our source in each specific case below.

Appendix

Quotes from *The Long Loneliness*

Note: We found the quote associated with the title of the section on Dorothy Day on the Catholic Worker website (see http://www.catholicworker.org/dorothyday/). There is no footnote for this quote.

For footnotes 7–10, 13, 18–19, 35: the quotes in the edition we used are located at the page number referenced in the footnote.

The following quotes were located on a different page. We did not change the reference in the footnote: footnote 33 (p. 37 in our edition rather than p. 40), footnote 34 (p. 38 rather than p. 37), footnotes 36–37 (p. 45 rather than p. 70).

Footnote 11: not found in the book we used. Found online in several books/articles about Dorothy Day—one cites a different edition of *The Long Loneliness*; we could not identify the sources for the others. The words were the same in all of them and we used those words.

Quotes from Day's Writings Other than *The Long Loneliness*

Footnote 15: We found a reproduction of the Ellsberg book on Google Books (see http://books.google.com/books?id=R9qApzGu3vMC&pg). The publication information in this version is the same as that in the footnote, but it shows the date of the letter as December 10, 1932, not 1935. We used this source for the English text, but we did not change the wording of the footnote.

Footnote 44: We found this in chapter 13 of *From Union Square to Rome* (see footnote 43) published on the Catholic Worker website (see http://www.catholicworker.org/dorothyday/daytext.cfm?TextID=213).

Quotes from Other Writers

Footnote 5: We found a reproduction of the Robert Coles book on Google Books (see http://books.google.com/books?id=gictbJZUk0EC&pg), and the English words are taken from there. The page and publication information in this version are the same as those in the footnote.

Footnote 20: We found this exact passage in an article by the same author on the website of the Catholic Worker (Forest, Jim, "Servant of God Dorothy Day," http://www.catholicworker.org/dorothyday/servant-of-god.html). We used this source for the English words.

Footnote 29: We were unable to obtain the O'Connor article. We translated this quote directly from the Portuguese.

Appendix

Etty Hillesum

In *O Mistério e o Mundo*, the quotes from Etty's diary and letters are taken primarily from the French version (*Une vie bouleversee*); see footnote 45. The author also refers in this same footnote to an English version (*Etty: The Letters and Diaries*), and this is the version from which most of our quotes are taken. We have changed the wording of footnote 45 to reflect this.

This is apparently the only completely unabridged version in English. We were unable to obtain a hard copy of the book, but we did locate a preview of the same version on Google Books (see htttp://books.google.com/books?id=UaMquRjHwcAC&pg). Since it is a preview only, it does not include all of the pages of the book. In the few instances when we were unable to find the quote in this version, we did one of two things:

1. There is another English version (*An Interrupted Life: The Diaries*) that appears in the bibliography, but not in the footnotes, of *O Mistério e o Mundo*. We did obtain a hard copy of this version, which is *not* unabridged. If we were able to find the quote here, we used it and changed the footnote to reflect this reference.

2. If we were unable to find the quote in either of the English versions, we kept the reference to the French version in the footnote, and translated the quote from the Portuguese into English ourselves.

Note: The quotes associated with the title of the section on Etty Hillesum are footnoted later in the text; see footnotes 95 and 81.

Footnotes changed to *Etty: The Letters and Diaries* (see footnote 45): 54, 61–67, 69–76, 78–81, 83–88, 90–96, 98–103, 106–8.

Footnotes changed to *An Interrupted Life: The Diaries*: 58, 60.

Footnotes that continue to refer to *Une vie bouleversee*: 55 (changed to spell out the reference), 56–57 ("ibid." unchanged), 59, 68, 72, 77, 82, 84, 89, 109 (spelled out). As noted above, we translated these quotes from the Portuguese into English.

Egide van Broeckhoven

In *O Mistério e o Mundo*, the quotes from Egide's diary are taken primarily from the French version (*Journal spirituel*); see footnote 110.

We were able to obtain a copy of the English edition of Egide's diary (*A Friend to All Men: The Diary of a Worker-Priest*). This edition appears in the bibliography but is not referenced in the footnotes. It is a translation of the French edition, *Journal de l'amitié*, which is referenced in the footnotes. It contains only a selection of the diary entries, and we were not able to find all the quotes.

For the quotes we found, we used the translation from the English edition. Those we could not find we translated from the Portuguese into English. We have indicated below the footnote numbers for the quotes we did not find, and for those we did find along with their page numbers in the English edition.

For quotes from other sources, we translated from the Portuguese into English.

We did not change the wording or page number references in any of the footnotes.

Note: For the two quotes associated with the title of the section on Egide van Broeckhoven, we found the first on page 24 of the English edition. It does not appear in any of the footnotes. We did not find the second quote in the English edition. A similar, but not identical, quote is referenced in footnote 140.

Footnote numbers for quotes not found in the English edition, and translated directly from the Portuguese into English: 115, 129, 131–33, 138–40, 143, 146–47.

Footnote numbers for quotes found in the English edition, with their page numbers in that edition:

#117, p. 42	#137, p. 50	#148, p. 111
#124, p. 19	#141, p. 110	#154, p. 108
#126, p. 23	#142, p. 62	#155, p. 108
#128, p. 35	#145, p. 106	#156, p. 101
#136, pp. 109–10		

Bibliography

ADORNO, T. *Critical Models: Interventions and Catchwords*. Translated by H. W. Pickford. New York: Columbia University Press, 2005.
———. *Minima Moralia: Reflections on a Damaged Life*. Translated by E. F. N. Jephcott. London: Verso, 2005.
ALBERSMEIER, S., ed. *Heroes: Mortals and Myths in Ancient Greece*. Baltimore: Walters Art Museum, 2009.
ALEMANY, V. *Saintes ou sorcières? L'heroisme chretien au feminin*. Paris: Les Editions de Paris, 2006.
ALENCASTRO, L. F. DE. "Esquecimento e memória." http://www.overmundo.com.br/banco/conferencia-esquecimento-e-memoria-luiz-felipe-de-alencastro.
ALEIXANDRE, D., et al. *La interioridad: un paradigma emergente*. Madrid: PPC, 2004.
ALLEN, D. *Three Outsiders: Pascal, Kierkegaard, Simone Weil*. 1983. Reprint, Eugene, OR: Wipf and Stock, 2006.
ALMOND, P. *Mystical Experience and Religious Doctrine: An Investigation of the Study of Mysticism in World Religions*. Berlin: Mouton, 1982.
AMARAL, L., et al. *Nova era. Um desafio para os cristãos*. São Paulo: Paulinas, 1944.
ANDRESEN, J., and R. K. C. FORMAN, eds. *Cognitive Models and Spiritual Maps— Interdisciplinary Explorations of Religious Experience*. Thorverton, UK: Imprint Academic, 2000.
ANDRADE, P. F. C. DE. "A crise da modernidade e as possibilidades de uma nova miltância cristã." Rio de Janeiro, ISER Assessoria, 2001. http://www.iserassessoria.org.br/novo/produtos/individuais.php.
———. "Encantos e desencantos: a militância do cristão em tempos de crise." Rio de Janeiro: ISER Assessoria 2001. http://www.iserassessoria.org.br./novo/produtos/individuais.php.
ANJOS, M. F. DOS. *Experiência religiosa: risco ou aventura?* São Paulo: Paulinas, 1999.
ARAUJO, W. S. *Navegando sobre as ondas do Santo Daime*. Campinas: Unicamp, 1999.
ARMSTRONG, K. *A History of God*. New York: Knopf, 1993.
ARRIBAS, A. A. (coord.) *Actas del II Encuentro de Filosofía y Educación*. Burgos: Instituto Superior de Filosofía San Juan Bosco, 1998.
ASSMANN, J. *Violence et monothéisme*. Paris: Bayard, 2009.
ASTI, F. *Dalla spiritualità alla mistica: percorsi storici e nessi interdisciplinari*. Vatican City: Libreria Editrice Vaticana, 2005.

———. *Spiritualità e mistica: questioni metodologiche*. Vatican City: Libreria Editrice Vaticana, 2003.
AUGUSTINE, ST. *Confessions and Enchiridion*. Translated and edited by Albert C. Outler. Library of Christian Classics 7. Philadelphia: Westminster, 1955.
———. *The Confessions of St. Augustine*. Translated by E. B. Pusey. Harvard Classics 7. New York: Collier, 1909.
———. *A Trindade*. São Paulo: Paulus, 1995, col. Patrística.
ÁVILA, Teresa de. *Livro da vida*. In: *Obras completas*. Madrid: Aguilar, 1957.
AZEVEDO, M. *Entroncamentos e entrechoques*. São Paulo: Loyola, 1991.
BADIOU, A. *Being and Event*. Translated by O. Feltham. New York: Continuum, 2005.
———. *Logics of Worlds: Being and Event, 2*. Translated by A. Toscano. New York: Continuum, 2009.
———. *Saint Paul: The Foundation of Universalism*. Translated by R. Brassier. Stanford: Stanford University Press, 2003.
———. *Theory of the Subject*. Translated by B. Bosteels. New York Continuum, 2009.
BALDINI, M. *Il linguaggio dei mistici*. Brescia: Queriniana, 1986.
BALTHASAR, H. U. von. *Explorations in Theology*. Vol. 1, *The Word Made Flesh*. Translated by A. V. Littledale with A. Dru. San Francisco: Ignatius, 1989.
———. *Explorations in Theology*. Vol. 4, *Spirit and Institution*. Translated by E. T. Oakes. San Francisco: Ignatius, 1995.
———. *The Glory of the Lord*. 7 vols. San Francisco: Ignatius, 1982.
———. *The God Question and Modern Man*. New York: Seabury, 1967.
———. *Herrlichkeit. Eine theologische Ästhetik*. Vol. 1, *Schau der Gestalt*. Einsiedeln: Johannes Verlag, 1988.
———. "Le Saint Esprit, l'Inconnu au-delà du Verbe." *Lumière et Vie* 13, 1964.
———. *My Work: In Retrospect*. San Francisco: Ignatius, 1993.
———. *Neue Klarstellungen*. Einsiedeln: Johannes Verlag, 1979.
———. "Teologia y espiritualidad." *Selecciones de Teologia* 13, 1974.
BARTHES, R. *Sade, Fourier, Loyola*. Paris: Seuil, 1971.
BARTHOLO, R. and A. E. CAMPOS, eds. *Islã: o credo é a conduta*. Rio de Janeiro: Iser, 1990.
BASLEZ, M-F. *Les persécutions dans l'Antiquite: victimes, héros, martyrs*. Paris: Fayard, 2007.
BASTIANEL, S. *La preghiera nella vita morale Cristiana*. Casale Monferrato: Piemme, 1986.
BATAILLE, G. *L'erotisme*. Paris: Minuit, 1957.
———. *L'expérience interieure*: Paris: Gallimard, 1954.
———. *O erotismo*. Lisbon: Antígona, 1988.
BAUDRILLARD, J. *Amerique*. Paris: Grasset, 1986.
BAUDRILLARD, J., et al. *Citoyenneté et urbanité*. Paris: Esprit, 1991.
BAUMAN, Z. *Alone Again: Ethics after Certainty*. http://demos.co.uk/files/alone again.pdf.
———. *Culture as Praxis*. New ed. London: Sage, 1999.
———. *Globalization: The Human Consequences*. New York: Columbia University Press, 1998.
———. *Intimations of Postmodernity*. London: Routledge, 1992.
———. *La sociedad sitiada*. Buenos Aires: Fondo de Cultura, 2004.
———. *Liquid Modernity*. Cambridge: Polity, 2000.

———. *Modernity and the Holocaust*. Ithaca: Cornell University Press, 1989.
———. *Postmodern Ethics*. Oxford: Blackwell, 1993.
———. *Postmodernity and Its Discontents*. New York: New York University Press, 1997.
———. *Society under Siege*. Cambridge: Polity, 2002.
BAUMGARTEN, M. *Ein aus 45 jähriger Erfahrung geschöpfter biographischer Beitrag zur Kirchenfrage*. Vol. 1. N.p.: Ernst Homann, 1891.
BEIERWALTES, W., et al. *Mistica, cuestiones fundamentales*. Buenos Aires: Agape, 2008.
BELDA, M., and J. SESE. *La "cuestion mistica": estudio histórico-teologico de una controversia*. Pamplona: Ediciones Universidad de Navarra, 1998.
BELL, R. H. *Simone Weil's Philosophy of Culture: Readings toward a Divine Humanity*. Cambridge: Cambridge University Press, 1993.
BERGER, P. *A Far Glory: The Quest for Faith in an Age of Credulity*. New York: Free Press, 1992.
———. *Questions of Faith: A Skeptical Affirmation of Christianity*. Oxford: Blackwell, 2003.
BERGER, P., and T. LUCKMANN. *Modernidad, pluralismo y crisis de sentido*. Barcelona: Paidos, 1997.
———. *Modernity, Pluralism and the Crisis of Meaning: The Orientation of Modern Man*. Gutersloh: Nertelsmann Foundation Publishers, 1995. E-book.
BERGSON, H. *Les deux sources de la morale et la religion*. http://www.wehave photoshop.com/PHILOSOPHY%20NOW/PHILOSOPHY/Bergson/Bergson%20-%20Les%20deux%20sources%20de%20la%20morale%20er%20de%20la%20Relig.pdf.
BÉRIAULT, Y. *Etty Hillesum, témoin de Dieu dans l'abîme du mal*. Paris: Médiaspaul, 2010.
BERNSTEIN, C., and M. POLITI. *His Holiness: John Paul II and the History of Our Time*. New York: Doubleday, 1996.
BERTELLI, G. *Mística e compaixão: a teologia do seguimento de Jesus em Thomas Merton*. São Paulo: Paulinas, 2008.
BINGEMER, M. C. "A aplicação de sentidos: assimilar o Mistério da Encarnação." *Revista de Itaici* 19 (2010) 43–57.
———. "A pneumatologia como possibilidade de diálogo e missão universais." In *Diálogo de pássaros*, edited by F. L. C. Teixeira. São Paulo: Paulinas, 1993.
———. *Alteridade e vulnerabilidade: experiência de Deus e pluralismo religioso no moderno em crise*. São Paulo: Loyola, 1993.
———. "Amar a Dios sobre todas las cosas: una invitación a todos." *Sal Terrae* 86/8 (1998) 603–14.
———. "Deus: experiência histórica e rosto humano—Alguns elementos sobre a questão de Deus no Concílio Vaticano II." In *Concílio Vaticano II: análise e prospectivas*, edited by P. S. Lopes Gonçalves and V. I. Bombonatto. São Paulo: Paulinas, 2004.
———. *Em tudo amar e servir*. São Paulo: Loyola, 1990.
———. "Jesus Cristo e a prática da não violência." In *A pessoa e a mensagem de Jesus*, edited by Mario de França Miranda. São Paulo: Loyola, 2002.
———. "O Deus inocente e a mortalidade humana." *Síntese Nova Fase* 21 (1994).
———. "Religions and the Dialogue among Cultures: The Brazilian Challenge." *Studies in Interreligious Dialogue* 16 (2006) 72–88.

---. "Simone Weil e os irmãos Grimm: elementos para uma soteriologia nas asas do mistério de um conto." 22nd Congresso internacional da Sociedade de Teologia e Ciências da Religião Soter, 2010. http://ciberteologia.paulinas.org.br.

---. "Simone Weil et Albert Camus. Sainteté sans Dieu et mystique sans Eglise." *Cahiers Simone Weil* 28 (2005) 365–86.

---. *Simone Weil: una mística en los límites*. Buenos Aires: Ciudad Nueva, 2011.

---. "Simone Weil. Une mystique pour Le XXeme siecle." In *Simone Weil*, edited by Chantal Delsol, 633–64. Cahiers d'histoire de la philosophie. Paris: Cerf, 2009.

---. *Um rosto para Deus?* São Paulo: Paulus, 2005.

---, ed. *Violência e religião: Cristianismo, Islamismo, Judaísmo; três religiões em confronto e diálogo*. Rio de Janeiro: Editora PUC-Rio, 2001.

BINGEMER, M. C., and P. F. C. DE ANDRADE. *Secularização: novos desafios*. Rio de Janeiro: PUC-Rio, 2012.

BINGEMER, M. C., and V. G. FELLER. *Deus Trindade: A vida no coração do mundo*. Valencia: Siquem, 2003.

---. *Deus Trindade: Graça que habita em nós*. Valencia: Siquem, 2003.

BINGEMER, M. C., and R. DOS SANTOS BARTHOLO, Jr. *Mística e política*. São Paulo: Loyola, 1992.

BINGEMER, M. C., et al. "Violência e não-violência na história da Igreja." *Revista eclesiástica brasileira* 59 (1999) 836–58.

---. "Violência e não-violência na história da Igreja (II)." *Revista eclesiástica brasileira* 60 (2000) 111–44.

BLACKBURN, V. *Dietrich Bonhoeffer and Simone Weil: A Study in Christian Responsiveness*. New York: Peter Lang, 2004.

BLANCH, A., ed. *El pensamiento alternativo: nueva visión sobre el hombre y la naturaleza*. Madrid: Comillas, 2002.

BLOECHL, J. *Liturgy of the Neighbor: Emmanuel Levinas and the Religion of Responsibility*. Pittsburgh: Duquesne University Press, 2000.

BLONDEL, M. *L'Action: Essai d'une critique de la vie et d'une science de la pratique*. 2 vols. Paris: F. Alcan, 1936–37.

---. "Le problème de la mystique." In *Qu'est-ce que la mystique? Quelques aspects historiques et philosophiques du problème*. Cahiers de la nouvelle journée 8 supplément, 1929.

BLONDEL, M., et al. *Qu'est-ce que la mystique? Quelques aspects historiques et philosophiques du problème*. Paris: Bloud and Gay, 1925.

BOELLA, L. *Cuori pensanti: Hannah Arendt, Simone Weil, Edith Stein, Maria Zambrano*. Mantova: Tre Lune, 1998.

BOFF, C. "A Igreja militante de João Paulo II e o capitalismo triunfante." In *Doutrina social da Igreja e teologia da libertação*, edited by F. Ivern and M. C. Bingemer. São Paulo: Loyola, 1994.

---. *Sinais dos tempos*. São Paulo: Loyola, 1985.

---. *Teoria do método teológico*. Petrópolis: Vozes, 1998.

BOFF, L. *Atualidade da experiência de Deus*. Rio de Janeiro: CRB, 1974.

---. "Constantes antropológicas e revelação." *Revista Eclesiástica Brasileira* 32 (1972) 26–41.

---. *Jesus Cristo Libertador*. Petrópolis: Vozes, 1994.

---. *Paixão de Cristo, paixão do mundo*. Petrópolis: Vozes, 1987.

---. *A Trindade, a sociedade e a libertação*. Petrópolis: Vozes, 1989.

BOFF, L., and F. BETTO. *Mistica y espiritualidad*. Madrid: Trotta, 1996.
BOLOGNE, J. C. *Le mysticisme athée*. Paris: Éditions du Rocher, 1995.
BONAVENTURE, ST. *Vita mistica* II. In *Mystical Opuscula*, translated by José de Vinck. The Works of Bonaventure v.i. Paterson, NJ: St. Anthony Guild Press, 1960.
BONHOEFFER, D. *Letters and Papers from Prison*. Rev. ed. New York: Macmillan, 1971.
BORGHESI, M. "Da queda do Muro à queda das bolsas." http://www.pucsp.br/fecultura/textos/fe_razao/2_depois_de_68_69.html.
BORRIELLO, L. *Esperienza mistica e teologia mistica*. Vatican City: Libreria Editrice Vaticana, 2009.
BOUILLARD, H. *Révélation de Dieu et langage des hommes*. Paris: Cerf, 1972.
BOURGEOIS, J. P. *The Aesthetic Hermeneutics of Hans-Georg Gadamer and Hans Urs von Balthasar*. New York: Peter Lang, 2007.
BOUYER, L. *Introduction a la vie spirituelle*. 2nd ed. Paris: Cerf, 2008.
———. *Mysterion: du mystère à la mystique*. Paris: O.E.I.L., 1986.
———. *The Spirituality of the New Testament and the Fathers*. New York: Desclée, 1963.
BOUYER, L., et al. *Christian Asceticism and Modern Man*. Translated by W. Mitchell and the Carisbrooke Dominicans. New York: Philosophical Library, 1955.
BRADY, J. A. "Dorothy Day: A Love of Fiction and Her Love of the Poor." *Religious Education* 105 (2010) 476–90.
BREMOND, H. *Histoire littéraire du sentiment religieux en France depuis la fin des guerres de religion jusqu'à nos jours*. Vol. 1, *L'Humanisme dévot (1580–1660)*. Paris: Armand Colin, 1967.
BRENNER, R. F. *Writing as Resistance: Four Women Confronting the Holocaust; Edith Stein, Simone Weil, Anne Frank, and Etty Hillesum*. University Park: Pennsylvania State University Press, 1997.
BRETON, S. *Philosophie et mystique: existence et surexistence*. Grenoble: Millon, 1996.
BRETON, S., et al. *Le mythe et le symbole*. Paris: Beauchesne, 1977.
BRETT, D. W., and E. T. BRETT. *Murdered in Central America: The Stories of Eleven U.S. Missionaries*. Maryknoll, NY: Orbis, 1988.
BROECKHOVEN, E. van. *Diário da amizade*. São Paulo: Loyola, 1978.
———. *A Friend to All Men: The Diary of a Worker-Priest*. Denville, NJ: Dimension Books, 1977.
———. *Journal de l'amitié*. Brussels: Lumen Vitae, 1972.
———. *Journal spirituel d'un jésuite en usine*. Christus. Paris: Desclée, 1976.
BRUNELLI, D. *Ele se fez caminho e espelho*. Petrópolis: Vozes, 1990.
BUBER, M. *I and Thou*. Translated by R. G. Smith. New York: Scribner, 2000.
BURITY, J. A. "Religião e política na fronteira: desinstitucionalização e deslocamento numa relação historicamente polêmica." *Revista de Estudos da Religião* 4 (2001) 27–45.
BURKE, P. J. *Contemporary Social Psychological Theories*. Stanford: Stanford University Press, 2006.
BURNHAM, S. *Ecstatic Journey: The Transforming Power of Mystical Experience*. New York: Ballantine, 1997.
BUTLER, E. C. *Western Mysticism*. London: Routledge, 1999.
BYCHKOV, O. V., and J. FODOR, eds. *Theological Aesthetics after Von Balthasar*. Burlington, VT: Ashgate, 2008.
CABAUD. J. *L'Expérience vécue de Simone Weil*. Paris: Plon, 1957.

———. *Simone Weil: A Fellowship in Love*. New York: Channel, 1964.
———. *Simone Weil à New York et à Londres: les quinze dernier mois (1942–1943)*. Paris: Plon, 1967.
CAFFARENA, J. G. "Aportación cristiana a un nuevo humanismo?" In *Ética dia tras dia*, edited by J. Mugueria et al. Madrid: Trotta, 1991.
CAFFARENA, J. G., and J. M. MARDONES. *Ateismo moderno: increencia o indiferencia religiosa*. Mexico City: Universidade Ibero Americana, 1999.
CAFFARENA, J. G., and J. M. VELASCO. *Filosofía de la religión*. Madrid: Revista de Occidente, 1973.
CALIN, R. *Levinas ou l'exception du soi*. Paris: Press universitaires France, col. Epimethee, 2005.
CAMPOS, L. S. *Teatro, templo e mercado*. Petrópolis: Vozes, 2000.
CAMUS, A. *La peste*. Paris: Gallimard, 1947.
CANGH, J.-M. van. *La mistica*. Bologna: DDB, 1991.
———. *La mystique*. Paris: Desclée, 1988.
CANO, M. *De locis theologicis, Liber VII: De sanctorum auctoritate*. In vol. 2 of *Opera*. Rome: Forzani, 1890.
CAPELLE, P. *Expérience philosophique et expérience mystique*. Paris: Cerf, 2005.
CAPOL, C. *Hans Ur von Balthasar: Bibliographie, 1925–1990*. Freiburg: Johannes Verlag Einsiedeln, 1990.
CAPUTO, J. D., and L. M. ALCOFF, eds. *St. Paul among the Philosophers*. Bloomington: Indiana University Press, 2009.
CAPUTO, J. D., et al., eds. *Questioning God*. Bloomington: Indiana University Press, 2001.
CARNEIRO, F., and R. SOARES, eds. *Corpo: meu bem, meu mal—III Seminário de Teologia e Direitos Reprodutivos: Ética e Poder*. Rio de Janeiro: Programa Sofia—Mulher, Teologia e Cidadania, Iser, 1995.
CAROZZO, C. "Mysticism and the Crisis of Religious Institutions." *Concilium* 4, 1994.
CARR, A. *A Search for Wisdom and Spirit: Thomas Merton's Theology of the Self*. Notre Dame: University of Notre Dame Press, 1988.
CARRARA, S. P. "A experiência cristã de Deus como resposta ao mal-estar religioso da pós-modernidade com especial referência à doutrina da oração de Santa Tereza de Ávila." MTh diss., Pontificia Facoltá Teológica, 2003.
CASALDÁLIGA, P., and J. M. VIGIL. *Espiritualidade da libertação*. 2nd ed. Petrópolis: Vozes, 1993.
CASARELLA, P. "Sisters in Doing the Truth: Dorothy Day and St. Therese de Lisieux." *Communio* 24 (1997) 468–98.
CASARELLA, P., and G. P. SCHNER, eds. *Christian Spirituality and the Culture of Modernity: The Thought of Louis Dupré*. Grand Rapids: Eerdmans, 1998.
CASTELLI, E., ed. *Le témoignage. Actes du colloque organisé par le Centre International d'Études Humanistes et par l'Institut d'Études Philosophiques de Rome*. Paris: Aubier, 1972.
CASTIÑERA, A. *A experiência de Deus na pós-modernidade*. Petrópolis: Vozes, 1997.
CATALAN, J. O. *A experiência mística e suas expressões*. São Paulo: Loyola, 2008.
———. *O inconsciente, morada de Deus?* São Paulo: Loyola, 2003.
CATHOLIC WORKER. http://www.marquette.edu/library/archives/day.shtml.
CAVANAUGH, W. *Being Consumed: Economics and Christian Desire*. Grand Rapids: Eerdmans, 2008.

Bibliography

———. *Être consommé. Une critique chretienne du consumerisme.* Paris: Editons de l'homme nouveau, 2007.

———. *Le mythe de la violence religieuse.* Paris: L'Homme Nouveau, 2009.

———. *Migrations of the Holy: God, State, and the Political Meaning of the Church.* Grand Rapids: Eerdmans, 2011.

———. *Theopolitical Imagination: Discovering the Liturgy as a Political Act in an Age of Global Consumerism.* London: T. & T. Clark, 2004.

———. *Torture et eucharistie.* Paris: Cerf/Ad Solem, 1998.

CERTEAU, M. *Fabula mistica—XVI-XVII secolo* (a cura di Silvano Facioni). Milan: Jaca, 2008.

———. "Historicites mystiques." *Recherches de Science Religieuse* 73 (1985) 325–54.

———. *L'Absent de l'histoire.* Paris: Maison Mame, 1973.

———. *La culture au pluriel.* Paris: Christian Bourgois, 1980.

———. *L'Écriture de l'histoire.* Paris: Gallimard, 1975.

———. *L'Étranger ou l'union dans la difference.* Paris: Desclée, 1969.

———. *La fable mystique. XVI–XVII siècle.* Paris: Gallimard, 1982.

———. *La faiblesse de croire.* Paris: Seuil, 2003.

CERTEAU, M., and J. M. DOMENACH. *Le christianisme éclaté.* Paris: Seuil, 1974.

CHADWICK, O., trans. *Western Asceticism.* Philadelphia: Westminster, 1980.

CHALIER, C. *Le desir de conversion.* Paris: Seuil, 2011.

CHAMPION, F. "La nébleuse mystique-ésoterique. Orientations psyco-religieuses des courants mystiques et ésoteriques contemporaines." In *De l'émotion en religion: Renouveau et traditions*, edited by F. Champion and D. Hervieu-Léger. Paris: Centurion, 1990.

CHAMPION, F., and D. HERVIEU-LÉGER, eds. *De l'émotion en religion: Renouveau et traditions.* Paris: Centurion, 1990.

CHANDLER, A. *The Terrible Alternative: Christian Martyrdom in the Twentieth Century.* London: Cassell, 1998.

CHATEAUBRIAND, F.-R. *Mémoires d'outre-tombe.* Paris: Hatier Parascolaire, 2004.

CHRÉTIEN, J.-L. *L'inoubliable et l'inespéré.* Paris: DDB, 2000.

CHRÉTIEN, J.-L., et al. *Phénoménologie et théologie.* Paris: Criterion, 1992.

CIPRIANI, R. *La religione diffusa: teoria e prassi.* Rome: Borla, 1988.

CIORAN, E. *Del inconveniente de haber nacido.* Madrid: Taurus, 1998.

CLARK, E. *Reading Renunciation, Asceticism and Scripture in Early Christianity.* Princeton: Princeton University Press, 1999.

CLARK, H. *The Ethical Mysticism of Albert Schweitzer: A Study of the Sources and Significance of Schweitzer's Philosophy of Civilization.* Boston: Beacon, 1962.

CLEMENT, O. *Roots of Christian Mysticism: Text and Commentary.* New York: New City, 1995.

CODINA, V. "De la ascética y mística a la vida según el Espíritu de Jesús." In *El Vaticano II veinte años después*, edited by C. Floristán and J. J. Tamayo. Madrid: Cristianadad, 1985.

———. *Teologia y experiencia espiritual.* Santander: Sal Terrae, 1977.

COETSIER, M. G. S. *Etty Hillesum and the Flow of Presence.* Columbia: University of Missouri Press, 2008.

COGNET, L. *Crépuscule des mystiques.* Paris: Desclée, 1991.

———. *Introduction aux mystiques rhéno-flamands.* Paris: Desclée, 1968.

———. *L'ascèse chrétienne.* Paris: Cerf, 1967.

———. *La spiritualité moderne*. Paris: Aubier, 1966.
COHN-SHERBOK, D., and L. COHN-SHERBOK. *Jewish and Christian Mysticism: An Introduction*. New York: Continuum, 1994.
COLE, G. A. *God the Peacemaker: How Atonement Brings Shalom*. Downers Grove, IL: InterVarsity, 2009.
COLES, R. *Dorothy Day: A Radical Devotion*. Reading, MA: Addison-Wesley, 1987.
COMBLIN, J. "As religiões hoje." http://www.servicioskoinonia.org/agenda/archivo/portugues/obra.php?ncodigo=228.
———. "O Cristianismo no limiar do terceiro milênio." In *A sedução do sagrado. O fenómeno religioso na virada do milênio*, edited by C. Caliman. 2nd ed. Petrópolis: Vozes, 1999.
COMTE-SPONVILLE, A. *L'Esprit de l'athéisme. Introduction à une spiritualité sans Dieu*. Paris: Cerf, 2006.
———. *O espírito do ateísmo*. São Paulo: Martins Fontes, 2007.
CONCILIUM. "Ateus de que Deus?" 2011.
CONGAR, Y. *Faith and Spiritual Life*. Translated by A. Manson and L. C. Sheppard. London: Darton, Longman & Todd, 1969.
———. *La foi et la theologie*. Paris: Desclée, 1962.
———. *Les voies du Dieu vivant*. Paris: Cerf, 1962.
CONGREGATION FOR THE DOCTRINE OF THE FAITH. *Orationis formas* ("Letter to the Bishops on Some Aspects of Christian Meditation"). http://www.vatican.va/roman_curia/congregations/cfaith/documents/rc_con_cfaith_doc_19891015_meditazione-cristiana_en.html.
COOK, J. *Bowery Blues: A Tribute to Dorothy Day*. New York: Xlibris, 2001.
CORTEN, A., and M. C. DORAN. "Immanence and Transcendence in the Religious and the Political." *Social Compass* 54 (2007).
COSTA, D. de. *Anne Frank and Etty Hillesum: Inscribing Spirituality and Sexuality*. Translated by M. F. C. Hoyinck and R. E. Chesal. New Brunswick: Rutgers University Press, 1998.
COURCELLES, D. *Les enjeux philosophiques de la mystique*. Grenoble: Jerome Millon, 2007.
COUSINS, E. H. *Global Spirituality: Toward the Meeting of Mystical Paths*. Madras: Radhakrishnan Institute for Advanced Study in Philosophy, University of Madras, 1985.
COWARD, H., and T. PENELHUM. *Mystics and Scholars: The Calgary Conference on Mysticism 1976*. SR Supplements 3. Waterloo: Corporation Canadienne des Sciences Religieuses, 1977.
COY, P. G., ed. *A Revolution of the Heart: Essays on the Catholic Worker*. Philadelphia: Temple University Press, 1988.
CRÉQUIE, G. *Religions et société: quelle perspective pour l'humanité*. Lyon: Aléas, 1995.
CROATTO, J. S. *As linguagens da experiência religiosa: uma introdução à fenomenologia da religião*. São Paulo: Paulinas, 2001.
CUNNINGHAM, L. "Authority and Religious Experience." *The Way Supplement* 92 (1998) 9–19.
——— et al. "Spirituality and religious experience." In: *The Way*, Supplement 1998/92 (whole issue).

CUSA, N. *Nicholas of Cusa on God as Not-Other: A Translation and an Appraisal of "De li non aliud".* Translation by J. Hopkins. Minneapolis: University of Minnesota Press, 1979.

———. *The Vision of God.* Translated by Emma Gurney Salter. 2nd ed. New York: Ungar, 1960.

DALY, M. *Beyond God the Father: Toward a Philosophy of Women's Liberation.* Boston: Beacon, 1993.

DALZELL, Th. G. *The dramatic encounter of divine and human freedom in the theology of Hans Urs von Balthasar.* 2nd ed. Bern: P. Lang, 2000.

DAMASIO, A. *Descartes' Error: Emotion, Reason, and the Human Brain.* New York: G. P. Putnam, 1994.

DANESE, N. *Ignazio Silone: Percorsi di una conscienza inquieta.* Turin: Effatà, 2007.

DANIELOU, J. *Platonisme et théologie mystique: doctrine spirituelle de Gregoire de Nysse.* 2nd ed. Paris: Aubier, 1953.

DAWKINS, R. *The God Delusion.* London: Bantam, 2006.

DAY, D. *All the Way to Heaven: The Selected Letters of Dorothy Day.* Edited by Robert Ellsberg. Milwaukee: Marquette University Press, 2010.

———. *By Little and by Little: The Selected Writings of Dorothy Day.* New York: Knopf, 1983.

———. *The Duty of Delight: The Diaries of Dorothy Day.* Edited by Robert Ellsberg. Milwaukee: Marquette University Press, 2008.

———. *The Eleventh Virgin.* New York: Cottager, 2011.

———. *From Union Square to Rome.* Silver Spring, MD: Preservation of the Faith Press, 1939.

———. *House of Hospitality.* New York: Sheed and Ward, 1939.

———. *In My Own Words.* Liguori, MO: Liguori, 2003.

———. *Loaves and Fishes: The Inspiring Story of the Catholic Worker Movement.* Maryknoll, NY: Orbis, 1997.

———. *The Long Loneliness.* San Francisco: Harper, 1990.

———. *Meditations.* Springfield, IL: Templegate, 1997.

———. *On Pilgrimage: The Sixties.* New York: Curtis, 1972.

———. *Therese.* Springfield, IL: Templegate, 1979.

DAY, D., with F. J. SICIUS. *Peter Maurin: Apostle to the World.* Maryknoll, NY: Orbis, 2004.

DE YOUNG, C. P. *Mystiques en action: Dietrich Bonhoeffer, Malcolm X et Aung San Suu Kyi.* Geneva: Labor et Fides, 2007.

DEBIDOUR, V.-H. *Simmone Weil ou la transparence.* Paris: Plon, 1963.

DELAMARRE, A. J.-L., et al. *L'experience et la conscience.* Arles: Actes SUD, col. Essais Littéraires, 2004.

DALAYE, A. *Sagesses concordantes: quatre maitres pour notre temps: Etty Hillesum, Vimala Thakar, Svami Prajananpad, Krishnamurti.* Paris: Accarias-L'originel, 2003.

DELBREL, M. *Oeuvres Complètes.* Paris: Nouvelle Cité, 2007.

DELEDALLE, G. *L'idée d'expérience dans la philosophie de John Dewey.* 2 vols. Paris: Presses universitaires de France, 1967.

DELP, A. *The Prison Meditations of Father Alfred Delp.* New York: Herder and Herder, 1963.

DELUMEAU, J. *História do medo no Ocidente.* São Paulo: Companhia das Letras, 1991.

DELVILLE, J.-P., ed. *Mystiques et politiques.* Brussels: Lumen Vitae, 2005.

DERRIDA, J., and G. VATTIMO, eds. *Religion*. Stanford: Stanford University Press, 1998.
DEVINE, G., ed. *New Dimensions in Religious Experience*. Staten Island, NY: Alba House, 1971.
DIEZ MERINO, L. *La passión de Jesucristo y de los martires pasionistas de Daimiel, Niceforo y XXV compañeros*. Zaragoza: Pasionistas, 1989.
DOCUMENTO DE APARECIDA. *Texto conclusivo da V Conferência Geral do Episcopado Latino-Americano e do Caribe*. São Paulo: Paulus/Paulinas, 2007.
DOMÍNGUEZ MORANO, C. *Crer depois de Freud*. São Paulo: Loyola, 1996.
———. "El Dios imaginado." *Razón y Fe* 231 (1995) 29–40.
———. *Los registros del deseo. Del afécto, el amor y otras pasiones*. Bilbao: Desclée de Brouwer, 2001.
———. *Orar depois de Freud*. São Paulo: Loyola, 1998.
DOU, A. *Experiencia religiosa*. Madrid: Comillas, 1989.
DOUGLAS, M. *Purity and Danger: An Analysis of Concepts of Pollution and Taboo*. Harmondworth: Penguin, 1970.
DOWNEY, V. M. "A Balm for All Wounds: The Spiritual Legacy of Etty Hillesum." *Spirituality Today* 40 (1988) 18–35.
DUCROCQ, A. "Etty Hillesum, une vie bouleversante." *CLES.com*. http://www.cles.com/enquetes/article/etty-hillesum-une-vie-bouleversante.
DUFRENNE, M. *Estética e filosofia*. São Paulo: Perspectiva, 1998.
DUPRÉ, L. *The Common Life: The Origins of Trinitarian Mysticism and Its Developments by Jan Ruusbroec*. New York: Crossroad, 1984.
———. *The Deeper Life: An Introduction to Christian Mysticism*. New York: Crossroad, 1981.
———. "Mysticism." In vol. 10 of *The Encyclopedia of Religion*, edited by Mircea Eliade, 245–61. New York: Macmillan, 1987.
———. *The Other Dimension*. New York: Doubleday, 1972.
———. *Religion and the Rise of Modern Culture*. Notre Dame: University of Notre Dame Press, 2008.
———. "Spiritual Life in a Secular Age." *Daedalus* 111 (1982) 21–31.
———. *Symbols of the Sacred*. Grand Rapids: Eerdmans, 2000.
———. *Transcendent Selfhood: The Loss and Rediscovery of the Inner Life*. New York: Crossroad/Seabury, 1976.
DUPRÉ, L., and D. E. SALIERS, eds. *Christian Spirituality: Post-reformation and Modern*. World Spirituality 18.New York: Crossroad, 1989.
DUPRÉ, L., and J. WISEMAN, eds. *Light from Light: An Anthology of Christian Mysticism*. New York: Paulist, 1988.
DUPUIS, J. *Rumo a uma teologia cristã do pluralismo religioso*. São Paulo: Paulinas, 2000.
———. *The Christian Faith*. New York: Alba House, 1973.
———. "Dialogo interreligioso nella missione evangelizzatrice della Chiesa." In *Vaticano II: bilancio e prospettive venticinque anni dopo (1962–1987)*, edited by R. Latourelle. Assisi: Citadella Editrice, 1987.
———. *Jesus Christ at the Encounter of World Religions*. Translated by Robert R. Barr. Maryknoll, NY: Orbis, 1991.
———. *Toward a Christian Theology of Religious Pluralism*. Maryknoll, NY: Orbis, 1997.

———. *Who Do You Say I Am? Introduction to Christology.* Maryknoll, NY: Orbis, 1994.
DUQUOC, C. *Jesus, homme libre.* Paris: Cerf, 2003.
———. *L'Unique Christ: la symphonie différée.* Paris: Cerf, 2002.
DURAND, G. *L'imagination symbolique.* 2nd ed. Paris: Presses universitaires de France, 1968.
DUTTER, C. *Etty Hillesum, une voix dans la nuit.* Paris: Robert Laffont, 2010.
DUVAL, A. *Etty Hillesum—Quand souffle l'Esprit.* Mesnil-sur-l'Estree: François-Xavier de Guibert, 2010.
EAGLETON, T. *Reason, Faith, and Revolution: Reflections on the God Debate.* New Haven: Yale University Press, 2010.
EDWARDS, D. *Human Experience of God.* New York: Paulist, 1983.
EDWARDS, Th. R. *Imagination and Power: A Study of Poetry on Public Themes.* New York: Oxford University Press, 1971.
EGAN, E. A. *Peace Be with You: Justified Warfare or the Way of Nonviolence.* Maryknoll, NY: Orbis, 1999.
EGAN, H. D. *Christian Mysticism: The Future of a Tradition.* New York: Pueblo, 1984.
———. *What Are They Saying about Mysticism?* New York: Paulist, 1982.
ELIADE, M. *Briser le toit de la maison: La créativité et ses symboles.* Paris: Gallimard, 1986.
———, ed. *The Encyclopedia of Religion.* New York: Macmillan 1987.
———. *Myth and Reality.* Translated by Willard R. Trask. New York: Harper & Row, 1963.
———. *The Sacred and the Profane.* Translated by Willard R. Trask. New York: Harcourt, Brace, 1959.
———. *The Two and the One.* Translated by J. M. Cohen. New York: Harper & Row, 1962.
ELIADE, M., et al. *Mystique, sexualité et continence.* Paris: DDB, 1990.
ELIE, P. *The Life You Save May Be Your Own: An American Pilgrimage.* New York: Farrar, Straus, Giroux, 2003.
ELLSBERG, R. "Dorothy in Love." *America*, November 15, 2010. http://americamagazine.org/issue/755/ideas/dorothy-love.
EMERY, G., and P. GISEL. *Le christianisme est-il un monotheisme?* Geneva: Labor et fides, 2001.
ENCYCLOPAEDIA UNIVERSALIS, numerical version, 2009.
ENDEAN, Ph. *Karl Rahner and Ignatian Spirituality.* New York: Oxford University Press, 2001.
ERLANDER, L. *Faith in the World of Work: On the Theology of Work as Lived by the French Worker-Priests and British Industrial Mission.* Uppsala: Uppsala University, 1991.
ESTRADA, J. A. *Razones y sinrazones de la creencia religiosa.* Madrid: Trotta, 2001.
EVANGELII NUNTIANDI, n° 41, 1974.
EVDOKIMOV, M. *Pereginos russos e andarilhos místicos.* Petrópolis: Vozes, 1990.
FABRI DOS ANJOS, M., ed. *Experiência religiosa—risco ou aventura?* São Paulo: SOTER/Paulinas, 1998.
FACKENHEIM, E. L. *To Mend the World: Foundations of Future Jewish Thought.* New York: Schocken, 1982.
FERNANDES, S. R. A. *Novas formas de crer.* Brasilia: Ceris, 2007.

FERRY, L. *O homem Deus ou o sentido da vida*. Rio de Janeiro: Difel, 1996.
———. *Vaincre les peurs: La philosophie comme amour de la sagesse*. Paris: Odile Jacob, 2006.
FESTUGIÈRE, A. J. *L'Enfant d'Agrigente*. Paris: Les Iles d'Or/Librairie Plon, 1950.
———. *L'Ideal religieux des grecs et l'Evangile*. Paris: Gabalda, 1932.
———. *La sainteté*. Paris: Presses universitaires de France, 1949.
FIORES, S. "Espiritualidad contemporanea." In *Nuevo diccionario de espiritualidad*. Madrid: San Pablo, 1983.
FIORUCCI, R. "A questão da memória na esfera pública global." *Revista Espaço Acadêmico* 86 (2008). http://www.espacoacademico.com.br/086/86fiorucci.htm#_ftn1.
FOREST, J. "Dorothy Day Servant of God." *CatholicWorker.org*. http://www.catholicworker.org/dorothyday/servant-of-god.html.
———. "The Living Legacy of Dorothy Day." *U.S.Catholic.org*. http://www.uscatholic.org/culture/social-justice/2009/02/the-living-legacy-dorothy-day.
———. *Love Is the Measure: A Biography of Dorothy Day*. New York: Paulist, 1986.
FORTE, B. *Jesus de Nazaré: História de Deus, Deus da história*. São Paulo: Paulinas, 1985.
———. *A Igreja, ícone da Trindade*. São Paulo: Loyola, 1987.
———. *A Trindade como história*. São Paulo: Paulinas, 1989.
———. *Trindade para ateus*. São Paulo: Paulinas, 1999.
FRANÇA MIRANDA, M. *Inculturação da fé: Uma abordagem teológica*. São Paulo: 2001.
FRANCIS, ST. *Francis and Clare: The Complete Works*. Edited by R. J. Armstrong and I. C. Brady. New York: Paulist, 1982.
FRANKL, V. *Man's Search for Meaning*. Rev. ed. New York: Washington Square, 1985.
FREIBERGER, O. *Ascetism and Its Critics: Historical Accounts and Comparative Perspectives*. Oxford: Oxford University Press, 2006.
FREUD, S. *The Future of an Illusion*. Translated by W. D. Robson-Scott. New York: H. Liveright and the Institute of Psycho-Analysis, 1928.
FRIEDMAN, T. L. *The World Is Flat: A Brief History of the 21st Century*. New York: Farrar, Straus, Giroux, 2005.
FUCHS, O., ed. *Theologie und Handeln: Beitrage zur Fundierung der practischen Theologie als Handlungstheorie*. Dusseldorf: Patmos, 1984.
FUKUYAMA, F. *The End of History and the Last Man*. New York: Free Press, 1992.
GAETA, G. *Le cose come sono: Etica, politica, religion*. Milan: Librischiwiller, 2008.
GAETA, G., et al. *Vite attive: Simone Weil, Edith Stein, Hannah Arendt*. Rome: Lavoro, 1996.
GAMARRA, S. *Teología espiritual*. Madrid: BAC, 1994.
GARCÍA RUBIO, A. *Unidade na pluralidade: o ser humano à luz da fé e da reflexão cristãs*. São Paulo: Paulus, 2001.
GARDET, L. *L'expérience du soi*. Paris: DDB, 1981.
———. *La mystique*. Paris: Presses universitaires de France, 1970.
GARRIGOU-LAGRANGE, R. *Perfection chrétienne et contemplation selon S. Thomas d'Aquin et S. Jean de la Croix*. 2 vols. Saint-Maximin: Vie Spirituelle, 1923.
GAUCHET, M. *Le désenchantement du monde*. Paris: Gallimard, 1985.
———. *Un monde désenchanté?* Paris: L'Atelier, 2004.

GAWRONSKI, R. *Word and Silence: Hans Urs von Balthasar and the Spiritual Encounter between East and West.* Grand Rapids: Eerdmans, 1995.
GEBARA, I. *As incômodas filhas de Eva.* São Paulo: Paulinas, 1993.
GEERTZ, C. "Religion as Cultural System." In *The Interpretation of Cultures*, 87–125. New York: Basic Books, 1973.
GEFFRE, C., ed. *Michel de Certeau ou la difference chretienne.* Paris: Cerf, 1991.
GELABERT, M. *Valoración cristiana de la experiencia.* Salamanca: Sigueme, 1990.
GELPI, D. *The Turn to Experience in Contemporary Theology.* New York: Paulist, 1994.
GENTILINI, P. B. *Psicologia de los santos.* Buenos Aires: Difusion, 1943.
GERGEN, K. J. *O eu saturado. Dilemas de identidade no mundo moderno.* Barcelona: Paidós, 2006.
———. *The Saturated Self: Dilemmas of Identity in Contemporary Life.* New York: Basic Books, 1991.
GESCHE, A. *O cosmo.* São Paulo: Paulinas, 2004.
———. *O ser humano.* São Paulo: Paulinas, 2003.
GIARD, L., et al. *Michel de Cearteau: Le voyage mystique.* Paris: Recherches de Science Religieuse, 1988.
GILLESPIE, M. A. *The Theological Origins of Modernity.* Chicago: University of Chicago Press, 2008.
GINZBURG, N. *Mai devi domandarmi.* Milan: Garzanti, 1970.
GOETZ, J. W. *Mirrors of God.* Cincinnatti: St. Anthony Menssenger Press, 1984.
GOLDSCHLAGER, A. *Simone Weil et Spinoza: essai d'interpretation.* Sherbrooke, QC: Naaman, 1982.
GOLEMAN, D. *Emotional Intelligence.* New York: Bantam, 1995.
GOMEZ, I. A. "Cristo, sacramento de Dios en la historicidad de los hombres." *Cuestiones Teologicas y Filosoficas (Medellin)* 33 (2006) 281–314.
GÓMEZ DE SOUZA, L. A. "Secularização e Sagrado." *Sintese* 13 (1986) 33–49.
———. "Secularização em declínio e potencialidade transformadora do Sagrado." *Religião e sociedade* 132 (1986) 2–16.
GONZÁLEZ BUELTA, B. *Bajar al encuentro de Dios.* Santander: Sal Terrae, 1988.
———. *Caminar sobre las aguas.* Santander: Sal Terrae, 2010.
———. *La utopia ya está en lo germinal.* Santander: Sal Terrae, 1998.
———. *Orar em um mundo fragmentado.* São Paulo: Loyola, 2007.
———. *Orar en un mundo roto.* Santander: Sal Terrae, 1999.
———. *Ver o parecer.* Santander: Sal Terrae, 2003.
GONZÁLEZ DE CARDEDAL, O. *Cuatro poetas desde la otra ladera.* Madrid: Trotta, 1996.
GONZÁLEZ FAUS, J. I. *Calidad cristiana: Identidad y crisis del cristianismo.* Santander: Sal Terrae, 2006.
GORT, J. D., et al. *On Sharing Religious Experience: Possibilities of Interfaith Mutuality.* Grand Rapids: Eerdmans, 1992.
GOSS-MAYR, H., and J. HANSSENS. *Jean Goss: Mystique et militant de la non-violence.* Namur: Fidélité, 2010.
GRAEF, H. *Histoire de la mystique.* Paris: Seuil, 1972.
GRAMSCI, A. *Os intelectuais e a organização da cultura.* Rio de Janeiro: Civilização Brasileira, 1981.
GREENE, G. *Collected Essays.* New York: Viking, 1969.

GREISCH, J. *Penser la religion: Recherches en philosophie de la religion.* Paris: Beauchesne, 1991.
GRESHAKE, G. *El Dios uno y trino: Una teologia de la Trinidad.* Salamanca: Herder, 2001.
GRIFFIN, D. R. *God and Religion in the Postmodern World.* Albany: State University of New York Press, 1989.
GRIFFIN, G. *The Influence of the Writings of Simone Weil on the Fiction of Iris Murdoch.* San Francisco: Mellen Research University Press, 1993.
GRIFFITH-DICKSON, G. *Human and Divine: An Introduction to the Philosophy of Religious Experience.* London: Duckworth, 2000.
GRIFFITHS, P., and R. HUTTER. *Reason and the Reasons of Faith.* London: T. & T. Clark, 2005.
GRIFFITHS, R. R., et al. "Psilocybin Can Occasion Mystical-Type Experiences Having Substantial and Sustained Personal Meaning and Spiritual Significance." *Psychofarmachology* 187 (2006) 268–83.
GRONDIN, J. *Du sens de la vie.* Montreal: Bellarmin, 2003.
GROTH, B. "Dal monologo al diálogo com i non-credenti o la difficile ricerca di interlocutori." In *Vaticano II: bilancio e prospettive venticinque anni dopo (1962–1987),* edited by R. LATOURELLE. Assisi: Citadella Editrice, 1987.
GUARDINI, R. "Der Heilige in unserer Welt." In *Lust an der Erkenntnis: Die Theologie des 20. Jahrhunderts,* edited by K.-J. Kuschel. Munich: Piper, 1986.
GUILLEBAUD, J.-C. *La trahison des lumières: Enquête sur le désarroi contemporain.* Paris: Seuil 1995.
———. *La tyrannie du plaisir.* Paris: Seuil, 1998.
———. *Le commencement d'un monde.* Paris: Seuil, 2008.
———. *Re-founding the World: A Western Testament.* Translated by W. D. Wilson. New York: Algora, 2001.
GUILLET, J., coord. *L'homme devant Dieu: Melanges offerts au Pere Henri de Lubac.* Paris: Aubier, 1963.
———. *The Religious Experience of Jesus and His Disciples.* St. Meinrad, IN: Abbey Press, 1975.
GUTIÉRREZ, G. *A força histórica dos pobres.* Petrópolis: Vozes, 1981.
———. *Beber no próprio poço.* Petrópolis: Vozes, 1984.
———. *Teologia da Libertação.* Petrópolis: Vozes, 1975.
HABERMAS, J. *The Structural Transformation of the Public Sphere: An Inquiry into a Category of Bourgeois Society.* Translated by T. Burger with the assistance of F. Lawrence. Cambridge: MIT Press, 1989.
HABERMAS, J., et al. *An Awareness of What Is Missing: Faith and Reason in a Post-secular Age.* Translated by C. Cronin. Cambridge: Polity, 2010.
HADEWIJCH. *Hadewijch: The Complete Works.* Translated by C. Hart. New York: Paulist, 1980.
HADOT, P. *Exercises spirituels et philosophie antique.* Paris: Institut d'Études Augustiennes, 1993.
———. *Philosophy as a Way of Life: Spiritual Exercises from Socrates to Foucault.* Edited by A. Davidson. Translated by M. Chase. Oxford: Blackwell, 1995.
HALBWACHS, M. *Le mémoire collective.* Rev. ed. Paris: A. Michel, 1997.
HALDA, B. *L'Evolution spirituelle de Simone Weil.* Paris: Beauchesne, 1964.

HAMMARSKJÖLD, D. *Markings*. Translated by L. Sjöberg and W. H. Auden. New York: Knopf, 1964.
HARNACK, A. *History of Dogma*. Translated by N. Buchanan. 7 vols. New York: Dover, 1961.
HAROCHE, C. *L'Avenir du sensible*. Paris: Presses universitaires de France, 2008.
HARRIS, S. *Letter to a Christian Nation*. New York: Knopf, 2006.
HART, K., and B. WALL, eds. *The Experience of God: A Postmodern Response*. New York: Fordham University Press, 2005.
HAUGHTON, R. *The Passionate God*. New York: Paulist, 1981.
———. *The Theology of Experience*. Paramus, NJ: Newman, 1972.
HAUTEFEUILLE, T. *Le tourment de Simone Weil*. Paris: DDB, 1970.
HAYEN, A., et al. *Melanges Joseph Maréchal*. vol. 1. Paris: DDB, 1950.
HAYES, M., et al. *Religion and Sexuality*. Sheffield: Sheffield Academic, 1998.
HAYES, V. C. *Religious Experience in World Religions*. Bedford Park, SA: Australian Association for the Study of Religions, 1980.
HÉBRARD, M. *Entre Nouvel âge et christianisme. Dix témoins racontent*. Paris: Desclée de Brouwer, 1994.
HEELAS, P., ed. *Religion, Modernity, and Postmodernity*. Oxford: Blackwell, 1998.
HEFLEY, J., and M. HEFLEY. *By Their Blood: Christian Martyrs of the Twentieth Century*. 2nd ed. Grand Rapids: Baker, 1996.
HEIDEGGER, M. *Qu'appelle-t-on penser?* Paris: Presses universitaires de France, 2002.
———. *What Is Called Thinking?* Translated by J. Glenn Gray. New York: Harper & Row, 1968.
HEISIG, J. W. *Diálogos a una pulgada del suelo: Recuperar las creencias en una época interreligiosa*. Barcelona: Herder, 2005.
———. "The Recovery of the Senses: Against the Asceticisms of the Age." *Journal of Ecumenical Studies* 33 (1996) 216–37.
———. "Six Sutras on the Dialogue among Religions." *Nanzan Bulletin* 25 (2001) 7–18.
HENRY, M. *C'est moi la vérité: Pour une philosophie du christianisme*. Paris: Seuil, 1996.
———. *L'Incarnation*. Paris: DDB, 2001.
HERVIEU-LÉGER, D. *La religon pour mémoire*. Paris: Cerf, 1993.
———. *Le pélerin et le converti: La religion en mouvement*. Paris: Flammarion, 1999.
HICK, J. *The Metaphor of God Incarnate*. London: SCM, 1993.
HICK, J., and P. KNITTER. *The Myth of Christian Uniqueness: Toward a Pluralistic Theology of Religions*. Maryknoll, NY: Orbis, 1987.
HILLESUM, E. *Etty: The Letters and Diaries of Etty Hillesum, 1941–1943*. Edited by K. A. D. Smelik. Translated by A. J. Pomerans. Grand Rapids: Eerdmans, 2002.
———. *Etty Hillesum: Essential Writings*. Selected by A. S. Kidder. Maryknoll, NY: Orbis, 2009.
———. *Etty Hillesum: une vie bouleversée*. Paris: Seuil, 2008.
———. *An Interrupted Life: The Diaries, 1941–1943; and, Letters from Westerbork*. Translated by A. J. Pomerans. New York: Henry Holt, 1996.
———. *J'Avais encore mille choses a te demander: L'univers interieur d'Etty Hillesum. Textes choisis*. Selected and translated by A. Pleshoyano. Paris: Bayard, 2009.
———. *Les ecrits d'Etty Hillesum: Journaux et lettres, 1941–1943. Edition integrale*. Paris: Seuil, 2008.
———. *Lettres de Westerbork*. Paris: Seuil, 1988.
———. *Une vie bouleversee, suivi de Lettres de Westerbork*. Paris: Seuil, 1995.

HITCHENS, C. *God Is Not Great: The Case against Religion*. London: Atlantic, 2007.
HOOK, B. S., and R. R. RENO. *Heroism and the Christian life*. Louisville: Westminster John Knox Press, 2000.
HOPKINS, J. *Nicholas of Cusa's Debate with John Wenck: A Translation and an Appraisal of "De ignota litteratura" and "Apologia doctae ignorantiae"*. Minneapolis: A. J. Banning, 1981.
HORKHEIMER, M. *Eclipse of Reason*. New York: Oxford University Press, 1947.
HORKHEIMER, M., and T. ADORNO. *Dialectic of Enlightenment*. Translated by John Cumming. New York: Seabury, 1972.
HORTAL, J. *O que fazer diante da expansão dos grupos religiosos não católicos?* Communication to the 30th General Assembly of the CNBB. Estudos da CNBB 62.
HOSTIE, R. *Religion and the Psychology of Jung*. New York: Sheed and Ward, 1957.
HOUTEPEN, A. W. J. *Dio, una domanda aperta: Pensare Dio nell'era della dimenticanza di Dio*. Queriniana: Brescia 2001.
HOUZIAUX, A., coord. *La mystique, une religion épurée?* Paris: Atelier, 2008.
HOWSARE, R. *Balthasar: A Guide for the Perplexed*. London: T. & T. Clark, 2009.
HOWSARE, R., and L. S. CHAPP, eds. *How Balthasar Changed My Mind: Fifteen Scholars Reflect on the Meaning of Balthasar for Their Own Work*. New York: Crossroad, 2008.
HÜGEL, F. VON. *The Mystical Element of Religion*. 2 vols. London: J. M. Dent, 1908.
HULIN, M. *La mística salvaje: En los antípodas del espíritu*. Madrid: Siruela, 2007.
HUNTINGTON, S. *The Clash of Civilizations and the Remaking of World Order*. New York: Simon & Schuster, 1998.
———. *Who Are We? The Challenges to America's National Identity*. New York: Simon & Schuster, 2005.
IACOPINI, B. and S. MOSER. *Uno sguardo nuovo: Il problema del male in Etty Hillesum e Simone Weil*. Milan: San Paolo, 2009.
IDEL, M., and B. McGINN, eds. *Mystical Union and Monotheistic Faith: An Ecumenical Dialogue*. New York: Macmillan, 1989.
IDINOPULOS, T.A. and KNOPP, J.Z. (eds.) *Mysticism, nihilism, feminism—New critical essays on the theology of Simone Weil*. Johnson City: Institute of Social Sciences and Arts, 1984.
IGNATIUS, DE LOYOLA, ST. *Exercícios espirituais*. São Paulo: Loyola, 1998.
———. *O relato do peregrino*. São Paulo: Loyola, 2001.
INGE, W. R. *Christian Mysticism*. Cleveland: World Publishing, 1964.
IRWIN, A. *Saints of the Impossible: Bataille, Weil, and the Politics of the Sacred*. Minneapolis: University of Minnesota Press, 2002.
IZUZQUIZA, D. *Rooted in Jesus Christ: Toward a Radical Ecclesiology*. Grand Rapids: Eerdmans, 2009.
JACQUIER, C., dir. *Simone Weil, l'expérience de la vie et le travail de la pensée*. Paris: Sulliver, 1998.
JAMES, W. *The Varieties of Religious Experience*. New York: Modern Library, 1929.
JANK, M. S. "A nova geografia do mundo, Presidente do ICONE." *O Estado de S. Paulo*, June 1, 2004, A2.
JANKELEVITCH, V. *Philosophie première*. Paris: Presses universitaires de France, 1986.
JAPIASSÚ, H., and D. MARCONDES, eds. *Dicionário básico de filosofia*. 3rd ed. Rio de Janeiro: Zahar, 1996.

JAVIER SANCHEZ RODRIGUEZ, F., ed. *Mistica y sociedad en dialogo*. Madrid: Trotta, 2006.
JOÃO DA CRUZ [John of the Cross]. "Chama de amor viva." In: *Poesias completas*. Lisbon: Assirio e Alvim. 1982.
———. "Llama de amor viva." In *Obras completas*. Madrid: BAC, 1974.
———. *Subida do Monte Carmelo*. São Paulo: Paulus, 1998.
JOHNSTON, W. *The Inner Eye of Love*. New York: Harper & Row, 1978.
———. *Mystical Theology: The Science of Love*. Maryknoll, NY: Orbis, 2004.
———. *The Still Point: Reflections on Zen and Christian Mysticism*. New York: Harper & Row, 1971.
———. *The Wounded Stag: Christian Mysticism Today*. New York: Fordham University Press, 1998.
JONAS, H. "The Concept of God after Auschwitz: A Jewish Voice." *The Journal of Religion* 67 (1987) 1–13.
———. *The Imperative of Responsibility: In Search of an Ethics for the Technological Age*. Translated by H. Jonas with the collaboration of D. Herr. Chicago: University of Chicago Press, 1984.
———. "Myth and Mysticism: A Study of Objectification and Interiorization in Religious Thought." *The Journal of Religion* 49 (1969) 315–29.
———. *O princípio da reponsabilidade*. Rio de Janeiro: Editora PUC-Rio/Contraponto, 2006.
JORDAN, P., ed. *Dorothy Day: Writings from Commonweal*. Collegeville, MN: Liturgical, 2002.
JOSSUA, J. P. *Seul avec Dieu: L'aventure mystique*. Paris: Gallimard, 1996.
JÜNGEL, E. *God as the Mystery of the World*. Translated by Darrell L. Guder. Grand Rapids: Eerdmans, 1983.
KAMITSUKA, M. D., ed. *The Embrace of Eros: Bodies, Desires, and Sexuality in Christianity*. Minneapolis: Fortress, 2010.
KANT, I. *Groundwork of the Metaphysics of Morals*. Translated and edited by M. Gregor and J. Timmerman. Rev. ed. Cambridge: Cambridge University Press, 2012.
KATZ, S., ed. *Mysticism and Philosophical Analysis*. New York: Oxford University Press, 1978.
———. *Mysticism and Religious Traditions*. Oxford: Oxford University Press, 1983.
KENDRICK, M. G. *The Heroic Ideal: Western Archetypes from the Greeks to the Present*. Jefferson, NC: McFarland, 2010.
KENT, D. *Dorothy Day: Friend to the Forgotten*. Grand Rapids: Eerdmans, 1996.
KERR, F. *Twentieth-Century Catholic Theologians: From Neoscholasticism to Nuptial Mysticism*. Malden, MA: Blackwell, 2007.
KESSLER, M., and Ch. SHEPPARD, eds. *Mystics: Presence and Aporia*. Chicago: University of Chicago Press, 2003.
KEYES, D. *True Heroism in a World of Celebrity Counterfeits*. Colorado Springs: NavPress, 1995.
KING, P. *Dark Night Spirituality: Thomas Merton, Dietrich Bonhoeffer, Etty Hillesum*. London: SPCK, 1995.
KING, U. *Christian Mystics: Their Lives and Legacies throughout the Ages*. Mahwah, NJ: HiddenSpring, 1998.
KIRK, K. E. *The Vision of God*. Cambridge: James Clarke, 1977.
KITAMORI, K. *Theology and the Pain of God*. Richmond: John Knox, 1965.

KLEJMENT, A., and A. KLEJMENT. *Dorothy Day and "The Catholic Worker": A Bibliography and Index*. New York: Garland, 1986.

KLEJMENT, A., and N. L. ROBERTS. *American Catholic Pacifism: The Influence of Dorothy Day and the Catholic Worker Movement*. Westford, CT: Praeger, 1996.

KOENIG-BRICKER, W. *Meet Dorothy Day: Champion of the Poor*. Ann Arbor, MI: Charis, 2002.

KOLAKOWSKI, L. *Bergson*. Oxford: Oxford University Press, 1985.

KRISTEVA, J. *Histoires d'amour*. Paris: Denoël, col. Folio, 1983.

KRUPA, S. J. "Celebrating Dorothy Day." *America*, August 27, 2001. http://americamagazine.org/issue/323/article/celebrating-dorothy-day.

KÜNG, H. *Christianity and the World Religions: Paths of Dialogue with Islam, Hinduism, and Buddhism*. Translated by P. Heinegg. Garden City, NY: Doubleday, 1986.

———. *O princípio de todas as coisas*. Petrópolis: Vozes, 2007.

———. *Proyecto de una ética mundial*. Madrid: Trotta, 1992.

KÜNG, H., et al. *A experiência do Espírito Santo*. Petrópolis: Vozes, 1979.

LABARRIERE, J. P. "L'homme et l'Absolu." *Archives de Philosophie* 36 (1973) 209–23.

LABBE, Y. *Dieu contre le mal: Un chemin de theologie philosophique*. Paris: Cerf, 2003.

LACOSTE, J.-Y., ed. *Dictionnaire critique de théologie*. Paris: Presses universitaires de France, 1998.

———. *La phenomenalité de Dieu: Neuf études*. Paris: Cerf, 2008.

LADARIA, L. *El Dios vivo y verdadero*. Salamanca: Estúdios Trinitarios, 2000.

LADRIÈRE, J. "Approcio filosofico alla mística." In *La mística*, edited by J. M. Van Cangh. Bologna: Dehniane, 1992.

———. *Articulation du sens*. Paris: Cerf, 1984.

LAMBERTH, D. C. *William James and the Metaphysics of Experience*. Cambridge: Cambridge University Press, 1999.

LASCH, C. *The Culture of Narcissism: American Life in an Age of Diminishing Expectations*. New York: Norton, 1978.

LE SAUX, H. *La montée au fond du coeur*. Paris: O.E.I.L., 1986.

LECLERC, E. *Le cantique des creatures ou les symboles de l'union: Une analyse de Saint François d'Assise*. Paris: Le Signe/Fayard, 1970.

LEVI, P. *Le devoir de mémoire*. Paris: Mille et une nuits, 2010.

———. *Si c'est un homme*. Paris: Julliard, 1987.

LEVINAS, E. *À l'heure des nations*. Montpellier: Fata Morgana, 1987.

———. *Autrement qu'être ou au-delà de l'essence*. La Haye: Martinus Nijhoff, 1974.

———. *Autrement que savoir*. Paris: Osiris, 1988.

———. *De Dieu que vient a l'idée*. Paris: Vrin, 1986.

———. *Difficile liberté*. Paris: Albin Michel, 1976.

———. *Du sacré au saint: Cinq nouvelles lectures talmudiques*. Paris: Minuit, 1977.

———. *En découvrant l'existence avec Husserl et Heidegger*. Paris: Vrin, 2002.

———. *Entre nous. Essais sur le penser-à-l'autre*. Paris: Grasset, 1998.

———. *Ethics and Infinity*. Translated by R. A. Cohen. Pittsburgh: Duquesne University Press, 1985.

———. *Ethique et infini. Dialogues avec Philippe Nemo*. Paris: Fayard-Radio France, 1983.

———. *Éthique comme philosophie première*. Paris: Payot & Rivages, 1998.

———. "Ethique et philosophie première. La proximité de l'autre." *Phréatique* 39 (1986) 121–27.

Bibliography 351

———. *God, Death and Time.* Translated by B. Bergo. Stanford: Stanford University Press, 2000.
———. *Hors-sujet.* Montpellier: Fata Morgana, 1987.
———. *Humanism of the Other.* Translated by N. Poller. Urbana: University of Illinois Press, 2003.
———. *Humanisme de l'autre homme.* Montpellier: Fata Morgana, 1972.
———. *Humanismo do outro homem.* Petrópolis: Vozes, 1993.
———. "Intentionalité et sensation." *Revue Internationale de Philosophie* 19 (1965) 34–54.
———. "Israel et l'universalisme." In *Dificile liberté.* Paris: Albin Michel, 1976.
———. "La laicité et la pensée d'Israel." In *Les imprévus de l'histoire.* Paris: Presses universitaires de France, 1960.
———. "Las tres formas de la esperanza." *La verdad es sinfónica.* Madrid: Encuentro, 1979.
———. *Le temps et l'autre.* Paris: Presses universitaires de France, 1983.
———. *Liberté et commandement.* Paris: Le livre de Poche, 1999.
———. *Totalité et infini: Essai sur l'extériorité.* La Haye: Martinus Nijhoff, 1968.
LIBÂNIO, J. B. "Cenários da Igreja." http://www.vidapastoral.com.br/artigos/eclesiologia/cenarios-da-igreja/.
———. *Crer num mundo de muitas crenças e pouca libertação.* Valencia: Siquem, 2003
———. *Eu creio, nós cremos: Tratado da fé.* São Paulo: Loyola, 2000.
———. "Fascínio do Sagrado." *Vida Pastoral* 41 (2000) 2–7
———. *Formação da consciência crítica.* Petrópolis: Vozes, 1984.
———. "Mística e missão do professor." http://www.infosbc.org.br/portal/index.php?option=com_content&view=article&id=364:mistica-e-missao-do-professor-por-j-b-libanio&catid=79:funcao&Itemid=97.
———. *Teologia da revelação a partir da modernidade.* São Paulo: Loyola, 1992.
———. *Volta à grande disciplina.* São Paulo: Loyola, 1980.
LIBÂNIO, J. B., and A. MURAD. *Introdução à teologia: Perfil, enfoques, tarefas.* São Paulo: Loyola, 1996.
LINDWORSKY, J. *The Psychology of Asceticism.* Baltimore: Carroll, 1950.
LIPOVETSKY, G. *A era do vazio.* São Paulo: Manole, 1985.
———. *A felicidade paradoxal.* São Paulo: Companhia das Letras, 2007.
———. *A sociedade pós-moralista: O crepúsculo do dever e a ética indolor dos novos tempos.* São Paulo: Manole, 1995.
———. *The Empire of Fashion: Dressing Modern Democracy.* Translated by C. Porter. Princeton: Princeton University Press, 1994.
———. *La culture-monde: Response a une societé desorientée.* Paris: Odile-Jacob, 2008.
———. *La societé de deception.* Paris: Textuel, 2006.
———. *Le bonheur paradoxal: Essai pour la societé d'hyperconsommation.* Paris: Gallimard, 2006.
———. *Le crespuscule du devoir: L'éthique indolore des nouveaux temps democratiques.* Paris: Gallimard, 1992.
———. *L'ere du vide: Essais sur l'individualisme contemporain.* Paris: Gallimard, 1983.
———. *Metamorphoses de la culture liberale.* Montreal: Liber, 2002.
———. *O futuro da autonomia: uma sociedade de indivíduos?* São Leopoldo/Rio de Janeiro: Unisinos/PUC-RJ, 2009.

———. *O império do efêmero: A moda e seu destino nas sociedades modernas*. São Paulo: Compahia das Letras, 1989.

LIPOVETSKY, G., and S. CHARLES. *Hypermodern Times*. Translated by A. Brown. Cambridge: Polity, 2005.

LITTLE, J. P. *Simone Weil: Research Bibliographies and Checklists*. London: Grant & Cutler, 1979.

LOBATO, A. *La pregunta por la mujer*. Salamanca: Sígueme, 1976.

LODI, E. *Estrela da minha vida: histórias do sertão caboclo*. Brasília: Edições Entre Folhas, 2004.

LONERGAN, B. *Insight: A Study of Human Understanding*. New York: Philosophical Library, 1958.

———. *Method in Theology*. New York: Herder and Herder, 1972.

LUBAC, H. de. *Affrontements mystiques*. Paris: Temoignage Chretien, 1949.

———. *Claudel et Peguy*. Paris: Aubier-Montaigne, 1974.

———. *The Discovery of God*. Translated by A. Dru. New York: P. J. Kenedy, 1960.

———. *Le drame de l'humanisme athée*. Paris: Spes, 1945.

———. *Le mystère du surnaturel*. Paris: Cerf, 2009.

———. *The Mystery of the Supernatural*. Translated by R. Sheed. Milestones in Catholic Theology. New York: Herder and Herder, 1967.

———. *Revelation divine: Affrontements mystiques; Atheisme et sens de l'homme*. Vol. 4 of *Oeuvres Completes*. Paris: Cerf, 2006.

LUZ, L. *Carnaval da alma: Communidade, essência e sincretismo na nova era*. Petrópolis: Vozes, 2000.

LYNCH, D. "Dorothy Day's Pro-Life Memories." Catholic Education Resource Center. http://www.catholiceducation.org/en/controversy/abortion/dorothy-day-s-pro-life-memories.html.

MACCINI, R. G. *Her Witness Is True: Women as Witnesses according to John*. JSOT Supplement Series 125. Sheffield: Sheffield Academic, 1996.

MAFFESOLI, M., ed. *Au creux des apparences: Pour une éthique de l'esthétique*. Paris: Plon, 1990.

———. *La connaissance ordinaire: Precis de sociologie comprehensive*. Paris: Librairie des Meridiens, 1985.

———. *La conquete du present*. Paris: Presses universitaires de France, 1979.

———. *Le reenchantement du monde*. Paris: La Table Ronde, 2007.

———. *Le temps des tribus: Le declin de l'individualisme dans les societés de masse*. Paris: Meridiens Klincksieck, 1988.

———. *Violence et transgression*. Paris: Anthropos, 1979.

MAITRE, J. "Les deux côtés du miroir. Note sur l'évolution religieuse actuelle de la population française par rapport au catholicisme." *L'Année Sociologique* 38 (1988) 33–48.

MANNHEIM, K. *Ideology and Utopia: An Introduction to the Sociology of Knowledge*. New York: Harcourt, Brace, 1936.

MANON, S. "Le divertissement. Pascal." January 11, 2008. http://www.philolog.fr/le-divertissement-pascal/.

MARCEL, G. *Homo Viator: Introduction to a Metaphysic of Hope*. Translated by E. Craufurd. Chicago: H. Regnery, 1951.

MARCOLIVIO, P. *Forme del destino Etty Hillesum*. Bari: Palomar, 2005.

MARCUSE, H., et al. *A la busqueda del sentido*. Salamanca: Sígueme, 1989.

MARDONES, J. M. *Análisis de la sociedad y fe cristiana*. Madrid: PPC, 1995.
―――. *Donde va la religión? Cristianismo y religiosidad en nuestro tiempo*. Santander: Sal Terrae, 1996.
―――. *El discurso religioso de la modernidad: Habermas y la religión*. Barcelona/ Mexico City: Anthropos/Universidad Iberoamericana, 1998.
―――. *El retorno del mito: La racionalidad mito-simbolica*. Madrid: Sintesis, 2000.
―――. *En el umbral del mañana: El cristianismo del futuro*. Madrid: PPC, 2000.
―――. *Fe y politica: El compromiso político de los cristianos en tiempos de desencanto*. Santander: Sal Terrae, 1993.
―――. *Hacia donde va la religión? Postmodernidad y postsecularización*. Mexico City: ITESO, 1996.
―――. *La indiferencia religiosa en España: Que futuro tiene el cristianismo?* Madrid: HOAC, 2003.
―――. *La transformación de la religión*. Madrid: PPC, 2005.
―――. *Las nuevas formas de la religión. La rconfiguración postcristiana de la religión*. Estella: Verbo Divino, 1994.
―――. *Matar a nuestros dioses: Un Dios para un creyente adulto*. Madrid: PPC, 2007.
―――. *Modernidad y postmodernidad: Posmodernidad y cristianismo; un debate sobre la sociedad actual*. Montevidéu: CLAEH, 1987.
―――. *Para comprender las nuevas formas de la religión: La reconfiguración postcristiana de la religión*. Estella: Verbo Divino, 1994.
―――. *Para un cristianismo de frontera*. Santander: Sal Terrae, Cuadernos Fe y Secularidad, 2000.
―――. *Postmodernidad y cristianismo: El desafio del fragmento*. Santander: Sal Terrae, 1988.
―――. *Postmodernidad y neoconservadurismo: Reflexiones sobre la fe y la cultura*. Estella: Verbo Divino, 1991.
―――. *Recuperar la justicia: Religión y política en una sociedad laica*. Santander: Sal Terrae, 2005.
―――. *Ser cristiano en la plaza publica*. Madrid: PPC, 2006.
―――. *Sintomas de un retorno: La religión en el pensamiento actual*. Santander: Sal Terrae, 1999.
―――. *Sociedad moderna y cristianismo: Corrientes socio-culturales y fe mesiánica*. Bilbao: DDB, 1985.
MARDONES, J. M., and J. REYES MATE. *La ética ante las victimas*. Barcelona: Anthropos, 2003.
MARÉCHAL, J. "À propos du sentiment de présence chez les profanes et chez les mystiques." *Revue des questions scientifiques* 14 (1908) 527–63.
―――. *Etudes sur la psychologie des mystiques*. 2 vols. Paris: DDB, 1937.
―――. *Le point de départ de la metaphysique*. 5 vols. Bruges: C. Beyaert, 1922–49.
―――. *A Maréchal Reader*. Edited and translated by J. Donceel. New York: Herder & Herder, 1970.
MARENZI, M. L. A. *Linguaggio e poesia: Paul Eluard, Simone Weil, Antoine de Saint Exupery*. Venice: Libreria Universitaria Editrice, 1966.
MARINUCCI, R., and R. MILESI. "Migrações internacionais contemporâneas." http:// www.migrante.org.br/migrante/index.php?option=com_content&view=article&id=143:migracoes-internacionais-contemporaneas&catid=87&Itemid=1203.

MARION, J. L. *Au lieu de soi: L'Aproche de Saint Augustin.* Paris: Presses universitaires de France, 2008.
———. *Certitudes négatives.* Paris: Grasset, 2010.
———. *De surcroît. Etudes sur les phénomènes saturés.* Paris: Presses universitaires de France, 2001.
———. *Dieu sans l'être.* Paris: Presses universitaires de France, 1991.
———. *Étant donné: essai d'une phénoménologie de la donation.* Paris: Presses universitaires de France, 1997.
———. *Le croire pour le voir.* Paris: Communio/Parole et silence, 2010.
———. *La croisee du visible.* Paris: Presses universitaires de France, 1996.
———. *L'idole et la distance.* Paris: Grasset, 1977.
———. *Le phénomène érotique—Six metitations.* Paris: Grasset, 2003.
———. *Le visible et le revele.* Paris: Cerf, 2005.
———. "Métaphysique et phénoménologie: une relève pour a théologie." *Bulletin de Littérature Ecclésiastique* 94 (1993) 189–206.
———. *Prolegomenes a la charité.* Paris: La Difference, 1986.
———. *Reduction et donation: recherches sur Husserl, Heidegger et la phénoménologie.* Paris: Presses universitaires de France, 1989.
MARION, J. L., and A. DE BENOIST. *Avec ou sans Dieu?* Paris: Beauchesne, 1970.
MARITAIN, J. *Distinguer pour unir: ou, Les degrés du savoir.* Paris: Desclée de Brouwer, 1932.
———. *Oeuvres Complètes.* Paris: Editions Universitaires, 1995.
———. *Redeeming the Time.* London: G. Bles, The Centenary Press, 1943.
MARLE, R. *Introduction à la théologie de la libération.* Paris: Desclée de Brouwer, 1988.
MARSHALL, I. H., ed. *Christian Experience in Theology and Life: Papers Read at the 1984 Conference of the Fellowship of European Evangelical Theologians.* Edinburgh: Rutherford House, 1988.
MARTELLI, S. *A religião na sociedade pós-moderna.* São Paulo: Paulinas, 1995.
MARTINELLI, P. *La morte di Cristo come rivelazione dell'amore trinitario nella teologia di Hans Urs von Balthasar.* Milan: Jaca Book, 1996.
MARTINI, C. M. *Nel cuore della Chiesa e del mondo: Dialogo con Antonio Balletto e Bruno Musso.* Genoa: Marietti, 1991.
MARTY, F. "Sentir et goûter." In *Les sens dans les "Exercices spirituels" de Saint Ignace.* Paris: Cerf, 2005.
MASIÁ CLAVEL, J., et al. *Pensar lo humano: Actas del II Congreso Nacional de Antropologia Filosofica.* Edited by J. Choza. Madrid: Iberoamericana, 1996.
MASLOW, A. *The Farther Reaches of Human Nature.* New York. Viking, 1971.
———. *Religions, Values and Peak-Experiences.* Columbus: Ohio State University Press, 1964.
———. *Toward a Psychology of Being.* New York: John Wiley, 1999.
MASON, M. G., and C. HURD GREEN, eds. *Journeys: Autobiograhical Writings by Women.* Boston: G. K. Hall, 1979.
MASSIGNON, L. *Parole donnée.* Paris: Julliard, 1962.
MATHON, G. "Sainteté." In vol. 61 of *Catholicisme: hier, aujourd'hui, et demain,* edited by G. Jacquemet. Paris: Letouzé et Ané, 1992.
MATTRE, J. "Les deux côtés du mirroir. Note sur l'évolution religieuse actuelle de la population française par rapport au catholicisme." *L'Année Sociologique* 38 (1988).

MAZZIOTTI, M. P., and S. LATTARULO. *La vita segreta delle parole.* Sant'Oreste: Apeiron, 2007.

MAZZIOTTI, M. P., and G. VAN OORD, eds. *Etty Hillesum, Diario 1941–1943: Un mondo "altro" è possible.* Sant'Oreste: Apeiron, 2002.

McCARTHY, T. *The Postconciliar Christian: The Meaning of the Priesthood of the Laity.* New York: P. J. Kenedy, 1967.

McCLENDON, J. WM., Jr. *Biography as Theology: How Life Stories Can Remake Today's Theology.* Philadelphia: Trinity Press International, 1990.

McCOLMAN, C. *The Big Book of Christian Mysticism: The Essential Guide to Contemplative Spirituality.* Charlottesville: Hampton Roads, 2010.

McDONNELL, K. "Spirit and Experience in Bernard of Clairvaux." *Theological Studies* 58 (1997) 3–18.

McGINLEY, P. *Saint-Watching.* Chicago: Thomas More Press, 1982.

McGINN, B. *Doctors of the Church: Thirty-Three Men and Women Who Shaped Christianity.* New York: Crossroad, 1999.

———, ed. *The Essential Writings of Christian Mysticism.* New York: Modern Library, 2006.

———. *The Flowering of Mysticism: Men and Women in the New Mysticism, 1200–1350.* New York: Crossroad, 1988.

———. *The Foundations of Mysticism.* New York: Crossroad, 1994.

———. *The Harvest of Mysticism in Medieval Germany (1300–1500).* New York: Crossroad, 2005.

———. Review of *Mysticism: A Study of Its Nature, Cognitive Value and Moral Implications* by William J. Wainwright. *Journal of Religion* 65 (1985) 306–7.

McGINN, B., and P. F. McGINN. *Early Christian Mystics: The Divine Vision of the Spiritual Masters.* New York: Crossroad, 2003.

McGINN, B., et al. *Christian Spirituality: Origins to the Twelfth Century.* New York: Crossroad, 1986.

McGUIRE, B. P. *Jean Gerson: Early Works.* New York: Paulist, 1998.

McINTOSH, M. A. *Christology from Within: Spirituality and the Incarnation in Hans Urs von Balthasar.* Notre Dame: University of Notre Dame Press, 1996.

McNAMARA, W. *Christian Mysticism: A Psychotheology.* Chicago: Franciscan Herald Press, 1981.

MEIER, J. P. *A Marginal Jew: Rethinking the Historical Jesus.* 4 vols. New York: Doubleday, 1991–2009.

MERLATTI, G. *Etty Hillesum, un cuore pensante.* Milan: Ancora, 1999.

MEROZ, C. "La vie des amants de Dieu: Une voix du désert et un témoin de notre temps." *Vie Consacrée* 54 (1982) 27–49.

MERRIMAN, B. O. *Searching for Christ: The Spirituality of Dorothy Day.* Notre Dame: University of Notre Dame Press, 1994.

MERTON, T. *The Ascent to Truth.* Harcourt, Brace, 1951.

———. *The Asian Journal of Thomas Merton.* Edited by N. Burton et al. New York: New Directions, 1973.

———. *At Home in the World: The Letters of Thomas Merton and Rosemary Radford Reuther.* Edited by M. Tardiff. Maryknoll, NY: Orbis, 1995.

———. *Basic Principles of Monastic Spirituality.* Bardstown, KY: Abbey of Gethsemani, 1957.

———. *Bread in the Wilderness.* New York: New Directions, 1953.

———. *Conjectures of a Guilty Bystander.* New York: Doubleday, 1966.
———. *Contemplative Prayer.* Garden City, NY: Image, 1971.
———. *The Courage for Truth: The Letters of Thomas Merton to Writers.* Selected and edited by C. M. Bochen. New York: Farrar, Straus, Giroux, 1993.
———. *Faith and Violence: Christian Teaching and Christian Practice.* Notre Dame: University of Notre Dame Press, 1984.
———. *The Hidden Ground of Love: The Letters of Thomas Merton on Religious Experience and Social Concerns.* Selected and edited by W. H. Shannon. New York: Farrar, Straus, Giroux, 1985.
———. *Honorable Reader: Reflections on My Work.* New York: Crossroad, 1989.
———. *The Nonviolent Alternative.* Edited by G. C. Zahn. New York: Farrar, Straus, Giroux, 1980.
———. *The Other Side of the Mountain: The End of the Journey.* Edited by P. Hart. San Francisco: HarperSanFrancisco, 1998.
———. *Peace in the Post-Christian Era.* Edited by P. A. Burton. Maryknoll, NY: Orbis, 2004.
———. *The Secular Journal of Thomas Merton.* New York: Farrar, Straus and Cudahy, 1959.
———. *Seeds of Destruction.* New York: Farrar, Straus, Giroux, 1980.
———. *The Seven Storey Mountain.* New York: Harcourt, Brace, 1948.
———. *Thomas Merton on Peace.* New York: McCall, 1971.
———. *Thoughts on the East.* New York: New Directions, 1995.
———. *Turning Toward the World: The Pivotal Years.* Edited by V. A. Kramer. San Francisco: HarperSanFrancisco, 1996.
———. *Witness to Freedom: The Letters of Thomas Merton in Times of Crisis.* Selected and edited by W. H. Shannon. New York: Farrar, Straus, Giroux, 1994.
MESLIN, M. *L'Expérience Humaine du Divin.* Paris: Cerf, 1988.
METZ, J. B., ed. *El clamor de la tierra: el problema dramático de la Teodicea.* Estella: Verbo Divino, 1996.
———. *Faith in History and Society: Toward a Practical Fundamental Theology.* Translated by D. Smith. New York: Seabury, 1979.
———. *Memoria Passionis.* Santander: Sal Terrae, 2007.
———. *A Passion for God: The Mystical-Political Dimension of Christinity.* Edited and translated by J. M. Ashley. New York: Paulist, 1998.
———. *Poverty of Spirit.* Translated by J. Drury. Rev. ed. New York: Paulist, 1998.
MEYER, C. *The Touch of God: A Theological Analysis of Religious Experience.* Staten Island, NY: Alba House, 1971.
MEYER, W. J. *Metaphysics and the Future of Theology: The Voice of Theology in Public Life.* Eugene, OR: Pickwick, 2010.
MIETH, D. "Alla ricerca de una definisione del concetto 'esperienza': che cos'è l'esperienza?" *Concilium* 13 (1978) 69–89.
MILITELLO, C. *Christianismo al femminile.* Milan: Dehoniane, 1995.
MILLER, W. D. *All Is Grace: The Spirituality of Dorothy Day.* Garden City, NY: Doubleday, 1987.
———. *Dorothy Day: A Biography.* London: HarperCollins, 1984.
———. *A Harsh and Dreadful Love: Dorothy Day and the Catholic Worker Movement.* New York: Liveright, 1973.

MIRABELLA, P. *Agire nello Spirito: Sull'esperienza morale della vita spirituale.* Assisi: Citadella Editrice, 2003.
MITCHELL, D. *Cultural Geography: A Critical Introduction.* London: Blackwell, 2000.
MOELLER, CH. *Littérature du XXe siècle et christianisme.* Vol. 1, *Silence de Dieu.* Tournai: Casterman, 1963.
MOINGT, J. *Dieu qui vient à l'homme.* Vol. 1. Paris: Cerf, 2003.
———. *Dios que viene al hombre.* Salamanca: Sígueme, 2004.
———. *El hombre que venía de Dios.* Bilbao: Desclée, 1998.
———. *L'homme qui venait de Dieu.* Paris: Cerf, 1997.
MOIOLI, G. "Mística cristiana." In *Nuevo diccionario de teología.* Madrid: BAC, 1982.
MOLTMANN, J. *The Crucified God: The Cross of Christ as the Foundation and Criticism of Christian Theology.* Translated by R. A. Wilson and John Bowden. New York: Harper & Row, 1974.
———. *God for a Secular Society: The Public Relevance of Theology.* Minneapolis: Fortress, 1994.
———. *God in Creation: An Ecological Doctrine of Creation; The Gifford Lectures 1984-85.* London: SCM, 1985.
———. *The Trinity and the Kingdom.* Translated by M. Kohl. London: SCM, 1987.
MOLTMANN, J., and E. MOLTMANN-WENDEL. *Passion for God: Theology in Two Voices.* Louisville: Westminster John Knox, 2003.
MONGRAIN, K. *The Systematic Thought of Hans Urs von Balthasar.* New York: Crossroad, 2002.
MOREIRA, R. "A reinvenção do mundo moderno e a nova forma da geografia." http://www.pucsp.br/~diamantino/circulocap4.htm.
MOREL, G. *Questions d'homme: l'autre.* Paris: Aubier-Montaigne, 1977.
MORO, U. V. *Orientação espiritual: Mistagogia e teografia.* São Paulo: Loyola, 2001.
MOUNIER, E. *Feu la chretienté.* Paris: Seuil, 1950.
———. *L'engagement de la foi.* Paris: Seuil, 1968.
———. *Le personnalisme.* 7th ed. Paris: Presses universitaires de France, 1961.
MOUROUX, J. *L'expérience chrétienne: Introduction a une théologie.* Paris: Aubier, 1952.
———. *The Christian Experience: An Introduction to Theology.* New York: Sheed and Ward, 1954.
———. "Language catéchétique et expérience chrétienne. Réflexion philosophique et théologique." *Catéchistes* 71 (1967).
MULLER-ARMACK, A. *El siglo sin Dios.* Mexico City: Fondo de Cultura Económica, 1986.
MUÑOZ, R. *O Deus dos cristãos.* Petrópolis: Vozes, 1985.
MURPHY, M. P. *A Theology of Criticism: Balthasar, Postmodernism and the Catholic Imagination.* Oxford: Oxford University Press, 2008.
NABERT, J. *Le desir de Dieu.* Paris: Cerf, 1996.
NEEFS, E. G. "Portrait d'un 'contemplatif dans l'action': Egide van Broeckhoven (1933-1967)." *Vie Consacrée* 45 (1973) 193-221.
NELSTROP, L, et al. *Christian Mysticism: An Introduction to Contemporary Approaches.* Burlington, VT: Ashgate, 2009.
NERI, N. *Un'estrema compassione: Etty Hillesum testimone e vittima del Lager.* Milan: Mandadori, 1999.
NEVIN, Th. R. *Simone Weil: Portrait of a Self-Exiled Jew.* Chapel Hill: University of North Carolina Press, 1991.

NICHOLS, A. *No Bloodless Myth: A Guide through Balthasar's Dramatics*. Washington, DC: Catholic University of America Press, 2000.
NIGG, W. *Heilige im Alltag*. Dusseldorf: Walter Verlag, 1976.
NIZNIK, J., and J. T. SANDERS, eds. *Debating the State of Philosophy: Habernas, Rorty, and Kolakowski*. Westport, CT: Praeger, 1996.
NOCELLI, G. *Oltre la ragione: Risonanze filosofiche dal pensiero e dall' itinerario esistenziale di Etty Hillesum*. Sant'Oreste: Apeiron, 2004.
———. *Se amare e chiedere troppo: Leggendo Etty Hillesum*. Rome: Pro Sanctitate, 2004.
NOLASCO, S. *De Tarzan a Homer Simpson*. Rio de Janeiro: Rocco, 2002.
NOONE, J., and C. GLAVAC. *Compañeras en el camino: Mártires de El Salvador*. San Salvador: UCA, 1999.
NOVAES, J. V. *Com que corpo eu vou?* Rio de Janeiro: Pallas, 2010.
———. *O intolerável peso da feiura*. Rio de Janeiro: Garamond, 2006.
NUMMINEN, T. *God, Power and Justice in Texts of Simone Weil and Dorothee Sölle*. Åbo: Åbo Akademis förlag, 2001.
NUVOLI, P. F. M. *Approccio antropologico all'esperienza cristiana nella riflessione teologica di Jean Mouroux*. Rome: Pontificia Universitas Gregoriana, 1988.
NYE, A. *The Thought of Losa Luxemburg, Simone Weil and Hannah Arendt*. New York: Routledge, 1994.
OBINU, S. *I dilemmi del corpo: Materia e corporeita negli scritti di Simone Weil*. Florence: Lalli, 1989.
O'BRIEN, R. *Global Financial Integration: The End of Geography*. New York: Council on Foreign Relations Press, 1992.
O'COLLINS, G. "Experience." In *Dictionary of Fundamental Theology*, edited by R. Latourelle and R. Fischella. New York: Crossroad, 1995.
———. *Fundamental Theology*. New York: Paulist, 1981.
———. "The Holy Trinity: The State of the Questions." In *The Trinity: An Interdisciplinary Symposium on the Trinity*, edited by D. Kendall and G. O'Collins. Oxford: Oxford University Press, 1999.
O'CONNOR, J. "Dorothy Day's Christian Conversion." *The Journal of Religious Ethics* 18 (1990) 159–80.
———. *The Moral Vision of Dorothy Day: A Feminist Perspective*. New York: Crossroad, 1991.
O'GRADY, J. *Dorothy Day: With Love for the Poor*. New York: Ward Hill, 1993.
O'HANLON, G. *The Immutability of God in the Theology of Hans Urs von Balthasar*. New York: Cambridge University Press, 1990.
OKURE, T., et al., eds. *Rethinking Martyrdom*. London: SCM, 2003.
OLIVERA, B. *How Far to Follow?* Kalamazoo, MI: Cistercian, 1997.
O'MALLEY, W. J. *The Voice of Blood: Five Christian Martyrs of Our Time*. Maryknoll, NY: Orbis, 1980.
ONFRAY, M. *Atheist Manifesto: The Case against Christianity, Judaism, and Islam*. Translated by J. Leggatt. New York: Arcade, 2007.
OORD, G. van, ed. *Con Etty Hillesum: Quaderno di informazione e ricercas*. Sant'Oreste: Apeiron, 2009.
OTTENSMEYER, H. *Le theme de l'amour dans l'oeuvre de Simone Weil*. Paris: Lettres Modernes, 1958.

OTTO, R. *The Idea of the Holy: An Inquiry into the Non-rational Factor in the Idea of the Divine and Its Relation to the Rational.* Translated by J. W. Harvey. London: Oxford University Press, 1923.

———. *Lo Santo: lo irracional y lo racional en la idea de Dios.* Madrid: Allianza, 2005.

OXENHANDLER, N. *Looking for Heroes in Postwar France: Albert Camus, Max Jacob, Simone Weil.* Hanover, NH: University Press of New England, 1996.

PACE, E. "Religião e globalização." In *Globalização e religião,* edited by A. P. Oro and C. A. Steil. Petrópolis: Vozes, 1997.

PANIER, L. "Pour une anthropologie du croire: Aspects de la problématique chez Michel de Certeau." In *Michel de Certeau, ou, La différence chrétienne,* edited by C. Geffré. Paris: Cerf, 1991.

PANIKKAR, R. *De la mística: Experiencia plena de la vida.* Barcelona: Herder, 2005.

———. *Entre Dieu et le cosmos.* Paris: Albin Michel, 1998.

———. *The Experience of God: Icons of the Mystery.* Translated by J. Cunneen. Minneapolis: Fortress, 2006.

PASCAL, B. *Pensées.* Paris: Edition Bibliothèque de la Pléiade, 1954.

PASCUAL, F. R., et al. *Vivencia mistica y tejido social.* Zamora: Monte Casino, 2006.

PASQUA, C. *Simone Weil, biographie imaginaire: Souvenirs de celle que je n'ai pas rencontrée.* Paris: L'Harmattan, 2005.

PASTOR, F. A. *A lógica do inefável.* São Paulo: Loyola, 1989.

———. *A semântica do mistério.* São Paulo: Loyola, 1982.

———. "L'uomo e la ricerca di Dio." In *Vaticano II: bilancio e prospettive venticinque anni dopo (1962–1987),* edited by R. Latourelle. Assisi: Citadella Editrice, 1987.

PEPLER, C. *The Three Degrees: A Study of Christian Mysticism.* London: Blackfriars, 1957.

PETITDEMANGE, G., and J. ROLLAND. *Autrement que savoir. Emmanuel Levinas.* Paris: Osiris, 1988.

PÉTREMENT, S. *La Vie de Simone Weil.* Vol. 2. Paris: Fayard, 1978.

PETROLLE, J. E. *Religion without Belief: Contemporary Allegory and the Search for Postmodern Faith.* Albany: State University of New York Press, 2008.

PIEHL, M. *Breaking Bread: The Catholic Worker and the Origin of Catholic Radicalism in America.* Philadelphia: Temple University Press, 1982.

PIERRON, J-P. *Le passage de temoin: Une philosophie du temoignage.* Paris: Cerf, 2006.

PINHEIRO, M. R., and M. C. BINGEMER, eds. *Mística e filosofia.* Rio de Janeiro: PUC-Rio/Uape, 2010.

PLESHOYANO, A. *Etty Hillesum: L'Amour comme "seule solution"; Une hermeneutique theologique au coeur du mal.* Berlin: LIT, 2007.

———. "L'heritage spiritual d'Etty Hillesum: 'Je me sens comme une des nombreuses heritieres d'un grand legs spirituel.'" *Studies in Religion/Sciences Religieuses* 37 (2008) 63–79.

POULAT, E. *Critique et mystique: Autour de Loisy ou la conscience catholique et l'esprit moderne.* Paris: Le Centurion, 1984.

———. *Histoire, dogme et critique dans la crise moderniste.* Paris: Casterman, 1979.

———. *L'ere post-chretienne.* Paris: Flammarion, 1994.

———. *L'université devant la mystique.* Paris: Salvator, 1999.

POULAT, E., and D. DECHERF. *Le Christianisme a contre-histoire.* Paris: Editions du Rocher, 2003.

POUPARD, P., ed. *Diccionario de las religiones.* Barcelona: Herder, 1987.

POWELL, S. M. *Participating in God: Creation and Trinity.* Minneapolis: Fortress, 2003.
PRETI, A. "Unanimity among Mystics: An Inquiry into the Phenomenology of Mystical Experience." PhD diss., Temple University, 2002.
PROUDFOOT, W. *Religious Experience.* Berkeley: University of California Press, 1985.
PSEUDO-DIONYSIUS, THE AREOPAGITE. *The Divine Names; and, Mystical Theology.* Translated by John D. Jones. Milwaukee: Marquette University Press, 1980.
PUJOL, O., and A. VEGA. *A revelação de Deus na realização humana.* São Paulo: Paulus, 1998.
———. *Creio em Deus Pai.* São Paulo: Paulinas, 1993.
———. *Do terror de Isaac ao Abba de Jesus.* São Paulo: Paulinas, 2000.
———. *Las palabras del silencio: El lenguaje de la ausencia en las distintas tradiciones misticas.* Madrid: Trotta, 2006.
———. *O fim do cristianismo pré-moderno.* São Paulo: Paulus, 2003.
QUEIRUGA, A. T. *A revelação de Deus na realização humana.* São Paulo: Paulinas, 1990.
———. *Creio em Deus Pai: O Deus de Jesus como afirmação plena do humano.* São Paulo: Paulinas, 1993.
———. *Fim do cristianismo pré-moderno: desafios para um novo horizonte.* São Paulo: Paulus, 2003.
RAHNER, K. *Christian at the Crossroads.* New York: Seabury, 1975.
———. *The Christian of the Future.* Translated by W. J. O'Hara. New York: Herder and Herder, 1967.
———. *Curso fundamental da fé.* Paulinas: São Paulo, 1989.
———. *Écrits de théologie.* Paris: Cerf, 1962.
———. *Éléments dynamiques dans l'Église.* Questiones disputatae 1. Paris: Desclée de Brouwer, 1967.
———. *Encounters with Silence.* South Bend, IN: St. Augustine's Press, 1999.
———. "The Experience of God Today." In vol. 11 of *Theological Investigations*, 149–65. New York: Crossraod, 1982.
———. "Experience of Self and Experience of God." In vol. 13 of *Theological Investigations*, 122–32. New York: Seabury, 1975.
———. "Experience of Transcendence from the Standpoint of Christian Dogmatics." In vol. 18 of *Theological Investigations*, 177–81. New York: Crossroad, 1983.
———. *Foundations of Christian Faith: An Introduction to the Idea of Christianity.* Translated by W. V. Dych. New York: Seabury, 1978.
———. *I Remember: An Autobiographical Interview with Meinold Krauss.* Translated by H. D. Egan. New York: Crossroad, 1985.
———. "La experiencia de Dios hoy." In *Escritos de Teologia IX*. Madrid: Cristiandad, 1970.
———. *La mistica ignaciana de la alegria del mundo: Escritos de Teologia III.* Madrid: Taurus, 1961.
———. "Los cristianos anónimos." In *Escritos de Teologia VI*.
———. *Mary, Mother of the Lord.* Translated by W. J. O'Hara. 2nd ed. Wheathampstead: A. Clarke, 1974.
———. *The Mystical Way in Everyday Life: Sermons, Prayers, and Essays.* Translated and edited by A. S. Kidder. Maryknoll, NY: Orbis, 2010.

———. *The Need and the Blessing of Prayer*. Translated by B. W. Gillette. Collegeville, MN: Liturgical Press, 1997.
———. *The Practice of Faith: A Handbook of Contemporary Spirituality*. Edited by K. Lehmann and A. Raffelt. New York: Crossroad, 1984.
———. *Theological Investigations*. Vol. 3, *Theology of the Spiritual Life*. Baltimore: Helicon, 1967.
———. *Theological Investigations*. Vol. 16, *Experience of the Spirit: Source of Theology*. New York: Crossroad, 1979.
RAHNER, K., and J. B. METZ. *The Courage to Pray*. New York: Crossroad, 1981.
RAMBLA, J. M. *Dios, la amistad y los pobres: La mistica de Egide van Broeckhoven, jesuita obrero*. Santander: Sal Terrae, 2007.
RAVIER, A., ed. *La mystique et les mystiques*. Paris: Desclée, 1965.
REES, R. *Brave Men: A Study on D. H. Lawrence and Simone Weil*. London: Gollancz, 1958.
REMY, G. "Etty Hillesum et Saint Augustin: l'influence d'un maitre spirituel?" *Recherches de science religieuse* 95 (2007) 253–78.
REY, J. M. *Les promesses de l'oeuvre: Artaud, Nietzsche, Simone Weil*. Paris: Desclée de Brouwer, 2003.
RHEES, R. *Discussions of Simone Weil*. Edited by D. Z. Phillips, with the assistance of M. von der Ruhr. Albany: State University of New York Press, 1999.
RICOEUR, P. *The Conflict of Interpretations: Essays in Hermeneutics*. Edited by D. Ihde. New ed. Evanston: Northwestern University Press, 2007.
———. "De la morale à l'éthique et aux éthiques." In *Un siècle de philosophie, 1900–2000*. Folio Essais. Paris: Gallimard, 2001.
———. *Freud and Philosophy: An Essay on Interpretation*. Translated by D. Savage. New Haven: Yale University Press, 1970.
———. "Herméneutique de l'idée de révélation." In Ricoeur et al., *La révélation*, 10–27. Brussels: Facultés universitaires St.-Louis, 1977.
———. *History and Truth*. Translated by C. A. Kelbley. Evanston: Northwestern University Press, 1965.
———. "Le sujet convoqué: A l'école des récits de vocation prophétique." *Revue de l'Institut Catholique* 28 (1988) 83–99.
———. "L'herméneutique de la sécularisation: Foir, idéologie, utopie." In *Actes d'un colloque organisé par le Centre International d'Études Humanistes et par l'institut d'Études Philosophiques de Rome*, edited by E. Castelli. Paris: Aubier, 1976.
———. "Nomear Deus." In *Nas fronteiras da filosofia*. São Paulo: Loyola, 1996.
———. *Soi-même comme un autre*. Paris: Seuil, 1990.
RICOEUR, P., and E. JÜNGEL. *Dire Dio: Per un'ermeneutica del linguaggio religioso*. Brescia: Queriniana, 2005.
RICOSSA, F., and M. L. GUERARD DES LAURIERS. *Cristina Campo, o l'ambiguità della tradizione: Risposta alla "Lettera ad un religioso" di Simone Weil*. Turin: Verrua Savoia, 2005.
RIEGLE, R. G. *Dorothy Day: Portraits by Those Who Knew Her*. Maryknoll, NY: Orbis, 2003.
RILEY, G. J. *One Jesus, Many Christs: How Jesus Inspired Not One True Christianity, but Many; the Truth about Christian Origins*. Minneapolis: Fortress, 2000.
RIOUX, J. P., and J. F. SIRINELLI. *Para uma história cultural*. Lisbon: Estampa, 1998.

ROBBINS, J., ed. *Is It Righteous to Be? Interviews with Emmanuel Levinas*. Stanford: Stanford University Press, 2001.
ROCHA, J. G. *Teologia e negritude: Um estudo sobre os agentes de pastoral negros*. Santa Maria: Pallotti, 1998.
RODRIGUES, D. DOS SANTOS. "Os sem religião no Censo nacional: investigações e ponderações acerca da ausência de pertencimento religioso no Brasil." http://www.espacoacademico.com.br/094/94rodrigues.htm.
RODRÍGUEZ PANIZO, P. "El caracter iniciatico de la experiencia mistica." In *Miscelanea Comillas* 53 (1995) 93–113.
ROGERS, H. J., ed. *Congress of Arts and Science, Universal Exposition, St. Louis, 1904*. Vol 1. Boston: Houghton, Mifflin, 1905.
ROMERO, Ó. *Homilías. Monseñor Óscar A. Romero*. Vols. 1 and 2. San Salvador: UCA, 2005–6.
RORTY, R. *Objectivity, Relativism, and Truth*. Philosophical Papers 1. Cambridge: Cambridge University Press, 1991.
RORTY, R., and P. ENGEL. *What's the Use of Truth?* Edited by P. Savidan. Translated by W. McCuaig. New York: Columbia University Press, 2007.
RORTY, R., and G. VATTIMO. *The Future of Religion*. Edited by S. Zabala. New York: Columbia University Press, 2004.
ROSANNE STONE, A. Preface to *Electronic Culture: Technology and Visual Representation*. Edited by T. Druckery. New York: Aperture, 1996.
ROSENZWEIG, F. *L'Etoile de la redemption*. Paris: Seuil, 2003.
ROY, L. *Le sentiment de transcendence, expérience de Dieu*. Paris: Cerf, 2000.
ROYAL, R. *The Catholic Martyrs of the Twentieth Century*. New York: Crossroad, 2000.
RUIZ DE LA PENA, J. L. *El don de Dios: Antropologia teológica*. Sal Terrae: Santander, 1991.
SADER, E. "Capitalismo: o que é isso?" *Carta Maior*, January 5, 2011. http://www.cartamaior.com.br/?/Blog/Blog-do-Emir/Capitalismo-o-que-e-isso-/2/23678.
SANCHIS, P. "O campo religioso contemporâneo no Brasil." In *Globalização e religião*, edited by A. P. Oro and C. A. Steil, 103–15. Petrópolis: Vozes, 1997.
SANTOS, L. *O sujeito encarnado: A sensibilidade como paradigma ético em Emanuel Levinas*. Ijuí: Unijuí, 2009.
SARGENT, L. T. "Utopianism." In *Routledge Encyclopedia of Philosophy*, edited by E. Craig. London: Routledge, 1998.
SARTRE, J.-P. *Huis Clos. Pièce en un acte*. Paris: Gallimard, 1945.
———. *L'etre et le néant: Essai d'ontologie phénomenologique*. Paris: Gallimard, 1943.
SAUDREAU, A. M. *L'Etat mystique: Sa nature, ses phases, et les etats extraordinaires de la vie spirituelle*. Paris: Amat, 1921.
SCANNONE, J. C. "Do símbolo à prática da analogia." *Stromata* 55 (1999) 19–51.
———. "Filosofia primera y intersubjetividad. El a priori de la Comunidad de Comunicación y el Nosotros Ético-Histórico." *Revista Stromata*. San Miguel: Facultades de Filosofía y Teología, 42, 1986, 367–86.
———. "Identidad personal, alteridad interpersonal y relación religiosa. Aporte filosófico." *Stromata* 58 (2002) 249–62.
———. "Racionalidad Ética, comunidad de comunicación y alteridad." *Stromata* 43/44 (1987) 393–97.
SCHAEFFER, F. *The God Who Is There*. London: Hodder & Stoughton, 1968.
SCHILLEBEECKX, E. *Revelação e teologia*. São Paulo: Paulinas, 1968.

Bibliography

SCHLEGEL, J.-L. "Retour du religieux et christianisme. Quand de vieilles croyances redeviennent nouvelles." *Études* 362 (1985) 89–104.
SCHLOSSBERG, H. *Called to Suffer—Called to Triumph*. Portland: Multnomah, 1990.
SCHLUTER RODES, A. M., and J. I. GONZALEZ FAUS. "Mística oriental y mística cristiana. XII Foro sobre el Hecho Religioso." *Cuadernos Fé y Secularidad,* 44. Santander: Sal Terrae, 1998.
SCHMITZ, K. L. *The Recovery of Wonder: The New Freedom and the Asceticism of Power*. Montreal: McGill-Queen's University Press, 2005.
SCHNEIDER, M. *Teología como biografía: una fundamentación dogmática*. Bilbao: Desclée de Brouwer, 2000.
SCHOLEM, G. *A mística judaica*. São Paulo: Perspectiva, 1972.
———. *As correntes da mística judaica*. Rio de Janeiro: Objetiva, 1982.
———. *The Major Trends in Jewish Mysticism*. New York: Schocken, 1995.
———. "Mysticism and Society." *Diogenes* 58 (1967) 1–25.
———. *On the Kabbalah and Its Symbolism*. New York: Schocken, 1965.
———. *On the Kabbalah: New Perspectives*. New Haven: Yale University Press, 1988.
SCHRIJVER, G. *Le merveilleux accord de l'homme et de Dieu: Etude de l'analogie de l'etre chez Hans Urs von Balthasar*. Leuven: Leuven University Press/Peeters, 1983.
SCHUMANN, M. *La mort nee de leur propre vie: Trois essais sur Peguy, Simone Weil, Gandhi*. Paris: Fayard, 1974.
SCHWEHN, M., and D. C. BASS. *Leading Lives That Matter: What We Should Do and Who We Should Be*. Grand Rapids: Eerdmans, 2006.
SCHWEITZER, A. *Humanisme et mystique*. Edited by J. P. Sorg. Paris: Albin Michel, 1995.
———. *The Mysticism of Paul the Apostle*. London: A. & C. Black, 1931.
SECOND VATICAN COUNCIL. *Dei Verbum,* n. 6.
———. *Dei Verbum,* n° 1, n° 2, n° 3, n° 8, n° 14.
———. *Gaudium et Spes,* n°11, n° 12, n° 29, n° 32, n° 36, n° 92.
———. *Lumen Gentium,* n° 1.
———. *Nostra Aetate,* n° 1, n° 3, n° 4, n° 5.
———. *Optatam Totius,* n° 8.
———. *Unitatis Redintegratio,* n° 1, n° 12.
SEMERARO, L. *Filosofia oppressiva e verita liberante: L'experienza intellettuale di Simone Weil*. Manduria: Capone, 1990.
SERVAIS, P. *La spiritualité du martyre: jusqu'au bout de l'amour*. Versailles: Saint Paul, 2000.
SFAMURRI, A. *L'umanesimo Cristiano di Simone Weil*. L'Aquila: Japadre, 1970.
SHELDRAKE, P. *Espiritualidade e teologia: Vida cristã e fé trinitária*. São Paul: Paulinas, 2005.
SILANES, N., et al. *Encarnación Redentora*. Salamanca: Secretariado Trinitario, 1999.
SIQUEIRA, D. "Pluralidade e trânsito religioso na atualidade." http://bmgil.tripod.com/sde47.html.
SITTSER, G. *Water from a Deep Well: Christian Spirituality from Early Martyrs to Modern Missionaries*. Downers Grove, IL: InterVarsity, 2007.
SMART, N. "Mysticism, history of." In vol. 5 of *Encyclopaedia of Philosophy*, edited by P. Edwards, 419–29. New York: Macmillan, 1967.
SMITH, J. E. *The Analogy of Experience: An Approach to Understanding Religious Truth*. New York: Harper & Row, 1973.

SMOLKA, A. L. B. "A memória em questão: uma perspectiva histórico-cultural." *Educacão & Sociedade* 21 (2000) 166–93.
SOBRINO, J. "Carta a Ignacio Ellacuria." *Adital*, October 31, 2008. http://www.adital.com.br/site/noticia.asp?lang=PT&cod=35809.
———. "Espiritualidade e teologia." In *Liberación con Espíritu*. Santander: Sal Terrae, 1985.
———. *Jesus na America Latina: Ensaio a partir das vítimas*. São Paulo: Loyola, 2000.
———. *No Salvation Outside the Poor: Prophetic-Utopian Essays*. Maryknoll, NY: Orbis, 2008.
SÖLLE, D. *The Silent Cry: Mysticism and Resistance*. Translated by B. Rumscheidt and M. Rumscheidt. Minneapolis: Fortress, 2001.
SPIER, J. *The Hands of Children: An Introduction to Psycho-Chirology*. Translated by V. Grove. 2nd ed. London: Kegan Paul, 1944.
STACE, W. T. *Mysticism and Philosophy*. Philadelphia: Lippincott, 1960.
STATNICK, R. A. "Dorothy Day's Religious Conversion: A Study in Biographical Theology." PhD diss., Notre Dame University, 1983.
STEIN, E. *Self-Portrait in Letters*. Translated by J. Koeppel. Washington, DC: ICS, 1993.
STEINER, G. *Real Presences: Is There Anything in What We Say?* New York: Faber and Faber, 1989.
STIRNIMANN, H. "Linguaggio, esperienza e incontro com Colui che parla." *Concilium* 13 (1978) 172–91.
STOLZ, A. *Theologie de la mystique*. Chevetogne: Editions des benedictins d'Amay, 1947.
SUDBRACK, J. *Mística: A busca do sentido e a experiência do Absoluto*. São Paulo: Loyola, 2007.
———. "Mística cristiana." In *Problemas y perspectivas de espiritualidade*, edited by T. Goffi and B. Secondin. Salamanca: Sígueme, 1986.
SUENENS, L. J. *Baudouin, King of the Belgians: The Hidden Life*. Translated by H. M. Wynne. Brussels: FIAT, 1996.
SULKUNEN, P., et al., eds. *Constructing the New Consumer Society*. London: Macmillan, 1997.
TARDAN-MASQUELIER, Y. *Les spiritualités au carrefour du monde moderne: Traditions, transitions, transmissions*. Paris: Le Centurion, 1994.
TAVARD, G. *The Inner Life: Foundations of Christian Mysticism*. New York: Paulist, 1976.
TAYLOR, C. *A Catholic Modernity? Charles Taylor's Marianist Award Lecture*. Edited by J. L. Heft. Oxford: Oxford University Press, 1996.
———. *The Ethics of Authenticity*. Cambridge: Harvard University Press, 2003.
———. *The Explanation of Behavior*. London: Routledge & Kegan Paul, 1964.
———. *Modern Social Imaginaries*. Durham: Duke University Press, 2004.
———. *A Secular Age*. Cambridge: Belknap Press of Harvard University Press, 2007.
———. *Sources of the Self: The Making of the Modern Identity*. Cambridge: Harvard University Press, 1989.
———. *Varieties of Religion Today: William James Revisited*. Cambridge: Harvard University Press, 2002.
TAZI, N., ed. *Experience: For a Different Kind of Globalization*. Keywords. New York: Other Press, 2004.

Bibliography

TERESA, MOTHER. *Come Be My Light: The Private Writings of the "Saint of Calcutta".* Edited by B. Kolodiejchuk. New York: Doubleday, 2007.
THÉRÈSE DE LISIEUX. *Story of a Soul: The Autobiography of St. Therese of Lisieux.* Translated by John Clarke. 3rd ed. Washington, DC: ICS Publications, 1996.
TEIXEIRA, F. L. C. "A experiência de Deus nas religiões." *Numen* 3 (2000) 111–48.
———. "A teologia no tempo." http://fteixeira-dialogos.blogspot.com/2010/04/teologia-no-tempo.html.
———, ed. *Diálogo de pássaros.* São Paulo: Paulinas, 1993.
———. "O Sagrado em novos itnerários." *Vida Pastoral* 41 (2000) 17–22.
———. *Teologia das religiões. Uma visão panorâmica.* São Paulo: Paulinas, 1995.
THELOT, J., et al. *Simone Weil et le poétique.* Paris: Kime, 2007.
THEOBALD, C., coord. *Le canon des Écritures: Études historiques, exegetiques et systematiques.* Lectio divina 140. Paris: Cerf, 1990.
———. *Le christianisme comme style.* 2 vols. Paris: Cerf, 2007.
THEVENOT, X. *Les ailes et le soufflé: Éthique et vie spirituelle.* Paris: DDB/Cerf, 2000.
THILS, G. *Existencia y Santidad en Jesus Cristo.* Salamanca: Sígueme, 1987.
THIOUT, M. "La recherché de la verité chez Simone Weil." *Archives des lettres modernes* 25–26 (1959).
THOMPSON, W. M. *Fire and Light: The Saints and Theology.* New York: Paulist, 1987.
THORN, W. J., et al., eds. *Doroth Day and the Catholic Worker Movement: Centenary Essays.* Milwaukee: Marquette University Press, 2001.
TILLICH, P. *Systematic Theology.* Chicago: University of Chicago Press, 1967.
TOMMASI, W. *Etty Hillesum: La inteligencia del corazón.* Madrid: Narcea, 2003.
———. *Etty Hillesum: L'intelligenza del cuore.* Padua: Messaggero, 2002.
———. *Simone Weil: Esperienza religiosa, esperienza femminile.* Napoli: Liguori, 1997.
———. *Simone Weil: segni, idoli e somboli.* Milan: Francoangeli, 1993.
TOURAINE, A. *Um novo paradigma.* Petrópolis: Vozes, 2006.
TRACY, D. "Afterword." In *Mystics: Presence and Aporia,* edited by M. Kessler and C. Sheppard, 239–43. Chicago: University of Chicago Press, 2003.
———. *The Analogical Imagination: Christian Theology and the Culture of Pluralism.* New York: Crossroad, 1981.
———. *Blessed Rage for Order: The New Pluralism in Theology.* New York: Seabury, 1975.
———, ed. "Celebrating the Medieval Heritage—A Colloquy on the Thought of Aquinas and Bonaventure." *The Journal of Religion* 58 (Supplement) 1978.
———. *Dialogue with the Other: The Inter-religious Dialogue.* Grand Rapids: Eerdmans, 1991.
———. *On Naming the Present: Reflections on God, Hermeneutics, and Church.* Maryknoll, NY: Orbis, 1994.
———. *Plurality and Ambiguity: Hermeneutics, Religion, Hope.* San Francisco: Harper & Row, 1987.
———. *Trinitarian Theology and Spirituality: Retrieving William of St. Thierry for Contemporary Theology.* Chicago: mimeograph, unpublished text.
———. "Writing." In *Critical Terms for Religious Studies,* edited by Mark C. Taylor, 38394. Chicago: University of Chicago Press, 1998.
TRESMONTANT, C. *La mística cristiana y el porvenir del hombre.* Barcelona: Herder, 1980.
———. *La mystique chretienne et l'avenir de l'homme.* Paris: Cerf, 1976.

TRITES, A. A. *The New Testament Concept of Witness.* Cambridge: Cambridge University Press, 1977.

TROELTSCH, E. *The Social Teaching of the Christian Churches.* 2 vols. New York: Harper & Row, 1960.

TULLY, J., and D. M. WEINSTOCK, eds. *Philosophy in an Age of Pluralism: The Philosophy of Charles Taylor in Question.* Cambridge: Cambridge University Press, 1994.

TÜRCKE, C. *Sociedade excitada: Filosofia da sensação.* Campinas: UNICAMP, 2010.

———. *What Price Religion?* London: SCM, 1997.

TURIJ, O., ed. *Church of the martyrs.* Translated by M. Matuszak. Lviv, Ukraine: St. John's Monastery/Publishing Division Svichado, 2004.

UNDERHILL, E. *Mysticism: A Study in the Nature and Development of Man's Spiritual Conscience.* Cleveland: World Publishing, 1965.

VALADIER, P. *Igreja e modernidade.* São Paulo: Loyola, 1991.

VALBERG, J. J. *The Puzzle of Experience.* Oxford: Clarendon, 1992.

VAN BUREN, P. M. "When Christians Meet Jews." In *Visions of the Other: Jews and Christian Theologians Assess the Dialogue,* edited by E. J. Fisher. New York: Paulist, 1994.

VANHOOZER, K., and M. WARNER, eds. *Transcending Boundaries in Philosophy and Theology: Reason, Meaning and Experience.* Burlington, VT: Ashgate, 2007.

VANNINI, M. *Introdução à mística.* São Paulo: Loyola, 2005.

———. *Mistica e filosofia.* Florence: Le Lettere, 2007.

VANSTEENBERGHE, E. *Autour de la Docte ignorance: Une controverse sur la théologie mystique au XVe siècle.* Munster: Aschendorff, 1915.

VAZ, H. C. DE L. *Antropologia filosófica.* Vol. 2. Filosofia. São Paulo: Loyola, 1992.

———. "A experiência de Deus." In *Experimentar Deus hoje,* edited by L. Boff, 74–89. Petrópolis: Vozes, 1974.

———. *Experiência mística e filosofia na tradição ocidental.* São Paulo: Loyola, 2000.

———. "A linguagem da experiência de Deus." In *Escritos de Filosofia: Problemas de Fronteira.* São Paulo: Loyola, 1986.

———. "Mística e política: a experiência mística na tradição ocidental." In *Mística e política,* edited by M. C. Bingemer and R. Dos Santos Bartholo Jr., 10–47. Seminários Especiais. São Paulo: Loyola, 1992.

———. "Religião e modernidade filosófica." In *O impacto da modernidade sobre a religião,* edited by M. C. Bingemer, 83–107. São Paulo: Loyola, 1992.

———. "Sinais dos tempos: lugar teológico ou lugar-comum?" In *Revista Eclesiástica Brasileira,* March 1972.

VEGA, A., et al., eds. *Estética y religión: el discurso del cuerpo y los sentidos.* Barcelona: Literatura y Ciencia, 1998.

———. *Utopia y esperanza cristiana.* Estella: Verbo Divino, 1997.

VELASCO, J. M. *A experiência cristã de Deus.* São Paulo: Paulinas, 2001.

———. *Cambio socio-cultural y cristianismo hoy.* Salamanca: Santuario de la Bien Aparecida y Secretariado Trinitario, 1980.

———. *El encuentro con Dios: una interpretación personalista de la religión.* Madrid: Cristiandad, 1976.

———. *El fenómeno místico: Estudio comparado.* Madrid: Trotta, 1999.

———. *El hombre y la religión.* Madrid: PPC, 2002.

———. *El malestar religioso de nuestra cultura.* Madrid: Paulinas, 1993.

———. *Hacia una filosofía de la religión cristiana: la obra de H. Dumery.* Madrid: Instituto Superior de Pastoral, 1970.
———. *Increencia y evangelización: del dialogo al testimonio.* Santander: Sal Terrae, 1988.
———. *Introducción a la fenomenología de la religión.* Madrid: Trotta, 2006.
———. *La experiencia cristiana de Dios.* Madrid: Trotta, 1995.
———. *La experiencia mística: Estudio interdisciplinar.* Madrid: Trotta, 2004.
———. *La religión en nuestro mundo: Ensayos de fenomenología.* Salamanca: Sígueme, 1978.
———. *La transmisión de la fe en la sociedad contemporânea.* Santander: Sal Terrae, 2002.
———. *Metamorfosis de lo sagrado y futuro del cristianismo.* Santander: Sal Terrae, 1998.
———. *Mistica y humanismo.* Madrid: PPC, 2007.
———. *Mundo en crisis, fe en crisis.* Estella: Verbo Divino, 1996.
———. *Ser cristiano en una cultura posmoderna.* Mexico City: Universidad Iberoamericana, 1996.
———. *Utopia y esperanza cristiana.* Estella: Verbo Divino, 1997.
VELASCO, J. M., et al. *Cambio socio-cultural y cristianismo hoy.* Salamanca: Ed. Santuario de la Bien Aparecida y Secretariado Trinitario, 1980.
VICTORINUS, M. *Traites théologiques sur la Trinite.* Vol. 1. Text prepared by P. Henry. Translated by P. Hadot. Sources Chretiennes 68. Paris: Cerf, 1960.
VISSER 'T HOOFT, W. *La paternité de Dieu dans un monde émancipé.* Geneva: Labor et Fides, 1984.
WAHL, J. *L'expérience metaphysique.* Paris: Flammarion, 1965.
WAINWRIGHT, W. J. *Mysticism: A Study of Its Nature, Cognitive Value and Moral Implications.* Wisconsin: University of Wisconsin Press, 1981.
WATKIN, E. I. *Poets and Mystics.* London: Sheed and Ward, 1953.
WEIL, S. *Attente de Dieu.* Paris: Fayard, 1966.
———. "Expérience de la vie d'usine." In *Ecrits historiques et politiques II—Ouvres Complètes,* edited by A. Devaux and F. Lussy. Paris: Gallimard, 1991.
———. *La connaissance surnaturelle.* Espoir. Paris: Gallimard, 1950.
———. "L'Illiade ou le poeme de la force." In *Oeuvres.* Quarto. Paris: Gallimard, 1999.
———. *Pensées sans ordre concernant l'amour de Dieu.* Espoir. Paris: Gallimard, 1962.
———. *Sur la science.* Paris: Gallimard, 1966.
WELTE, B. *El hombre entre lo finito e infinito: reflexiones para una interpretación de la existencia humana.* Barcelona: Labor, 1968.
———. *La luce del nulla.* Brescia: Queriniana, 1983.
WENNINK, H. *The Bible on Asceticism.* De Pere, WI: St. Norbert Abbey Press, 1966.
WESTHELLE, V. "Modernidade, mito e religião. Crítica e reconstrução das representações religiosas." *Numen* 3 (2000) 11–38.
WHITE, G. A., ed. *Simone Weil: Interpretations of a Life.* Amherst: University of Massachusetts Press, 1981.
WHITE, J., ed. *La experiencia mistica y los estados de conciencia.* Barcelona: Kairos, 2005.
WIGGINS, D. *Solidarity and the Root of the Ethical.* The Lindley Lecture 2008. Lawrence: Department of Philosophy, University of Kansas, 2008.
WILBER, K. *Integral Spirituality.* Boston: Integral Books, 2006.

WILDER, S. *Un sujet sans moi: Psychanalyse et expérience mystique*. Paris: EPEL, 2008.
WILLIAMS, R. *Christianity and the Ideal of Detachment*. Oxford: Clinical Theology Association, 1989.
WIMBUSCH, V., and R. VALANTASIS. *Asceticism*. New York: Oxford University Press, 1995.
WINKLER, M. G., and L. B. COLE, eds. *The Good Body: Asceticism in Contemporary Culture*. New Haven: Yale University Press, 1994.
WITTGENSTEIN, L. *Tractatus Logistico-Philosophicus*. São Paulo: Edusp, 1993.
WOODS, R., ed. *Understanding Mysticism*. Garden City, NY: Image, 1980.
WRIGHT, B. D., and A. M. YONKE. *Hero, Villain, Saint: An Adventure in the Experience of Individuality*. New York: P. Lang, 1989.
YON, E. *L'homme selon l'Esprit*. Paris: DDB, 1995.
YORK, T. *Living on Hope while Living in Babylon: The Christian Anarchists of the Twentieth Century*. Eugene, OR: Wipf & Stock, 2009.
ZAEHNER, R. C. *Mysticism, Sacred and Profane: An Inquiry into Some Varieties of Praeter-natural Experience*. Oxford: Clarendon, 1957.
ZAMBONI, C. *Interrogando la cosa: Riflessioni a partire da Martin Heidegger e Simone Weil*. Milan: IPL, 1993.
ZIESLER, J. A. *Christian Asceticism*. Grand Rapids: Eerdmans, 1973.
ZIZEK, S. *For They Know Not What They Do: Enjoyment as a Political Factor*. London: Verso, 1991.
———. *The Fragile Absolute, or, Why Is the Christian Legacy Worth Fighting For?* London: Verso, 2000.
———. *In Defense of Lost Causes*. London: Verso, 2008.
———. *The Metastases of Enjoyment: Six Essays on Women and Causality*. London: Verso, 2005.
———. *On Belief: Thinking in Action*. London: Routledge, 2001.
———. *Violence*. New York: Picador, 2008.
———. *The Zizek Reader*. Edited by E. Wright. Oxford: Blackwell, 1999.
ZIZEK, S., and F. W. J. von SCHELLING. *The Abyss of Freedom/Ages of the World*. Ann Arbor: University of Michigan Press, 1997.
ZUNDEL, M. *Morale et mystique*. Sainte-Foy, QC: A. Sigier, 1999.
ZWICK, M., and L. ZWICK. *Mercy without Borders: The Catholic Worker and Immigration*. New York: Paulist, 2010.

Index

Adamov, 226n4
Adorno, T., 34, 34n83
Aleixandre, D., 142n63
Alencastro, L. F. de, 35n86
Almond, Philip, 178–79, 178nn217–18, 179n220
Amaral, L., 82n82
Andrade, P. F. C. de, 5n8, 62n17, 63n19, 81n79, 143n67, 274n166
Anjos, M. F. dos, 83n85
Antor, 26n75
Aquinas, Thomas (saint), 100–101, 100n136, 146, 156, 175, 175n201, 187, 197n308, 216
Araujo, W. S., 68n40
Aristotle, 31, 43
Armstrong, K., 169n174
Assis, Andre, 73n54
Asti, Franco, 193
Augustine (saint), 32, 32n80, 97n123, 112, 141, 145n76, 152, 156n124, 182, 212, 256–57, 257nn108–9, 272, 272n162, 273, 286, 294, 301–2
Azevedo, M., 58n7

Bakunin, 284
Balthasar, Hans Urs von, 191–92, 192n284, 193n287, 217, 252n91, 260n121, 276, 276n175, 311, 311n112, 314–15, 315n121

Bareau, 227nn9–10
Barth, Karl, 182, 275
Barthes, Roland, 262, 262n134
Bartholo, R. dos Santos, Jr., 163n147, 241n47
Basil of Caesarea, 244n53
Bastos d'Avila, Father Fernando, 129n9
Bataille, Georges, 104n148, 106n151, 134, 134nn33–34, 184n246
Baudrillard, J., 11n28, 18, 18n56
Bauman, Zygmunt, xiiin7, xviin16, 6, 6n11, 9–12, 9n18, 9n19, 9n20, 10nn21–25, 11nn26–28, 12n30, 16–17, 16nn44–47, 17nn48–50, 18n56, 24–25, 24nn67–70, 25nn71–74, 39n93, 41n101, 41n103, 42nn105–7, 56nn1–56n2, 57n3–4, 64n23, 138, 138n43, 140n54, 225n3
Baumgarten, M., 222n380
Benedict XVI (pope), 40, 103, 103n145
Benjamin, Walter, 6
Berger, Alan L., 258n115
Bergson, Henri, 174–75, 175n197
Bériault, Y., 307n96, 309n104–9n106
Bernard of Clairvaux (saint), 214, 217
Bernstein, C., 5n7
Bertelli, G., 251n88

Bingemer, M. C., 62n17, 63n19, 73n53, 78n72, 78n74, 79n75, 81n79, 82n80, 163n147, 168n173, 198n311, 202n325, 204n327, 207n331, 208n333, 241n47, 253n94, 267n146, 275n170
Bloch, Ernst, 4
Bloechl, J., 48n133
Blondel, Maurice, 118, 174, 174nn191–96, 234, 234nn31–32
Boff, C., 5n9
Boff, Leonardo, 22n63, 69n43, 146n78, 196n305
Bonaventure (saint), 207n332, 214, 214n350
Bonhoeffer, Dietrich, 309n103
Borghesi, Massimo, 7–8, 7n15–7n16
Borriello, Luiggi, 193–94, 193nn289–91, 194nn242–94
Bouillard, H., 118, 118n196
Bouyer, 217
Brady, J. A., 288n25, 289n28
Braudel, 251n85
Bremond, Henri, 184
Brenner, Rachel Feldhay, 258, 258n112, 258n113
Broeckhoven, Egide van, 310–23, 310nn109–10, 312nn113–14, 313nn115–16, 314nn119–20, 315nn122–23, 316n125, 316nn127–28, 317nn130–31, 318n132, 318n135, 319nn136–39, 320nn140–42, 321nn144–47, 323nn153–55, 331–32
Brunner, 182
Buber, Martin, 39n96, 198n309, 255, 255n102
Bultmann, 118
Burity, J. A., 52n144, 249n75
Bush, George W., 86
Butler, Edward, 185, 185n252

Caffarena, J. G., 194n296
Campos, L. S., 66n34, 79n77

Camus, Albert, 25n72, 100, 100n135, 275
Cano, Melchior, 221, 221n376
Carozzo, C., 254n98, 254n100
Carrara, S. P., xiin3, xivn8, xivn10, xvn12, xvinn13–14, xviin18
Casalis, 201nn320–21, 202n322
Casarella, P., 180n222, 292n42
Castiñera, A., xin2, xiin5, xiin6, 63n21
Cavanaugh, W., 64n24, 131n15
Certeau, Michel de, 13–15, 13nn32–34, 14n35, 14nn38–39, 15n40, 15n42, 16, 78n73, 103n144, 160n141, 176, 176nn205–8, 181, 181n228, 234–35, 235nn33–34, 235n36, 257, 257n110
Champion, F., 250n82
Chaplin, Charlie, 132n22
Charles, S., xivn11
Chateabriand, F. R., 35, 35n84
Cipriani, R., 250n78
Clark, H., 183n238, 233n26
Clarke, Maura, 259n116
Coles, Robert, 282n5, 330
Comblin, J., 66n31
Comte-Sponville, André, 64n24, 64n26, 99n133, 251n86
Congar, Y., 118, 118n196
Cousins, Ewert, 180, 180n225
Cunningham, L., 252n90

da Vinci, Leonardo, 68
Daly, 202n323
Damasio, A., 63n22
Danese, N., 252n89
Daniélou, Jean, 188–89
Dawkins, Richard, 82n80, 82n81, 84, 84nn87–88, 85n90
Day, Dorothy, 251n88, 261n131, 280–93, 280n1, 281n2, 283nn7–8, 284nn9–12, 285nn13–14, 286n15, 287nn17–19, 288nn21–24, 290nn33–35, 291nn36–37, 292n40, 292n42, 293n43, 329–30
Delbrel, Madeleine, 239, 251n88

Derrida, J., 81n79
Descartes, 110n163, 149
Desroche, 2nn1–2, 3, 3nn3–4
Dickens, Charles, 289
Dilthey, 118
Dionysius the Areopagite, 181, 194, 212
Domínguez Morano, C., 89n100, 110n160, 121n203, 122n204, 122n206, 161n144, 162n145, 197n306
Donovan, Jean, 259n116
Dostoievsky, 288–89
Douglas, Mary, 9, 9n19
Downey, V. M., 294n46
Ducrocq, A., 297n52
Dupré, Louis, 152–54, 152nn105–7, 153nn109–10, 154, 154nn112–15, 179–80, 180nn222–24, 210, 210n339, 211, 211nn340–42, 212n343, 213nn344–46, 214nn348–49, 214n351, 215nn353–54
Dupuis, J., 82n82
Duquoc, C., 253n95
Durand, G., 143n69
Dutter, C., 296n49, 297n50

Eagleton, T., 98n128
Eckhart, Meister, 180, 212–13, 273
Egan, 189n268
Einstein, A., 73, 73n54
Eliade, Mircea, 79n76, 81n79, 158, 158n130
Ellsberg, R., 286n16
Encrevé, 233n24–33n25
Engel, 126n3
Estrada, J. A., 54n150

Fackenheim, Emil, 258, 258n112
Feller, V. G., 208n333, 267n146
Fénelon, 215
Fernandes, S. R. A., 68n39
Festugière, A. J., 106n150, 208n336
Fiores, S., 99n133
Fiorucci, R., 36n88, 44n109
Ford, Ita, 259n116

Forest, Jim, 287, 287n20, 290n32, 292n38
Forte, Bruno, 57–58, 57nn5–6, 82n80, 83n83
Francis of Assisi (saint), 214, 292
Freud, S., xix, 6, 112, 160, 161n143
Friedman, T. L., 14n37
Fukuyama, F., 4n6

Gadamer, 118
Gamarra, S., 181n227
García Rubio, A., xvin15
Gardet, Louis, 189
Garrigou-Lagrange, Reginald, 186, 186n255
Gauchet, M., 49n135, 50n139, 52n146, 59n10, 59n136, 143, 143n69, 144n70
Geertz, C., 94n112
Gelabert, M., 145n76, 146nn79–80, 147nm81–83, 148n84, 196n305
Genio, Maria Rosario del, 193
Gergen, K. J., 18n54, 130n10
Gerson, Jean, 152
Gesche, A., 98n127, 99n131
Glavac, C., 259n116
Goleman, Daniel, 136, 136n39
Gómez de Souza, L. A., 81n79
González Buelta, Benjamin, xivn9, 7n14, 16n43, 17nn51–52, 18nn54–55, 20n58, 101nn137–38, 102nn141–43, 128–29, 128nn6–7, 129n8, 130n12, 130n14, 135n36, 138n48, 139, 139nn49–52, 140n55, 245n59, 246n62, 247nn63–66, 248n68, 322–23, 323nn151–52
González Faus, J. I., 123n209
Gracián, Father, 257n111
Gramsci, A., 3, 3n5
Gregory of Nyssa, 212, 244n53
Greisch, 231n20
Griffiths, R. R., 153n111
Gröning, Philip, 90n102
Guardini, Romano, 209–10, 210n337
Guevara, Ernesto "Che," 4

Guibert, Joseph de, 186
Guillebaud, Jean-Claude, 133–34, 133nn27–28, 134nn29–32, 134n34, 135n35
Gutiérrez, Gustavo, 220, 220nn371–72, 233, 233n23
Guyon, Jeanne, 215

Haas, 264nn139–40
Habermas, J., 77n70, 95n115, 98n128, 111, 143n69
Hadewijch of Antwerp, 213, 214, 312
Halbwachs, M., 36n89
Harnack, Adolph, 181–82, 182, 182nn232–34
Haroche, C., 139n53
Harris, Sam, 82n80, 84, 85n90
Hébrard, M., 82n82
Heidegger, Martin, 33, 33n82, 118
Heisig, James W., 65n27, 84n86, 131, 131nn16–18, 132–33, 132n19, 132nn23–24, 133n26, 135n37, 253n96
Henry, M., 198n313
Hervieu-Léger, Danièle, 51n142, 67, 67nn35–36, 250n79
Hick, J., 79n76
Hillesum, Etty, 174n196, 251n88, 253, 258–59, 265n141, 272n159, 293–310, 293nn44–45, 297n50, 297n53, 298n54, 299nn55–60, 300nn61–64, 301nn65–71, 302nn72–75, 303nn76–77, 304nn79–82, 305nn83–85, 306nn86–93, 307nn94–97, 308nn98–99, 308nn100–101, 309n102, 309nn105–6, 310nm107–8, 326, 331
Hitchens, Christopher, 82n80, 84, 85n90
Hoffman, Abbie, 282
Horkheimer, M., 34n83
Hortal, J., 79n77
Houtepen, A. W. J., 144n71
Hügel, F. von, 150, 171–72, 171n181, 172n182, 175
Hugo, Victor, 289

Huntington, Samuel, 20, 20n60
Husserl, 118

Ignatius of Antioch (saint), 183
Ignatius of Loyola (saint), 155–56, 155n116, 237, 244, 249n74, 252, 252n93, 257n111, 262n134, 270, 270n154, 277n180, 317, 317n129, 322
Inge, William Ralph, 184, 184n244–84n245
Irenaeus (saint), 87
Isaiah, 220
Izuzquiza, D., 261, 261nn130–31

James, William, 117, 117n193, 150, 150n95, 152, 152n108, 163–64, 163n149, 171, 171nn179–80
Jank, M. S., 21n62
Japiassú, H., 127n4
Jaspers, 118
Jeauneau, Édouard, 199nn317–18, 200n319
John (saint), 183, 263n136
John of the Cross (saint), 104, 104n148, 122n205, 122n206, 155, 174, 175, 186–87, 214–15, 215n352, 244, 249n74, 252, 252n92, 272, 272nn160–61, 312
John Paul II (pope), 5, 119
Johnston, W., 188n262
Jonas, Hans, 75, 75n59, 159, 159n136, 231, 231n19
Jung, 294

Kant, I., 29–30, 29n76, 127, 149, 225
Katz, Steven, 179, 179n219, 179n221
Kazel, Dorothy, 259n116
Kierkegaard, 118
Kirk, Kenneth Escort, 184–85, 184n250, 185n251
Krebs, Engelbert, 175n201
Krupa, Stephen, 281, 281nn3–4
Küng, H., 80n78, 107n152, 208n335
Kurz, Robert, 23–24

Index

La Taille, Maurice de, 186
Labarriere, J. P., 148n87
Lacoste, J. Y., 81n79
Ladrière, J., 77n69, 181n226
Lasch, C., xviin17
Lattes, Cesar, 73n54
Le Saux, 251n87
Legaut, Marcel, 315
Levinas, Emmanuel, 39–42, 39n97,
    40n98, 40n99, 40n100,
    41n102, 44–48, 45n112,
    45n114, 46nn116–22,
    47nn123–27, 48nn128–32,
    70–71, 70n46, 71nn47–51,
    95, 95n115, 95n117, 96n119,
    108n154, 109n155, 110–11,
    111n165, 112, 113–14,
    113nn175–78, 114n180, 115,
    115n181, 198n310, 227n7,
    231, 277, 277nn178–79
Lewinska, Pelagia, 258n112
Libânio, João Batista, 53n149,
    55n153, 66n32, 69n43, 78n73,
    78n74, 84n89, 110n162,
    111n167, 119nn197–98,
    232n22, 266n145
Lipovetsky, Gilles, 19–20, 19n57, 38,
    38nn90–92, 39nn93–95, 130,
    130n11, 130n13, 251n85
Lipovetzky, G., xivn11, xviin16
Lodi, E., 68n40
Lonergan, Bernard, 179, 188,
    188nn263–64
Lossky, Vladimir, 187
Lubac, Henri de, 189, 189nn266–67,
    217
Luz, L., 79n77
Lynch, D., 281n2

Madalena, Gabriele di Santa Maria,
    186
Maitre, J., 250n81
Mannheim, Karl, 4, 43n108
Manon, S., 140n56
Mao Tse Tung, 42
Marcel, G., 95n116, 118
Marcondes, D., 127n4

Mardones, J. M., 12n29, 30n77,
    49n134, 49nn136–37,
    50n140–50n141, 58n7,
    64n24, 65nn28–29, 66n30,
    66n33, 67nn35–36, 67n37,
    68nn38–39, 75nn60–61,
    76nn62–65, 77n67, 88n96,
    137n41, 138n44, 142nn64–
    65, 143n66, 143nn68–69,
    149n60, 250n80, 254n97,
    273n165, 274n167
Maréchal, Joseph, 172–73,
    172nn184–86, 173nn188–90
Marinucci, R., 24n66
Marion, Jean-Luc, 111n169, 115–16,
    115n182–15n183, 115n185
Maritain, Jacques, 175–76,
    175nn199–200, 175n202,
    176nn203–4, 186
Maritain, Raïssa, 251n88
Marty, F., 246n61
Marx, K., 4
Maslow, A., 95n115
Massignon, L., 251n87
Mathon, G., 107n153, 208n336
Matthew (saint), 207
Maurin, Peter, 282, 289
Mayor, 75n58
McClendon, J. Wm., Jr., 260–61,
    260n122, 261nn123–27
McDonnell, K., 252n90
McGinn, B., 151, 151nn101–3, 152,
    152n104, 159–60, 159n135,
    160nn137–40, 160n142,
    162–63, 163n146, 171–93,
    171nn177–78, 172n183,
    173n187, 175n198, 176n204,
    178n214, 178n216, 178n218,
    181nn229–30, 182n231,
    182n233, 183n237, 183n242,
    184n243, 184n246, 184n248,
    185n253, 186n254, 186n256,
    187nn259–61, 189n268,
    190n272, 191n278, 191n281,
    192nn283–86, 193n288,
    233nn28–29, 234n30
Merleau-Ponty, 118

Meroz, C., 244n51, 316n124, 316n126
Merton, Thomas, 221n378, 251n88
Methodius of Olympus, 182
Metz, Johann Baptist, 34, 34n83, 123n210, 219n367, 220n375, 236n37, 237–38, 237nn42–44, 238nn45–46, 244–45, 244nn55–56, 248n70, 260n121, 262n132
Mieth, D., 144n72
Milesi, R., 24n66
Miller, W. D., 288n24, 292n39
Mitchell, D., 20n59
Moingt, Joseph, xiin4, 52n145, 53n147, 210n338, 219n367, 248n70
Moioli, G., 181n227
Molinos, Miguel de, 215
Moltmann, J., 52n146, 81n79, 148nn85–86, 196n305, 197n307, 267nn147–48
More, Thomas, 1–2
Moreira, R., 22n64
Moro, Ulpiano Vásquez, 270, 270n153
Mounier, Emmanuel, 14n36, 252n89, 255n105
Mouroux, Jean, 118, 118n196, 145n75, 148nn88–89, 149n90, 163–67, 163n148, 164nn150–56, 165n157, 165nn159–63, 166nn164–68, 167n169, 169
Muller-Armack, A., 63n20
Murad, A., 69n43

Neefs, Georges, 313–14, 314nn117–18, 315n121, 318n133
Neumann, Erich, 160
Newman, 112
Nichols, David E., 153n111
Nietzsche, 85
Nigg, W., 222n380
Nolasco, S., 67n36
Noone, J., 259n116
Novaes, J. V., 130n11, 132n20

O'Brien, R., 21n61
O'Collins, G., 117n191, 118n194
O'Connor, June, 288–89, 288n26, 289nn27–30, 330
Onfray, Michel, 82n80, 85–86, 86n92
Origen, 211–12
Oster, 256nn106–7
Otto, Rudolf, 118, 118n195, 149–51, 149n91, 150nn92–94, 151nn96–99, 151n100, 158, 165, 178, 179

Pace, E., 250n77
Panier, L., 52n146
Panikkar, Raimon, 157, 195–96, 196n303, 245n57
Parrilla, Lana, 139n49
Pascal, B., 94n113, 101–2, 101n139, 102n140, 140, 140n56, 140n58, 269, 269n150
Pastor, F. A., 120n201
Paul (saint), 42, 78, 78n71, 88, 88n97, 108, 109, 183, 187, 211, 219, 220, 241, 253, 303, 303n78
Paul VI (pope), 123, 219n368, 222, 222n381, 248nn71–72, 249n73, 292, 292n41
Pepin, 31nn78–79
Perrin, Father, 275n173
Petitdemange, G., 71n52
Philoxenus of Mabbug, 257
Pierron, Jean Philippe, 226, 226nn5–6, 227n8, 229n13, 244n54, 259n118, 260nn119–120
Pius XII (pope), 103
Plato, 31
Plotinus, 211
Politi, M., 5n7
Poulain, Augustin-François, 186
Poupard, P., 81n79, 242n49
Price, J. Randall, 188
Price, James, 179

Queiruga, A. Torres, 60nn11–13, 81n79, 83n84, 86–87, 86n93, 87n94, 88n95, 119n198

Index

Radhakrishnan, Sarvepalli, 178
Rahner, Karl, xx, xvin14, 53n149,
    54nn150–52, 55n153, 61,
    61n15, 83n84, 88–89, 88n98,
    89n99, 89n101, 92n104,
    99, 116n187, 117n190, 118,
    118n196, 146n77, 156–57,
    158n129, 188, 189–91,
    189n268, 189n270, 190n271,
    190nn273–77, 191nn278–80,
    191n282, 199n314, 220,
    220n374, 235–37, 236nn37–
    39, 237nn40–41, 244, 244n52,
    266nn143–45, 322, 322n150
Rambla, J. M., 318n134, 322n148
Ravier, A., 189n266
Ricci, Matteo, 33
Ricoeur, Paul, 35, 35n85, 44, 44n110,
    45, 45n114, 64n25, 81n79,
    103n146, 111–13, 112nn170–
    72, 112n174, 114, 116,
    269n152
Rilke, 226n4
Rioux, J. P., 36n87
Ritschl, Albrecht, 181
Rocha, J. G., 51n142
Rodrigues, D. Dos Santos, 52n144
Rof Carballo, Juan, 95n115
Rolland, J., 71n52
Rolland, Romain, 160
Romero, Monsignor, 259n116
Rorty, R., 10, 10n25
Rose, Anne Carver, 258n114
Ruiz de la Pena, J. L., 157nn126–27,
    158n128
Ruusbroec (Ruysbroeck), 180, 213,
    214, 312

Sader, Emir, 5n9
Saliers, D. E., 180n222
San Joaquin, Antonio de, 257n111
Sanchis, P., 250n83, 251n84
Sargent, L. T., 7, 7n12
Sartre, Jean-Paul, 9n19, 70, 70n45,
    93n111
Saudreau, Auguste, 186
Scannone, Juan Carlos, 44n111, 45,
    45n113, 45n115, 110n159,
    110n164, 111n166, 112n173,
    114n179, 115, 115n186,
    117nn188–89
Scheler, Max, 118
Schimmel, Anne Marie, 160n138
Schlegel, J. L., 82n82
Schleiermacher, 117, 117n192
Schneider, Michael, xxn23, xxiin27,
    219n366, 219nn369–70,
    220n373, 248n69, 260n121,
    261, 261nn128–29, 262n133,
    262n135, 263n137, 264n139,
    265n142, 276n175, 276n177
Schner, G. P., 180n222
Scholem, Gershom, 159, 159nn131–
    32, 159n134, 175n201
Schultze, 137, 137n41, 138n42
Schweitzer, Albert, 183–84,
    183nn239–41, 192, 233–34,
    233n27
Silone, Ignazio, 252n89
Sinclair, Upton, 289–90
Siqueira, D., 52n144, 250n76
Sirinelli, J. F., 36n87
Smart, Ninian, 178, 178n215
Smolka, A. L. B., 32n80, 33n81
Sobrino, Jon, 123n210, 219n367,
    225n2, 248n70
Spence, 33n81
Spier, Julius, 294–95, 294n48,
    298–300
Stace, Walter Terence, 177–78,
    177nn209–13
Stein, Edith, 258–59, 272, 272n163,
    303
Steiner, G., 99n132
Stirnimann, H., 145n74
Stolz, Anselm, 186–88, 192
Sulkunen, P., 137n41

Tanquerey, Adolphe, 186
Taylor, C., 58n7
Teilhard de Chardin, 312, 313
Teixeira, F. L. C., 78n74, 82n82
Teresa, Mother, 122n205
Teresa of Avila (saint), 121, 155,
    155n116, 186, 187, 215, 244,
    249n74, 257n111, 270n155

Theobald, C., 53n149
Thérèse of Lisieux (saint), 292, 292n42, 303, 303n78
Thils, G., 110n158
Tillich, Paul, 99, 182, 182n235
Tolstoy, Leon, 288–89
Touraine, A., 143n69
Tracy, David, 214n347, 255n101, 255nn103–4, 274–75, 274n168, 275n169, 275n171
Tresmontant, C., 241n48, 271n157, 272n158
Troeltsch, Ernst, 182–83, 182n236
Türcke, C., 138, 138nn45–47

Underhill, Evelyn, 178, 184, 184nn247–49

Valadier, P., 109nn156–57, 223nn382–84
Vannini, M., xixnn20–21, xxn22, xxiiinn31–32, xxiii–xxiv, xxivnn33–37
Vattimo, G., 64n24, 81n79, 251n85
Vaz, Father Henrique de Lima, xixn19, xxinn24–25, xxiinn26–29, xxiiin30, 52n146, 58, 58nn8–9, 83n85, 119n199, 120, 120n200, 145n73, 167–70, 167n170, 168nn171–72, 169nn175–76, 175n202, 196n304, 196n305, 197n308, 198n312
Velasco, Juan Martin, 77n68, 91n103, 92nn105–6, 92n108, 93nn109–10, 94, 94n114, 95n115, 95n118, 96n119, 96n121, 97nn122–25, 98n126, 98nn128–29, 100n134, 110n161, 155, 155nn117–19, 156nn120–23, 157n125, 194–95, 194nn245–97, 195nn298–302, 196n305, 204n326, 216nn355–58, 217nn359–62, 218, 218nn363–65
Visser 't Hooft, W., 202n324
Vitruvius, 68n41

Wainwright, William, 178
Weil, E., 230n18
Weil, Simone, 63n22, 132nn21–22, 140–41, 141n59, 164n156, 174n196, 221n377, 222n379, 239, 253, 258–59, 264, 265n141, 271n156, 272n159, 273, 273n164, 274–75, 275–76, 275n169, 275nn172–73, 276n174, 276n176, 278n181, 303, 320, 320n143
Westhelle, V., 81n79
William of Saint-Thierry, 213–14
Wiseman, J., 180n222
Wittgenstein, L., 98–99, 99n130

Xavier, Francisco, 121

Zaehner, Robert, 159–60, 177, 178
Zolkiewski, 13n34

www.ingramcontent.com/pod-product-compliance
Lightning Source LLC
Chambersburg PA
CBHW022226010526
44113CB00033B/514